ALSO BY GARRET KEIZER

GETTING SCHOOLED

GETTING SCHOOLED

THE REEDUCATION *of* AN AMERICAN TEACHER

GARRET KEIZER

METROPOLITAN BOOKS

HENRY HOLT AND COMPANY NEW YORK

[m]

Metropolitan Books
Henry Holt and Company, LLC
Publishers since 1866
175 Fifth Avenue
New York, New York 10010
www.henryholt.com

Metropolitan Books® and [m]® are registered trademarks of
Henry Holt and Company, LLC.

Library of Congress Cataloging-in-Publication Data

Keizer, Garret.
    Getting schooled : the reeducation of an American teacher / Garret Keizer.
       pages cm
    ISBN 978-0-8050-9643-9 (hardback)—ISBN 978-0-8050-9644-6 (electronic copy)
    1. High school teaching—Vermont—Case studies.   2. High school teachers—
Professional relationships—Vermont—Case studies.   3. Public schools—Vermont—
Case studies.   4. Keizer, Garret.   I. Title.
    LB1607.52.V5K45 2014
    373.110209743—dc23   2013042594

Henry Holt books are available for special promotions and
premiums. For details contact: Director, Special Markets.

First Edition 2014

Designed by Kelly Too

Printed in the United States of America
1 3 5 7 9 10 8 6 4 2

For the Teachers

I know nothing about education except this: that the greatest and the most important difficulty known to human learning seems to lie in that area which treats how to bring up children and how to educate them.

MONTAIGNE

CONTENTS

NOTE TO THE READER

Getting Schooled grew out of an essay of the same title that was published in the September 2011 issue of *Harper's Magazine*. The adults mentioned in these pages have been given their real names or pseudonyms or have been left unnamed as judged best by the author. No student appears with his or her real name. Certain details have been altered to camouflage identities, but none of the incidents recounted have been invented, exaggerated, or otherwise distorted.

GETTING SCHOOLED

BEGINNERS

You go back, Jack, do it again.

—Steely Dan

In the fall of 2010, after a fourteen-year hiatus from the class-room and at the unpropitious age of fifty-seven, I began a one-year job filling in for a teacher on leave from the same rural Vermont high school that I'd entered as a rookie thirty years before. I signed on mainly because my wife and I needed the health insurance. The reason I trained to be an English teacher in the first place was my parents' insistence that I graduate from college with a trade, "poet" falling short of the mark in their eyes. It's fair to say that I have never gone to work in a school with what might be called purity of heart, though much of what I know about purity of heart I learned there.

It can still surprise me that I became a teacher at all. I could have satisfied my parents' requirements by pursuing a different trade; sometimes I wish I had. With a push in either direction, I think I could have managed to become a halfway decent attorney or machinist. I am not one of those high school teachers whose teenage years evoke such an irresistible nostalgia that they enter the ranks mainly in the hope of chaperoning a prom.

Nor, when I say "surprise," do I mean to suggest that mine is the well-worn path of the marginal student who feels called to the classroom in order to help kids have an easier time than he had. That is often a noble story, among the noblest in the field of education, but it is not my story. I was a good student at school, and when I applied myself, an exceptional student. At the risk of sounding immodest, I should probably add that there are people who would tell you that I am an exceptional teacher. There are former students of mine who would find it difficult to imagine that I could ever have wanted to do anything else.

I never had that difficulty. In fact, there was never a time during the sixteen years I taught when I didn't imagine doing something else. Even in the best moments, when teaching gave me the kind of rush some people find in skydiving or cocaine, I yearned to be at home writing. In the worst, I would imagine putting my name in at the local furniture plant, which I might well have done but for the impossibility of lying about my white-collar credentials to bosses whose kids, nieces, or nephews I'd had in class. I can't recall a single year of teaching that I didn't begin with a burst of enthusiasm accompanied by the fervent hope that come June I'd be done with teaching for good.

There is no simple way to account for that contradiction. From my earliest grades, I was fascinated with teaching and repulsed by school. By second grade I was asking my teacher's permission to "teach the class" about my scientific passions at the time: dinosaurs, rocks, and planets. I still marvel at the number of times she yielded the blackboard—to say nothing of the rarity with which my classmates rewarded my efforts with a black eye. But as early as first grade, I was throwing up my breakfast every morning out of anxiety before the school bus arrived. I had no trouble holding down my food on weekends and holidays. To this day the mere act of entering a school—that first whiff of disinfectant, that crackling interplay of regimentation and anarchy—is enough to turn my stomach.

Becoming a professional teacher intensified, and complicated, the emotions I'd felt as a kid. Teaching could be wonderful, and even when it wasn't, the students I taught could be wonderful. It made me sad to see some of them graduate, though in time I realized that part of my sadness had to do with being left behind. They were going on to do what they "really wanted to do," whereas I wasn't. In a ridiculous but palpable way, I felt less grown up than the gowned graduates who shook my hand and embraced me. After all, an adult is someone who's finished with high school. The distinction tends to blur when you find yourself matching wits with a mouthy fourteen-year-old or asking a principal if you can pretty please leave the building on your lunch break to run home and retrieve the corrected papers—your "homework"— that you left on the kitchen counter. The greatest challenge of teaching is not, as is so often averred, finding a way "to relate to kids." It is rather finding a way to relate to yourself in a process that often leaves you feeling like a kid.

A good part of that challenge has to do with the burden of evaluation. A child's acute awareness of measuring up, and of failing to measure up, exists for few adults with the same remorseless constancy as it does for a teacher. Everything a student fails to learn is something a teacher has failed to teach. (And everything that might be construed as wrong with the society at large can be placed, and inevitably will be placed, at the feet of its teachers.) Work harder, you tell yourself, but hard work is not always enough. Knowledge of material and technique is not always enough. You can still fail. What is more, you *will* fail. Certain social conditions combine with certain working conditions to make failure a foregone conclusion. The realization that I could work every waking hour of every day and still fall short of the most modest expectations was the first great lesson of my teaching career. I ought not to have found it so stunning. A teacher in the ancient world might have had a handful of pupils; he would have eaten and even lodged with them throughout their tutelage. Jesus Christ had twelve. In his first year of teaching, Garret Keizer had around a hundred.

The teaching position to which I applied in 2010 would give me a mere eighty. And I knew more about how to teach English than I did as a beginner. I was also better at the math. I knew, for example, that asking my students to put pen to paper only once a day would give me four hundred pieces of paper by week's end. Giving each piece of paper a scant ten minutes of my attention would require sixty-seven hours of correction. That's a lot of homework, and it doesn't count as preparation, which at its best ought to exceed correction by a factor of no less than two.

Within days after the principal called to say that I had the one-year job if I still wanted it, which is to say, within days after refusing my wife's final plea not to take it, I began having nightmares. I often have nightmares, but these were less obscure in their meanings. Even the fantastic ones weren't hard to figure out.

For instance, I am on a raft on the ocean a short distance from another raft. There is a creature slumped on that other raft that I surmise is either dead or close to it. Still, I hoist and flex the long metal pole in my hand so as to bring one of the leaden balls attached to either tip thudding down on its bowed shaggy head. I don't know how long I've been at this methodical braining, but as soon as I deliver one blow, I hoist the undulating rod above my head, watching intently for when the ball is in the right position for me to deliver the next. I don't dare to relax my concentration for even a second. If I don't make sure to kill this thing, it will kill me. It is easily five times my size.

Suddenly, the creature comes to life, furious, rearing up on its hind legs and sucking the breath from my lungs in the same instant. With one easy leap it bounds over the water from its raft to mine. The weapon in my hand, awkward at best, is now utterly useless, too long to wield in close quarters. With my heart pounding, I wake just as I am about to be eaten alive. Right away I know that the beast is the job I "killed" fourteen years ago and will resurrect in less than six months' time. The symbolism of the weapon takes longer to parse. Perhaps it is the ballpoint pen by which I have managed to earn my precarious living, mockingly elongated and flaccid, my years of hired scribbling revealed in all their humiliating impotence. Or maybe it is simply the ten-foot pole with which I had sworn never to touch teaching again.

Determined to enter my classroom as prepared as I can be, I make an appointment to meet with the principal and department head before the snow is gone. Here in northeastern Vermont that can mean a date as late as May, especially on the higher elevations where I live, but it's March when I make my way off the mountain, along the winding ridge road, and under the narrow railroad overpass that still feels, as it did during my last years of teaching, like the arch of a castle gate: protective coming in, ominous going out. Four miles of the trip are done at that point, followed by another seven that will take me along the train tracks and over the county line, past a lonesome pond and defunct sawmill, the cluttered dooryards and sagging roofs of South Barton, toward the neater lakeside houses laid close to Crystal Lake. Hidden by foliage but known to me are a rusted, battered trailer and backyard scrap-metal business toward the south end of the lake and, with a grand view from a perch above the northern shore, a palatial house of stone and glass in which one of my students once lived. I remember climbing the steep drive to visit her parents one winter night, the tall windows blazing into view just as the radio began to play Mozart's *Requiem*. It was like entering Camelot.

Today, though, I'm entering the village of Barton in Orleans County, its outskirts marked by the turreted Blue Seal feed store and the western-style Crystal Saloon, nicknamed the Snake Pit in former days, when it boasted numerous brawls and at least one homicide on the premises. In the very beginning, before my wife and I had managed to buy our long-desired "house in the country," I had come from the opposite direction, driving south from our apartment in the mill town of Orleans.

Either way requires a turn, left from the present direction, right in the past, onto an uphill road that passes under the interstate. Route 91 reached the heart of northeastern Vermont a few years before our arrival in 1979, changing much though not all of what was then regarded as a wild place. By wild I mean both wooded and lawless. Some of the lawlessness was indigenous, typical of what one might expect of a region at the northernmost tip of Appalachia. Some of it came with the countercultural migrations of the early seventies, the disillusioned hippies and radicals on the lam. No doubt closeness to a desolate border was a factor too. Not far from the high school or all that long ago the maverick inventor Gerald Bull built the long-range "super guns" he sold illegally to South Africa and Saddam Hussein.

The abutments of the underpass were thick with black graffiti when I first saw them, the school's vice principal brazenly proclaimed as an inveterate sucker of "wet donkey dinks" on one cement surface and a more generic "big pud" on another. In later years a depressing run of suicides and drunk-driving accidents lent a morbid, almost macabre tone to the graffiti until the school authorities, apparently as dispirited by the memorials as I was—though I had taken my leave by then—inaugurated the custom of having each graduating class paint a mural on one of the four faces as a legacy to the school. Among those I pass this afternoon is a depiction of rainbow trout jumping the falls, one of the region's more celebrated sights. People still gather every April on the banks of the Willoughby River and watch salmon and trout as long as two feet leap their way upstream to spawn. The iconic trout is also pictured on a granite marker outside the Ethan Allen furniture mill, the area's largest employer, once the destination of most of the able-bodied young males who weren't marked at birth for college or their fathers' barns.

The trout is not the high school's mascot, however, that honor falling to the coonskin-capped "Ranger" of Roger's Rangers, a group of colonial expeditionaries best known for their raid on a tribe of St. Francis Indians beyond the northern shores of Memphremagog and their ill-fated retreat thereafter. I make my turn onto high school property past a granite monument with the Ranger logo carved under the school's name, an addition since I left Lake Region Union High School in the midnineties, when only a few gray hairs salted my head.

The building that emerges as I round the corner is a flat-topped brick structure typical of regional high schools built in the 1960s. But for an occasional tractor parked outside the garage doors of the ag shop, little about the place gives a clue of its geographical location or the diverse sociological profile of its roughly four hundred students. The sprawling grounds suggest an active athletic program and a conscientious maintenance crew. There are tennis courts. Acts of vandalism are not unheard of, but they're painted over or repaired as quickly as possible and, perhaps for that reason, infrequently repeated. There are probably other reasons too. For most of the students, high school represents a heady expansion from the smaller, often less well-funded, small-town elementary schools they attend till eighth grade. For at least a few of them, Lake Region is the warmest, brightest, safest space they know. Kids cry at their graduations all over the world, but they do not cry for all the same reasons.

When Kathy and I first ventured into "Ranger Country" in our late twenties, with newly earned master's degrees from the state university and our New Jersey accents even more noticeable than neighbors claim they still are today, we were searching for two openings in the same school or at least in geographic proximity, one for an inexperienced English teacher and one for a new speech pathologist. Candidates for the first were a dime a dozen, but the latter were and in some ways continue to be a rarity in rural parts of the state. I recall occasions when, after being perfunctorily instructed by a superintendent's secretary to send a résumé and letter of application to such and such an address by such and such a date, I would casually mention that my wife was a master's-level speech pathologist also in search of a job (and therefore able not only to meet new state requirements for special education but to pull in state funding as well), whereupon I was told to hold the line until the superintendent could come to the phone. It seemed we would get some interviews, perhaps even a few choices, though Kathy felt strongly that the state fellowships that had paid our tuitions and duty-free stipends at the state university obliged us to look at school districts where "the need was greatest," or at least beyond the relative affluence of the Champlain Valley.

Not to worry, it was only beyond the Champlain Valley, and quite a ways beyond, that we found a district able and willing to see us as a package deal. We were hired by the Orleans Central Supervisory Union in Orleans County, one of three that make up Vermont's so-called Northeast Kingdom, and one of the state's poorest. That distinction has not changed, notwithstanding the presence of some large prosperous farms (often the aggregated acquisitions of smaller, failed holdings), a solid middle class of small business owners, skilled tradespeople, and white-collar professionals willing to trade an upscale income for a down-home lifestyle, and even a few millionaire squires seeking the same dream on larger acreage. As of the last census, only one of Vermont's fourteen counties (Essex County, also in the Kingdom) showed a slightly higher percentage of its population living below the poverty line than Orleans. Orleans County leads the state in accidental deaths and in the percentage of its children receiving food stamps, is last in the state for longevity among males, next to last for longevity among females. It ranks third for suicides and prominently for drug abuse, domestic abuse, and teenage pregnancy. When Kathy and I announced to our professors where we were going to work, one of them claimed that the region's most popular graduation gift used to be a set of false teeth.

I began doubting the rumor almost as soon as we arrived—if only because I couldn't see how many of the parents could have afforded the teeth. We were not much better off. With a master's degree each, Kathy's and my combined gross salaries were a little over $18,000. We located a high-ceilinged upstairs apartment roughly two blocks from where the rainbows jumped and as many blocks from the furniture mill, whose humming sawdust chutes would become a familiar sound of our summer nights. (We were also within walking distance of a hilltop country club, though we'd live in town for over a year before we knew it existed and would never have guessed from our immediate surroundings that it did.) Our landlords, a first-grade teacher and a school custodian more newlywed than we, though neither was young, sized us up and charged us a rent even less than what our pathetic salaries could have borne.

Theirs was not untypical of the kindness we would meet in that town and in those years. In defense of an eighteenth-century schoolmaster accused of being overly harsh in his discipline, Samuel Johnson notes "with how little kindness, in a town of low trade, a man who lives by learning is regarded." In a region where zoning disputes periodically arise over unregulated junkyards and whose collective memory reserves a hallowed place for game poachers and whiskey runners, the Northeast Kingdom has plenty of what Johnson might have considered "low trade," but the disdain he observed was in our experience mostly confined to harangues against the school budget and mock-wistful references to our long summer vacations. *So you folks are all done work now, are you? Mus' be nice.* What might have been said behind our backs in those first years after our arrival we didn't know, but our faces rarely met with anything but respect. Carolers tramped up our wooden steps and sang outside our door at Christmas. Occasionally students dropped by unannounced, including one endearing, academically challenged lug who, when I choked on a morsel of food one evening, sprang up from our kitchen table and might have broken my ribs had I not recovered my voice in time to spare myself a bruising application of the Heimlich maneuver. When our daughter was born, the minister's wife, a no-nonsense mother of four who handled a baby with the businesslike dispatch of a pizza chef tossing dough and as slim a chance of dropping it on the floor, volunteered to give us a kitchen-table demonstration on bathing an infant (we jumped at the offer) and the owner of the local furniture store came by with his wife and a dozen of her homemade rolls, still warm from the oven. From the other side of the cultural divide, the founders of the famous (or infamous, depending on your politics) Bread and Puppet Theater in Glover showed up with congratulations and a silk-screened banner bearing a militant red flower and the word *YES* to hang above her crib. I was a great eater of pancakes in those days, but I can't recall that we ever bought a container of maple syrup. It came to us, the way venison steaks and fresh raspberries would have come to a doctor's back porch in previous generations.

But we were always mindful of something anarchic in the shadows, rooted mostly in stories of "what things were like back then," before the interstate was laid and the down-country bourgeoisie began arriving in droves to seek "a simpler way of life" or "an old house with character," but still in living memory and sometimes on open display. Even in our tamer time, Halloweens fell just short of what would have justified calling out the National Guard. Wooden bridges and abandoned barns were set ablaze, and the house of one unpopular teacher was so mercilessly egged that he'd gotten into the habit of suspending large canvas tarps from the eaves to the driveway. In the smaller hamlets on the farther edges of the district, the older ways lingered on, not only in midnight devilment but in the comparatively staid conduct of school business. A veteran teacher's aide we came to know liked to tell the story of showing up for her first day on the job in the 1960s, only to find the village school locked and empty. When she went to the superintendent's office to ask if she had misread the school calendar, his deputy ventured an educated guess that "Dottie must not have felt like starting school today. Try going over tomorrow."

The larger point here is that Dottie was still a few years from retirement when my wife and I arrived at the end of the 1970s. She no longer used a large handbell to call the students in from recess, perhaps in consequence of a mishap involving a small boy who'd ventured too close to the arc of her swing and been

KO'd on the spot. As the story goes, the boy, questioned at dinner by his father as to the plum-sized lump on his scalp, began by saying, "Mrs. J. hit me in the head with a bell." Before he could elaborate further, his indignant father demanded, "What were you doing when she hit you?" The boy said he'd not been doing anything except standing too close to his teacher, but the father was unconvinced. "You must have been doing something pretty bad if your teacher had to bean you with a bell." The child might have gotten some additional knocks had Mrs. J. not rapped on the door just then, dropping by to check on her hapless pupil's head. She assured the parents that he'd done nothing to deserve a hiding.

When we first heard the story, it was used to illustrate how much times had changed—*a parent wouldn't be so quick to side with a teacher these days, that's for sure, call a lawyer more likely*—but it underscored how recently they had changed, recently enough for us to be part of the transition. Of course, we too were destined to be changed by our assignments, as much taught as having taught. By my count I have taken the equivalent of four degrees in my life, one from a college, one from the glue and plastics factories I worked in during college, one from a university, and one from teaching at a public high school in the Northeast Kingdom of Vermont, a region alternately as close to and as far from the Kingdom of God as any place I have ever known.

I walk from my car to the building with my resurrected briefcase (a leather, brass-buckled KPMG "audit bag" given me by my accountant brother and a signature accessory in my former teaching days) and an empty milk crate for lugging home as many course texts as I can carry. On the way I check to see that my old friend Donna Underwood is still included among the various memorials in the grass circle under the flagpole. It seems the school's untimely deaths are now consolidated in one upright monument, and Donna's name is there. Much beloved at the school, she was my department head until she died of cancer in between my seventh and eighth years of teaching. She'd been missing from my application interview—on medical leave to handle her first, nonfatal bout with breast cancer—and was reportedly against the hire, her disapproval probably overruled by my charmed status as the husband of a speech pathologist. In addition to my lack of teaching experience, she was concerned, as she later told me when we had become friends and could treat her confession as a joke, by the number of straight-A semesters on my transcripts. "You proved me wrong, but frankly, I didn't think our kids would relate to an egghead."

I sense the current department head also has reservations about me, and she does, though hers are of a different order, having to do with my ability to adjust to current trends in education rather than with any distinctions of my transcript or deficiencies in my toolbox. I will not learn of her caveats until later, when she no longer has them and I am just beginning to. For now I'm hoping that by showing up so early to learn the details of next year's assignment, I will put her at ease.

All trends aside, one thing has stayed the same. As I'm crossing the parking lot, the intercom squawks an announcement from the outdoor speakers. I have timed my visit to correspond with the end of the school day, so I can sense the more driven of the teachers inside the building sighing as the last three minutes of their lessons are lost—can feel something sigh deep in myself. "Without the loudspeaker we never would have conquered Germany," Hitler said, and on that point I've always been willing to give the führer his due. I hated that sound almost as much as anything else in the school routine, even if I liked the person whose voice was barking into the microphone. The kids knew I hated it, and the more sympathetic ones would join in groaning with me, a few hinting that in exchange for some extra credit they might be able to arrange a little accident with the wiring. This afternoon's message, "Seniors, remember your picture money for tomorrow," comes with a subtext: *Garret, are you sure you want to do this?*

I am no stranger to the question. I heard it even in the Donna days. After seven years of teaching, I took a sabbatical to write my first book—*No Place But Here: A Teacher's Vocation in a Rural Community*—returning to my classroom refreshed but more convinced than ever that I wanted to write full-time, wanted to work alone, wanted to wake up early with a tranquil feeling in my stomach and to work with no intercom squawking above my desk. I was now the head of my department, Donna having died near the close of my sabbatical. I had fewer classes to teach and thus fewer papers to correct, but more headaches, which is to say, more exposure to problems that were not of my making. What had been my working motto all the years before—stay in your own classroom and out of other people's affairs—no longer sorted with my job description. Nevertheless, I managed to last another eight years, six beyond the two-year commitment required by the sabbatical, largely by alchemizing what was supposed to be "administrative time" into extra tutoring time with kids. But the chairmanship was the beginning of the end for me. I don't think I was an especially awful chairperson, just an awfully unhappy one.

It was my daughter who helped me escape. One evening when she was in fifth grade, slumped as usual over her prodigious homework—it is virtually a natural law that the less educated or educationally involved the parents of school-age children are, the more they will tend to see "lots of homework" as a sign of effective teaching and the more likely their teachers will be to take the hint—I heard her say tearfully to her mother: "I'm not good at anything."

At that point in my career, I was teaching mostly advanced-level courses, a newly devised AP English among them, filled with kids who were "good at everything," or at least had been led to believe they were. Every year I added to my vanity files letters from college admissions offices *written to me* in praise of the detailed letters of recommendation I had written for my students. Every year I received a visit or a letter from a former student or a former student's parent, thanking me for my part in their preparation for college. *You were a good teacher*—but was I an attentive father? If teaching was the best thing I knew how to do, didn't my own child deserve a better share of it?

With my wife's support, in both paychecks and lesson plans, and our daughter's poignantly enthusiastic assent—her only question was whether homeschool would also include "snack time" and if that might be scheduled a little earlier in the day—I took the plunge, requesting a year's unpaid leave and forfeiting a salary that was at the time roughly equivalent to a year's tuition at Harvard. Thus began a labor of love and what I recall as one of the happiest years of my life. I divided the days into halves, with mornings given to conventional, skill-based lessons in basic subjects, and afternoons devoted to hands-on, long-term projects: an archaeological excavation at an old house site in the woods, running our own restaurant for an evening (on the premises of an actual restaurant and after weeks of lessons on foods and finance), and studying "babies" (which included shadowing a pediatrician on his hospital rounds). The local public school agreed to let our daughter come for art and music classes and thus to maintain ties with her classmates. I turned our tanklike '78 Malibu (destined to end its long and illustrious life as the winner of a demolition derby) into a mobile classroom, outfitting it with map assignments and flash cards for long trips and a jerry-rigged bike rack for physical education classes. I resisted the urge to draw up and affix a perverse if altogether accurate bumper sticker—"I'm a homeschoolin' gun-totin' Bible-bangin' . . . *SOCIALIST*"—though I was not always able to resist giving my stock rejoinder to some acquaintance's sniffing, hackneyed caveat about "the loss of peer interaction": *The inmates at Walla Walla state prison get peer interaction too.* There are few more trenchant giveaways as to the lack of confidence so many parents have in their local public school, and the anguish they experience in consigning their children to its care, than their readiness to construe another parent's homeschooling as a personal attack.

It had always been our intention that our daughter should return to public school, an institution we strongly believe in. Accordingly, she rejoined her classmates the following year. It had been my plan to return as well, but due to a fortuitous publishing opportunity, I did not—except for teaching an elective first-period course gratis for a single semester, a parting gesture of thanks to a school system that had treated me well. By the end of my semester with an overcrowded and dubiously motivated class, I was readier than ever to be done. And done I was, at least for the foreseeable future. What I could not have foreseen was walking back into the very same school, fourteen years later, and also on another mission I like to think was motivated by love.

Kathy and I had started our teaching careers in the same school district, with the same level of preparation and on the same salary step; for a while we even drove the same type of car, a VW Bug, mine beige and hers white, with a child car seat passed back and forth between them. Notwithstanding the unfair advantage

I had in teaching upper-track teenagers capable of singing my praises or at least remembering my name, both of us managed to achieve a comparable level of excellence according to our formal evaluations and community standing. Beyond that our trajectories were very different. For one thing, hers lasted twice as long as mine.

She had started out as the itinerant speech pathologist for seven schools, with a seventeen-mile spread between the most outlying two. One of our first chores after moving into our apartment was to construct a user-friendly map of their scattered locations and various dirt-road connections, to be kept in her car along with a snow shovel, a thick blanket, and a candle (the heat of a single candle flame reputedly sufficient to prevent hypothermia in a storm-trapped car). After a while her position shifted from working with students K through 12 to working exclusively with preschool children. This had been her aim even before taking her degree. At first she was dividing her time between students enrolled in a preschool classroom and children who received their services at home. When the preschool program began to move away from home visits toward the safer model of site-based delivery, she was also able to reduce her time on the road.

She would soon be spending most of her time in the rented rooms of a church basement, not an ideal site, though preferable to some she had known in the past. In her itinerant years, for example, she had given therapy on the stairwell of a two-story school that would soon be condemned as unfit for human occupancy and had delivered services at another school through whose playground a farmer took his dripping manure spreader every spring.

There was no manure in the church basement but that's not to say it was free of shit. The gatekeepers of the congregation were habitually snapping at the teachers—this trifle or that falling short of their standard of "acceptable" housekeeping—even as the Sunday school felt free to leave the classroom areas in disarray for Monday mornings. Basically there was one classroom and an adjoining room that served the dual purpose of storage space and office for as many as six teachers, aides, and specialists. Whenever I dropped by to deliver some teaching tool forgotten at home or to make a car switch, I'd enter a small metropolis of stacked toys and games, hang a left and then a right past the rainbow-colored skyscrapers, and find my wife (or a chair with just her sweater) sitting in a corner at a broken wooden desk that most people would feel embarrassed to leave on the curb with a FREE sign.

And yet, in spite of the physical circumstances, those years in the basement would be viewed in retrospect as the heyday of an exemplary program. Kathy's closest partner, the program's early-education specialist, was a master teacher (once the district's Teacher of the Year) and also her dearest friend. The other teachers and even the teacher's aides were all seasoned and impressively knowledgeable, as aides often are. (The widespread use of so-called paraprofessionals as underpaid substitutes for teachers is public education's best claim to a racket.) If it's cant to say that women work together more collegially and less "hierarchically" than men, it's a cant these women made it easy for me to believe.

But, just as the beginning of the end came for me when I was promoted to the head of my department, the golden age of my wife's thirty-year job came to a close with what felt at first like the fulfillment of a dream. The program was going to have its own building. The preschool was going to have the amenities of every other school in the district and perhaps even an approximation of the same respect.

The idea and much of the labor that followed came from

Kathy's teaching partner, who at times was working round the clock on the project while still holding her full-time job. Her colleagues took on extra duties in order to free her up for writing grants, consulting with architects and early childhood experts, and pacifying state officials whose greatest single fear seemed to be that a new building funded for direct services to children and families would wind up shanghaied by school administrators for their own purposes. Her colleagues also stirred their ideas into the brew.

Though the plans were repeatedly scaled down from the Reggio Emilia–inspired structure called for in the original blueprint, the building eventually came to be. It included multiple classrooms, individual or small-group therapy rooms, a storage space worthy of a medium-sized hardware store, office space for teachers, additional office space for social agencies (who it was hoped would offset building costs by paying rent and provide the equivalent of one-stop shopping for parents in need of broad-spectrum social services), a combination cafeteria/activities room (for work with gross motor skills), and a cushioned playground with brand-new equipment. Parents of the children, husbands of the teachers, and local business owners all lent a hand in assembling furniture, putting up shelves, moving equipment from former sites, and donating materials not covered by grants. It gave me particular pleasure to sit on the polished floor one evening and screw together my wife's new desk.

With the public declaration of an innovative new model for early childhood education—including the coordination of services between the public school, Head Start, and a nonprofit agency devoted to the area's migrant-worker families—reporters came to snap the pictures and write down the names of the superintendent, the director of special services, the state legislator for our district, and a host of other luminaries (say "cheese," as in "big")—everyone, need I add, but the women who had brought the building to birth. But the building was a reality. A new day had dawned.

It would be a short one. You can build a school from the ground up, but the directing of its destiny will always move from the top down. You can say "the kids come first" till the cows come home, but in practice the kids come fourth behind administrators, parents, and teachers—or fifth, in a dairy economy, behind the cows. Within the space of about three years, a new superintendent relocated his offices to the building. The social service agencies vanished. The storage room was emptied and its contents squeezed into outdoor storage sheds in order to make additional office space. The office for the preschool staff became nearly as cluttered as before with the overflow from the storage sheds. At least one treatment room was rededicated as a transition space for obsolete computer equipment. The spacious "gross motor room," to which children would go for their exercise on days too cold for them to have recess outdoors, was regularly commandeered for district-wide principals' meetings. Worst of all, three out of three extraordinarily gifted preschool teachers had left for other jobs. First to go was the woman whose brainchild the building had been and whose visionary capabilities included that of being able to read the writing on the wall.

Kathy stayed. Now the most senior member of the operation, the go-to person for day-to-day problems, though never for any programmatic decision that might plausibly require some rudimentary knowledge of early childhood development, she was often the first to arrive at the building and the last to leave. She was also one of the few people left under its roof who could recall what the place was originally intended to be. Returning from a sabbatical granted for the purpose of adding to her already considerable knowledge of autism spectrum disorders, she found the building altered and her new proposals ignored. The sabbatical felt like a practical joke. By then the "new initiative" within the district was for "all-day" (as opposed to half-day) preschool, ostensibly predicated on the belief that pre-K education is of vital importance and actually predicated on the belief that pre-K education is nothing more than glorified day care anyway. No one troubled to ask Kathy or any of her frontline colleagues about the appropriateness of a thirty-five-hour school week to a four-year-old. And why should they, given that a teacher of four-year-olds is frequently afforded the status of a four-year-old?

When Kathy dared to tell her imperious new supervisor that she was always open to constructive criticism but not to being snapped at like a stray dog, she was rewarded with the added chore of helping to set out hot lunches, buttering crackers, and wiping plates while postponing the treatment needs of the quasi- and nonverbal children who crowded her roster. Unlike my wife, the quasi- and nonverbal children could be counted on not to complain.

As my daughter had once awakened me from my stupor by saying "I'm not good at anything," my wife roused me to wakefulness by an equally affecting refrain. "Just once before I die, I would like to have a job where I'm treated like an adult."

William Carlos Williams told us that "so much depends upon a red wheelbarrow," and I have wondered if he said so because, as a physician, he wanted to distract us from the fact that so much *more* depends on a Blue Cross insurance policy, glazed with J-Rider, beside the chickenshit job. As my wife continually reminded me when I told her to quit and that I would welcome her home with roses and a loud hurrah if she did, we needed health insurance. My quoting of Thoreau's magnificent line about the folly of working yourself sick in order to have money to pay the doctor wasn't much help. Though Kathy never would have said so, the simple fact was that for years I'd been able to play Thoreau *and* pay the doctor thanks to her.

Indignant and discouraged but not yet beat, I devised two plans of emancipation. Neither one involved my return to Ranger Country, I might add. First, I would try to write my way out of our problem. I seemed close to a solution when the offer of a magazine column promised more income stability than I can usually count on as a freelance writer. The offer seemed almost too good to be true, and it was. The column was given to someone else.

The second plan was to parlay my modest publishing credentials into some kind of prep school or college teaching job. (The expiration of my teaching certificate several years previous made my employment at a public high school seem unlikely.) True, I had no college teaching experience, no PhD either, but creative writing positions sometimes waived those requirements. And hadn't I prepared kids for college for years, including some who were now professors with PhDs?

Knowing this was a long shot but not without confidence, I shelled out for a year's membership (at the peon level) in the Modern Language Association, without which mortals are not permitted even to weep over its want ads, and applied for positions at universities, colleges, and private secondary schools. I'd love to tell you some of the impressive things I said in my interviews, but that would require me to have been invited to an interview.

After every option I could think of had dead-ended, I learned there was to be a one-year opening at the high school where I'd taught, the only place I'd ever taught for pay. Suddenly there was a new and fateful nuance to the title of my book about teaching, now more than twenty years old: *No Place But Here*. For a fee and some hoop jumping, and with the superintendent's approval, the state was willing to grant me a two-year provisional license.

So, you might ask—echoing Dylan's taunting refrain in "Like a Rolling Stone"—*how does it feel* to be walking across the high school parking lot on a balmy spring day in the autumn of my life, just ahead of the school buses now blocking any chance of a hasty retreat, with my old nemesis the intercom blaring at me across the lawn? How does it feel to be back in the building from which I'd ventured fourteen years ago to earn my living with my pen? How did it feel to sit at a table at the one interview I'd managed to garner after all my exhaustive searching, across from a principal, a director of guidance services, and two out of four school board members who are all not only younger than I but also former students of mine and, without telling any lies outright, hedge the desperation that led me to apply? And what did I feel when one of the board members, not a former student, I'm relieved to say, expressed her concern that I might treat the post as a poor relation to my writing career, shortchanging the students while living on the taxpayers' dime, as had been the case with one schoolteaching real estate agent she'd known in the past—a bitterly ironic insinuation given that my refusal to do that very thing in all the years I taught at this school is quite possibly a reason for the arrested development and equivocal success that have brought me hat in hand to the interview?

Ambivalence. That's what I felt at the interview, that's what I feel walking into the school this afternoon, and that as much as any other single word is my best recommendation to whoever gets the chore of coming up with the Library of Congress subject classifications for this book. Teachers—rural high schools—midlife predicaments—freelance hacks, plight of—ambivalence.

On the one hand, I feel a sense of futility and failure, a sense of having been cut down to size, the victim of bad luck, of "systems" both educational and economic, of my own delusions most of all. This has nothing to do with thinking that the profession of teacher is beneath me; I have always said that no book I've ever written or will ever write is as important in the scheme of things, as venerable in the firmament of human accomplishment, and as much sheer fun in its finer moments as teaching the young. I will believe that till the day I die. I would believe it were my name to eclipse that of Joan Didion or Philip Roth. Rather, my discouragement has to do with my apparent failure to live up to the motto I now find blazoned in large letters in the school's main lobby: MOVE FORWARD.

At the same time, I feel an emotion difficult to express without sounding maudlin. As happened more than half my lifetime ago, when no one seemed to want my services or to be willing to give me a chance, this small rural high school is once again opening its doors—and not reluctantly, or on the whole suspiciously, but rather as if little besides its own good fortune has drawn me (what other word can I use?) *home.* I never felt it was a sin to leave the school behind once I was brave and solvent enough to do so, but somehow coming back calls to mind the parable of the prodigal son. Unworthy as I am, Lake Region Union High School has put a ring on my finger and health insurance under my feet. And there may be a more applicable parable. Even as I write this I wonder, honestly for the first time, if I have misinterpreted that nightmare about the beast I was trying to bludgeon to death out on the open sea. Had I dreamed but a moment longer, might I have realized that it leapt to my imperiled raft for no other purpose than to take me in its arms?

AUGUST

High school is closer to the core of the American experience than anything else I can think of.

—Kurt Vonnegut

I lose my black-and-white picture postcard of Malcolm X somewhere in the aisles of Bed, Bath and Beyond, a predicament as ludicrous as I'm starting to feel. I'm in Bed, Bath and Beyond in the hopes of finding some inexpensive picture frames for decorating my classroom. I've brought Malcolm in for a fitting. I'll have his photograph in my classroom for what I tell myself are several compelling reasons; I've gone so far as to memorize them in anticipation of the first time a student asks, "Who's that guy?" and, more to my purposes, "Why do you have his picture here?"

I'll tell them that Malcolm was a pimp and a drug pusher who became the leader of a liberation movement and thus a symbol of every person's potential for redemption. (I'll probably need to define *redemption*; I doubt I'll need to define *pimp*.) I'll tell them Malcolm was an avid reader who found at least some of his redemption in books. "If I weren't out here every day battling the white man, I could spend the rest of my life reading." I'll tell them that although he may at one time have been the most feared man in America, he defied our pop stereotype of the badass rebel by dressing in dark suits and ties and leaving us a body of published work in which you'll search in vain for a single four-letter word.

Not least of all, I'll tell them that until a bullet cut him down, he continued to change and grow, renouncing his own racism no less than that of his opponents. And if I feel the need, I'll tell them that unlike his justly more celebrated counterpart, Martin Luther King, he was no pacifist and nobody's idea of a saint, and neither (all young knaves, take note) am I.

Probably I won't wonder aloud in their presence if hanging his portrait in my classroom amounts to my own bid for badass cachet—the lame attempt of a compliant, middle-aged, middle-class white man to convince himself that he's an edgier customer than he really is. Except that Malcolm seems to have said as much already by vanishing into thin air and leaving me to cope with the embarrassment of losing him in Bed, Bath and Beyond.

Kathy tells me not to be discouraged. For all we know, she says, some bored-to-tears kid who got dragged along on a shopping trip will pick up the picture, ask his mother whose face it is, and turn to Google for whatever his mom doesn't know. I'm braced by her faith, the faith of a teacher, though I feel a bit like a tagalong kid myself to be so much in need of soothing.

If I'm testy this afternoon it has to do with more than a stifling parked car and my general disinclination to shop. The summer is quickly slipping away. Much of it has been taken up with promotional events for my most recent book, published the preceding May like a last hurrah before my writing output dries up to a few doodles. I am using the rest of my time to prepare for my classes, only one of which (Composition) I've ever taught before. Given that I began to do so in March, I'm dismayed not to be further along. I know from experience that while preparation is no guarantee of success, there is no sustained success without it. You can be as prepared to teach *Of Mice and Men* as Milton was to write *Paradise Lost* and still be shot down by a host of exigencies, equipment malfunctions, last-minute changes in the schedule, the wrong thing said to the wrong kid on the wrong day, but you're doomed from the start without an adequate plan.

Any teacher worth his or her salt will tell you that there are gains to be had by laying the plan aside and going with the flow of a class's sudden inspiration, but show me a teacher who sees this as the norm, and I'll show you a teacher living in a pipe dream of delusional serendipity. In a word, I'll show you a slacker. The problem is that time and energy are finite, and the need to be prepared isn't, so that sooner or later even the most conscientious teacher, and most certainly the rookie teacher, walks into a class less prepared than she needs to be, which means anxiously expectant of the moment when the whole thing will begin to unravel at the drop of a hat, or more precisely at the drop of a sheaf of test papers, a roiling test tube, or a photograph that was in your hand just a minute ago and where in God's name did you put it?

I'm gratified to discover that I will have a classroom mostly to myself and that it is one of the few retaining an old-fashioned blackboard. Most of the others have been outfitted with those white glossy panels that take erasable felt markers. I've always found chalk more sensuous, its sound on slate more authoritative than a marker's mousey squeak. I'll be stationed three doors down from the room that was once mine, but with the same view out the windows, the same hilly pastures under the wooded horizon. I might even see cows.

Other details have changed, including the presence of a

television in the room, and a desktop computer that I'm instructed never to turn off. Its wires run up to the ceiling and out to a power strip like an unruly grapevine. The venetian blinds all work; I'll have light through all my windows. For a few bleak years in the mideighties the school directors decided to conserve energy by boarding up one window in every classroom as well as the skylights over the gym. The boards went out on the orders of a new principal. It was during his term that framed pieces of student art began to appear in the lobby and hallways. Now there is scarcely a wall without a painting, though most of the wall space on the floors of the academic wing is taken up by lockers. I don't look forward to the sound of them slamming throughout the day or to the compulsive time wasting they occasion. But the students have always loved them—a small private space in a zone where almost nothing is private—and it is probably still possible to connect with a few freshmen through a bit of extemporaneous safecracking when the combinations fail.

For now my business takes me to the main office, which I find has been reorganized and much brightened since I was there in the mid-1990s. The remnants of someone's birthday cake and a bouquet of flowers are on the counter beside the clipboard on which the staff are expected to sign in and out. Where there had previously been one main office secretary, there are now two, one close to the door and another pulled back slightly from the traffic, but neither invulnerable to constant interruption. By way of a good omen, I'm greeted warmly by two veterans from my first years at Lake Region.

"Back for some more abuse?" asks the music teacher, while the math teacher gives me a bear hug. I always admired these two, especially after I had a chance to see their skills with my own daughter. I'd asked the one to get her through some difficulties with her clarinet and the other to help her prepare for a geometry exam. In both instances, I was struck not only by the deft mid-wifery that characterizes a master teacher but also by the realization that after years of teaching in the same building with these men I had in fact never seen them teach. I fear this is the norm for most schools. You rate your colleagues by your students' praises, by what you're able to deduce from lunchroom conversations or assignments left behind on a photocopier, but you rarely see them in action. Perhaps I'll be more fortunate this time around. For now, it's enough to hear them say "Glad to have you back."

My first appointment is with another past acquaintance, though not a former colleague. I first met Andre Messier as a fourteen-year-old farm boy in my freshman English class, at which age he could have done a competent job of leading the school, though it is only recently that he's become Lake Region's principal. Prior to that he served the school as a math teacher and later as vice principal, the unexpected death of his ranking supervisor putting him at the helm. Well over six feet, with a halogen smile and the broadest shoulders I have ever seen on a human being, he is deferential, resolute, and charismatic to such a degree that he trumps my usual suspicions of charisma. Apparently, the kids like to call him Mr. Mess, and one of my first questions to him is what he would prefer me to call him.

He replies that however I address him, he can't bring himself to call me anything but Mr. Keizer, so he is Mr. Messier to me from then on.

I've never considered myself to have "a problem with authority"; most of my tussles have been with men who presume an authority they don't officially have. With authority figures who know their place and honor mine, I have a history of doing well, perhaps too well, to the extent that I wonder if I might in some past life have been a cavalier or a samurai, fierce in my lord's or lady's defense and deferential in their retinue, feudal to the marrow of my professedly democratic bones. Any potential for that dynamic to be strained by the difference in age between Mr. Messier and me is more than compensated by the courtly respect on both sides. That doesn't mean that I won't be held accountable or have my challenges adjusting to what Mr. Messier refers to as "a twenty-first-century school."

As I anticipated, one of these adjustments will be to a computerized grading system, which has been in use at school for a few years now, though this year's version will be new, something called PowerSchool. Mr. Messier is quick to assure me that as long as grades are duly recorded online, teachers are free to keep an old-fashioned paper grade book, as most of the older members of the faculty do.

The demonstration he gives me is less reassuring. I am put off by the feature that allows one to check a student's progress in every course he has. In other words, while I am still not likely to observe my colleagues at work in the classroom, I will be only a few keystrokes away from being able to peer into their grade books. If I so choose, I can cast an appraising eye on how regularly they give tests and assignments and how timely they are in recording their grades. Experience tells me that this will be a favorite pastime with the sort of teacher who looks for any diversion from doing his own job, especially if it affords him the opportunity of learning that another colleague is even lazier than he is. My tongue gets the better of me, and I blurt out, "I'd as soon go through your wife's purse" (the wife in this case being the chair of the math department) "as look into her grade book."

This is received calmly, without visible irritation, and possibly with the trace of a smile—three descriptors I can't claim for my utterance—and I am sorry for my comment. But not entirely so. In time, thanks to some good tutelage from two long-suffering colleagues, I will become a competent PowerSchool user, praised by several of my peers for the number and timeliness of my recorded grades. But I will never be able to return their compliment because I will never be able to bring myself to the point where I would look into Mrs. Messier's purse.

I do better at holding my tongue when the principal sketches out the direction he would like to see the school take in regard to the grades themselves. He sums it up with the motto "Failure is not an option." As I will soon learn, this does *not* mean that no student can receive a failing grade, though the more cynical among the faculty will from time to time contend that it might as well. The principal is rather talking about a shift in emphasis from the grade earned to the material learned. Giving a student a zero for missing work—something Mr. Messier freely admits was his own policy during his years as an esteemed math teacher—he now regards as "the easy way out." It may fulfill some standard of justice or bookkeeping, but if the student is allowed not to hand in an assignment or pass a test, doesn't that mean he or she is being "let off the hook" of learning the material or the skill?

Mr. Messier wants to see a more aggressive approach, one he grants is a difficult sell "for some of the older people on staff." As an example he cites how he searched out a student who'd failed to hand in an assignment for a given class, brought him into the main office during a lunch period, and saw that he did not rise from his desk until the work was done. It seems that leading a horse to water is no longer enough; the horse is going to drink, even if it requires a trip to the principal's office to lower his lips to the trough.

This runs counter to my own philosophy, which has always put a high premium on free will. Based on what Mr. Messier says about the resistance he meets among the older faculty, I gather that free will still has its adherents. But perhaps philosophy is too exalted a word for what boils down to professional pride: I have always seen compulsion as a poor substitute for a teacher's motivational powers. When the school first introduced a policy on athletic eligibility years ago, I was adamant in my opposition: Why ruin something a kid does well on the basis of what he is failing to do well? And why usurp my prerogative to inspire a good ballplayer to write good essays about playing ball?

I should be listening to my principal, not ranting in my head, and what I hear is his heartfelt concern over the drop-out rate at the school (on the rise in recent years) and the bearing that standardized tests have come to have on its reputation and financial well-being. (Taxpayers are less apt to support a school they perceive as "failing.") On his side of the argument are some laudable successes in reducing the premature exits and raising the scores. In the year before my arrival, Lake Region ranked first in the state in its writing tests. Wasn't I the one who said at my application interview that I did not have an educational philosophy so much as a work ethic? So why am I wanting to quibble over philosophy now?

I try to bear in mind that I am little more than an overnight guest here, with an obligation to cause as little disruption as possible to my hosts. As for educational philosophy, I have taught long enough to know that it resembles political philosophy in depending a great deal on the personnel involved. If the king is Buddha, then long live the king, and if Hitler is elected by popular vote (as in fact he was), don't ask me to give three guttural cheers for democracy. If Andre Messier says failure is not an option, I'm ready to bend my beliefs, if only to do my part in seeing that failure is never an option for him.

Sara, my department head, was the second person I saw in March and we have been in regular touch throughout the spring and summer. She says she appreciates the time I'm putting in before the job starts. If she has reservations about the hire, as I'm told she has, she doesn't show them to me. I don't expect her to. Very fond of sports, she is also a good sport. She is the only member of the department who is older than I, though not by much. Voluble with peers, maternal with students, and seemingly inexhaustible in everything she undertakes, Sara appears to be the kind of supervisor who for every thing she asks you to do does three herself of the same kind—or four, if you include her assistance with the one thing she's asked you to do.

What I've asked Sara to do is to bring me up to speed on my teaching assignments and the current English curriculum. She has everything in readiness on my first visit. In addition to copies of the required texts for all my courses, I receive three-ring binders outlining the 2009 Vermont Common Core of "standards-based instruction," the department's own "scope and sequence" for its 9–12 offerings, and the NECAP (New England Common Assessment Program) test, an annual examination given since 2005 in order to comply with the federal No Child Left Behind Act.

One thing is clear from the outset: the biggest change in education since my departure from the classroom, bigger even than the place of technology in the curriculum, is the move toward uniform instruction. Students and teachers are obliged to be on the same page, or the same screen if you will, in terms of the "desired outcomes." In many ways the changes are mutually supportive: the technology allows for greater standardization and oversight; it also provides the rationale for greater standardization and oversight. *Our kids need to be prepared for the digital age and we need to be sure our teachers are preparing them.*

Despite some strong misgivings—the "digital age" is not my god any more than the "global marketplace"—I want to work in concert with my colleagues. I want to do a good job. I recognize the dangers of the self-styled contrarian whose "different drummer" lesson plans amount to little more than a list of pet peeves and arbitrary waivers. I've met more than one English teacher, for example, who claimed that "writing can't be taught" or that "grammar isn't important." At the same time, I'm not sure students are best served by a faculty of conformists, by teachers who are less shepherds than sheep. Sara probably imagined me raising just such a caveat when she objected to my hire.

Nevertheless, it's obvious she wants me to succeed. She has seen that my teaching assignment includes three sections of the same class, midlevel tenth-grade English, and has assured me that I will have a sufficient number of the required texts to teach the same book to all three classes at the same time. Effectively this means that for a five-class teaching assignment, I will have only three preparations, perhaps as close as any public high school teacher ever gets to the teaching load of a tenured university professor, which admittedly is about as close as Neptune ever gets to the sun.

My semester-long elective courses, offered exclusively to juniors and seniors, are Literature of Vermont and Popular Fiction in the fall, and Composition and another section of Popular Fiction in the spring. These, too, are geared to students of average ability, who account for roughly half of the school's total enrollment. While that doesn't discourage me, it does make me slightly uneasy. In general my preferences run to the advanced (top third) and the remedial (bottom fifth) tracks of the school's ability groupings, where the stakes tend to be higher, though they're not often the same stakes. The brighter kids are driven to succeed; the more challenged kids are driven not to fail. The middle are more complacent; it can take a heap of kindling to set them afire.

As if reading my mind, Sara tells me that I can choose a new book to add to my Popular Fiction class. It seems she wants the course to be an elective for me as well as for my students, though it's just as likely that she wants to add a little fresh blood to the reading syllabus. I'm happy to oblige, and I know, as Sara undoubtedly does, how much the students stand to gain if I can teach a book I love. But I have other criteria besides my own enthusiasm. I want the book to be recent enough in copyright date to qualify as contemporary. I would also like a book written by a woman or at least a book in which a fully drawn female character figures prominently. Few of the books at my disposal meet this requirement. Not least of all, I'd like a book that might do for my students what *The Autobiography of Malcolm X* did for me.

It so happens I have recently read what seems like the perfect selection: Elizabeth Strout's *Amy and Isabelle*, a poignantly class-conscious predecessor to her Pulitzer Prize–winning *Olive Kitteridge*. The book has two major female characters, a mother and a daughter, a working-class setting not unlike the grittier parts of our school district, and an author whose unsentimental compassion for her characters is on a par with Thomas Hardy's. As a bonus, the novel contains what is possibly the sleaziest teacher in all literature, a sexual predator who seduces the daughter. The problem is that some of the students I teach may already have met his type. Sara suggests as much, with little commentary but with a strong recommendation that I select another book. She's afraid of reopening old wounds. This is classic Sara in its sensitivity, but it also strikes me as indicative of a major change between schools now and schools then. The self-censorship that once was predicated on the wish to spare students exposure to aspects of life they were "not ready for" now is based on the dismal job we've done in providing that very sort of protection. In other words, much of what we now deem "inappropriate for children" is deemed as such because it depicts what

has already happened to children. The unmentionable is no longer the same thing as the unthinkable.

Anyway, *Amy and Isabelle* is out. When Kathy and I go up to
school one night at the end of August to make final adjustments
to my classroom, I lay another novel on my department head's
desk for vetting, with the juicy passages flagged to save her time.
I'm surprised by the number of flags; I'd never thought of the
book as racy. *You're in a different setting now*—it occurs to me
that I will need to flag some of my own daily expressions. I'll
need to relearn the skill of listening with the ears of a child and
the ears of a parent too.

Kathy and I set down the plants we've carried up through the
stuffy, darkened halls and throw open the windows to the air
and the moths. When the students show up in another week, I
intend to have a bouquet of fresh flowers on the sill. I hang up
framed photos of the Vermont poet James Hayford and his wife,
Helen, both deceased, who befriended Kathy and me in our first
teaching years, as well as a new Malcolm X (with a more suitably
priced frame from the Dollar General) and a flyer from an
ACLU Banned Books Week event in which I'd participated the
previous year. I tape up larger posters of Billie Holiday and Eleanor Roosevelt, the latter quoted as saying that no one can
demean you but yourself, the former seeming to say "I'm not so
sure of that." I roll up two large sheets of paper into horns and
tape one to each side of the TV. If I have to give the devil his due
in my classroom, I'm also going to give him his proper insignia.

My predecessor has left the room in immaculate shape,
including the desk and filing cabinets. There's a rumor that his
year's leave is in fact a prelude to his farewell—that he's not coming back after this year is done. Judging by the shape the room is
in, that seems plausible, though an equally plausible explanation
is his regard for his former department head. He liked to call me

Boss in those days, which he explained was not a gesture of subordination but a tip of his hat to my Jersey roots and our shared love of Springsteen. In front of his room stands an artifact from my old boss, Donna Underwood, who died before he joined the faculty, a massive wooden podium built for her by a former student in his shop class. I'm cheered by the sight of it, a bit worse for wear but still solid and, to my eyes at least, still Donna's.

Tomorrow will be the first official day of duty for district teachers and staff, all of whom will meet in the high school cafeteria en masse before going to their separate buildings. The program will be the usual mix of orientation, goal setting, and possibly a speaker, workshop, or activity designed to hone our skills and boost our morale but almost certain to depress me. For the past fourteen years Kathy has come home from these staff development days and said, when I asked how they went, either "It wasn't so bad" or "It was pretty awful" but always "I am so glad you're not there anymore." Now it's my turn to be thankful, though hardly Kathy's turn to gloat. Her eyes are wet, the next morning, when she kisses me good-bye.

By custom, staff development days begin with the introduction of new staff and the noting of departures. The superintendent makes a statement to the effect that the district has lost one Keizer and gained another, and it takes just about all the self-control I possess not to blurt out that the district has hardly broken even. Several others speak of Kathy's "retirement," and I want to correct them with the word *resignation* but I'm committed to holding my tongue as much as I can.

Not much of the morning will pass before I become aware of my need to exercise another kind of self-discipline: that of holding my bladder and bowels. I won't need to ask permission to use the restroom during staff development days, but once school starts, I'll not be able to step away from my room without asking another teacher to keep watch on my class. There are four minutes between class periods, roughly five hundred students and staff spread out on three floors, and a single toilet for each gender on mine. This is going to pose a challenge, especially since my only proven strategy for avoiding what were once almost daily headaches is constant hydration.

For her part, the "retired" Kathy Keizer is doing well in a new job. After my acceptance of the teaching position and shortly before resigning from her own, she located a part-time position as the speech-language pathologist in the pediatric neurology department at Dartmouth-Hitchcock Medical Center, an hour and a half's drive from home and several light years away from what her public school job had become. The headiness of the change is hard to describe. Courted and now regularly consulted by a former Georgetown specialist and a PhD-level nurse practitioner with multiple tours of humanitarian work in Colombia and Afghanistan, shadowed by earnest interns in their first white coats, Kathy has found herself in what is commonly called "another orbit" though "different universe" might be more apt. Where once her insights counted for naught among supervisors with little or no knowledge in early childhood development, now among specialists with breathtaking credentials she is asked to weigh in. Of more surprise to her than me, her decades of frontline work with underprivileged children and families amount to gold-standard currency among people smart enough to know their own limitations, which is to say, among people whose advanced degrees are not in education.

My low opinion doesn't lessen with the superintendent's address. It strikes me as typical of the profession's schizoid synthesis of lamentation over prevailing trends—"the newspaper is dead," "the World Wide Web is dead" (presumably a casualty of social media), on-site classroom instruction by teachers will soon be dead—and zealous promotion of the same. But "typical" is the whole point: the schizophrenia is not the superintendent's so much as the profession's. We teachers will make the world a better place, our masters tell us, and we will do so by finding more effective ways to keep our students in lockstep with the world as it is.

Consider, for example, the "30-million-word gap." Citing statistics from a famous study, the superintendent notes that students from the lower strata of society reach the age of three having heard 30 million fewer words than their middle-class counterparts. They've also heard 400,000 fewer parental expressions of praise. Possibly because I'm scrambling to get these figures into my notebook, I'm not sure what point they're intended to illustrate. That this is what we're up against, or that this is what will ultimately defeat us, or that this is the wrong that a handful of people armed with Ho-Hum State diplomas and Payless shoes are responsible for making right? Or perhaps, given that we are one of the poorest schools in the state according to the criterion of students who qualify for "free or reduced lunch," the implication is that the wrong has already been righted. After all, our topnotch students perform satisfactorily on their AP tests; nearly two-thirds of our graduating seniors go on to some kind of college or technical school.

In vain I wait for someone to remark that if our students are subject to such appalling inequalities, even before they enter school, then educational reform is a pathetic substitute for social revolution. At the least, I want someone to assert that the best reason for educating children is not to put them and their descendants on the winning side of the 30-million-word gap but to equip them to destroy the gap altogether. As the lecture continues, and throughout the school year, I will repeatedly be struck by the sense that the professed goal of creating "a level playing field" through education is little more than the goal of sorting winners from losers with a steady hand and a clear conscience. The single greatest expression of the American project, American public education is also its most cynical lie.

I'm still straining to keep my mouth shut (for all I know, dozens of my colleagues are engaged in the same struggle) and figure that if I've made it silently through the 30-million-word gap, I'll probably manage the same feat with the segments given over to technology, though that is likely to be a longer slog. Here, too, I wait in vain for what strikes me as the ultimate, unavoidable question. As we're told that 10 percent of all high school education will be computer-based by 2014 and rise to 50 percent by 2019, and as the PowerPoint throws up aphoristic bromides by the corporate heroes of the digitally driven "global economy"— the implication being that "great companies" know what they're doing, while most schools don't—and as we're goaded mercilessly to the conclusion that everything we are, know, and do is bound for the dustbin of history, I want to ask what kind of schooling Bill Gates and Steve Jobs had. Wasn't it at bottom the very sort of book-based, content-driven education that we declare obsolete in the name of their achievements?

Like an act of clemency, we're informed that after a short break we will have a presentation on blood-borne pathogens by the same school nurse who used to do the program when I taught here before and has done it ever since. Fair, freckled, and willowy, looking only a little older than I remember her, and with the same fetching display of good-humored embarrassment she's always shown in front of a group, Joannie steps on stage to sing her old standards about what to do when a kid starts bleeding all over your shoes. It's not easy to describe the effect this has on me, after so many years away and after several hours of biting my tongue, though it's clear that my companions are also moved, especially the old timers. Our cheering only serves to make Joannie more blushingly adorable, which brings on a whistle or two besides. Joannie and the Blood-Borne Pathogens. Bennie and the Jets. It's like coming back to your hometown and finding so much altered, the storefronts new, the gas pumps automated, and the dogs all dead, but then, just around a corner is your old bar, still open, with the same girl at the taps. Just as she did in years past, Joannie's handing out the rubber gloves, offering extra pairs to anyone who wants them. It was Joannie who told me to drink more water and I'd need fewer Excedrin, Joannie who will tell me to go easy on myself as I get back in harness. I'd as soon start the day over as miss a minute of what she has to say about her old buddies the blood-borne pathogens. So glad I am to see her that it takes me a few moments to realize that I'm less than a week away from walking elbow-to-elbow in a tense throng of jostling adolescents, where the eruption of a fistfight is always possible, to say nothing of contracting a case of hepatitis from a combatant's bloody nose.

On the second day of staff development, the district's teachers report to their respective schools, with each building principal in charge of the day's agenda for his crew. I greet the prospect with relief, though the agenda item labeled "Let the games begin" gives me pause. I tell myself it is probably a metaphor, something like "play ball" or "to your marks, get set, go" and completely in keeping with the athletic sensibilities of our administration. Even when the vice principal appears before us dressed in a catcher's outfit, I wonder if this is merely a theatrical touch, no more, something to raise the hungover spirits of those still sobering up from their summer breaks. I ought to know better.

The vice principal tells us that no one has to participate in the game he is about to describe but urges us to consider the number of times each of us, in our role as teacher, has asked students to do things they found uncomfortable and even embarrassing. In short, he asks us to consider whether feeling like a fool might not, in the long run, be preferable to looking like a hypocrite.

It is acting like a prima donna that I fear most and so I resolve that I am going to play along, though I will never in the course of the year feel more tempted to walk out of the building than I do right then. Without going into tedious detail, the game is basically a treasure hunt that each team of tablemates is to conduct while holding on to a length of clothesline. Since this is a timed race, it behooves each team to move quickly, which is to say, as quickly as its slowest member allows. Since the clues are scattered throughout the school and over the sprawling school grounds, and since I have spent the last weeks of the summer taking medication for an injury to my feet, it does not take long for me to be in some pain. It takes even less time for me to feel humiliated.

Finally, I drop out and return to my table. I tell my teammates that I can only slow them down. I rather feel as though I've let them down. This has been my first real challenge on the job, and I have failed—something I'd not have done had I either flatly refused at the beginning or followed through to the end.

I also see it as an occasion for repentance. Over the past fourteen years of my self-employed life, I've gotten rather smug about my appetite for work. Well, Garret, this is what "work" means for most people. Although the vice principal's words about putting on the shoe we often ask our students to wear conjures up few

associations for me, I find I'm thinking of a whole array of wage
earners: the HarperCollins sales people I saw at a book conference who'd been forced by the publisher to wear Lemony Snicket
armbands, the junior executives ordered to examine one another's auras in sleepover seminars on Gurdjieff, the counter clerks
who risk reprimand and even the loss of their jobs for failure to
get you your burger and fries within one minute flat or to ask if
you want a hot apple turnover to wash down with what remains
of your supersized soda, my teacher colleagues today not least of
all, who fall into the drill without complaint and perhaps with a
more informed sense than my own that this could be, and in some
years has been, a whole lot worse.

These are my musings at the time, though not at present,
when my thoughts are mostly of the vice principal. I made a note
to keep my eye on "that guy" then, little knowing that his eye was
already on me and that he was showing me with as good a metaphor as any I can imagine how our relationship would work. In
the ensuing nine months he would stand with me in every difficulty I brought to his attention, as though a rope were holding us
together, and he would never once let me go.

After almost a week of meetings, the arrival of the students is
like a breath of fresh air. Their voices course through the hallways
like molecules of oxygen through tired blood. Literally, though,
the air is hot beyond belief. The temperature in my classroom,
which is directly above the flat tarred roof of the downstairs
lobby, hovers around 90, which is to say, a few degrees above
what the temperature is outside. I have a fan for my room, but
turning it on makes hearing more difficult, and opening the
door to the classroom exposes us to noise in the halls. I lower
the blinds to block as much sunlight as possible and turn off the

overhead fluorescent lights, leaving students with barely enough light to see. The last time I recall working in heat of this intensity was during the summer after high school, when I worked in a glue factory. Even there we had an open garage door and a handy water hose for dousing ourselves.

One of the rooms adjacent to mine is fully air-conditioned. It contains several banks of classroom computers, which will run erratically if they get too hot. I remark to my students that if they were made of wires and silicon instead of nerves and blood, they would be sitting in a cooler room. They do not seem to grasp the irony. Born at the close of the twentieth century, they know their lowly place in the Great Chain of Being. They show remarkable patience as the day drags on, complaining as well they might, but not whining or using the heat as an excuse to slack off or misbehave.

Much remains to be seen, but the kids seem fairly similar to those I taught in the past. The voc-ed boys still carry baseball caps, putting them on between passing bells, and stalk through the hallways in high-topped boots. The girls still take hot weather as an invitation to bare as much skin as the dress code allows, though décolletage was never the rage it is now: one has the impression of being in the court of Louis XVI on a casual Friday. Everyone seems to have a cell phone; school rules dictate they be turned off throughout the academic wing. There's also more obesity than I recall in past years, though that was probably always more prevalent in this region than in other parts of the state. (Only someone utterly unacquainted with the cruel ironies of underclass life would see a contradiction between high rates of obesity and the fact that an estimated one child in four in the Northeast Kingdom is "food insecure"—that is, unable to take the likelihood of three meals a day for granted.) If anything, the students seem more cooperative, even more friendly on first

contact than I remember kids being in my first years, but I am of
the same generation as their grandparents now, and I was a mere
nine years older than my oldest student when I first started out.
Toward the last half of my first tenure I enjoyed the benefits of a
cumulative reputation, of dos and don'ts handed down from older
siblings—I'll enjoy less of that benefit now. It turns out I might
have something better. "Do you remember having a student named
Mary LaClare?" "Yes, and fondly"—and a sudden perceived resemblance tells me what's coming next. "She's my mom."

Unlike most of the men on the faculty, especially on those first
sweltering days, I wear a tie, and a jacket too, hanging up the latter
as soon as I enter my room. In an offhand expression of solidarity
with the blue-collar parents of our community, but mainly as a
concession to my falling arches, I add a pair of well-oiled work
boots. For the first time in many years, I have what might be
called a look—like me and like the white-collar trade of teaching
itself, a strange amalgam. A girl passing in the hall tells me I look
"spiffy." "I'd have thought I looked *old*," I say, and she counters by
asking, "How old are you, thirty?" I take this as a compliment and
beam accordingly, though she may in fact be doing nothing more
than agreeing that I am old.

I have decided to begin each class period with a selection of
music chosen for that day, writing the selection and artist on the
board above my class agendas and keying the selection into a
small CD player. For the students' first day, I choose John Coltrane's "Welcome," at the closing bars of which a hush comes
over my chattering students, proof of what I've always believed
about the divinity of Coltrane's inspiration and the wellsprings
within even the dopiest-seeming kid. "This is nice music," one
boy remarks, and no one sneers.

As I imagine is true for most teachers, I believe in stating my
expectations from the start and in getting out of the gate as fast

as possible with a first assignment. I stress the importance of courtesy and mutual respect. I stress that I will expect reading assignments to be read, a requirement I've been given to understand is alien to the experience of some of my older students, whose past English teacher is no longer employed at the school.

I also lay down what has always been one of my firmest rules: students who've been absent are to see me *on the morning* of their return to school, before classes begin. Few things can deflate a class period like devoting its first ten minutes to catching up students who were absent the day before—at the cost of neglecting students who were there. Often with the best of intentions, schools consistently telegraph the message that missing school is more advantageous than attending it. The suckers who show up live by the deadlines; the rest do their work and take their tests according to their own convenience. The trick is to convince students that you value their presence, you value the class period, you value the taxpayer's dime as the equivalent of a sacred trust. I personify that trust by asking my students not to forget "the man who works in the woods." As I explain, I mean any local logger who cuts pulp in a cedar swamp at thirty degrees below zero in order for us to have light and heat and books and in order for yours truly to have the health insurance and pension fund that the logger doesn't have. (Please, somebody, ask "Why not?") We insult his sacrifice if we waste our time.

Strict as I sound, and decent as most of these kids seem, it doesn't take them but a day to learn that as a matter of principle I will not refuse anyone's request to go to the restroom. I find the request itself demeaning, to me no less than to the student, and my answer has always been yes. It takes an explanation from another member of the faculty for me to realize that the requests are about answering the call of a cell phone as much as the call of nature. Texting in the boys' room is the new version of smok-

ing in the boys' room, though to their lasting credit the addicts
of yesteryear were usually able to go an hour without taking a
puff. My strategy, at least initially, is the same as the one I used
in years past when dealing with the Marlboro Man: keep the
classes focused enough and intense enough that there's really
something to be missed by staying away. Make the students *want*
to be there. But already I can see that this approach may prove
inadequate. Given that my classes this year are on the whole "less
academic" than those I used to teach (now designated, to my considerable distaste, as "honors"), test scores and report card grades
may not be the sticks and carrots they were for me in the past.

What is more, I'm competing for students' attention on no
firmer foundation than I'm competing for air-conditioning. In
other words, I'm up against the orthodoxy of a virtual religion,
much more powerful than any narcotic, of which teachers themselves are the chief apostles. My comparison of texting today with
smoking in years past amounts to a weak analogy unless it can be
shown that schools in times past were evaluated by how thor-
oughly they integrated tobacco products into every aspect of the
curriculum. With some teachers conducting class discussions via
keypads and others following their students on Facebook, decrying the students' obsession with their cell phones seems disingenuous at best—like Al Capone decrying the amount of time
Chicagoans are spending in speakeasies and brothels.

At the end of that first sweltering week, with the Labor Day
weekend bobbing like a life raft at the end of it, a large boy, tall
and wide, stops by my door and asks if it's true what he's heard,
that I'm a writer. I tell him it is, at least insofar as I've managed to
make a modest living doing that work. He says he's a writer too. I
say I'm glad to hear it. I could be meeting myself as I was forty
years ago, though I was much skinnier and not so tall. I probably
can't expect to have the same effect on his literary aspirations as

young and lovely Miss Pombo had on mine, but maybe I can have a small one. The boy is not in any of my classes. I shake his hand.

When I ask his name, he says that everyone calls him Ox. I search his face to see if I can detect whether he is happy about that, but it's possible he doesn't know himself. I tell him I'm not sure I'm going to be able to call him Ox, but that in the absence of a given name—he doesn't seem to want to tell me his—I might decide to call him Writer. Would that be okay?

It would. He says that maybe he will show me the book he is writing. I tell him I would love to see it. I will restate my willingness at least once more in the coming weeks. As time goes on, I will realize I am not going to see Writer's book—no more than I am going to see any of the other books my students claim to be writing, including one incredible tome that reportedly vanishes into cyberspace during the composition of its final, 700-and-somethingth page.

But now is only the first week of school, when I stand ready to assist and possibly rechristen every one of the budding authors who I am almost certain will approach me as a matter of course, ready for that moment when a framed photograph of El-Hajj Malik El-Shabazz, formerly Malcolm Little and best known as Malcolm X, will incite a life-changing discussion that in fact never occurs.

SEPTEMBER

Americans must resist the coming of fall, . . . because Americans want to remain individual. The classroom will teach us a language in common. The classroom will teach a history that implicates us with others.

—Richard Rodriguez, *Days of Obligation*

Within a few days after classes begin, I've formed my routine, which for all its appearance of self-discipline is grounded mainly in my desire to avoid panic. I rise most mornings by 4:00, hoping to carve a few more productive hours out of the day and also to convert the psychic energy that might otherwise go into making nightmares to creative energy for making assignments and tests. It occurs to me that had I risen as early to write during the past ten years, I might be writing still.

By 4:30 I'm showered, dressed, and at my upstairs desk, where I can usually accomplish a couple of hours of solid work. I know from experience they'll be worth twice that many spent at the tail end of a tiring day. By 6:30 I'm out the door, toting a full briefcase and a lunch cooler my wife has carefully packed for me, including at least three containers of fluid, usually two of water and one of iced tea. I could easily have another hour at my desk and still be to school by 8:00 as required, but I have my

reasons for leaving when I do. I can get situated with fewer interruptions if I'm there by 7:00 and possibly have first dibs on the
photocopier. I can blow some of the stale air from my classroom
and suck the last of the cool morning air in. I probably won't be
the first to arrive—there seem to be more early birds on staff
these days than in the past—but I'd prefer not to be. I'd prefer
not to risk setting off the school's security alarm when I punch
in the code that deactivates it.

Once I've unlocked my classroom, opened the windows, and
observed a moment of silence, I set up my fan and head down
the hall to the photocopier in the teachers' workroom. I'm a regular there, having no leftovers from past terms to fall back on. In
addition to being fast, the magnificent machine collates, staples,
and punches holes for a three-ring binder. The first automatic
washing machine could not have looked more magical to a laun-
dress than that copier looks to me. I came up through the ranks
in the days of mimeograph machines, typing my masters on a
typewriter without a ribbon in order to maximize the clarity of
the keys' impressions, correcting mistakes with a razor blade
and a fresh scrap of inked backing, and creasing the sheets carefully onto the drum lest the slightest wrinkle lay a blue jagged
scar across each page. Then it was staple, staple, staple, or find a
kid willing to staple for a few bucks. Even when the first copiers
arrived, they were reserved for use by the administration. Now
there are four copiers in the building; if there's a queue at this
one, I can try my luck downstairs.

With the copies warm in my hand, I walk quickly back to my
room to set up for my first class. This includes writing an agenda
on the blackboard, posting the title and artist for that day's
music, and arranging my desk and worktable as neatly as I can.
A teacher's battle with chaos follows the lines of Norse mythology: we know that the frost giants will eventually win but that

doesn't mean we can't smack a few down in the meantime. I uncap one of the water bottles my wife has prepared, the bottom third of its contents frozen solid against the heat. I chew an Altoid left over from the gift bag I took home from a television interview last summer. There was a bottle of vodka in that bag too, but I'm not to that point yet. I wait for my first arrivals.

I ask absent students to see me at the start of the day for the reasons I gave above, reasons I will have to repeat before the rule sinks in, along with warm praise whenever the rule is followed, but the fact is that I might keep the rule even without the reasons. Seeing a student first thing in the morning, telling him that he was missed the day before, asking her how she is feeling today, basking for a couple of minutes in the backstage banter that the audience of a classroom seldom allows—this is the only shot of spirits I need. There are school days that would seem close to wasted but for that first half hour with a few sparkling, sometimes still damp-haired kids.

At some point before the first passing bell I will need to turn on my laptop and log onto PowerSchool in order to take attendance as quickly as possible. The process is always slower than I hope. My habit in past years was to take a few minutes at the start of each period to set a positive tone, tell a joke, praise a student's achievements in another school activity, recount a current event, or read a passage I'd come across that seemed worth reading aloud, all the while taking attendance out of the corner of my eye and noting it in my grade book. The present system is more jealous of my attention. Often my first words to the class are related to the minutiae of the record keeping. We are expected, for example, to record missing homework, so that teachers in subsequent study halls can follow up and see that it gets done. To start a class by asking for a show of hands from those who haven't done their homework (something I've always preferred to do confidentially and at least a few minutes into the period by walking discreetly among the students) is hardly the best way to set a positive tone. If I hit the wrong key, I need to cancel out my notations and do all of them again. If a tardy student walks into the room a minute after I've hit "submit," then I need to call up the screen and do the entire roster over. As noted by the outside consultants who manage the system, it "currently lacks the capability" of maintaining a daily record of absences beyond "total to date"—a must for any teacher who hopes to keep track of when a student was and wasn't in class and therefore was or wasn't responsible for a missing assignment or on hand for an essential presentation of material. This means I must take attendance twice, once on the computer and once in a notebook I consult whenever I wish to know for sure what a student may have missed on a given day.

The bottom line here—and I use the phrase with an eye to the mind-set that promotes these "systems"—is that I am increasingly devoting more time to the generation and recording of data and less time to the educational substance of what the data is supposed to measure. Think of it as a man who develops ever more elaborate schemes for counting his money, even as he forfeits more and more of his time for earning the money he counts.

At least I do not lose more of my first period to morning announcements, which come at second period, when I have off. Instead of being read over the intercom by the principal as in years past, they're presented as a televised newscast by students in a media class. Included are a weather report and a notice of student birthdays. Thus the reason for a television in every room. I dehorn mine on the day of the first broadcast, sorry for my snarky gesture, not that it arouses much notice. Neither do the bulletin boards I've put up, including one that displays a medley of pop culture profiles, arresting photographs, incredible statistics, and hilarious cartoons and another that provides a space for students to write their "blues" (right next to Billie), complaints, and suggestions. The space will remain as blank as a broken TV for the next nine months; apparently no one has the blues but me.

My first-period class, Literature of Vermont, is small (ten students), docile, mostly unmotivated, and overwhelmingly (though not boorishly) male. Our one young woman sits in the middle, geographically, academically, and as a sisterly moral center. Among the texts I inherit, all of them chosen with the strictest regard to the permanent Vermont residency of their authors, I choose to begin with the longest, an all but forgotten novel by Mari Tomasi called *Like Lesser Gods*. It represents one of the state's first ambitious works of fiction (1949), was written by a woman, is based on almost-local history (that of the Barre granite quarries), and treats two themes not commonly associated with Vermont: Italian ethnicity and organized labor. The latter seems especially pertinent. The local furniture plant has no union, nor do the region's numerous underpaid child care workers (though an effort is afoot to organize them), nor do many of those employed in the building trades. Tomasi also develops a theme remarkably missing in much of the literature we assign to young people: the choice of a life's vocation. Study of the novel in years past has included a field trip to Barre, where Tomasi lived and where granite is still quarried and carved—an incentive for students to read the book but also for the teacher to assign it early, before any snowstorm can cancel a bus.

On the other hand, the book is long, the exposition dense, the vocabulary ponderous, the allusions plentiful—obstacles that seem all the more daunting after I've spent more time with the class. One student tells me flat out that he has never read a book in his life. Even over the summer, ignorant of my students and about a quarter of the way into my exhaustive annotation of the book, I began having doubts as to the wisdom of teaching it, but I told myself that if "midlevel students" in the past had managed to read it, students in the present should be able to do the same thing. I bet an awfully big wad of confidence on what proves to be a monumentally big *if*.

I consider bailing at one point, but conclude that would be a mistake. Abandon a book because it's stupid, not because it's hard, which always risks sticking the "stupid" label in the wrong place. I press forward, using almost every trick I know—study guides, character lists, in-class oral readings, real-life tie-ins, pop quizzes, alternatives to quizzes, student-designed quizzes, student-designed crib notes to be used on quizzes, close analysis, revised syllabi, donuts, imaginative identification with the novel's sentimentally drawn characters—but for most of the students, most of the time, the book is a loss. I'm an experienced teacher, but it seems I have a few lessons to learn.

Some of them come to me in offhand, stunning ways. I've been instructed that the policy for study halls requires teachers to assist students with their work before attending to their own (which was always my practice anyway) and prohibits allowing students to catch a few winks at their desks (something I never minded, especially once I discovered how taxing a school day could be to my own child). I have a small, highly cooperative lunch-period study hall, and a most delightful girl on the list, someone whose studiousness and affability seem to rub off on her neighbors. One day she has nothing to do, claiming she's managed to complete all of her homework. I have no reason to doubt her. Either because I've noticed her drawing or because I know she has a class in the art room, I ask her if she likes art. Yes, she likes art very much. Music to my ears—among several of the books I've brought to school for browsing is an expensive coffee table compendium of painting and sculpture by three

Italian masters, Leonardo da Vinci, Michelangelo, and Raphael, costing more than even I would shell out for a book (it was a gift) and including (though I don't mention this in my pitch) some very buff guys depicted as only a gay Italian genius could depict them. The girl glances at the book without opening it. "Thanks," she says, "but I guess I'll just draw," by which she means penciling in the scribbled loops on a torn-out page of lined notebook paper. So much for the Renaissance.

More troubling is the small fiasco I cause in the Vermont Lit class by pulling out my old chestnut on the fallacy of saying you're "no good with grammar." Every class I teach does some writing, and I try to offer a few pointers in composition and usage whenever I return a batch of papers. One thing I've always enjoyed impressing upon students is the idea of language as a cultural inheritance—it doesn't belong to English teachers, it belongs to them—buttressed by a demonstration of the fact that they know more "grammar" than they realize, however alien grammatical terminology may be.

"For instance," I will ask, "which of you can tell me the difference between an objective case pronoun and a nominative case pronoun?" (Few people then, no people now.) "All right, no surprise there, most people can't. Yet every single one of you knows the difference, and, not only that, you've known it most of your lives, since you were about two or three years old, which is to say long before you began to be intimidated by the word *grammar* or the likes of me. Look at these two sentences, please."

> I will go to the store this afternoon.
> Me will go to the store this afternoon.

"If I speak the first sentence, what does *I* refer to? And if I speak the second sentence, what does *Me* refer to? Exactly. The pronouns mean the same thing because they refer to the same person. But one of them is used correctly in its sentence and the other one isn't, and all of you know that, even if you don't know why. A show of hands, please. How many of you say the first example is right?" Hands up, all around, as always, ready to catch the big eureka. "How many of you say the second example is right?" Of course, no one will.

Except that a hand shoots up.

Wise guy? No, sir. Just a boy, often in trouble, or so I've heard, though never with me, frequently absent, always dressed as though he's just got out from under the chassis of a car, with his hand raised boldly, proudly, not afraid to be different or, in spite of my prefatory remarks, wrong.

I backpedal as fast as I can, as far as possible from the insinuation that he doesn't know what most people know by the age of three—and what he certainly seems to know based on his spoken language. Fearing I've done him harm, I go after class to the specialist he sees for academic support, prepared to make full confession of my sin and do whatever penance she prescribes.

"He has some challenges," she says, which are compounded by poverty and a very tough past. But I shouldn't be worried. "In fact, he really likes you. I've rarely seen him this motivated." Moving as this is, it leaves me unable to picture him reading *Like Lesser Gods*.

In the weeks to come he will give evidence of doing just that—with some tutorial help, I'm sure—but even now I'm impressed by his answers to questions and his contributions to discussions, and I tell him so. Outside of class, we talk about cars, the truck he'd like to buy if he can pull together the dough. But his attendance grows more sporadic, probably because he is out working when he ought to be in class, and I can see already that he's going to fail. He gets into some kind of trouble I don't fully understand, and suddenly he is gone from school, leaving the objective *me* and the nominative *I* to parse their anger at the world's injustice from the shame (admit it!) of their own relief.

Martin Luther King said that a person who doesn't know what he would die for doesn't know what he's living for, and I decide I'm going to live or die on the value of books. That's a pretty tame stand for a high school English teacher, though perhaps no more so than that of a twenty-first-century Democrat who stands by organized labor or a twenty-first-century husband who stands by his wife. The girl who refused to open the art book is a partial inspiration; so is the sight of a school library that resembles a NASA control center in which the technicians occasionally break for a little light reading after lunch. More provocative than either is a curious window display outside the library prepared by our energetic first-year librarian and grossly misunderstood by the older man in necktie and work boots whom she treats with the kindest regard. The display consists of a dozen or so new acquisitions, graphic novels and topical books of particular interest to teens, standing on a pyramid of steps made from the glossy black volumes of the Library of America, laid flat like bricks. The library began collecting these volumes, each devoted to the works of an American literary master, some years back and has managed to amass an encyclopedia-sized collection. What can the display be if not a celebration of the old and the new, and perhaps an acknowledgment that the new stands on the old, "on the shoulders of giants," to use an ancient metaphor. Faulkner, Whitman, Dickinson, and Wharton are the building blocks of our American literary project, our stepping stones to the future . . .

Actually, what they are is discards. The symbolism of their position under *Pride and Prejudice and Zombies* is comparable to that of the dragon under the foot of St. George. As the librarian has explained to my department head, her space is limited, the books are hardly ever used, and so she's decided to give the library a freshening up by moving the Library of America out of the Lake Region collection.

I decide at once that one of my goals for the year will be to find a tactful way of persuading her to restore the volumes. I say tactful because I understand her predicament: she has a budget she must either spend or lose, she oversees a space that no electorate has agreed (and at least one has adamantly refused) to expand, and she has even fewer shelves for books than there were twenty years ago because of the space required by the computers. I'm also mindful of her prerogatives; this is her classroom, this is her first year, and if I would not take kindly to her telling me how to teach, I imagine she might not take kindly to my telling her how to run her library, a presumption that would be compounded by our respective genders and ages. I'll need to bide my time on this.

What I want to say to her is that school libraries exist to serve all the students, yes, but they also exist to serve that student who comes along once every twenty-five years, who is likely to go almost totally unnoticed during his four years of haunting the stacks and is about as likely to be the graduate who puts his small-town alma mater on the map. I'm thinking in particular of a former student of mine from years back, now a professor, writer, and dear friend, who probably would have set herself the task of reading as many of those Library of America volumes as she could carry in two arms had they been around in her day. By her sophomore year she was dropping by my classroom to discuss what she'd newly gleaned from Plato and Montaigne, a good deal more in both cases than I'd received in my formal education. When she asked me whether I'd recommend Saul

Bellow's *Herzog* as a suitable read for her and when I confessed that it was but one of many gaps in my background, we made a pact to read it at the same time and discuss it as we could, an arrangement in which I was often scrambling to catch up. She prompted me by leaving whimsical reminders hidden in places where I was likely to find them; more than twenty years later, I will still pull a book off my shelf only to have a scrap of colored calligraphy fall to the floor: *Herzog!* I won't try the same stunt with the librarian, though if I did, I might use my former student's name.

Faculty meetings, always a trial for me, are softened only slightly these days by my affection for the person leading them. What most vexes me, ironically enough, is that we have been asked to read a book. Mr. Messier has assigned us monthly chapters in a text called *Raising the Bar and Closing the Gap: Whatever It Takes*, the first time in my experience (another irony, to be sure) that an administrator has given teachers a book for homework. I love the gesture, but I hate the text. Its four authors, two of whom are married and share the surname DuFour and all of whom self-identify as "active consultants" (i.e., those who've managed to figure out that there are easier and more lucrative ways to make money in the education racket than by teaching kids), have devised a program for organizing faculties into "professional learning communities" (PLCs) and schools into a network of "intervention strategies" dedicated to the premise that every student can—nay, must—learn. The goal is laudable; its underlying assumptions trouble me.

I am troubled, first of all, by the pseudoscience of the authors' "evidence," according to which a successful (usually middle-class) school is invariably one that has adopted their nomenclature and bought into their program. I see no hint of a suggestion that a rose by any other name, which is to say a PLC in everything but their franchised acronym, can smell as sweet. Equally unscientific is the utter absence of any evidence that doesn't support their hypotheses or any measure of success besides such dubious indicators as performance on standardized tests or the number of students signed up for Advanced Placement courses. Surely any "educator" worthy of the name would be scholar enough to raise an eyebrow at this.

I'm also troubled by the repeated, snide, and almost sinister references to those recalcitrant teachers who insist on acting as "lone wolves" and on treating their classrooms as "personal kingdoms." Admittedly, these are fair descriptors of one of the worst kinds of teacher: the self-described maverick whose primary aims are to amuse himself and do as little work as possible. Not for him a plan book or a comprehensive exam; such trivialities are at odd with his "style," his "philosophy," his plans for the weekend. At the same time, the authors seem to indict the very teachers who played the biggest role in my own formation. Those teachers were never lazy but they were indeed lone wolves, sleek-furred beauties who preferred howling at the moon of their own lunatic inspirations to sniffing hindquarters among the faculty pack. One of their type, a foreign language teacher still going strong after my last stint at the school, still whisking kids away to France on a wing and a bake sale, even as she brings France to them by the vivaciousness of her instruction, will say to me, "I'm afraid the day of the teacher as artist is dead."

More than anything else I'm offended by what seems to be the main subtext of the authors' argument—and no doubt the principal reason that they're getting plugged by such luminaries as Lawrence W. Lezotte, "CEO of Effective Schools Products, Ltd." and embraced by school reformers who count past presidents as personal friends—which is that poverty need not deter achievement (*Stand and Deliver* redux) or overly concern us so long as we can get the children of dysfunctional families and blighted neighborhoods to achieve grade-level proficiencies and have a few AP courses under their belts when they get shipped off to their fourth tour of duty in Afghanistan. We must shift "from an external focus on issues outside the school," the authors assert, to what business consultant Jim Collins calls "the brutal facts" of our "organization."

Taken at its best and shucked of its corporate jargon, the authors' argument sounds like a modest and perfectly reasonable appeal for schools to focus on what they're actually able to do (impart basic skills and information) as opposed to what they might wish to do (guarantee a decent life for all of their graduates). But taken as an overarching solution to the "problem of American education"—our preferred euphemism for the problem of creating a democratic society within a decidedly undemocratic economic system—the DuFour agenda strikes me as an argument for ignoring every "brutal fact" save those that can be blamed on poor teaching. Out with the pedagogical lone wolf! In with the political ostrich!

I've often said that it's a good thing Jim Jones wasn't an educational consultant, else the halls of America's schools would be littered with the corpses of self-poisoned teachers. As if reading my mind, some of the teachers who've returned from the DuFour workshop held in Boston the previous summer jokingly refer to having drunk the Kool-Aid. They mean having replaced their initial skepticism with unconditional conversion. They're only half joking. I don't hear a single caveat or criticism when we break into small groups to discuss the reading assignment, and I don't expect to. Excepting the misfits and the burnouts, public school teachers are the original true believers: show them the latest thing in education and they'll soon be bowing down to it as to a god.

The reasons are not hard to discern. For one thing, educators are naturally predisposed to hope that someone better educated than they are will have a better method for addressing the vexing challenges of universal public education. The key word here is *method*—usually an implication that people up a creek without a paddle can be taught a strategy for maneuvering their boats that eliminates any need of buying them paddles. Teachers see method as an alternative to going mad; politicians see method as an alternative to spending money.

For another thing, anyone who can go to work each day believing that every student can learn, which every good teacher needs to believe as an article of faith (and which, to their credit, the authors of *Raising the Bar* seem to believe without reservation), has to have cultivated a prodigious capacity for belief. Students marvel at their teachers' gullibility in the face of lame excuses, and skeptics like me sometimes marvel at their colleagues' willingness to imbibe the most noxious concoctions of snake oil, both of us failing to appreciate that the best teacher has already fallen for something much more outlandish: the potential for magnificence in every human being.

So it happens that even as I'm inwardly fuming at passages I've underlined and asterisked as "tripe," "crap," and "what every Republican wants to hear" (for I make it a point of honor to read every assignment, a resolution I have good reason to suspect is not universally shared by those of my colleagues who take their seats whispering, "What chapter were we supposed to read?"), I'm moved by the heartbreaking earnestness of men and women who, after years of being bored and bamboozled by every sort of con artist, from those with pimples to those with PhDs, still worry over their students enough to hope for a messiah, or at least a miracle or two. No less than I'm convinced that Jim Jones had what it takes to be a successful educational consultant, I'm convinced that the fishermen Jesus chose for disciples in his day would have been schoolteachers in ours. True to type, they'd have misunderstood much and wrangled among themselves not a little, yet they would have held on to their implausible faith with a fervor sufficient to subvert an empire, which is what I in my own credulous way am always waiting for teachers to do.

Meanwhile, back in the classroom, I have smaller subversions to deal with. Going to school is like going to prison (as generations of schoolyard songs attest): you have about two weeks to establish your credibility, failing which you're either a punk or as good as dead. Depending on the school, some students can manage to avoid those stark alternatives, but even at the best school, no teacher does.

I seem to be doing all right so far. I have nothing that could fairly be described as a discipline problem. Experience helps. Age helps. Good class size helps. (None of mine exceed twenty.) Mr. Messier sticking his head in the doorway now and again to tell my students how lucky they are to be in my class certainly doesn't hurt. And to give the devil his due, having a school dedicated to the idea of being a "professional learning community" doesn't hurt either. I've never before seen so much collaboration among the faculty. Lone wolf I might be, but I never feel alone.

Not least of all, I'm helped by the relative good nature of a student body served by a well-functioning school, and, as I'll show, by particular students who are pulling for me every bit as much as I'm trying to pull for them. It's a tentative negotiation day by day, like the courtship of an unlikely pair. At our first meeting I told all of my classes that they were going to have to remind themselves at least once a day that I was not seventeen years old, and I was going to have to remind myself at least once a day that they were not fifty-seven.

The reminders are more or less built in, of course. Some of our differences are "generational" in terms of the normal stages of human development, and some of them generational in the sense of cultural changes between historical generations. It's not always easy to parse which is which, and it doesn't make much of a difference in practice. For instance, I'm repeatedly struck by what seems a compulsive, almost uncontrollable communicativeness on the part of my students. It's curious to watch a class taking a test. No sooner does a student turn over his completed test than his head goes up like a prairie dog sniffing the wind. Who else is done? Whom else can I talk to? According to a rule I enforce with inflexible strictness, the answer is no one—not until everyone is finished. It's tempting to ascribe the failure to respect a neighbor's concentration as nothing more than adolescent solipsism—and in my more sarcastic caricatures, I sometimes do: "The most important person in the whole wide world has just finished *his* test, so, like, what's the problem?"—but that is to pay short shrift to all the ways in which students show touching concern for one another's welfare. A true solipsist wouldn't be so charitable as to slip his needy neighbor the correct answers during a test. What drives my students is rather this ahormonal lust for communicativeness, this need to fill up silence with any kind of sound, something that's always been true for adolescents, to say nothing of adults (just watch a group of teachers trying to settle down for a meeting), but that I suspect is also the technologically conditioned enhancement of a habit (what human beings are likely to do) into *a habit* (what junkies have no choice but to do).

There sits my student Jack, sideways in his seat, his sizable forearm resting on the desk behind his, and his attention directed to the girl beside him, not in admiration as nearly as I can tell but in constant solicitation. *Talk to me.* I tell him to turn himself forward; he does so, and the next time I look back from the blackboard he's turned sideways again. This goes on to the point that I invite him into the hall for "a word." I can't figure out if he is playing dumb or is dumb, but there's a denseness in his responses that I find unsettling—is this a tactic or a disability? (I've already checked with the school nurse to see if he has problems hearing.) I tell him that along with violating his neighbor's right not to be eyeballed for forty-five minutes a day, he's starting to get on my nerves. I'm quick to add that I like him personally. "I like you too," he says. "You're a good teacher." *Then why can't you just shut the fuck up and turn around in your seat!* Not what I say, but the substance of it. "I'm not comfortable sitting the other way," he says. Well, he's a big kid, though I've taught bigger specimens who had no trouble fitting into a desk. Eventually, I offer a compromise; I'll sit him in the back, next to an empty desk, and he can sit however he wants. He likes that idea, perhaps because it affords him greater license for scribbling on his desktop on those days when he manages to bring a pencil. Now the girl who sits in front of him starts turning sideways in *her* desk.

But something else besides communicativeness or restless youth may be contributing to the occasional disruptions surrounding tests and in-class assignments. Increasingly I design the latter as cooperative exercises in the hopes of exploiting communicativeness in a positive way. But just as the tests are not proofread by the early finishers, the group exercises are often completed in a slapdash way—leading to the same disruptions I observe on tests. Probably the slapdash aspect is also cultural, but in a more localized sense. My wife's friend, the one who worked with her in the district preschool program, once said that she moved out of the region because she had gotten sick of hearing the expression "Good enough." Another she might have cited is the quasi-obscene "Get-R-Done," prominent not only on the bumpers of innumerable pickup trucks in the Northeast but also and shockingly on one of the superintendent's PowerPoint slides. I do want my students to "Get-R-Done," but not at the expense of producing quality work or working in concert with their less speedy peers.

Cashing in on both their sociability and their love of the screen, I take my Popular Fiction students to the library for an online treasure hunt relating to the scores of allusions in Sue Monk Kidd's *The Secret Life of Bees*. What happened at the bombing of the Birmingham church? What was Apollo 11? Who were the Supremes? Immediately, I see I've taken the right tack: they go to the computer banks like little children set loose on a beach, diving into Google images as into a surf, splashing one another with hints and links, chattering happily but mostly on point. I make a mental note to incorporate a visit like this into our weekly routine, add a competitive element, say two "hives" with two "queens," prizes, presentations the next day. But even in this case, communicativeness joined with a Get-R-Done ethos works against us, augmented by the Internet-fostered illusion of a world at your fingertips, instant gratification, no sense in lingering, no need to dig. "We're done!"

Also observable, especially among some of the more sullen students and especially though not exclusively among the boys, is a kind of built-in defeatism. "I ain't smart enough to take this course," says one of the boys in Popular Fiction, to which I reply that if I were the one saying so, he'd be within his rights to knock me down. I wonder, though, how much of what he says is an attempt to describe not his intelligence but his having grown up without books. Even more I wonder how much his having grown up without books is the result of his belief that as a natural-born "redneck" he has no business reading one. We shake hands after I sign his drop slip, and I tell him he'd be welcome back to try again, with all the help I can give, if he changes his mind. When he turns to join his friends out on the sidewalk, I notice the NASCAR insignia on the back of his shirt. Does he see it as the obvious emblem of a young man "not smart enough" to take my course? If he does, I want to tell him that I don't.

No doubt some of his attitude can be explained as the passive fatalism that has dogged working-class life since the dawn of the proletariat. But there is another, more recent factor at work. So much of what passes for authentic "redneck" culture—the Confederate flags, the macho strut, the trailer-park mores—like so much of what passes for authentic inner-city culture, is in fact a fabrication of the market. This first dawned on me several years ago when I realized that certain former students of mine seemed more "local" in their dress, speech, and mannerisms than their parents. How could that be, given that the students were generally less insulated in their rural environment than their parents had been? The answer is that what I took for local wasn't really local at all. Instead it was a countrified getup created by the savvy (and, needless to say, nonlocal) marketers of beer, mass entertainment, and motorized recreation. This is the flip side of the truism that capitalism destroys local cultures in its relentless drive to dominate the globe; it also *creates* cultures, mostly caricatures of the tribes it has displaced. The self-described rednecks, more likely to be young folks than old, see themselves as the "real Vermonters," the last of the Northeast Kingdom holdouts, when in reality they are no more indigenous than a Quebecois truck driver line dancing in cowboy boots. The sad irony in all this is that on some deep level the self-identified redneck wants to rebel against the economic forces that have run roughshod over small-scale agriculture and agriculturally based community, even as he buys his prepackaged rebellion from those very forces.

Suffice it to say, the brokers of those forces would much prefer rebels who shop to rebels who read. More than once it occurs to me how many of my conflicts revolve around a book. I come to understand why some of my predecessors, if I'm to believe what I've been told, gave up and simply read the texts to the students or had them watch based-on-the-book movies instead.

I try to remain flexible, with reading as my constant and the approaches up for grabs. Discovering that a mere handful of the sophomores in my last period have read an assigned short story, I opt for a different-strokes-for-different-folks agenda: those who've yet to read it can have today's class for a grace period, provided they will stay on task; those who have read it are invited to hold a literary powwow with me on the floor outside the room. I know this is going to be dicey, but it works rather well. The kids reading need only a reminder or two to settle down, and the kids on the floor become positively dazzling in their insights. So far, so good.

The next story on the syllabus is more difficult, and so I forgo the quiz and suggest we read the story aloud together, strengthening whatever comprehension each of us achieved the night before and discussing passages as we go. Immediately, one of the girls from yesterday's hallway symposium balks at having to sit through the oral reading of a story she's already read. It seems that without meaning to I've created an elite. Within the next thirty seconds several other girls, all friends of the first one who spoke, claim the same conscientiousness with respect to reading assignments and the same distaste for reading a story twice. They want to leave the room and discuss the story out in the hall.

My best course here would be to say that today we are doing something different, that good literature stands up to repeated readings, and end it there. But I make the mistake of giving way to baser motivations, namely, guilt over having created a false expectation, fear of offending a kid who seems to have gotten the message about reading assignments, and vanity in wanting to show that if you try to play poker with me you best be ready to have me call your bluff. I might be amenable to some people going out into the hall, I say, but just so there's an appearance of good faith all around, I'll ask those who've applied for the privilege to answer a few questions about the story or simply to formulate a few relevant questions of their own that the rest of us might use in our close reading of the text.

That's enough to set off a sniping contest with several students, one of whom volunteered to kick off our oral reading but now refuses to do so. I'm not at my best; it hasn't been an especially good day, I'm running on four hours of sleep and unfortunately find less humor than humiliation in the thought that at almost sixty years of age I am reduced to debating my professional prerogatives with fifteen-year-olds. One of them has been yanking my chain for weeks now. In time, she is going to become one of my best, most reliable students, but at the moment I'm wondering how much more of her I can stand.

Until—another girl stuns the class, and me, with a remark that I must say, at the risk of sounding older than I feel, no girl would have said back when I was going to school:

"Ladies, it's starting to get a bit estrogeny in here."

This isn't the only time a kid saves my bacon; in fact, it isn't even the first time today. I got off to a bad start by losing my cool with a boy in my first-period class whom I had to remind for the third or fourth time that school rules prohibit food and drink in the classroom. There he was with his can of Monster drink in his mitt, and there I was in the doorway, standing next to my department head and feeling especially ineffectual in her presence. We all have our triggers, and one of mine is feeling that my courteous requests are being ignored, all the more galling because I've gone out of my way to be so courteous. After barking that I wasn't going to tell him about the rule again (a rule he probably and accurately sensed was of complete indifference to me beyond the school regulation), I added in sheer frustration, "It's like talking to a tree stump!"

One is often startled by the sensitivity of the seemingly insensible, which is to say, by all the life that remains latent in the roots of a tree stump. I clearly hurt his feelings. After class began, I apologized to him for my harshness. I meant it too. I walked to his desk and offered him my hand. He took it warmly, to the relief of us both I think, and everything between us would be good thereafter. Still, there was an awkwardness in the room as I tried to get on with the class as though nothing had happened.

Then, out of the blue, with no pretext in anything I have ever said or intend to say in this or any other class, one of the students blurted out, "Mr. Keizer, somebody told me you were on Comedy Central."

I was, I said. When I'm not making an ass out of myself here, I like to do it for a television audience—I didn't say that but wish I had. Instead I revealed that last summer I'd briefly appeared as a guest author on a program called *The Colbert Report*. In contrast to yours truly when his publicist had first told him of the show, everyone in the room was familiar with it. They wanted to hear the details. There was more light in their eyes than I'd seen since the start of school. Even the guy with the Monster drink seemed to feel an extra buzz. In a New York minute, and as the result of what I have to believe was a very calculated maneuver on the part of a very sympathetic student, I went from a testy old

fart to a television star, someone who just might be worth listening to after all. I was so relieved at the change in the atmosphere
that it took me a while to realize that my larger problems were
still waving in my face, that it was not my authorship of a book
that gave me credibility in an English class but the six minutes I
spent as a straight man on TV.

I often stay late. It's not uncommon for mine to be the last car in
the faculty parking lot. Sometimes I stay to meet with students
who want extra help, though the good work of the tutors in the
academic support areas throughout the day and the transportation needs of a regional high school tend to keep their numbers
down, as do the constraints of after-school jobs. Just as often I
stay to record my grades and tidy up my school e-mail account.
The dial-up Internet service at my house doesn't permit me to
do much with the Lake Region site or the PowerSchool account
it links to. There's a certain unfairness to this: I'm kept from
going home because broadband Internet service hasn't gotten
there yet. It can feel especially sharp when the 4:30 display on
my classroom clock marks my twelfth hour on the job. But it's a
trifle compared with the predicament of students who lack personal computers or Internet of any kind. Social inequality has
gone digital along with everything else—disguised somewhat
by the fact that even the poorest of the poor seem to have cell
phones.

One of the kids who lives in an "unwired" household is my
former nemesis Jack. I say former because by the end of September he's gone from one of my daily irritants to one of my daily
delights. His detention today is for a brief relapse; I heard him say
"Fuck you" to another student just before class was dismissed. As
I explain to him, and as he readily agrees, I have to respond in

the same way I'd want my daughter's teacher to respond if another kid said the same thing to her. The at-home digital handicap doesn't surprise me because I know he lives as far out in the boonies as I do and because he admits to interests of an off-screen nature. For example, he tells me he's interested in World War II. I haul out another coffee table book on the subject, fully prepared for him not to open it. He doesn't at first—because, he says, he was working down in Ag Shop, and he ought to wash his hands before handling such a nice book. I ask if he'd like to take it home. It will not come back for a while, the reason being a little brother who's interested in the same stuff. "Then maybe you better keep it," I will tell him.

Ag Shop gives us another thing to talk about. He tells me he loves everything to do with farming and works part-time for a farmer after school. He doesn't live on a farm, however. In this he is typical of most of the handful of students I have who belong to the FFA (Future Farmers of America). At first the sight of their regulation dark blue corduroy jackets seems like a thread of continuity between the present and the past, when kids came to school after a round of morning chores with the barn smell still in their clothes and sometimes the muck still in the tread of their boots, but it's not long before I realize that most of the members I have in class are children of the Past Farmers of America. Like other businesses in the nation, small-scale agriculture has increasingly been displaced by larger operations and consolidated holdings. In my first year at Lake Region, there were well over three thousand dairy farms in Vermont (compared with three times that many in the year I was born); now there are slightly over a thousand, about a quarter of them in the Northeast Kingdom. But the dream of "a family farm" remains. Jack makes a statement that will stay with me as much as anything that anybody will say to me in the course of the entire year—this rough-and-tumble young man who tosses off a "Fuck you" for a fare-thee-well and says he's going to join the military straight after high school. "I wish I was a farm child."

Unlike "Fuck you," this is the sort of endearing, unaffected utterance one seldom gets to hear during class. It sounds more natural after school. No less than a city after dark, a school after hours is a different place, at once spent in its disheveled appearance and flexed for more passionate engagements. The student body's complacent middle class is mostly gone, leaving the felons and the stars, the former in detention and the latter running drills down in the gym or practicing their scales in the band room. Usually, you can get more than a scheduled minute with the colleagues you need to see, you can carry a cup of hot tea through the hall without risking catastrophe, you can finish a thought before someone interrupts it with "Can I quick go . . . ?" Custodians who drop by to empty the trash cans and dry-mop between the desks pause to talk politics and sports. Better still, the children of younger teachers occasionally stick their heads in the doorway, either because they've got the wrong room—*Whoa, you're not my mom*—or because the right room has gotten pretty boring over the last ten minutes and they're wondering if your plant might need watering or your blackboard want some chalk-drawn daisies by way of decoration.

One of the things I find I need to relearn, want to relearn, is the art of casual visiting. This is seldom a challenge where a student of mine is concerned—in that case even "irrelevant" exchanges count as productive—but occasionally an annoyance when I'm scrambling to finish work that another person seems not to have. For years I have worked entirely at home, by myself, where my few conversations have been confined to my family, a writer friend who phones, and editors or agents who are usually even more eager to get off the phone than I am. My situation has changed. For very different reasons but with very similar results, not a few of a school's denizens, both students and staff, are starved for adult conversation. I try to cultivate the practice of feeding that hunger without opening an all-you-can-eat buffet. As for my hunger, hungers, I should say—all of them bend toward home.

I enjoy coming home from work, which I've not done for years, setting down my valise like Willy Loman and collecting my breadwinner's kiss, though it turns out my wife is still kneading her half of the loaf. Against my advice, Kathy has cut short what I had hoped would be a time for vocational self-exploration and has added another job to her Dartmouth gig, delivering speech services several days a week to children at an elementary school. They're older than the preschoolers she's used to and perhaps, she worries, too far from her core of expertise. At least it won't be just one of us talking school over our predinner glass of wine. And we certainly won't lack for money, though each of us earns what would be a beginner's salary in another profession or in the school system of a warmer state.

Never so sweet as the destination, the drive home is still sweet. When we first moved from Orleans to another county in the Kingdom, I appreciated the longer drive to work, the opportunity to warm up going and cool down coming, and I appreciate it even more this year. September is my favorite month—if youth is wasted on the young, September is wasted on the academic year. Make us sweat out July in a classroom if we must, but leave us September in which to roam free. The leaves at this latitude begin turning midway through the month; I see red and orange tinges in the mountain, a small litter of yellow maple leaves on our lane. In my happy-hour mood I might stop for a drink—not at the saloon and not in a bottle, maybe a fortifying cup of coffee at the convenience store, where I can also buy gas—for the sensation of my real-world tie blowing like a signal flag as I operate the pump. If I see someone I know, a former student or the parent of one, they're likely to have heard I'm "back teaching" and almost as likely to ask me how that feels. "Good," I'll say, as expected, though I refuse to give the stock response when someone starts to hold forth, possibly in sympathy, on how incorrigible "kids these days" can be. Not really, I tell them. Only if you expect them to read a book, I say to myself.

If someone should add, "Thank God it's Friday"—an expression that's always tasted to me like a watered-down death wish—all I have to offer is a devout amen. Friday nights have never seemed so luminous. I've never felt such a Sabbath ease as I sit down to my meal. I ask my wife to light the candles before we eat. My peace has to do less with not having to get up early the next morning (something I'm likely to do anyway) than with not having to be prepared to go on stage. I need offer nothing to the next two days but myself. I try my best to do nothing school-related once the sun goes down.

By Saturday morning, though, I'm no longer taking my cues from the Mishnah. I'm correcting papers, planning lessons, developing assignments, my goal a fully unloadable briefcase come Monday morning and enough materials to get me partway through the week. One of my first batches is the four-page student-interest questionnaire I've given to all eighty-plus of my students, not only to get to know them better but also to assess their proficiency at following directions, writing complete sentences, forming good paragraphs. I'm up to speed enough to know I should refer to the last of these as "constructed responses," the current state jargon for a unified block of prose. It won't occur to me until much later how my questionnaires must strike at least some of the kids as a horse-and-buggy version of a Facebook page. I don't ask them who their friends are, true, but I do ask them to weigh in on some of their likes and dislikes. I also invite them to post a comment, as it were, advising me on how to be an effective teacher.

I write my responses sitting in my easy chair, with the books I used to read on weekends close at hand but effectively out of bounds. By Monday, I know much of what can be gained by asking students their favorite foods ("macaroni and cheese"), their future plans ("to go into the militerry"), their mailing addresses ("don't know"), their greatest weaknesses ("math and reading"), their greatest strengths ("being a good friend"), their heroes ("my dad"), their hopes ("that my parents would get along better"), their writing (better than I'd have dared to expect in the past), and I've finished my quota. I've also learned what comes of keeping a middle-aged hand and elbow in the same position for the waking hours of two whole days. When I go to write Monday's agendas on the blackboard, I can scarcely raise my arm.

counterparts in math and science, the other content areas to be tested along with reading and writing. Although I don't think highly of teaching to the test, I do admire how the school as a whole acknowledges the game it's been forced to play without yielding any more ground than necessary to out-and-out crassness. There are no General George S. Patton–style pep talks from the principal about the enemy we have to kill, no directives to the students other than to do their best and not to fret. Nor is there any pretest automated robocall such as comes to our house from the school where my wife is now working part-time, reminding parents to see that their children "eat a nutritious breakfast and have a good night's sleep" because . . . *tomorrow is the day when the elementary schools take their NECAP tests.* Let no child be left behind for a good breakfast on the day of a standardized test. The message stops short of suggesting that children might also have shoes on their feet and kisses on their foreheads, but then there is less data to support that such amenities raise scores.

If I'm impressed by the sobriety of my colleagues, I'm even more impressed by the dedication of the students. I expect many of them to blow off the pregame drills, but there's almost none of that. Granted, those who perform exceptionally well on the reading and writing parts of their NECAPs will get the option of not taking their final exams in English, a privilege formerly extended by some teachers for high academic performance in a given course but now denied by school policy in all cases except the one mentioned. Still, it's doubtful that many students expect to win that plum. The motivation seems to derive more from pride in their school, affection for their principal, and not least of all from having performed above par in the recent past. Success with taking tests is not unlike success in making money: the more you have, the more you want and the more you're likely to get. Regardless of the reasons, any evidence of motivation for a test that "doesn't count" among students conditioned from the age of nine to regard grades as the only reason on earth for lifting a pencil strikes me as pretty remarkable.

The strategies we employ are remarkable, too, if not so inspiring. The five-paragraph model of an essay (each paragraph consisting ideally of five sentences) is by this stage totally ingrained—not only as a way of taking standardized tests but as the definitive taxonomy of English prose. I meet no student who believes the universe was created in six days, but Darwin himself never saw so many open mouths as greet my meek suggestion than an essay might once in a while achieve six paragraphs or, more shockingly still, complete its work in four. Among the recommendations that come from the teacher who seems to be the department's NECAP guru are "address the prompt" (i.e., feed the question back to the examiners in your first paragraph, a virtual death sentence for any impulse toward writing a captivating lead) and "fill the space provided," which means precisely what it says. He's made a study of test results and has determined that the higher scores invariably go to those students who fill the space. Perhaps because our department head senses that some of us, including the guru himself, might be a little embarrassed by this observation, she attempts to dull its edge by noting that there are occasions in life that require a person "to bs" and that our kids might as well learn that now. This is realism, to be sure, though hardly an inspiration to teach rhetoric.

For all my grousing, the NECAP process hands me one reward and one small vindication, both in an offhand way. My elective courses contain junior and senior students, but only juniors take the tests, and so I must have an alternative activity for the seniors. Sara suggests that we coach them in writing college application essays while juniors are at work on their practice tests. This means I get to do some of the intensive one-to-one work with

students that was once a mainstay of my routine (especially when
I was department head and shamelessly devoted most of my
"administrative" periods to giving extra help to students) but is
now a less frequent occurrence, at least outside of class, because of
a full teaching load and because the school's academic support
areas have absorbed much of the tutorial work that used to fall to
classroom teachers. Refreshingly, the act of coaching a college
essay is in some particulars the exact opposite of coaching a
NECAP essay. In a standardized test, you're urging kids to conform to a template; on a college application, the trick is rather to
inspire the drowsy admissions officer who's slogged through scores
of generic essays to open his eyes and ask, "Who's this and where
did she come from?" In other words, part of the coaching boils
down to convincing students that their own lives are interesting.

I need no convincing to believe that some of their lives are
hard. Reading over these essays amounts to a refresher course on
social dysfunction. Two of my seniors have a parent in prison; not
a few of them have at least one parent who might as well live on
the moon, and the phrases "lost his job" and "drinking too much"
occur often enough to make an out-of-town teacher suspect plagiarism. At the same time, there is a movingly recurrent theme—
especially from the kids who have only one functioning parent—of
admiration for a mother's or father's struggle to provide enough
emotional and financial support for a child to thrive.

None of the essays are defeatist. On the contrary, some seem
to strain for a sense of triumph unsupported by the details of the
narrative. I'm given a better understanding of my Popular Fiction class's standoffish response to Russell Banks's *Rule of the
Bone*, the novel I thought they'd connect with most easily. A few
kids do, though just as many seem to hold it at arm's length,
refusing to infer its grittier implications. In the prevailing view
of my students, the novel's young delinquent protagonist owes

all of his troubles to his abuse of drugs—not to his parents' virtual abandonment of him, much less to his society's virtual abandonment of his parents. As they see it, he needs to give up doping and try harder in school. *He needs to make up with his mom*, some write, even though his mother has essentially told him that she'd rather hang on to her pedophiliac boyfriend than to her emotionally needy son. The tendency of at least some of my students to blame themselves for predicaments they did not create seems all too clear. Not that I'd want them to become fatalistic—I'm encouraged that they believe in the merits of "making the right choice." But to believe that every calamity results from a poor choice is fatalism of another kind, existence reduced to a standardized test with a karmic scoring key.

The vindication I mentioned comes in the form of one of the essay questions on this year's NECAP. Essay questions are framed according to specifically designated modes of discourse—"procedural" (what we used to call process analysis), "persuasive," etc.—and one of this year's turns out to be a "reflective essay," a type my colleagues have seldom seen on past NECAPs, to be written in response to a quotation, a subtype my colleagues can't remember seeing at all. As reports of the test's contents begin trickling back from students to teachers, one hears a grumbling in our department, and among some of the kids too, as might be heard among baseball fans who've just seen an umpire call a third strike on a player who any idiot could see was pitched a ball. I can't resist mentioning to my department head—having at least enough decency not to mention this to my peers—that though the past tests and practice exercises gave us no forewarning of such a prompt, I've been having my Popular Fiction students write reflective essays on quotations taken from the novels we've studied. Ironically, I may have made my best contribution to the NECAP effort when it was furthest from my mind.

Of course, the joke is on me in that the vindication seems less mine than the test's. *See, this emphasis on standardized testing isn't just a matter of teaching to the test, as cynics like to claim. The testing has a much broader focus, and your own assignment proves that!* Sara doesn't say this, but someone else might. Parse it either way, the two most pertinent questions remain. First, how much better might my students be at writing reflective essays if they and I were permitted to get on with our work? And second, how confidently can we assume that the sort of people who sign on to score NECAP tests would know a decent reflective essay if it hit them in the head?

Whatever the answers, one is left with the "brutal fact" that the headquarters from which educational policies emanate are always at a comfortable distance from the frontline troops. At a department meeting I watch as two of my colleagues have a heated disagreement over the creation of our own mandatory "summative assessments" for year-end mastery of the English curriculum, not over the mandate itself but over the best way to implement it and interpret the data. This is not the sort of turf war that erupts between the teacher who wants to do things in a new way and the teacher who wants to stick to the old, nor is it the more dismal sort of turf war that erupts between the teacher who wants to do things in a new way and the teacher who doesn't want to do anything at all. These are two accomplished and highly dedicated practitioners, neither of whom appears to have a cynical or lazy bone in his or her body. They also happen to be young parents. Often I see them working late into the day as their children, dropped off by the bus, sit dangling their feet in the big kids' desks while munching on carrot sticks and crackers and wondering aloud when it will be time to go home. I never see either one of them with a child in tow that I don't recall with an ache what my own daughter once said when she was small: "I wish I could make two daddies, one who would grade the kids' papers and one who would play pirates with me." And it's impossible for me to witness their dispute this afternoon without wondering which of the tipsy potentates reconvening at the Red Lobster after a day of designing NECAP exams or writing "new state standards" or conducting a workshop for school administrators has ever in his or her life or wildest dreams worked as hard as either of my colleagues or cared half as much as they do about the well-being of their students. In short, it's impossible for me to stand among the frontline troops without dreaming of a mutiny. And wishing I'd been a better pirate.

In total the NECAP tests and preparations cost me nearly two weeks of teaching time and a considerable loss of momentum in our study of literature. At first I tried to combine goals, sticking to the reading syllabus while devising multiple-choice exercises based on our texts and modeled on questions in the reading section of the NECAP test:

The closest meaning of the word homely *as it appears in the first paragraph of* Like Lesser Gods *is*

> A. ordinary and domestic
> B. plain and unattractive
> C. familiar and comforting
> D. foreign and strange

In the end, I lacked both time and confidence; I couldn't be sure that my NECAP impersonations were on the mark. I laid the books aside and went with the canned materials from previous tests.

Even without the NECAPs, October has a way of impeding September's best-laid plans. It takes but a few weeks for enthusiasm to make the acquaintance of entropy. I begin the year with two ideas for enriching my connections with students and for superimposing some of my own rhythm on that of the regular school day. First, I invite students (and their friends and parents if they wish to come) to have breakfast with me every Thursday before school. For a meeting place I choose a luncheonette in the village of Barton, roughly midway between my house and the school. It opens at 6:00 a.m. and sits catty-corner to a stop on the school bus route. (I am advised by both the principal and my own judgment that giving rides to students, as I used to do without scruple, is probably not a good idea.) I plan to be drinking my coffee by 6:30 a.m. and leaving for school an hour after that. Students are free to drop by at any time and leave whenever they want. I'm careful to emphasize that there is absolutely no credit to be gained or lost, academic or otherwise, by coming or by staying away. In the unlikely event that we pack the place, I might ask my guests to kick in a small amount as they are able, but otherwise the cost of the breakfast is on me.

I know enough to keep my expectations low. I'm not surprised when no one shows on Thursday. I sit by myself at the long table in the back room kindly provided by the owner. He is probably more disappointed than I am by the lack of takers. I eat my bacon and grade my tests with easy resignation, reminding myself that no one ought to go fishing who isn't prepared to get skunked. After a few weeks of this, a new kid appears in my homeroom, a tall and affable young man who divides his coursework between the high school, community college, and home-school instruction from his mother and who seems to have no of some student who has distinguished him- or herself during the course of the week by an insightful remark, an extraordinary effort, or a remarkable courtesy. I buy a small box of note cards embossed with the image of a golden tree bearing red fruit and keep it in the left top drawer of my desk. I use the student questionnaires, which I've kept on file, to determine the names and addresses to which the notes should go. I stamp them at my own expense because I want the gesture to be mine alone. I assume the notes reach the parents, and I hope they're gratifying to the students, though I hear nothing to indicate that the notes ever make it home. I don't expect to. It takes a bold adult to compose a note to a red-pen-wielding English teacher, and it takes an even bolder kid to acknowledge a teacher's appreciation where another kid might overhear. The proof is in the repetition of the action praised, and I see plenty of proof. Still, I wonder if my gesture is so eccentric as to arouse suspicion. Is it but a step down from offering to drive a student home—or, for that matter, to buy him a plate of scrambled eggs and toast? I wonder now and then what the regulars at the Parson's Corner counter make of the "spiffy" middle-aged man who waits for the blue-eyed boy with curly hair to join him for breakfast, though I suspect their dirtiest thought is that we're eating our sausage patties on the school's tab, as if my long summer vacation weren't extortion enough.

My notes home become a moot point after a while because my Friday afternoons—chosen for my latest stays because of the hour and a half it takes my wife to get home from her Friday job at Dartmouth—are soon taken up with other tasks, many of them occasioned by the modern school's almost insatiable thirst for "data" and the timely (i.e., as close to instantaneous as possible) recording of the same. In addition to grades and homework assignments, we are required to do a "productivity rubric," which must be tallied for each student for each marking period and for the "progress report" periods in between; in other words, eight times a year. The productivity rubric is a feature of the PowerSchool grading system that allows teachers to assign numbers of 1 to 4, with 4 being the highest, to criteria presumably not subsumed by academic grades, such as "initiative," "cooperation," "attendance," "behavior," and "responsibility." A faculty committee has designed a two-page spreadsheet that defines the meaning for each criterion of "productivity"—what distinguishes a 3 for behavior from a 2, for instance—and also attempts to reduce the vexing overlap between categories like "initiative" and "responsibility." It goes without saying that the guide creates as many questions as it answers. What score should I give to a student who is missing far too many days of school but who does a better job of meeting her deadlines than a number of students with close to perfect attendance? Do I give her a number that amounts to a wink at truancy or a number that turns a blind eye to the efforts of a kid who's anything but a deadbeat? What conclusions will she, or her parents, draw from the word *unsatisfactory* or the word *acceptable*? I can only give a number that designates a word; I cannot put the word into a sentence.

Though I approach the process with as much care and diligence as I can, vowing to myself that I will never allow skepticism to be a cover for shoddiness, I resent the chore deeply. I see it as part and parcel of the way in which "the school of the twenty-first century" is continually trying to mask the ambiguities of evaluating student performance by a pretense of rigorous objectivity. In English classes, for example, we avoid assigning an "arbitrary" grade for a piece of writing by constructing a "scoring rubric" of roughly ten criteria and assigning ten no less arbitrary scores to each, adding them up to achieve a grand total of subjectivity that is undoubtedly as solid as a Freddie Mac mortgage or a Miss America scoring card.

Even more I resent the way in which our jobs are increasingly dictated by the tools we employ. Form doesn't follow function; form dictates function. I don't want to sound dogmatic or, worse, ungrateful. Without a doubt, the PowerSchool program, once mastered, offers a more efficient way of recording grades than I've ever encountered. Every time you add a grade to the roster, the student's average for the marking period is automatically computed and displayed. The end-of-marking-period all-nighter with a roped-in spouse doing backup duty on a calculator has mercifully gone the way of the mimeograph blues. But digital technology abhors a vacuum even more than nature does; it insists on reinvesting whatever time it saves, and it insists on doing so according to its own agenda. The purchaser's need to justify the cost of the technology also plays a part. If a school system invests money in a sophisticated computer program that includes a feature for calculating the daily growth rate of a user's moustache, then don't we owe it to the taxpayers to see that every man, woman, and child capable of growing a moustache begins doing so at once?

The first time I try to do my productivity rubric it takes me several hours. I have roughly eighty students and five criteria, which means four hundred separate considerations and data entries. Times eight, that comes to thirty-two hundred by the close of the year; I try not to think too much about that. There are few people still left at school on a Friday afternoon, but I have received a good tutorial in advance. I should note that I never find myself floundering with a computer task because someone has handed it off with an attitude of sink or swim. But somewhere in the inner sanctums of the school's IT system, or in the empyrean of cloud computing, or perhaps in the domain of PowerSchool itself, there resides a spore of latent indignation. Suddenly my screen is taken over by red headlines accusing me of things I'm not sure I even understand. The launching of a North Korean nuclear warhead could hardly produce a more alarmist screen. I'm unable to give a precise account of the wording because my screen goes black before I can read it a second time. Fearing that one inadvertent keystroke may have caused a digital meltdown, I run for the English teacher in the room next door, who is also working late, and ask for her help. She is a compassionate, careful woman who teaches both Advanced Placement and remedial-level English with the gentle hand that each requires, and I can tell that my stress is causing stress for her. I can also tell that she is doing her best to avoid any insinuation of stupidity on my part when she asks, "As you were going along, did you happen to hit save?"

Not once. I feared that saving before I could double-check my entries would lock in mistakes that I might not be able to change, a foolish notion perhaps, though not inconsistent with what I've seen so far of the system's potential for capricious finality. As for the Armageddon screen display, it strikes my colleague as nothing more than *what these machines will sometimes do*. Every so often a gargantuan gorilla will seize a woman in his paw and climb to the top of the Empire State Building—just the nature of the beast, I guess, no different from the way that an exhausted human being overcome by a sense of futility will sometimes break down and sob. I will do that only once in the entire school year, and I keep myself under control until my colleague leaves the room. Anyone who stops in thereafter might wonder which member of my family has died. But there are no casualties to speak of beyond the loss of an hour or two with my wife and the jettisoning of a few quaint intentions. I entered the scores first in my paper grade book, so it seems I've "saved" them after all. I'll find some other use for the fancy note cards.

———

Like a scene changer in a situation comedy, the sky opens up
and rains to the point of flooding on the day scheduled for my
Vermont Literature class's field trip to Barre. We've been preparing for the trip for weeks, holding sessions in the library to
research the sites we hope to visit, and voting to decide the
weighty matter of where we'll eat. Our plan is to tour the Rock
of Ages quarry, the plant where the quarried granite is carved,
the renowned town cemetery where generations of stone carvers have left monuments to their skill and to one another, and,
if there is time, a museum that promises to pay more attention
to labor history than the novel does. By the time I get to school
it's raining so hard that some of my wryer colleagues can't resist
a bit of ribbing—brought on, in part, by the hubris of the enter-
prise. Field trips are not for the superstitious. I know of more
than one teacher whose career was suddenly on the line because
of some shenanigans involving an AWOL kid or a bottle of
booze smuggled onto a bus. But drowning, not drunkenness, is
my concern today.

In spite of the miserable weather, I'm reluctant to cancel, and
any teacher can tell you why. Canceling a field trip is like calling
off an invasion. We have had to reserve a bus, a guided tour, and
a restaurant. I've had to notify the main office several weeks in
advance and have the trip approved on three tiers of administration. My department head has had to submit a purchase order,
the school has had to hire a sub, and I have had to devise lesson
plans comprehensive enough to prevent her from being eaten
alive. The students have had to obtain their parents' signatures
on permission slips from home in addition to a sheet signed by
all their teachers indicating that they've taken the trouble of
finding out what they're missing on the day of the trip. These
documents are only a little less difficult to get signed than a stay
of execution; repeatedly they're lost, misplaced, forgotten, and

often, I have no doubt, forged. The thought of starting the process all over again, perhaps only to be drenched on some other date or in some other way, is too much to bear. I'd rather get wet today.

At the last minute, it seems that a couple of students have decided not to take the trip. Loath to leave anyone behind, I check to be sure. I'm especially sorry to learn that one of those who've opted out is probably the novel's most devoted reader, a notable distinction given that he spends a good part of his time jockeying between the households of separated parents, one of whom lives beyond the borders of the school district. At one of his way stations he reportedly received a quantity of fleabites sufficient to keep him out of school for a week. There's no time or pretext to discover his reason for not going on the trip today. It isn't money; all costs are covered by the school. His classmates have already boarded the bus, a large one for our handful. I've asked the school's female guidance counselor to come with us as an extra chaperone, believing we ought to have at least one woman along for the sake of our lone girl. The windows are fogged and streaming when I take my seat, the aisle mats muddy from the morning's pickups on dirt roads. I make it a point to tell our driver that we're leaving in plenty of time so there's no need to rush. The roads are bound to be slick with wet leaves.

The students are in good spirits in spite of the rain; if anything, the weather outside makes ours a cozier ark. Plus we're leaving school grounds, and I share their sense of release. The worst thing I have to contend with is a couple of boys with a fondness for coarse language. I dutifully reprimand them, but not harshly since it's not directed at another kid. By now they've probably been with me long enough to deduce the distinction I make between saying that life's a bitch and calling someone else a bitch, my greater tolerance for *shit* than for *shithead*. It is virtually a ritual for kids to swear and for teachers to tell them not to, where-upon the kids say "sorry" and keep a lid on things only to begin swearing again—and I have wondered sometimes if adolescents swear for the same reason that baby animals bawl, as a way of making sure they're alive and that their mothers haven't forgot-ten them. So it's "fucking this," and "fucking that" followed by a "Gentlemen, watch your language." After a while, they do.

Our first stop is the Rock of Ages hangar-sized workroom. From a catwalk visitors can watch the craftspeople carve and polish monuments, mostly for graves, though a master sculptor in the distance is at work on a statue of the Virgin destined for the Vatican. None of them seem in a hurry. They walk their massive blocks along tracks of rollers with all the studied non-chalance of Frank Sinatra strolling onto a stage. Music from dif-ferent work stations drifts up to us along with the drone of the dust collectors. The silica dust that once disabled quarrymen and stone carvers as early as their late twenties and is virtually a character in Tomasi's novel, an airborne angel of death, is now controlled by air-filtration systems, their effectiveness certified by routine visits to a doctor. I expect the students to grow antsy after a short time but I underestimate them along with the sus-tained fascination that comes of watching a skilled person at work. They, too, are in no hurry.

I wonder if they feel the same twinge of envy that I do. I won-der if they have the sense of watching an elite. Like the charac-ters in Tomasi's novel, and their Italian contemporaries in the textile mills of Paterson, New Jersey, where I was born, the people on the floor below us are proud masters of a craft and members of a union. Schools devote too little time to labor history, but a decent labor-based curriculum would also need to address the awkward subject of labor's debasement, not least of all in the popular conception of what it means to be a "manual laborer."

The workers of Paterson and Barre who wove the cloth and cut the stone also played musical instruments in their spare time and attended public lectures, they dressed in their Sunday clothes to have their pictures taken in front of the grape arbors they'd planted, they made their own wine and drank it, they went on strike believing in nothing so much as their own worth. They sent their children to school with the same belief. They would have had a hard time seeing their reflection in the stereotype of the Joe Sixpack proletarian. The symbolism of what is being chiseled on the floor below is not lost on me—I keep waiting to see a grave marker inscribed with the words "Meaningful Work," "Collective Bargaining," "Made in America"—"Rest in Peace."

If the cemetery above town isn't one of Vermont's best-known tourist attractions, it deserves to be. There you can see a life-sized married couple holding hands in their granite bed, a rare gendered angel with her legs crossed demurely as she sits atop a stone, an entire grove of stylized granite tree trunks (symbolically cut off like the lives of those interred beneath, but putting out shoots for the future), and the likeness of socialist Elia Corti, victim of an anarchist bullet in the days when the Left was robust enough to have family feuds, sitting in contemplative dignity with his elbow resting on a pillar and a palm branch spread over his carving tools. Unlike most of my students, I have been to the cemetery several times before, but this is the first time I see the monument erected to Louis Brusa, wasted by silica dust and dying in his wife's arms, the curve of her hip, the cuffs on his pants, a worker's pietà. Brusa agitated for the recognition of silicosis as an occupational hazard and was instrumental in getting the quarry owners to acknowledge the disease and take steps to prevent it. His image finds its way onto several smart-phones, along with the cross-legged angel he created. I wish I could give their photos a caption.

"What does labor want?" asked Samuel Gompers in 1893, in a passage I encountered, also for the first time, several weeks before our trip. "We want more schoolhouses and less jails; more books and less arsenals; more learning and less vice; more leisure and less greed; more justice and less revenge; in fact, more of the opportunities to cultivate our better natures, to make manhood more noble, womanhood more beautiful, and childhood more happy and bright." And what did labor get? Fleabites. Obesity. NAFTA. My kids live in a country that holds more of its citizens under correctional supervision than the gulag did under Stalin, that at one point spent two billion dollars a week on a war in Afghanistan, that has experienced the most devastating financial meltdown since the Great Depression, that counts childhood lucky, if not happy and bright, if it manages to avoid being raped in its bedroom or shot dead in its school. The roads are washing out. Wires are down. Sports and drama practice have been canceled due to weather. I don't want my students driving home after sunset, and so after making a call to the school, we skip our visit to the labor museum and head straight home from the cemetery. The sky looks even darker than it did when we started out.

Sometimes I wonder what my students will do for work and what I ought to be doing to help prepare them. The simplest answer is that I ought to be teaching them the basic skills they'll require to get into college or hold down a job: how to communicate, collaborate, and reason. How to comprehend an assigned task and see it through. I would like to go further. I would like to think I can play a role in helping my students to discern and develop their talents. At the very least, I want to help my students to resist any notion of their lives as a done deal. I hope that in the course of my teaching career I've managed to do both.

But if teaching has taught me anything, it is to be wary of any easy assessment of my influence, for better or for worse. "For us, there is only the trying," T. S. Eliot said. "The rest is not our business."

A student hands me a rambling short story loaded with every imaginable error and only marginally suited to the assignment I gave, but that's what creative kids often do, and this kid is clearly trying to announce her creativity. I already know that one of her dreams is to become a writer. So I attach what amounts to an editorial letter to her story, showing that I've read the work and care for the work, trying with all my might not to patronize the work or belittle its shortcomings. I also include several recommendations—all with this intended subtext: "I take you and your aspirations seriously." In short, I write the letter I wish an English teacher had written to me. The student receives it with a single comment: "I find it hard to read your handwriting." She has never mentioned this difficulty before.

Another student in the same class hands in a quiz fifteen minutes after all the papers have been collected, claiming that in her absent-mindedness she stuck it into her notebook instead. This sounds a bit suspicious, but I tell her I believe her, though I also believe in holding to certain matters of form for the sake of a classroom's collective good faith. Therefore, I'd like to give her a different quiz during her next free period. Would she be willing to do that? Yes, she says, and she takes it, performing about the same as she did on the first one. But in the process I have made an impression I hardly expected to make.

"No teacher has ever given me another chance like this," she says. I doubt this is so—especially in a school that prides itself on accommodating the needs of individual students. It would have made more sense coming from the student with the short story. But this is the student it comes from; my job is to be ready for what comes next.

Eventually she will volunteer to write news articles for the local paper on her after-school club's activities and enlist my editorial help. We go over her efforts line by line. Watch her be the one who wins the Pulitzer Prize, which is not to say my help was all that important, merely that the ultimate result of our help is unknown.

I decide that it might be a good idea for me to devote the twenty minutes I usually have between lunch and study hall to taking a walk around the building as opposed to doing a bit more work at my desk. I need the exercise, for one thing, and it wouldn't hurt me to keep the school's big picture in view.

My usual route takes me past the academic support area at the foot of the stairwell, two flights down from my second-floor classroom and several steps up from the level of the lobby and the main office. It's the one where I'm likeliest to find my students though not the only place they can go for help. After the ubiquity of technological devices, the school's tutorial component is the most notable of the changes I've seen. What was previously one highly stigmatized "special ed" room is now a bustling network of four study areas, all staffed by unflappable, die-hard tutors, most of them proficient in several subjects. Some of those areas are devoted to students with identifiable special needs, but there's a laudable blurring of the boundaries, at least on the surface, that seems to make it easy for kids to feel comfortable in any given room. The word *retard* sadly persists in the hallways but is used mostly as an all-purpose, gender-neutral alternative to *peckerhead*.

It's rare for me to walk by these areas without at least sticking my head in. Sometimes I can help clarify one of my assignments for a kid or his tutor, but mostly I stop by simply to enjoy the heady sight of so much application, to breathe the easy camaraderie in the air. Everybody's welcome, and so am I. I also go for the no less heady sight of three of my former students running the show. One of them tells me that my class played an important part in her youth. "I always felt safe in your English class, and at that time in my life I couldn't say that about every place." She's glad her niece has me for a teacher this year, she says, though she can hardly be more delighted than I am to teach that bright and intrepid child, who sports a "Girls Rule!" T-shirt about once a week.

Today her aunt is working on math with a small group of students, one of whom, a big kid in short pants, is complaining bitterly about how much "things suck" in his life. She is sympathetic but doesn't gush. Summoning an authority for which she's paid her dues in full, she says to him, "Then what you need to do, Charlie, is get a good education. It was the way out for me."

The ag shop is at the farthest reach from my classroom, at ground level on the opposite side of the building, so I make it the turnabout for my walks. I've already reestablished my credentials as an honorary member of the FFA by prominently displaying my old blue cap above one of the blackboards in my room. (The honor was bestowed on me in response to a chapter I'd written in my first book, and so it counts as one of my first literary awards.) I'm happy to see that the garage bays still hold tractors in various stages of repair, though no students are working on them today; they're in their classroom with their backs to the door, lined up at a bank of computers. It's fall so there are no new chicks in the incubators, though I'm greatly relieved to learn that they still hatch chicks in the spring.

As for seeing the country's future farmers glued to computers, it's no different from what I witness everywhere else. Teachers I would have seen one-on-one with a kid fifteen years ago are
now as likely to be seen one-on-one with a laptop, though the
picture is somewhat misleading in that some of them are communicating with their classes in that way, updating course blogs
and teacher Web sites. In spite of official discouragement from
the National Education Association, some of the faculty also
social network with their students. EST (Educational Support
Team) meetings, convened so teachers can discuss students in
academic jeopardy, are as likely to include mention of what a kid
has posted on his Facebook page as what he's missing for homework. Teachers have always been aware of their students' existing
in a world outside of school; the difference now is that there are
multiple, mostly virtual worlds, and teachers move in them too.

So do bullies, which may be another reason, besides the generally friendly climate of the school, why one sees less evidence
of hazing in the halls. You can always stick it to somebody
online. What one does see (and always saw) are kids who can't
seem to say anything that wins the approval of their peers, kids
who've met some orthodox and perhaps disability-based criteria
for "weird" or "annoying," and other kids too socially invisible to
be either, who seem always to be alone. I try to seek these kids out
when I walk, as other teachers do, and some begin seeking me.
My after-lunch walks will be short-lived for that reason; there's a
boy who starts coming to see me at that time, and I want him to
find me "at home."

For now I have the young woman sitting on one of the benches
in the main lobby to deal with. She's been testing me almost since
the year began. Today she complains that our current writing
assignment is a great trouble to her, which is why her first draft
is late.

"I can help you if you'd like," I say, but she accuses me of not wanting to. She says that I "turned my back" on her the other day when I was preparing to leave class early for a medical test. Knowing I had an appointment to keep, with the sub already in my room, she'd repeatedly raised hand to summon me to her desk to answer a series of bogus questions. They grew more insistent—nearly desperate—in tone as I began to put on my coat and glance nervously at the clock. I wound up rushing to my appointment precisely because I refused to do the very thing she's now claiming I did. I won't let her fluster me again.

Well, I can help you now, I tell her calmly. What's your subject? (Something she hates.) Well, what do you like? (Guys! Especially this new one.) Well, why don't you write about a guy then? (Yeah, but what about this illustrating a general thing with a specific thing that you want us to do?) Is the guy fun to be around? (He is.) Well, then give me an example . . . not now, in your essay.

"And one more thing," I add, walking back to her bench a few seconds after walking away. "If you really believe that I refused to help you the other day, I think you should complain about it. You might go see Mr. Messier or your guidance counselor. Both of them have a long-standing acquaintance with my notorious habit of turning my back on students who need my help. Tell them exactly what you've told me. And I'll make you a deal. If they don't smile when you say it"—as I'm careful to smile now—"you don't have to do your essay, and I'll give you an A for it besides. How's that?"

Mr. Messier will be easy enough for her to find; I just passed him down in the gym, shooting hoops with kids on their lunch hour. The guidance office is even closer. I'll make a visit there myself to find out what on earth might be eating this kid. It turns out to be a good deal more than anything I had to deal with at her age. For her part, she elects to take the old-fashioned route to an A. She will write four successively better drafts about the young man of her dreams and will soon become a teacher's dream as well, a leader in her class, a student I can always count on.

My walks at school are not reflective—public high schools are not designed for that. Reflection comes afterward, on the drive home, in the very few minutes it takes me to fall asleep. It rarely brings comfort.

Though my interaction with the girl who questioned my willingness to help her will prove successful in all kinds of ways, I do not know that tonight, and even when the outcome seems to vindicate my instincts, I will continue to believe what is dawning on me now, that I didn't handle her well. I want to think that by pushing back on her manipulations, by showing her my limits, I broke through to a place where she might be able to respect me, which is to say, that I showed some respect for her. Male teachers often make the mistake of thinking that the best way to deal with recalcitrant adolescent girls is with flirtatious condescension, which may work in the case of a dimwit, but it can backfire too, and this girl is anything but a dimwit. It's my firm belief that the last thing an intelligent girl or young woman wants from an older man is condescension.

No less is it my firm belief that any teacher who fails to take a put-up-or-shut-up stance against a groundless accusation, however petty, is setting himself up for something more serious, with potentially ruinous consequences. I've followed through on both beliefs, and if I want to, I can let that be my sole conclusion and go to sleep.

But although events will prove that my hunch was right, my response to the girl was far too reactive to qualify as a hunch.

For one thing, my refusal to be manipulated was in fact the evidence that I'd already been manipulated. Why would she have accused me of refusing to help had she not perceived, rightly, how much of my ego is wrapped up in my reputation for sparing no effort in helping any student who asks? I was telegraphing that message last week when I played her game instead of leaving promptly for my medical appointment. A more secure teacher would simply have said, "Not now." So, I took her bait, and though I did it with such a yank as to pull her off the dock and give her a good, sobering dunk, it's only because I felt the barb of the hook, as I'd been meant to.

Not only that, but in alluding to my personal history with certain key figures at the school, I risked implying that her options for seeking recourse were slight. Provoked though I was, that can never be good. And I meant to imply no such thing. I know quite well that no one at the school, however high their esteem for me, is prepared to give me a free ride, just as they know, if they know me at all, that I'd disdain employment with anyone who would. But does the girl know that?

It comes back to me now in a sickening wave—what I hated most about teaching, not the loss of free time and the weariness of the work, the absurd pettiness of a thousand minutiae, the hurry-up-and-wait inertia of the school routine, the interruptions tugging and blaring at you every other minute but the constant second-guessing of oneself. Anything you do is bound to be, on some level and for some kid, wrong. You do not have the right to remain silent, but anything you say can be held against you. Because you teach the young, who are both unformed and vulnerable, you are constantly exposed to the arousal of every imaginable emotion: pity, anger, delight, humiliation, exasperation, gratitude, remorse, impatience, wonder, despair, but for that same reason—because you teach the young, who are both unformed and vulnerable—your integrity depends in large part on holding your emotions in check, an object that the average human being is less likely to achieve through the exercise of self-discipline than through the ruthless cultivation of numbness.

I want to believe my students are better served by the actuality of a human being than by the impersonation of a robot. In the case of my own humanness, that means laughing when I'm amused, holding forth when I'm excited, crying out when I'm hurt, and apologizing when I'm wrong. Do these propensities make me a good teacher or a poor one? It is far too glib, if true enough, to say they make me both. What they make me most of all, at least in my private hours, is a wreck.

On a morning shortly before Halloween I unlock my classroom and find that a digital projector has been installed on my ceiling, the kind that allows one to make presentations off of a laptop, the kind that most teachers have and that I don't want. *Trick or treat.*

Now I have even more wires running up my wall, a mess of debris on the desks and floors, and a remote control device lying in the center of my desk. The effect is like that of a red cape waved in front of a bull. I know this is not my room beyond this year, though I sense that my chalkboard-retaining predecessor did not want one of these machines, and I resent what feels like an implication that I should or that my temporary watch should form an acceptable pretext for doing an end run around him.

Ungenerously, I suspect that someone—the librarian perhaps or one of the "techs," a man who enters an occupied classroom with all the insouciance of a shop foreman who needn't knock to inspect the work on "his" floor—has presumptuously made the suggestion that Mr. Keizer ought to have (i.e., ought to be coaxed into using) a digital projector. I regard the machine as no more than an upgrade of the old overhead projector, one more excuse for a teacher to hide in the dark, a telltale accessory of the most inept of my college and high school instructors, something I am proud never to have used in my life. The culprit cannot possibly be my department head and is probably not my principal, neither of whom is a technological evangelist. And what about this mess on the seats and floor, left here like coal dust in a one-room schoolhouse for the schoolmarm to sweep up after she's finished breaking the ice on the water bucket?

A gentle knock interrupts the fury of my reverie, and one of the students employed part-time on the school's custodial staff, a soft-spoken junior who's taking tenth-grade English for the second time, pokes his head in and asks if he might come in. Mr. Messier has asked him to clean up the mess left from the installation. He goes about his business, asking me if I had a good weekend. Listening to jazz records after we read the short story "Sonny's Blues" was a cool idea, he says. He used to play the trumpet, but eventually it got to be too much with everything else he had going on. He still loves Louis Armstrong, though. Not like Sonny in the story, who's more of a Charlie Parker guy. He's glad I played a song by Louis. Did I know that because of the music I played for "Sonny's Blues" and the music I've been playing before class Jenny Martin has downloaded a bunch of John Coltrane songs onto her iPod? She plays the tenor sax in band. She's pretty good too. "I'll see you later in class, Mr. Keizer," he says, and then he and his broom are gone.

He's blessed my morning, left me his peace. Those were supposedly my offices in the days when I supplemented my teaching income by working as a part-time (ordained but untrained) Episcopal priest. I don't do that work anymore, and if any students at the school know I did it once, they make no mention of

it to me. I'm glad. It was over the hills, in another county, and
they'd have been no older than ten when I took my last service.
It could have no meaning for them beyond a few cautionary
tales, and I can make those points with other examples, including those in books.

But there are a few advantages that come of having been a
jack of all trades and a master of none, some little more than the
motor memory of a useful gesture. I move my hand through the
air in a pattern I have not made for a long time, placing the slide
projector in the crosshairs of my benediction. Pinned to the
ceiling like a fish-eyed bat and twice as ugly, the machine is nevertheless the sign of someone's good intention, the fruit of someone's careful work. The kids will like it, as they do anything that
blinks and hums. Churches bait their hooks with bingo, why
shouldn't I bait a few of mine with digital bling? I can show my
students the possibilities of their own sentences; I can fiddle for
their edification with a few sentences of my own. At the very
least I can give them a few laughs as I press the buttons with all
the wincing apprehension of a man detonating dynamite. And if
an old dog can be taught a new trick, what possible excuse can a
young dog have not to learn a few old ones? *Let's watch the
screen, please, gentlemen. And our language.*

"his wife") and point us to our assigned places in two of the orchestra section's wooden fold-up seats. Think art deco without much art but with hints of the early twentieth century seeping through the bricks, just as the Jazz Age must have seeped northward in its heyday, though mostly it came in the form of Quebec whiskey smuggled south. My imagination doesn't go back that far, but I do see ghostly showstoppers from twenty years ago— a waggish performer yanking up his trousers to produce those castrato high notes, a model student and future drama major transformed into such a credible witch that she almost needed to sing to keep the little ones from running in terror out of the theater, a boy in the audience so overcome with admiration that he let loose the most lifelike rendition of a bawling heifer I've ever heard, and I've heard some of the best.

I find the same magic I remember from previous shows— and some of the same teachers, still playing in the orchestra and doing makeup backstage, most of them gray-headed now—the magic of kids stepping out of their daytime roles and into new ones, the latter sometimes closer to their most authentic selves. Not always recognizable in their costumes, still less so when they sing, they seem charmed and immortal, happily lost in that thin place that is both school and not-school because it exists outside the scheduled day. The student elite are well represented among the cast, but there are also a few surprises, kids you never would have expected to see in a play, kids you never imagined could sing, kids whose mere attendance at rehearsals seems little short of miraculous. Moving in shadow are those who work the lights, change the sets, hand out the programs—the crew of "cast and crew," and an even more motley crew than the cast. Kathy recognizes kids she knew in preschool, including some who came to her for speech therapy—now delivering flawless lines in deeper voices—and others more severely disabled but also matured and in their carefully cued movements no less splendid than the leads. "From each according to his ability, to each according to his need"—if I didn't know better, I'd swear that Marx jotted the line on the back of a program at a high school play.

At the end of the last ovation, as the audience files out of the theater, mothers of actresses identifiable by the bouquets in their hands, the vice principal calls me aside and says that the principal wants to speak to all the faculty in the basement under the stage. When we gather, Mr. Messier announces that Frank Smith, a thirty-nine-year-old teacher and a former student of mine, has died suddenly at home from heart failure. Visibly shaken, Mr. Messier wants us prepared for the next school day. Smith taught some of his social studies classes in an alternative, hands-on program at the school, gathering his students around a woodworking table in the shop area downstairs. A special education aide who works with many of the same kids begins to wail. "He was so young. He'd just gotten married."

Veterans on the staff might breathe a guilty sigh of relief that we have been spared a suicide, a disastrous auto accident, the death of someone not yet kissed, all occasions they have seen before. There is no mourning like mourning in a school. It's another kind of theater, another ensemble piece. Every conceivable human response to death, from the heartrending outburst to the opportunistic excuse, struts and frets its hour upon the stage. Adults are fond of saying that kids are too young to comprehend death, which may be true, though high school kids are at least old enough to grasp their own incomprehension. They're at sixes and sevens to know what they should feel. Outside counselors join the guidance staff to handle the overflow of referrals. The main office hands out round blue buttons with Smith's initials written in the script of the New York Yankees logo, a tribute to him and his favorite team. School is canceled for half a day to fill the Orleans Catholic church to standing-room-only capacity, the standers spilling to the outside steps and sidewalk. The eulogies are long and tender, spiced with jokes; but for the setting, one would think the deceased had retired with decades of golf on his horizon. Perhaps because I distrust sentimentality, something in me tends to harden at a funeral, something of which I've never been proud. Where better people hold back tears, I am often holding back bile.

But what is my job about if not holding back? On the day of the funeral a girl in one of my classes asks me if I could "use a hug." Of course it is she who could use one, bereaved as she is, not so much by the death of a teacher she scarcely knew as by the recent absence of a father who keeps in touch mainly through disparaging remarks about her falling grades and increasing weight. I would gladly oblige, but what might her classmates say about her if I do, and how many of them will assume that hugging their teacher is either the ticket to his good graces or a likely risk of coming to see him for extra help? "You've already hugged me by offering to," I say, only to see the disappointment of yet another rejection on her face. Once again I yield to my recurring fantasy of receiving a phone call from her father, a demand to know why she's failing my course and a chance to see if my way with words is sufficient to throttle a human being long distance or, failing that, to dupe one into hastening my retirement. ("I'm afraid we can no longer employ a teacher who would address a parent as 'you philandering piece of shit.'") I'll hug you then, my sad darling, and everybody else I pass on my way out the door, but for now you don't want to put your arms around anyone like me. It'd take you another year at least to get warm again.

My heart begins to thaw when a knock comes at the door

project, the more hands-on the better. Since our culture increasingly regards manual work as the domain of toddlers and dolts, transcendence just as often translates to shedding the chrysalis of false sophistication—which if you're an American teenager is probably better described by the metaphor of a straitjacket. Simply put, learning is sometimes abetted by giving self-conscious young adults permission to remember what it means to play.

I hand out markers and invite students to deface enlarged photographs of my face (taken with perverse pleasure from the jacket of my last book), awarding one blacked-out tooth or booger per part of speech accurately identified, and everybody wants to find a passive-voice verb. At the close of our unit on the American short story, I ask my students to make a museumlike display of projects based on the literature we have studied. Though I encourage the use of technology, their overwhelming preference is for projects made with tangible stuff, perhaps because more than one person can touch it at a time. The more macabre stories seem to inspire the most projects: there's more than one black lottery box loaded for Shirley Jackson's famous tale and even an edible diorama of the lottery itself. (Instead of stoning a single villager, we get to eat them all.) Among several references to Poe's "The Black Cat" are an ambitious short film and a high-decibel dramatic monologue that brings the principal rushing to the classroom door in the expectation of preventing bloody murder. Flannery O'Connor's racially charged "Everything That Rises Must Converge" inspires two depictions of the purple hat that Julian's mother and her black antagonist both wear, one of them perched atop a Styrofoam head symbolically painted half white and half black. A boy with a passion for computer games builds one based on Hemingway's "The Killers" that allows a player to search for doomed Ole Andreson through several rooms, including the diner where Nick Adams and his coworkers are taken hostage. Other games are in the conventional mode, with playing pieces and question cards—good review for our upcoming unit test, assuming the information on the cards is correct, which it mostly is except for spelling.

We invite other members of the school to visit our display, treating them to baked goods and asking them to sign a guest book and leave their comments. I like to think we're giving them a chance to play as well—if only to pretend that the established order has been shaken for a day. "Honors" students are our spectators for a change; the office secretaries and cafeteria cooks seem touched that we've gone out of our way to invite them upstairs. The vice principal gets to ask his hot-seat regulars a different sort of question than "Where were you second period?"

"Had you read any other stories by Poe before?"

The students seem to have as much fun as I do, though mine is counterbalanced by the bother involved, no small part of which entails finding vacant rooms for the classes displaced by the activity. The cleanup is protracted—many of the kids seem equally indisposed to taking their projects home or chucking them out—and the productions are going to be a devil to grade. Effort has to count for a lot, the quality of the materials for relatively little. To do otherwise comes down to grading the resources available in a student's household (though I'd like to know what manner of grading *doesn't* come down to that in the end).

On top of this, I've allowed students to do their preapproved projects (without the requirement of preapproval, special projects amount to whatever quasi-relevant artifact can be yanked off a living room wall on the morning of the due date) in preapproved groups. So I need to take into account what one student did on her own versus what three students did together, which in the latter case can come down to what one student did on her own and two other students tried to take a free ride on. "If you're going to team up," I tell my classes, "make sure you hold up your end of the deal and make sure you choose somebody who's capable of doing the same. Have a reason for working together besides your fear of being alone." I wonder if, for some kids, this is the most valuable takeaway of the whole assignment. To drive home the point, I grant few divorces once the groups are formed and none after the projects come in.

What a complicated mess it all can be—I don't wonder that some teachers fall in love with the illusory precision of standardized tests, the tidiness of a daily worksheet, the radical individuation of the report card. The little clay figurines that topple over after a day or two, the glue that gives way along crookedly folded seams, the cardboard pieces that go sliding onto the floor, so lovely for bearing our human thumbprints, turn out to be sad for the same reason.

I have no illusions about the retro nature of some of my methods, but it takes a special faculty meeting devoted to swapping ideas for "using technology in our classrooms" to make me understand just how retro I am.

"We've just about eliminated class discussions," one colleague notes, as though class discussions were a rare strain of malaria. In lieu of verbal exchanges, his students record their comments on something called Moodle, sitting shoulder to shoulder at their screens like mute commuters on a crosstown bus. Since everyone seems to know what Moodle is, I decide not to waste the group's time by asking. I couldn't trust myself not to ask what's wrong with a class discussion. My colleague also notes that his students like to vote in class polls using their cell phones, which requires a waiver of the rule prohibiting cell phone use in class and also, needless to say, possession of a cell phone. The matter of possession surely accounts for the "mere four students" who opt to keep a paper journal for another teacher's class, in which the majority do their journals online. Thus a paper journal takes on the stigma once attached to patched pants. Recently I took a confidential classroom poll to see what I could conscionably expect of my students in terms of online research at home, and I could easily have predicted which of the kids had the equipment and which did not, based on their clothing, their attendance, and the sadder narrative details of the paper journals I require all of them to keep.

Fairness is not the only basis for my requirement. As the months go by, I come to recognize the extent of my naiveté in regard to the brave new world of digital cheating. It is not uncommon, I'm told, for students to photograph exams on their smartphones and send the photos to classmates who will take the same exam later in the day or on the day following an absence. I find that some of my practices are in woeful need of an upgrade. It has always been my policy, for example, this year and in the past, to permit students to use their notes on any pop quiz based on their reading assignments. My aim is to see that conscientious application gets its wages, with no penalties for poor retention. "So if you're worried about forgetting what you read, jot down a few notes. And if you're still worried after you take the quiz, then pass your notes in with it. If I can find something accurate—or, better still, something insightful—in your notes, I'll see you get credit for that too." Surprisingly, many of the students with the most expansive notes elect not to pass them in. Just as surprisingly, a number of students phrase their answers with identical wording, even though the wording is not from the text and even though none of them appear to be glancing at one another's quizzes.

What they're doing, though it takes me a little while to catch on, is downloading plot summaries from online sites like

SparkNotes and using them in lieu of the notes I've encouraged them to take on their own. The sharper kids cut and paste the information into what appear to be their own word-processed documents; the duller ones don't even bother to do that. An orderly society could hardly exist but for the natural affinity of dishonesty and laziness: thieves steal because thievery is easier than work, and they get caught because it's too much work to be a good thief. In that regard at least, technology fosters order.

As for discouraging the use of SparkNotes and its ilk, that is done easily enough, as in the following quiz, which derives its rationale from the folk remedy for dissuading children from smoking cigarettes by having them smoke cigars:

> Printed below is the text of a summary of chapters 6 and 7 for
> *The Secret Life of Bees* as found on a sleazy Internet rip-off site
> specially designed for students who have more important things
> to do in their lives than read books. I apologize for making you
> even *look* at such a thing, but I'm hoping we'll have some fun
> with it.
>
> Read over the summary and then, based on your own reading of
> the chapters, list 7 details, events, exchanges, or other informa-
> tion that the summary misses or waters down. Your 7 items can
> include details of description, the narrator's thoughts, a charac-
> ter's words, or anything else, however small, that is not found in
> the synopsis below. A full page of hints follows the summaries,
> but feel free to use your own material.

It takes but a few such stratagems and counterstratagems before teachers and students alike are missing the point of read-ing literature in the first place. To say nothing of missing some glaring ironies: the likelihood that the same companies producing the crib notes are marketing all kinds of expensive software to address illiteracy, the fact that educators who can't speak three consecutive sentences without using the phrase *critical thinking* almost never encourage, much less model, critical thinking in the adoption of technological tools. And this irony too: that in my tortuous efforts to get my students to enjoy reading, I am making it less than enjoyable for them and me alike. This is what kills me more than anything: the loss of pleasure as an admissible reason for doing anything, its utter insignificance in the ethos of Get-R-Done.

Nevertheless, a strange poetic justice can occur when disadvantaged students who lack the tools for online cheating turn to their books and almost by default begin to shine on their quizzes and in our class discussions, however anachronistic the latter may be. Still, it's cold comfort: even the principled refusal to cheat winds up belonging to the technologically entitled. How can we have allowed so much of *public* education to rely on *private* property? Perhaps because our whole conception of public education, originally intended to prepare students for the obligations of democratic citizenship, is to foster the acquisition of private property. You need a laptop to get a good education, so you can get a good job, so you can buy each of your children a laptop.

The young librarian, whom I've gotten to know well enough to find a number of affinities in our politics but not yet well enough to broach the subject of restoring the Library of America to the library of Lake Region Union High School, asks me what I think of the idea of writing a grant that would provide every student with a laptop. She's full of energy and commitment, and the last thing I want to do is slam a good idea. At least she recognizes the educational inequality that exists when every student doesn't have a laptop. I'm not sure this is a recognition shared in the school at large. I would indeed like to see every student with a laptop—or at least every student with equal access to one. But, I go on to say, how about starting with a grant that allows every student to do his or her homework in an adequately heated house? (A social agency rescued one of my students last winter from living with her boyfriend in an unheated trailer behind her grandparents' house, which, for all I know, might not have been any warmer than the trailer.) In fact, there are such things as fuel assistance grants, but they seldom cover the heating demands of a northern winter and are always subject to unanticipated spikes in the price of oil, in the numbers of eligible applicants (an additional ten thousand Vermonters will join the poverty rolls this year), and in the cost-cutting zeal of the Congress. By January, if not before, some residents will be spending their food money on fuel, hoping to make up the difference by scrounging at community food shelves. In such a context, "let them have laptops" comes dangerously close to "let them eat cake."

The librarian sees my point; I'm not sure she sees the writing on the digital wall. As an enrichment experience, I set up an after-school showing of Atom Egoyan's film of *The Sweet Hereafter*, the Russell Banks novel I wish were on the Popular Fiction syllabus in place of his *Rule of the Bone*, though I admire them both. I require parental permission slips (the film is rated R) and send out for pizzas. At one point in the story, what is arguably its thematic climax, a lawyer who's come to an Adirondack town to litigate in the aftermath of a tragic school bus accident stands in the snow next to the demolished bus and soliloquizes that "something has happened to the children." He doesn't mean just the victims of the accident, one of whom was a victim of father-daughter incest before she lost the use of her legs. He means the children of America, his own drug-addicted daughter not least of all.

"What has happened to the children?" he demands of the dark winter sky. What indeed? I look up from the papers I'm correcting at the back of the room to see what effect this bleak soliloquy might be having on my students. All but one are staring at their cell phones.

After the film is over, the leftover pizza is distributed, and the students are dispersed (not before they've thanked me and said how much they enjoyed the movie), I go down to the locked main office to sign myself out of the building. I find two girls seated on the bench in the lobby, not my students, just kids waiting for a ride. As I approach they ask if they might be allowed to come into the main office and use the secretary's phone to call home. This is somewhat irregular, but since I'm able to stand outside in plain view, I see no harm in granting the request. It should take no more than a minute.

But it takes much longer, and not because the girls are taking advantage of my time. It takes longer because the person they've called, a father, I assume, or someone else in the house who goes by the name of Dad, is proving doggedly reluctant to come to school and drive them home. From the girls' responses coming to me through the glass, I can infer his list of suggested alternatives, which seem to stop short of hitchhiking in the dark but veer close enough. "Can't a friend drive you?" "What about a teacher?" All the options that any parent with even the slightest capacities for worry would jump off a moving train to avoid. "Come on, Dad," the girl on the phone implores, shifting from one foot to another, grimacing at her friend. She's at school too late to have stayed for a detention; my guess is that she's just gotten out of a sports practice or perhaps been seeking extra help from a teacher. In other words, she's been trying to make the most of her school day. If there's any supper waiting on the other side of the phone line, it's likely to be cold by now. If there's homework to be done, the girls will get a late start. But the negotiations continue, as if in a hostage crisis, except the hostages are negotiating for themselves. *Why not? Please! Just come, will you?* Finally, it seems a ride is on its way. The girls come out of the office and thank me for letting them use the phone. Am I mistaken to think they're ashamed at what I have overheard—could not help but overhear, given my responsibility to keep them in view—or am I the one who's feeling ashamed for their sake?

I don't need to teach to know this feeling; I need only go to the supermarket, need only wait in line for a stamp. I seem to have become more sensitive to it over the years: the spectacle of parents without a single kind word to say to their kids. But what was that stat that went with the 30-million-word gap, the one about the class differences in what children hear by way of praise or blame? *Quit it, cut it out, smarten up, you're gonna be sorry—* the soundtrack of my world. Sometimes it's pure display: Look at me, I'm a strict parent; I make my kids mind. Other times, it's probably little more than a grudge against life. Even when there's no apparent annoyance, the sheer inattention can be staggering. I will never forget my daughter's elementary school science fair, all the little scientists standing by their rabbits and soil-filled soda bottles, their eyes fishing for the slightest notice, the alacrity with which they seized on the briefest show of interest, while their parents, the ones who'd even bothered to come, yakked and flirted among themselves like attendees at a junior high dance. The children and all their paraphernalia could have vanished without a trace and hardly been missed.

With report cards come parent-teacher conferences, and a corrective to my dismay. True, there are many more parents who stay away than come, not untypical for high school (as opposed to the younger grades) or for the midlevel classes—or, it ought to be said, for a school in which parents have a passing level of confidence. If all is well, there's no need to check things out. But enough parents come to keep me busy for most of the night. A handful show up the next day, which has been set aside for the same purpose. Some of these are former students of mine. One of them, a freshman in the first year I taught, hobbles into my room on crutches, the result of her playing King of the Hill with her athletic teenaged son. She's impressed that I can recall the position of her desk on my 1979 classroom seating chart (which I could also do for the boy's father, but he is out of the picture now) and quote the first line of an essay she wrote that same year. My remarks about her son are more guarded. He's making progress, academically and behaviorally, but not without bumps. She's been keeping close track of those. So strange for me to see the teenaged girl's face superimposed on the mother's, a few wrinkles now and a great deal more worry, but not without that indefatigable smile. "Keep me informed," she asks, the devoted parent's perpetual refrain.

I can give a more stellar report to the next mother who comes through the door. She, too, is a former student, one so quiet I might have forgotten her by now, or at least her name, except for her memorable parting years ago—when she took my hands at the end of her senior year and tearfully thanked me for "everything you did." I wondered for years thereafter what on earth I might have done out of the ordinary for this conscientious student who took a one-semester course in which I gave her no extra help I can remember, not even a letter of recommendation. Long before I realized I had her daughter in my class, she had come to occupy a symbolic place in my mind—the little Goddess of Unaccountable Thanks. Now here she is a good twenty years later, wife, mother, coach, community pillar, taking my hand again and saying how glad she is her daughter has me in class. And how glad I am to have her daughter—I can say so without reservation. And what a wonderful movie she and her friends made about "The Black Cat" for our museum project. "I hope they didn't leave you to clean up all the blood."

Other conferences are more fretful—one boy hurries upstairs ahead of his parents and asks if I intend to tell them about "that stupid thing with the SparkNotes I did today." I assure him the thought never crossed my mind; it runs entirely counter to my code. No cheap shots on parent-conference night, no ingratiating bullshit either, but no cheap shots, especially with a kid who I'm almost positive has learned an important lesson. Not a few of the tenser exchanges involve mothers who are at wits' end to know what to do with the surly young men who've suddenly emerged in their hitherto man-free houses. Without their sons in tow, they're at liberty to confess. This may have something to do with my age, but I don't recall many times in my first years teaching when a lone parent came out and said, "I don't know what to do with him. What should I do?" I venture no advice beyond urging them not to give up on the question, "which you're obviously not going to do if you bothered to come here tonight."

Parent conferences help to remind me that good parenting defies all ideologically based predictors. Social conservatives, I'm sure, would like to see a better correlation between "intact [heterosexual] family" and happy child, just as my socialistic convictions would rest easier with a stronger correlation between class deprivation and family strife. No doubt, we each have ample evidence for making our case. But the exceptions make mischief with our best arguments: the illiterate parent who sees to it that the homework gets done, the village brawler who never once strikes his kids, the mother who shows up at school looking like a refugee from Cold Comfort Farm but who will get her daughter, and eventually herself, through college, whatever it takes. Kathy brings me more than one of these stories home from her work at Dartmouth, my favorite having to do with a mentally impaired divorced father with a menial job and a sympathetic boss who gives him the day off so he can drive all night across four state lines every time his child has a school conference or a doctor's appointment. He may or may not grasp what it means to have a kid "on the autism spectrum" or an advanced degree in pediatric neurology, but he knows enough to grasp his child's hand and not to let it go.

The matter of "how much to say" comes easier to me in parent conferences than it sometimes does in individual exchanges with kids. With the parents, there's an etiquette, a scripted agenda: the grades, the behavior, the things that are causing difficulty, the potential I see that I hope the parent sees with me and that we want the child to see as well. "Call me anytime" takes the place of a formal bow among the Japanese: the parent says it, I repeat it, we go back to our respective sides of the teahouse, me to my desk and the parent to the door. With the kids, it's a dicier proposition, and *dicey* provides the right metaphor, because often the exchange takes the form of a game.

For instance, the game of "Do you believe me?" The student makes the first move by pretending not to have understood the difference between taking notes while reading an assignment and downloading prepackaged notes off the Internet. "You said we could use notes." Or the student pretends to have believed that "you wouldn't mind" if she went AWOL for half a class period. The apparent object here is to place the teacher in the position of losing no matter how he responds. Refuse my excuse, and you're calling me a liar. Accept my excuse, and you've as much as called one of us an idiot, since it would take an idiot to believe what I've just told you. Or, worse, you've shown that you're much more concerned about smooth relations than you are about an honest student-teacher relationship.

Too often this amounts to an accurate depiction of a school's priorities. Behind a pretext of "mutuality" and "giving students the benefit of the doubt," the institution winds up convincing any student with half a brain that he scarcely matters at all. It's the pretense of rectitude we care about, the idol of ourselves as "caring people" that we worship instead of the latent god in the living kid. So we allow a kid to negotiate his way to functional illiteracy, then congratulate ourselves on our fair dealing. For the moment, the kid believes that he has conned us, but I fear he often grows up to understand that we have conned him. A bitter epiphany if he does.

I try to explain that to my students when I disallow certain dodges. "I don't want you looking back ten years from now and saying to yourself, Mr. Keizer seemed like a pretty nice guy at the time, but he was just going through the motions and picking up a paycheck and laughing at me all the way to the bank. In fact, he must have thought I was pretty stupid." Sometimes this connects. Sometimes it doesn't. The problem of how much to say is complicated further by the problem of how much is likely to be heard. A teacher should never underestimate the factor of selective listening. Simply to use the word *stupid* risks having a kid believe, or claim to believe, that you've called him stupid. He hears the word and nothing else. A failure in auditory processing, as much as any willful recalcitrance, lies at the root of more than a few classroom conflicts.

Many of these are innocuous enough, even comical, but others play out in more disturbing ways. In fulfillment of an ice-breaking assignment I inherited years ago from my department head—"Talk to a Chair" (that is, to someone you imagine sitting in it)—a girl talks to her father's new wife. I've explicitly warned the students at the outset and in writing that they should not use the assignment as a therapy session or to violate anyone's confidentiality, including their own. Use your imagination, keep it light, be discreet. But the girl who steps to the front of the room has either not heard what I said (a real possibility given that she's often running to the nurse's office or her guidance counselor at the start of class) or else has chosen to ignore me. She makes unflattering references to the new wife's ethnicity and her wiles in catching her husband. In a class with more than a few step-children, the girl's no-holds-barred attack plays like a battle cry. The kids seem thrilled, and I have to admit that the talk is strong. For the girl I imagine it represents a kind of catharsis. But in the midst of my praises for her diction, her dramatic delivery, her use of specific examples to illustrate general statements (a point of special emphasis for this class, notwithstanding the examples that made me squirm), I feel it necessary to caution her about matters of confidentiality and the real danger that certain kinds of remarks might be construed "by someone who doesn't know you as well as we do" as racist.

Later in the term a colleague tells me, "Deidre thinks you hate her. She says you think she's a racist." Should I have made my remarks to her privately? Would it have made any difference? And didn't the audience for her remarks oblige me to address my caveats—and my praises—in front of the same impressionable audience? I can't help but wonder if the wicked stepmother doesn't feel the same exasperation as I do. *Say what I will, the child never hears me.*

The best I can do is to make the points I think need to be made as clearly as I know how to make them and, no less important, to be as keen to listen as I am to talk. In other words, I need to be as ready to learn as I am to teach. I'm presented with an opportunity to do both in an exchange with a trumpet player who hails me from the band teacher's office. He's overheard some of the jazz I played for my sophomores in connection with "Sonny's Blues" and thinks it was cool stuff. With an eye to his trumpet, I ask if he knows Miles Davis. He doesn't, and so I offer to lend him *Kind of Blue*. Pointing to the name and face on the front of his T-shirt, I ask if he'd care to requite my Davis with a bit of Dr. Dre. If he's willing, I wouldn't mind a lesson or two in hip-hop, a genre about which I know little and would like to learn more. Would he be willing to teach me, in other words. He would.

"You made Mike's day by asking about Dr. Dre," the student's English teacher tells me. But my request remains in limbo for a while. Eventually, I'm given to understand that the delay owes to Mike's difficulty in finding tracks suitable for a teacher's ears. The problem of selective hearing works both ways, you see, and he's fearful that I'll hear "the rough parts" and nothing else. I tell him he should give me what I asked for and not worry about offending me; his only concern should be with giving me a good introduction to the music.

That he does, and it's no strain to find some songs that I like and some well-turned lines that I admire. But how far should I go in tackling the misogyny in some of the lyrics? The last thing I want to do as a white teacher talking to an African American student is to play the dozens with his music—especially when he has fewer than a dozen schoolmates, and no instructors, of his color. But I'm playing the same game with his intelligence if I simply nod my head in bland approval, adopting that tolerant mien Emerson so memorably describes as "the gentlest asinine expression." I have to say the word *women* at the least. I have to speak to what disturbs me.

Mike knows what I'm talking about, and it disturbs him too. He tries to give the issue some historical context, parts of which I find more convincing than others, but I don't need to tell him so. Perhaps the best antidote against selective listening is selective talking: say no more than what's most important to say. In this case, that includes "thank you," and not just for teaching me. He has also trusted me.

So has the girl who comes to me to tell me why she's been missing so many classes. How without saying too much do I suggest that she may be revealing too much? The word *medical* is quite sufficient, I want to tell her, all I need in order to understand why I ought to cut her some slack. I'm quite willing to do so without any reference to her ovaries. But there's a thin, thin line here between helping her to understand that she doesn't have to barter intimate details of health history in exchange for some compassion and driving her back to that zone of misogyny in which women are supposed to regard their bodies as unmentionable. It would take a self-defeating number of words to make the first point while disclaiming the second, so I say less than I could.

I wish I'd said more when I overhear—when everyone in class overhears—several girls gabbing that the reason Rhonda is out of class again is that she's got gross things growing on her ovaries. "Let's let our classmates' medical matters be their own business," I say, though I can tell from the ensuing facial expressions that what I meant to say and what was heard are at considerable variance. *Let's let our classmates die of ovarian cancer and not give a damn about them because our homework is all that counts around here*—that's likely to be what got heard, not merely or even primarily because the kids are not listening but because so much of what I say is filtered through the larger culture, in which knowing the details of other people's pain increasingly becomes the substitute for relieving it. "Knowledge is power," gossip is compassion, attitude is protest, doing nothing what-soever is doing everything imaginable so long as you're well-informed. But you can't say that to a bunch of sophomores, and they'd miss the irony even if you did.

Stick to the curriculum, focus on the task at hand, that's what you tell yourself, but even that bumps up against certain cultural norms that you either swallow or push back on. I have a student who comes to school every day after only a few hours of sleep. He sometimes dozes off sitting upright in his desk. In addition to doing chores on his family's farm, he reports to another barn at 2:00 a.m. and milks for several hours there. "Your studies need to come first"—that's what I want to say, but the matter is more complicated than that. I know from talking to him, as I will learn again on a deeper level when I have him in a second-semester Composition class, that his sole vocational goal is to become a farmer. In that light, his time in the barn *is* his "stud-ies." In fact, his father has purchased the farm—a perilous step at best in the current agricultural economy—with the plan of giving him the training he desires and a place to put that train-ing to profitable use once the farm passes from father to son. What to do, then, but talk to a guidance counselor and talk ever so gingerly to the student, lauding his work ethic and sense of vocation while reminding him of his need for sleep and for the literature that is no less his inheritance than the farm, no less nourishing than milk.

A girl in another class explains to me, not without frustra-tion, why her grades have fallen from best in class to failing. I know something of her background, and so I have no reason to disbelieve her when she says, "I've been raised to believe that your family and your friends come first." In other words, when a parent tells you to involve yourself in some ridiculous kinship drama as opposed to reading a book about someone else's kinship drama, you don't disobey. How does a teacher question a value so irreproachable as "family loyalty"? Perhaps by expanding it. "I agree with what you've been brought up to believe," I tell her, "but only if you include your future family in the mix. It's possible to let down your yet-to-be-born children by being too afraid to let down your parents. A mother with a good education is less likely to be forced to choose between caring for her kids and earning a living." As feminism this is pretty thin gruel—what about the young woman's obligation to herself?—but it's the message she's likeliest to digest. It is her future welfare, not my ideological purity, that's at stake. I cite my wife as an example; her education has allowed her some options that other women, other mothers, don't enjoy.

If I'm dangerously close to undermining a parent's authority, I'm even closer to undermining my own argument. It's the same sad paradox that every teacher faces: "Get a good education—so you can be more like me." Are teachers the happiest, most esteemed and prosperous people that a kid is likely to meet? We are certainly among the best educated, at least in a community like mine. At times I try for a better exhortation, spicing it with a bit of sardonic humor: "Get a good education—or else you could end up like me." I'm telling them to lay hold of every educational opportunity at hand. *Surpass your teacher.* But is that what they hear? Quickly, lest they draw the wrong conclusion, I add that I consider myself very fortunate, as indeed I do, to serve as their teacher and to spend time with them every day.

Finally, I make time to drive to Burlington for dinner with my grown-up daughter, a biweekly custom in my freelance life but increasingly rare in my schedule now. I look forward to it all day. For one thing, I'll be on the road in daylight, out of work early—I've asked for and been granted permission to leave school when the students do—and for another, I can count on being a better conversationalist than usual. Often I find myself casting about for topics beyond the usual paternal remarks about maintaining tire pressures and keeping the door open for graduate school. A writer's regimen provides little in the way of anecdote. Today, though, I'll be coming to the table full of stories; both of us are teaching now.

Within moments after driving out of the busy school lot, I find myself in the middle of an ominous caravan snaking along the winding, damaged road that goes past the school toward Irasburg. Two cars ahead of me, at the head of the line, is a school bus. Directly behind me, practically in my backseat, is a car driven by a student who appears to be tripping on some drug. He is gesticulating crazily—at me, at another car, to his music, who knows? I could read his lips in my rearview mirror if I took my eyes off the road long enough. Behind him, swerving frequently into the oncoming lane, is another car with a student sitting with his body outside the passenger side window and his hands on the car roof. Should the driver brake abruptly, his buddy's as good as airborne. A third car behind those two is also jockeying for position, driving the others up against my back. The thought flashes through my mind that at fifty-seven years old, with a salary of less than fifty thousand dollars per year and very little to leave my loved ones in the way of wealth, I am going to be killed in a wilding incident on a secondary road in Podunk. That the car threatening a head-on collision with any vehicle coming the other way has the grille of a late-model Volvo only makes the thought more bitter. I am going to be sideswiped or run off the road by a seventeen-year-old kid whose parents can afford to send him to school in a Volvo. I am going to be eulogized in spray paint on a bridge abutment as people weep their eyes out for the poor teacher who lost his life in the unfortunate "accident," to say nothing of the damage to the goddamn Volvo.

I'm out of my car almost before the school bus has come to a full stop at the next T intersection. I tap the driver's side of the car behind me until the driver, who does not look at me at first, rolls down his window. I shout out to the other drivers behind him, all of whom are looking at me now and who seem surprised to see me. Some kids have just gotten off the school bus and they're watching too. I ask what anyone would like to bet me that any of these cars is going to be allowed a parking space at school tomorrow. I have no takers. I have at least one apology—I don't remain long enough to hear any others.

Instead I drive back to the school. On the way into the lot, I nearly collide with another teacher approaching on my right; neither of us sees the other till we hit our brakes just in time. This shakes me up further, though I'm already pretty shaken. I doubt Mr. Messier has ever seen me this upset. "I don't mind not having a life for a year," I say melodramatically, "but I draw the line at *losing* my life." He smiles when I add "to a Volvo no less." He knows which student drives a Volvo, along with the names of the others who fit my descriptions. Within fifteen minutes he has spoken by phone to every parent connected with the incident. He doesn't get any blowback. He says he intends to speak to all of the students tomorrow, informing them that although his jurisdiction does not extend beyond the school grounds, the sheriff's does, and he will notify the sheriff. When he gently voices his concern about my driving so many miles in such a bad state of mind, I say that I will probably abort my trip.

"If you still would like to have dinner with your daughter, and you want a driver, you've got one." He is talking about a round trip of 180 miles, six hours out of his day at the least. And he means what he's said—I almost can't bear to register how sincerely he means it. He also offers me his phone and the privacy of his office to call my daughter.

The next day passes without incident. Mr. Messier has told me he will not order the drivers to apologize; wisely he intends to "see what they do." He probably knows how little a forced apology would mean to me: less than none at all. One of my students does ask what was happening behind the school bus yesterday, which he saw when he'd gotten off at his stop, tactfully adding "Are you okay?" I'm fine, I tell him. "I just don't like being crowded." I can't help recalling a character in the novella we're reading, Howard Frank Mosher's *Where the Rivers Flow North*, who shares a similar dislike. "Don't crowd him, you," says his common-law wife, before he drives a cant hook through the hand of a man who ought to have heeded her warning. Perhaps my favorite scene in the book.

At the close of the day, three penitent young men appear at my door and ask if they can speak to me. I'm listening. When one of them swears that he'd never have tailgated my car had he known a teacher was driving it, I have the cue I need to say what matters most. Though my own safety was uppermost in my mind at the time, I urge them to think of how much more was at stake in the case of their own lives. I do not want to die, I tell them, and yet if I died now, I'd die in the satisfactions of a happy marriage, of having watched a child of mine grow to adulthood, of having seen most of my ambitions fulfilled. All of these satisfactions came to me when I was older than they are now. To die before one is even fully conscious of his own capacities for happiness—and to die stupidly into the bargain, what a terrible waste that would be. "Your friend, the guy leaning out the window—what if he'd lost his balance?" and so on. They've heard all of this a hundred times, I'm sure, but there is always the chance it will sink in on the 101st try.

I impart no other life lessons before shaking their hands and telling them we're square. All in all, not without the help of my principal and probably of some parents too, I've managed to bring the whole business to a satisfactory close. I've seized what educators are fond of calling the teachable moment and used it to good effect. I should be feeling better about things than I do.

For the truth is that the slowest learner to have entered this classroom at the end of the day is the one left standing in it. Maintaining professional detachment, setting boundaries between work life and personal life—a time to punch in, and a time to punch out—at these I'm still an apprentice. A decade and a half since my previous year of teaching I remain stuck in the same rut on the near side of wisdom. I'm still ready to grasp the teachable moment even as I lose the livable one. I should have waited for the school bus to make its turn and made mine in the opposite direction. I should have shaken my head in disgust and driven on to Burlington. *But someone might have died*—to hell with that. We're all dying. *I'm* dying. The daughter who once wished aloud that she could make two daddies, one to grade the kids' papers and one to play pirates with her, ate dinner without her father last night, just as she did so many nights in the past when his body was at the kitchen table and his mind still at school. Who am I to lecture anyone on the subject of a terrible waste?

DECEMBER

There is nothing like tempting the boy to want to study and to love it: otherwise you simply produce donkeys laden with books. . . . If it is to do any good, Learning must not only lodge with us: we must marry her.

—Montaigne, "On Educating Children"

Not long before the Thanksgiving recess I begin what will prove the most arduous task of the year: teaching my three tenth-grade classes how to write a research paper. Another member of the department, no shirker and perhaps the best trained of any of us in the art of teaching students how to write, insists that tenth graders are still too young to handle such an assignment. He may well be right about that, though there are precedents that might refute him.

At one time, roughly concurrent with my last tenure at the school, a research paper was a standard requirement in the tenth grade for both English and social studies. Attempts to coordinate between the departments and allow students to write a single paper for both classes probably did as much as any factor to discourage the assignment in subsequent years. Naturally enough, social studies teachers tended to see "content" as their prerogative, which greatly restricted the range of acceptable subjects, and "form" as belonging to their colleagues across the hall, which prompted English teachers to feel they were being asked to run an editorial laundry service. In retrospect, the disagreement was probably no more than the inevitable outcome of any team teaching effort involving more than one team.

Many things have changed since then, not least of all the emphasis on writing across the curriculum. These days it's not unusual for me to be invited to admire a piece of student writing generated by a phys ed class. Sara has said the time has come to revive the requirement of a tenth-grade research paper. She has asked if I will help. Her wishes are enough to get me going, though I have my own inducements. I've recently written an intensively researched book, so I feel up to speed on the process. I'm also vain enough to want a crack at anything deemed too difficult to teach.

Not to say I ever found the unit easy. Research writing is the decathlon of the language arts, requiring a range of skills that most teachers can hardly claim to possess themselves, let alone know how to teach anyone else. The simple act of defining a topic can amount to a procrustean bed of adjustments, either because the topic is too broad for adequate treatment in a short paper or too narrow for the limited resources of a high school library. The Internet goes a ways toward helping with the latter, but only as far as a teacher's willingness to allow students to rely exclusively on Internet sources—in my case, not very far. The topic should ideally be of interest to the student (a toughie with students who claim to have no interests whatsoever or to be interested "only in sports," which as often as not means only in the statistical profile of a favorite player or team) and covered by at least one source that might plausibly be deemed reliable. Not least of all, the topic should be within the student's conceptual grasp.

Beyond that hurdle, which includes the ability to work one's way not only through the library catalog but also through the indices of books with no more than a tangential relation to the topic, lies the formidable matter of learning how to take notes. This, too, has its component parts: learning the difference between paraphrasing and direct quotation and when to opt for one or the other, learning to construct note cards in such a way as to be able to document the information accurately. In the past I used to tell my classes that research writing was mainly about telling the truth. It's also about constructing a usable memory of one's work, taking notes in such as way as to permit their flexible organization once the student reaches the outlining stage, which is yet another skill, another lesson plan, another potential pitfall.

Still, I agree with Sara in thinking the assignment worth the trouble. The reasons go far beyond that of "getting students ready for college." Not all of mine will go to college, and some will probably wind up in colleges where writing research papers is as much the exception as the rule. All the more reason for initiating students now. Learning how to write a research paper is the educational equivalent of a Bar Mitzvah or First Communion, the rite of passage when students make the giant leap from passive learning to aggressive learning, from the familial cave of the classroom to a larger assembly of scholars. And "form" is not the least part of it, in spite of the understandable temptation for the creatively minded teacher to play down form as persnickety and pedantic. Few people would see writing a research paper as an artistic endeavor—I certainly wouldn't—yet it has this much in common with many works of art: the struggle to find self-expression within the confines of material limits and traditional conventions. The need to make *this thing*—this canvas, this chorus, this genre—*mine*. And the need to follow incremental steps, the recognition shared by Darwin and Moses alike that few things worth our wonder are constructed in a day.

But that has never stopped us from looking for ways to abridge a process. There are computer programs that allow you to build Rome in an hour. I know that some of my younger colleagues have their students use a Web site called Noodle Tools to enter information and have it automatically arranged on the screen on virtual note cards, which can then be formatted and sequenced. The program also arranges bibliographical data—authors, titles, publishers, etc.—into one or another standardized format for footnotes and bibliography. It acts something like a magical hopper: you throw the raw materials in and the desired product emerges on the other side fully assembled. To the chagrin of a few students—and probably to the puzzlement of some of my colleagues—I announce that we are not going to be using Noodle Tools. We're going to learn how to take notes the old-fashioned way, on 3×5 note cards. I precede the announcement with the first of several raids on the school supply closet, knowing better than to require students to go foraging in the nearest convenience store, and pass out the booty as I speak.

I spare them an account of my complete rationale, including my distaste for anything so absurdly named as a Noodle Tool. I tell them I'm teaching them how to be chefs, which is not to my way of thinking the same thing as teaching them to preheat an oven to 350 degrees and peel back the foil on the peach-cobbler side of an aluminum tray. Cooking involves knowing how to choose ingredients, how to prepare and combine them, how to exercise the judgments of one's eyes, tongue, and nose. You need to blow on your noodle and put it in your mouth to know when it's done. I want them to learn the actual process for which Noodle Tools is merely the metaphor. Indeed, how would a kid fully comprehend such a program who hadn't first performed the process in three dimensions?

I have other unspoken reasons beyond that spiel. I want students to feel that *they* achieved the work, that they were more than acolytes of their digital tools. I want students without Internet access or computers at home to be on the same footing with their better-equipped peers. I want students with learning disabilities to have the advantage of being able to manipulate their information in three dimensions. I want them to be able to lay it out and turn it over in such as way as to see it all at any given time.

Finally, I want to preempt another Web wonder: a bogus research paper delivered whole cloth for a fee. The opportunities are legion. Given my approach, with its step-by-step benchmarks along the way, a student determined to cheat would need to construct by hand an entire counterfeit "preparation" of his research paper backwards from the one he obtained online. I don't rule out the possibility that a student might try to do just that—cheating has other motivations besides the avoidance of work—though I doubt he could do so without learning something along the way.

In the faculty workroom, the head of the social studies department watches me tape two handwritten sample note cards to a sheet of paper that I will then lay on the photocopier to make yet another handout. I ink in arrows to various parts of each card and write in labels: "topic heading," "author's last name," "page number for where the material was taken," "quotation marks for direct quotation," "slash to indicate that quotation continues on a new page of the source," "note from source, one per card," "your comment about the note (optional)," etc.

"So you're teaching them to do it with actual note cards," he says.

"I am." My ears are tuned for a note of disapproval. I know he has a Web site for each of his classes and posts all of his assignments online. I doubt he thinks very highly of my approach.

"I'm so glad to see that," he says. "I think the kids do much better when they can actually hold the cards in their hands."

I'm slightly surprised—though I shouldn't be; good sense was always his trademark—and more than slightly gratified by his warm approval. Something else occurs to me, which must have occurred to him first since he obviously tolerates the use of Noodle Tools in his own department. With physical note cards on my side of the hall and virtual note cards on the other, our students will have the best of both worlds—like having a hip younger aunt and a stubbornly opinionated grandpa both living on your street. What fun to be adored by them both, even as you tell tales about each in order to scandalize the other.

All in all the range of topics that the students choose to research is not disappointing. Neither is the number who choose topics of particular relevance to their own interests and plans: a paper on depression by a student whose uncle committed suicide; a paper on the life of John Deere by a self-described "redneck"; several papers on occupations that students hope to pursue, from real estate agent to obstetrician; a history of one of the oldest farm families in the region, including an account of why they stopped farming. The suggestions I provide at the outset run the gamut from the Matewan coal strike to the revival of farmers' markets, from Somali pirates to surrogate motherhood. In three classes I have only two takers: a girl who may be my most consistent high performer, who chooses the rescue of Jews in the French village of Le Chambon during the Second World War; and a student who's retaking tenth-grade English after failing it the year before, who chooses the giant squid. The rest of my topics go unexplored, quite possibly because some would require preliminary investigation to be understood, though others would seem like easy sells, especially given the brief oral teasers I provide as I go over the list after handing it out. But if the main reason has to do with students wanting as much ownership of the assignment as possible, then we're off to a good start.

In any case, the topics students choose on their own are often as intriguing as the ones I've suggested: traditional clothing in India, the early Negro baseball leagues, the bubonic plague. Sometimes the topic comes out of a dialogue between a student and me; the student supplies an area of general interest, I supply some avenues for further investigation. These hybrids are my favorites and make me feel as though I'm really teaching, though one of them leads me to worry if I've forgotten the age level I teach.

A girl tells me she is interested in the subject of self-mutilation. "People who do weird things to their bodies." Her interest seems more anthropological than psychological. I doubt the topic is in any way personal—she's definitely not a cutter; as far as I'm aware, she doesn't even have a tattoo. I feel I have the perfect suggestion for her, at once topical and relevant to her interests. Taking care to see that another female student is with us and employing the most tactful, nonexplicit language I can muster, ready at the slightest show of discomfort to segue to another topic, I suggest she examine the subject of female circumcision, or female genital mutilation, as it's also called. She's immediately enthusiastic, though I'm not sure if this is mainly in response to the subject itself or to the implication that she's mature enough to handle it. In any case, I seem not to have offended or shocked her. I feel I've taken an appropriate risk, one that might pay dividends beyond a decent five-page paper. *I*

trace the roots of my work with Egyptian women's groups to a
project I did for a high school English class . . .

But after school lets out for the day, I begin to wonder if I've assessed the risks from the right perspective. My spontaneous thoughts during class were focused almost exclusively on gauging current standards of propriety and the girl's level of maturity, which I'd rated as fairly loose and fairly advanced, respectively. On those criteria, I've probably managed to stay abreast of the times and to take an accurate measure of my kids. Where I have surely been more clueless, as usual, is in the area of technology, where my imaginative grasp continues to be perilously weak. More to the point, it does not conjure the high-resolution image of a raw, infected, newly mutilated vulva thrown up on a fifteen-year-old's computer screen by the simplest combination of keystrokes—to say nothing of the variety of sadomasochistic monstrosities that might be harvested by a comparable number of clicks.

Not yet panicked but beginning to perspire, I go to the guidance office and look up a phone number for the girl's house. I know her mother works at another school in the district, so it's likely she'll be home by this hour. I decide I'll start with the mother if I can, though I also decide that I'll need to speak to the student herself if she answers. I'll only create needless anxieties if I say "I need to talk to your mother." Sure enough, the girl answers and is home by herself. I keep my tone light and my message brief. I'm calling, I tell her, because I want to ask that she wait to begin her online research until our school librarian can help. I hadn't given enough thought to the likelihood of such a topic leading her to inappropriate sites, which the librarian will know best how to avoid. I also tell her that I hope she realizes she's free to change her topic if she comes to have any doubts about it. "I know that whatever you do is going to be thoughtful and well done; it doesn't have to be this one."

The girl takes my call in stride. I get off the phone thinking I've done the right thing—and making a mental note to inform the librarian of my recommendation tomorrow morning at the latest—though I also have the sensation that I keep digging myself into an ever deeper hole. *Male teacher suggests lurid topic to teenage girl, then phones her at home the same day.* I wonder if I have ever had a proper appreciation of the fact that I'm teaching *kids*.

This perpetual need—not only to interpret every manner of adolescent grunt, grimace, and gesture but to anticipate how my most carefully articulated sentences might be *mis*interpreted—it makes me tired, and after a while it makes me sick. The work I can do, the misbehaviors I can handle, but the self-imposed prohibition against thinking clearly, speaking frankly, and reacting honestly—that, most of all, is what's beginning to wear me down. Plus the nagging insinuation that conscientiousness may be my worst liability. In terms of professional survival, upping the intellectual ante is almost always less advisable than keeping your head down and letting the students find their own way.

Well, a few class periods of doing research in the library are enough to qualify that notion. Letting students "find their own way" is just a euphemism for abandonment. Small wonder it's the lazy teacher's favorite cliché. The deadbeat parent's too. With the help of our excellent librarian, my student finds a number of good sources, along with a tidy abbreviation for her subject: "I'm doing my paper on FGM," she'll say with a touch of archness, though she has no qualms about identifying the letters and she exhibits not the slightest inclination toward sensationalizing the subject matter for her peers. I'm proud of her. And for the most part I'm proud of the way my students commit to their subjects and to the deadlines ahead, of their attention to detail when they show me their first note cards, and, not least, of the assistance they offer to one another.

I suppose I shouldn't be surprised, though I am, at the reluctance of many students to consult books. I expected that *locating* books might be an issue for some of them, but the unwillingness even to *open* the books I help them locate still puzzles me. I recall times in past years when a student stumped over a research paper would take a newfound source from a teacher's hands as if it were a rich uncle's will. Not so much now. I bring in books from my personal library, naively warning students not to let even an excellent source—or any single source, for that matter—take over their paper. I needn't worry. In one case—when I bring in an article about computers that beat chess champions for a boy who wants to do research in the area of computer games—the source is refused outright. "Thanks, but I think I'm okay."

I'm even more surprised when some of my few overtly bookish students resist looking beyond some book they already know. I'm happy to learn that one of my students wants to do a paper on chakras, a topic that seems right down her New Age alley while also offering plenty of interesting side streets. But I can't seem to get her interested in any sources having to do with Hinduism, including one with an ornate diagram of kundalini rising through the chakras of a yogi's spine. Instead she wants to rely almost exclusively on a chiropractic manual that contains not a single footnote for its several glib assertions about "ancient traditions of the East." Another student, who reads assiduously if not widely, takes meticulous notes from a single online source describing the esoteric meanings of mythical Chinese animals but shows no interest in a lavishly illustrated book on Chinese mythology that I find for her on the library shelves.

At bottom I'm seeing a truth too easy for teachers to forget. Learning something new—especially about a subject you already know something about—can be a terrifying thing. Research is not for the lazy, our teachers and professors tell us, but it might be more pertinent to say that above all else it is not for the timid. No less than discipline, it takes courage to reconfigure your view of the world. If you're perfectly satisfied that the earth is flat, you're not in any great hurry to sail beyond the horizon. And falling off the edge of the earth is not the worst thing you fear.

Not for the first time I organize an after-school workshop, this one devoted to the research paper. Adhering to the principle that failure is not an option, I make the session mandatory for students who've failed to keep pace with the various deadlines in the process and optional for those who'd simply like some extra help. Or perhaps what they'd like is an after-school snack. No matter, they come, volunteers and conscripts alike. At the end of the year one of my colleagues will inquire how I managed to motivate so many students to stay after school, to which I will reply, "I fed them." Never all they could eat, though. Any messiah who took it upon himself to feed five thousand of these guys wouldn't have had twelve baskets left over, I can tell you that. It seems they are always ravenous. On a whim I've gotten into the habit of hanging a bunch of green bananas over the blackboard and there's as much interest in their status of ripeness as in anything written underneath. For the after-school workshop, I bring extra bananas, potato chips, cookies, apples, whatever I can grab out of our household cupboards or off the shelves of the mini-mart on my drive to work. A few of the students add provisions of their own. One girl will almost always bring in a tray of home-baked goodies whether she herself is staying or not.

I sign laptops out of the library for kids who will need them. I ask if they'd like music, and when they say they would, I put on Bach's *Well-Tempered Klavier* (highly rated by one conspicuously pierced and purple-haired underachiever in my study hall who said she liked working to it). And Herbie Hancock gets a turn at the piano too.

I park myself next to an empty desk and take customers as they come. I open my laptop next to theirs for some "floor time." My wife's old friend and preschool teaching colleague says that she hardly ever sees preschool teachers on the floor with their kids anymore. In her work as a college instructor of novice practitioners she's just as likely to see a teacher, even a mentoring teacher, recording data. In our case, two open laptops side by side count for a floor. So does the after-hours library. I take the students down in relays, unlocking the doors and helping them to canvass the stacks. Back in the classroom, I write a few note cards "for free."

It's easy to underestimate how much these small steps can mean, especially when they're *first* steps. One boy with more than adequate ability to perform the assignment but lacking a single of the twenty-five note cards he was supposed to have completed by the end of last week, slides in beside me and sighs with frustration and self-disgust. "You know what I wish, Mr. Keizer?" he says. "I wish I could stack your firewood for you and get out of doing this paper." Well, bud, I won't say that isn't a tempting offer, though it wouldn't be all that good for your education or my waistline. Let's try a stack of note cards instead. May I do the first one? How long did that take me? Watch this. Here's number two. And keep your eye on three because it's going to be finished before you know it happened. Now your turn. Look at this: card number four. One more and you're 20 percent done. How many do you think you can do before your ride shows up or we run out of food?

It's that invisible net of helplessness that perplexes me, though I am no stranger to it. I'm simply old enough to have learned how to extricate myself from procrastination, how to rip it open with one decisive swipe. A girl whose recently changed topic has to do with her intention of becoming an obstetrician tells me that she's "looked" but there's "nothing on the Internet" about obstetricians. I assume she means that there is *so much* on the Internet that she has no idea where to begin. She stands beside my desk in an absurd pose of languorous disaffection: Why must life be so impossibly cruel? Here's where a book or a magazine might have served her better, something definite she could hold in her hand, but I put that aside for the moment and give her some hints on refining her search. As with the boy and the note cards, I find her a first link and telegraph the article to the teachers' room printer. I also suggest that she interview an obstetrician as one of her sources, which at the least might give her some idea of the radical change she'll have to make in her work habits if she hopes to get into, to say nothing of finish, medical school.

Not that I would say such a thing, and I'm not exactly pleased with myself for thinking it. Even in this funky little tutorial I am reminded of how hard it is to predict when and how a girl or boy is going to catch fire. I'd as soon predict the weather on a day thirty years from now as predict the achievements of any student walking into his ten-year class reunion. I'm reminded as well of how hard-won an achievement a kid's mere attendance can be relative to the forces keeping her down. Another girl who's also way behind on her research paper—and in fact will never hand one in—stops in the middle of our conference to receive the first of several importunate text messages . . . "from my father's new girlfriend." If you want to talk to me, you need to turn that thing off, I tell her. And if you want to accomplish almost anything else—I don't tell her that. After all, she's *here*, she showed up, with everything she has on her plate. And perhaps, who knows, my greatest contribution to her life may be the remembrance of a single late afternoon when she glimpsed what it means to be part of a community of scholars. It will be my fondest remembrance too: I know even as I'm sitting here that the year will hold nothing better than this.

I make sure the door stays open. Students not in my classes also drop by to visit—and munch—always welcome so long as they don't interfere with our work. They rarely do. Nor do the kids in the workshop seem to waste much time. Of course, the compulsory attendees are eager to get themselves caught up and out from under their obligation. "Am I done now?" But even the volunteers stay pretty much on task. The socializing is quiet, convivial, proportionate—*natural*. We're at our ease. Ever mindful of the ways in which any given classroom approach models a type of society, I find in these workshops what may be the best case for anarchism. How wonderful if the formalities of my assignment were to wither away like the nation-state, leaving us to learn and write without coercion. Yet it is partly coercion that has brought us here.

Not entirely, though. Nor is it entirely vanity that brings me to this paragraph. A forgivable vanity if it is. A passerby sticks his head in the door, momentarily dumbfounded by what he sees, a gathering too late to be class, too loose to be school, too full of books and paper to be a club. "What are you doing?" he mouths to the girl sitting nearest the door, the girl who baked the cupcakes. "We have Mr. Keizer with us," she says. "Otherwise it would be detention."

My impromptu workshop isn't the only school activity that takes place after hours and off the activities pages of the yearbook. This is not a school where teachers hit the parking lot running at the end of day. I'm invited to a poetry reading organized by a couple of seniors in collaboration with our librarian. I doubt many of my students will attend—the big draw will come from the honors classes and the upper grades—but I'm happy for two or three of my sophomores who've professed artistic aspirations. This will be a good venue for them to showcase their talents and, perhaps even more important, to find their community. At the very least, it might encourage them, as I have been gently encouraging them, to consider taking a crack at the honors-level electives next year.

Two of them drop by my room before the reading. The less friendly of them, a girl who seems to believe that creativity is most reliably authenticated by an air of haughty disdain, though I would guess she's a sensitive kid who lives in daily fear of being found out as less intellectual than she appears, asks if I would be willing to read three of her poems. She wants to read two of them this evening, and she wants my opinion as to which of the three she should choose. I've read enough of her class assignments to know she is talented, and she's read enough of my comments to know that I think so, but this tentative overture outside of class is something new between us. A younger teacher would likely be more inclined to see it as a breakthrough. For my part, I think she may be seeking my judgment only to have an opportunity to overrule it. But even that would mark some progress.

I read the poems. Unlike her precocious short fiction, her poetry is on a par with what you'd expect from an adolescent with literary aspirations. That probably means no more than that she's read more fiction than poetry. One of the poems has for its subject how bored she is in my English class, a theme belied by her attention and participation, though probably truthful enough in the area of certain assignments she deems beneath her. Fortunately the poem about her boredom in my class is one of the stronger of the three, so rendering my judgment is a simple task. "These two," I say, and hand them back to her without further comment.

When I go to the library, I find it set up like a coffeehouse, separate tables, intimate lamps. One of the English teachers has brought his guitar. I hope no one expects me to sing. I can't stay long; I have a ton to do this evening. I'm putting in an appearance mainly as a show of support. It's a good half hour before anyone stands to read, most of it taken up by eating and fraternal chitchat among the college-bound. My two sophomores must feel out of place, yet they may have a better claim on the activity than the kids for whom this is at best an evening's diversion, another kind of dress-up event, like Spirit Week or the prom. I'm not surprised that the girls have gravitated to our young librarian, who wants her library to be a hub of cultural activity at the school, a gathering place for kids who might not find an appropriate gathering elsewhere. I laud her objectives. They might even provide me with a jumping-off place when I work up the nerve to suggest reinstating those exiled volumes from the Library of America.

I expect the event to stir some nostalgia. I always participated in the poetry readings at my state commuter college and always looked forward to them, but in retrospect they seem like sad affairs. Imitating their Beat idols, the readers frequently showed up stoned. Halfway through my freshman year, I already knew most of the repertoire; new material was in short supply. Yet there were a few bright lights among us, and I wonder where they are now. Possibly in situations similar to mine: teaching high school English and waiting for their nostalgia to kick in at a student poetry slam. The thought doesn't cheer me.

I'm sure my mood has been tainted by having read the girl's disparaging poem. I suppose that in some ways she's done me a favor: without the in-your-face preview, I might have been tempted to hang around long enough to hear her read, which is to say, long enough to be late for dinner. I have no intention of making such a sacrifice now. Are my feelings hurt? A little, I suppose. But I've taught long enough to know that these affronts are almost never personal in the strictest sense. They have to do with needs and grievances way beyond any teacher's powers of interpretation. And I know as well that if little irritations can still irk me, then breakthroughs just as little can elate me too.

The next day one of my tenth graders tells me that someone may have stolen her English binder. She suspects it was tossed into the garbage by one of her enemies. This is especially worrisome because midyear exams are just around the corner and because all the materials about doing the research paper were in the binder. The loss is also worrisome because her grades have been falling, the reason she's now required to spend her free period in one of my lunchtime study halls. In the beginning of the year she seemed flippant at times, certainly not very motivated for school and evidently not much taken with me. Lately, though, we have enjoyed a better rapport. Today we'll seal it.

I tell her that we are going to reconstruct her binder. We're going to do it in study hall, she and I, and we're going to finish it in one period. We won't be able to restore any of her homework papers, but there were too few of those to begin with. At least now she'll have a clearer idea of the assignments she needs to make up.

I clear my desk and lay out labels for the different categories: literature, vocabulary, composition, etc. I cut out and tape together some makeshift dividers. I go through my promiscuous bundle of handouts and have the student sort them into the appropriate piles as I give them to her one by one. We discuss the best placement for pieces that might go in more than one category. We make use of scissors, paper clips, markers. This is floor time, high school style, and the most fun I've had all day. Does the student notice? All she seems to see is the "extra trouble" she's given me. But what I see is the slow eureka dawning in her eyes: *With something this pulled together, I might actually be able to pass.*

I can't resist adding a didactic note when I hand her the finished notebook, neat as a freshly barbered head. Like all my didactic notes, it's one I need to hear as much as any student does. "I'm willing to wager this notebook is in way better shape than the one you lost or had stolen ever was." She doesn't deny it.

"If somebody did steal your notebook, then you and I just turned their theft into an advantage, didn't we? That's the best way I know to deal with crap like that." I choose a verb I know she'll understand. "*Defy* it."

Soon it will be the winter solstice. For weeks now I've been driving home after dark, enjoying the Christmas lights as I go. Many of them have been up since Halloween and some will stay lit for months into the bleak New Year. I drink them in as I drive through Barton and along Crystal Lake, where there are additional lights glistening across the ice from the fancier digs on the opposite shore. "Santa Claus is coming to town," Springsteen sings on my car radio, one of the few popular Christmas songs I'll endure, though I'll probably warm up to "Little Saint Nick" in another week. What's coming to town for me is a recess, neither fat nor particularly jolly but welcome just the same.

We have some Christmas lights at school as well, mostly in the main office, though by rights we're not supposed to have any. The superintendent decreed several years ago that as a public school district we were not to pay homage even to secularized religious holidays. The ruling seems to be honored more in the

breach than in the observance, at least beyond the confines of
the central office. Since the central office is located in the same
building as the preschool (which used to make a point of teaching the region's mostly gentile children about Hanukkah), this
essentially means that the only students in the district lacking
tokens of holiday cheer are three and four years old. For my
part, I tack a string of unadorned white lights around my blackboard, hoping they'll do for my students what the lights in Barton do for me. Hang on, kids, your break is coming.

The Christmas spirit at school does seem more subdued than
I recall from years past. I get a few small presents—homemade
cookies and handmade ornaments to hang on my tree at home—
some very touching cards, including one or two from boys,
though fewer of the edible presents that used to come my way.
I'm just as glad; I could hardly bear with the sugary largesse of
the old days, when the girls presented me with tins and trays
and tinfoil pouches of fudge, peanut brittle, cookies, brownies—
enough to keep my family and our guests flush with desserts
for a week. By the close of the last day of school, I'd go down to
the gym for Christmas assembly (still allowed in those days),
vaguely nauseated and probably several pounds heavier than
when I walked in the door that morning. But the parting good
wishes are as frequent and amiable as they ever were, including
a few from students who are not even in my classes but stick
their heads in my door on the way to the buses to wish me the
joy of the season.

I know it will be a sad holiday for some. Their parents will
have split up earlier in the year or lost their jobs or both. Some
asked-for presents will not be under the tree or else will materialize in spite of all expectation, not miracles so much as dire
omens, the reckless parental generosity that can take a child's
breath away. Low men on the retail totem pole, some students

will spend their holidays minding the store, tending the drive-up window at the fast food joints on Christmas Eve. Friends whose parents have more money will decamp to Orlando and Cancun; their poorer counterparts will lack transportation to come over and hang out. Younger siblings will be home and require babysitting, the decoration-deprived three- and four-year-olds making up for lost time with a vengeance. Parties will be happening all over the county, with some kids invited to all and many invited to none. A girl might get engaged, most likely because her older beau is on his way to Afghanistan. Some houses will be less than warm. A few will be less than safe, mistletoe hanging like a noose when a certain uncle is lurking about. Somewhere in some hollow, like a lottery number waiting to be called, a trailer is going to catch fire. People will "lose everything." All their presents. Maybe even their pets. There will be a coffee can with their name on it in the mini-marts, next to the chocolate Santas, a day past season and priced to go.

For weeks now I've been haunted by the memory of walking to the faculty parking lot one late autumn afternoon to find an uncomfortably obese woman wedged behind the steering wheel of her wreck of a car jabbering into her cell phone. It would appear she doesn't have a pot to piss in, but of course she has a cell phone. In the back seat are two filthy, bedraggled children, a boy and a girl looking for all the world like Ignorance and Want under the green robe of the Ghost of Christmas Present. They are not dressed warmly enough for the cold. They stare at me as if I might have food to give them, a blanket—a word—anything to acknowledge their existence on earth. I catch myself growing angry at their mother, only to recognize she is merely the same neglected child under the robe of Christmas Past.

I read somewhere that the Puritans had a crier go through the streets on Christmas Eve and cry "No Christmas tonight."

This was to prevent any backsliders from reverting to "popish" calendars and pagan entertainments. The most sterile of all carolers, he made his way through the song-starved lanes. I've always imagined him with a handbell, though perhaps I've misappropriated that detail from the Salvation Army. I'd want to knock him down if I met him; I look forward to my turkey and my tree, to our daughter coming home for the holidays, and to the gifts I know I am going to like because I always do. Still there is something in me—the memory of those children in the car, the sad faces of some of my students as they trudge with their token candy canes to the school bus—that wants to borrow a page from the Puritans and from the superintendent too and walk through the streets of the Orleans Central Supervisory Union on the twenty-fourth of December crying, "No Christmas tonight!" No Christmas, no Hanukkah, no Kwanzaa, no New Year's Day . . . "nor shall my sword sleep in my hand, till we have built Jerusalem in [New] England's green and pleasant land."

— 7 —

JANUARY

But the more he thinks of educating them . . . the more he has
to ask himself: by what right do I do this? It is not certain that
it will make them socially happier.

—John Berger, *A Fortunate Man*

As I was at Thanksgiving, I was sick for most of the Christmas
vacation, for a few days almost too sick to move. Except to take
meals or stoke the furnace, now and then tossing a grocery bag
of spent Kleenex onto the fire, I rarely rose from my living room
chair. My condition was familiar from past years of teaching—
the way vacations give a stressed mind and body permission to
ail. On more than one Christmas my wife and I would drive to
visit our families in New Jersey, only to have me spend a feverish
week in bed. I wasn't hit that hard this time but hard enough to
keep me from returning to school as refreshed as I'd hoped to be.

Fortunately, I don't have anything to make me dread my
return. Just as I know from experience that a school vacation is a
likely time to get sick, I also know from experience that the mel-
ancholy of a Monday morning will probably not last beyond the
arrival of the first bus. I have two boys in my first-period class
who come into my room early and visit, often finishing the last

bits of their outrageously nonnutritious breakfasts as they dribble boy talk and lob the rolled-up greasy wrappers into my trash can. They're not my best students by any stretch, and they're not brownnosers either, but they seem to enjoy my company. I certainly enjoy theirs, and I'm happy when I learn that I'll have them next semester in a Composition course. I've already gleaned a few of the topics they might write about—metal bands and football teams, fathers and cows, cars and tattoos. Later on, in my third-period class, there's a girl who always returns my "good morning" to the students with a rousing "Good morning, Mr. Keizer!" that seems intended and is definitely received in the spirit of a cheerleader's hurrah. I think that on some level the students sense that I'm trying my best and often tried to my limits, that I can use every little boost I can get. I get plenty of boosts, in any case.

Lately they take the form of a few wistful queries as to the possibility of my returning to teach again next September. I've only been hired for the current year, I say. As I'm sure they know, I'm filling in for a teacher on leave, a teacher that none of my sophomores have had in the past. They have no basis for comparison and thus no more than a provisional reason for wishing me back.

"But what if he decides not to come back?" one of them says, adding that she and a few of her pals might be willing to make "the other guy" an offer he can't refuse. I'm touched by this, though I'm careful to appear no more than amused. And they're only asking what others at school have asked—including a custodian who I imagine is missing his after-school chats with my more garrulous predecessor—something I've lately been asking myself. What if the other guy doesn't come back? What if I'm invited to apply for the position and, as some of my colleagues have assured me would happen, I get it?

My official response is that I'm going back to my desk to resume my work as a writer. On most days that is also the sincere response. But it weighs on me—how could I conscionably turn down the stability of a job with salary and benefits, including retirement benefits, in order to return to the precariousness of my previous work? If a permanent position were to open here and I were hired to fill it, Kathy would be free to explore more adventurous options than the part-time elementary school speech position she's taken to cover our health insurance next year, including a possible expansion of her consulting work at Dartmouth, where she continues to thrive. The catch-as-catch-can, hand-to-mouth nature of freelance work would be behind me. No more humiliating queries to newspapers about delayed payments, no more rug-merchant negotiations with libraries and academic departments looking for ornamental talks. How many of the writers I admire most have shored themselves up with teaching work—admittedly in cushier places than the one I'm toiling in now—and who am I to imagine I can sustain myself another way? As for the writing itself, no doubt my output would be radically curtailed to what I could churn out during the summer, but might its quality improve just as radically? "Having time to write" is not always an unqualified advantage. I have sometimes thought that I was a better writer, or at least a more socially useful one, when my daily life was pushed up against harsher realities. I'd never want for those here.

Nor would I be without teaching's less dubious perks, not the least of which is being loved or, failing that, being "on." I have to admit that I like an audience. No less do I like the one-to-one instruction, the narcotic high of coaching a skill. I like my gratuitous exchanges with students not in my classes, who have nothing to gain by seeking me out. Though I am and always was a solitary teacher, a shut-the-door and get-on-with-the-work teacher, eating alone and rarely devoting much time to off-duty gab with my colleagues, I enjoy having colleagues. I feel a mutual respect with most of them. And I find the presence of youth invigorating—sometimes, yes, in the way that youth reverts to childhood and to childlike delight in simple discoveries and small surprises, but more often in flickering revelations of adulthood. I apologize to a girl for having been short with her about her failure to complete an assignment when I ought to have been more sensitive—how could I have forgotten she has just lost her grand-mother? "I accept your apology," she says, "but I ought to have been more responsible than I was. And I shouldn't have been so snotty to you." This from a kid, and a kid who's grieving besides.

At times I begin to be gripped by a sense of destiny closing in. I've come here for a reason, and the reason is that I am meant to stay. This is where I belong, this is where I can do my best work. I've had a good run with my books and articles, more than most late bloomers get to accomplish. I've proved whatever it was I had to prove, and if I had any aptitude to achieve great-ness, surely I would have realized it by now. There is no shame in the fact that I haven't. My little trophies are honorable enough and will remain so; time now to put them on an attic shelf and resume the work that will see me through to a solvent old age.

I almost can't believe what I'm thinking. When I broach the possibility to my wife, she refuses to see it as anything but a delu-sion. It would be a mistake, she insists, and I would wind up very unhappy. *She* would be unhappy. "This is *not* your real work."

Fortunately, any thoughts of continuing past the current year are hypothetical and sporadic, little more than passing moods and possibly nothing more than my ego's infantile predilection for regular feedings. All it takes is a class of unprepared kids— half of whom are clambering for a third copy of an assignment sheet to replace the loss of the previous two, for a book to replace the one that's been left behind in a locker, for permission to use the restroom, for a Band-Aid, for an extra day to complete the homework, for the repetition of directions I've already given twice—to make me ask myself if I'm out of my mind. Do I really think I could enjoy spending the rest of my working life like this? And would I have the staying power to devote myself to the work with the intensity it requires? To say nothing of the patience. I make up detailed syllabi for several of my classes, a day-by-day roster to help my students plan the time remaining till the end of the semester—only to have it knocked askew by an unanticipated school closing when the temperature dips to 30 below. These disruptions happen all the time. Teaching, which grants few successes without careful planning, hates nothing so much as a planner.

When I'm most conscious, most on top of my game, I can appreciate my moments of frustration and my most exasperating kids as aids to clarity. The pains in the ass are in fact my muses and angels, sent to deliver me from temptation, sent to remind me that the work I most want to do is elsewhere. And in the semester to come I will meet my share of angels.

Surprisingly, the high point of my enthusiasm for teaching comes at one of the least likely junctures, the time of midyear exams. Normally, this would be just the time when a teacher would have the wind taken out of his sails. But I've trimmed my sails to avoid that.

I no longer see midyear exams as a confirmation of "mastery"—as if mastery of any meaningful kind were the provenance of sixteen-year-olds, as if mastery could be ascertained so soon after imparting the material. Instead, I see the exams as a chance to instill the hope that mastery is *possible*, that whatever slow progress we've made has been worth the effort. On the crasser level of "the data," I see the exam process as a chance for my foundering students to redeem their grades. This doesn't mean that I intend to give easy exams or to weigh them too heavily in computing my semester grades. It means that I plan to do a fair amount of review and to construct my exams more than I ever have in the past out of the review exercises. In a few cases, I will write pages of the exams from the review sheets with virtually no alteration. I've taught long enough to know that even this will fall short of a complete giveaway: some students won't do the review work either. But those with their chins still above deep water may sense the life preserver I've tossed within their reach—and take hold of it.

As I've been doing with the research paper (still in progress), I hold some additional preparation periods after school. To those students who attend, I'm especially generous, though I still hold my cards close to my chest. "Here's something I'd especially want to study if I were in your shoes." I'm somewhat surprised by the makeup of these sessions. I'm not surprised that some of the kids who show up hardly need the help; I'm surprised that they're not, in the usual way these things go, in the majority. Most of those who come are underachievers who've taken a sober measure of what they need to pass. I credit at least some of their sobriety to the work of the tutors in the academic support areas, who encourage this kind of self-assessment and strategy. I'm especially moved by the earnestness of a few of my sophomores and amazed, as ever, by their appetites for food, which might in this case be partially attributable to nerves. Only four show up at one of the sessions, but they demolish a whole tin of cookies within the first half hour. What they don't know yet is that they've also devoured most of what my exam is going to contain within a half hour after that.

To my satisfaction no one in any of my five classes fails his or her exam. Among the juniors and seniors taking half-year electives, I have only one student who fails the course, a bright senior with a history of standing as close as he can to the precipice. His exam performance is good but not good enough to cover weeks of missed work, even with the bonus points I always add to any major test as a cover for possible mistakes I might have made in correction. The boy takes his F with an attitude that another generation would have called "manful"; I only wish he'd taken his studies in the same way. In that regard, I'm glad he failed. A passing grade would have insulted his intelligence, which is to say, it would have affirmed his overreliance on intelligence at the expense of hard work.

His peers who drop by to learn their grades are not so stoical. More than a few receive the news of a C or even a D by pumping their fists with a vocal rendition of Meg Ryan's orgasmic *yes!* I'm sad to note the survival of a shortcoming that always dismayed me in years past: the school provides no class day in the schedule for teachers to go over midyear exams with juniors and seniors in semester-long courses. There's no feedback beyond the giving of a grade, no chance to clarify mistakes for students who don't bother to pick up their tests. After such an investment of time and labor, the exercise winds up feeling like a sham.

It's a different story with my sophomores, who are back in the classroom after the conclusion of exam week and with whom I'm able not only to go over the test results but even to have some fun. I can't resist teasing them just a bit before rejoicing over their good performance. In my most somber tone, and with an unwavering deadpan expression, I say, "Well, I have finished grading your exams." No one dares to ask, though some faces do: "Were they bad?" "There's much I could say about the class's overall performance, but I find that the words don't come easily." Uh-oh.

"Therefore, I thought it might be advisable to have someone else speak for me, more particularly one Mr. Marvin Gaye."

Still stone-faced I depress the button on my boom box and detonate the opening piano notes, pointing to the class on "You" and not allowing myself to smile until the words "pride and joy," at which point, with a flick of my wrist I send the pulled-down projection screen snapping upward to reveal the tally I've written on the blackboard behind it: many As and even more Bs, a few Cs, and no Ds or Fs. I'm not quite dancing as I go up and down the aisles handing back the tests, though I may be as close as a middle-aged white man with weak arches and work boots ever gets to a "groove." I hold the standout performances briefly in front of some noses before slapping them down on the desks and "movin' on down the line." There's laughter, most of it in relief, the rest occasioned by the sight of me so animated and happy. There's no instance where "the first are last"—the world is not overthrown so easily, and I hardly want my highest achievers to be overthrown—but there are at least a few where the last are first, or damned close to it, and the pride and joy on their faces speaks even more eloquently than Mr. Gaye or his superb backup chorus to what I feel.

When things settle down, we go over the tests, item by item, with special emphasis on those tasks that required more attention to the directions than they sometimes got and on the distinguishing features of the better essays. I note the places where students supplied correct answers I did not anticipate when I made up the test, and other places where a bit of logic on their part could have prevented some goofs. Inspired by the Mosaic prohibition against picking up any stray sheaves dropped in the act of harvest, I instruct students not to tell me about any correction errors I've made in their favor. The gleanings must be left on the ground for "the poor and the stranger." But the poor and the stranger are still inclined to ask if you're sure you want to let the errors slide. For every cheater a teacher might have in a given class, there are usually half a dozen students who'd rather take a hit than an unfair advantage. Perhaps a few can't resist telling me that I'm less than perfect, but I'll go with the more generous interpretation.

That doesn't come hard, given the generosity of some of their remarks. For one of the "constructed responses" that made up the written section of the exam, I called for a journal entry of the type we've been doing on a regular basis throughout the semester. Above a photocopy of a ruled page from a paper journal, I wrote the following: "This exam is based on material you have learned in class. But in most classes, students learn things that were not taught, not intended, or not noticed by the teacher. On the journal page below, write a thoughtful entry on something 'extra' you have learned in class. It might be about your own study habits or learning style, about getting along with others, about your own pleasure or displeasure, or about the effects of literature."

The answers I receive are not all on point—some address central elements of the school curriculum—but few miss the point entirely, and many suggest that there is indeed some "extra" learning going on here:

I have not ever studied too hard but the tests we have been given this year have made me change that. For a reading quiz I actually have to read the book and can't just scim it. This class has tought me better studying techniques I will use for other classes as well.

When different types of music is played that most teenagers do not listen to it exposes them to new music. While listening to the various songs played I've learned that I like some of the different types that I never thought I would like.

"Can you give an example of a piece of music you enjoyed?" I write at the bottom of the page, illustrating by example being one of the skills I've tried to emphasize during the semester. If I don't subtract at least one point, the comment won't carry any weight, so I do. Other students show a better knack for following the general with the specific, though not always with the best syntax:

> Something I have learned in class this semester is I learned new studying methods. I was introduced to 3×5 note cards and I found it to be much easer to gather info I didn't know and place them on a card. I found I could study myself this way and it was a convient way to learn things. Next semester I will probally do this in many other classes because I think it benefited me on this exam!

> I don't really like writing but when you write about something you like it is much more enjoyable. An example would be when we had to write a journal entry of our own topic, I had writen about my horse and that was the easest thing I had to write.

> This class has opened some doors for me. As an example, I've started reading more, I look for similare authors like the ones we have read in this class because I find their book/short stories intreaging. I learned that a lot of literature can be touching, especially about the black History and what they went through, not only that but some of the fiction stories were interesting and I didn't find them boring because they always kept me on edge.

Much to my delight, others echo the last sentiment. "I have learned that reading really isn't that bad," one student writes, while another goes so far as to claim that reading has led her to a major recognition: "I now believe that the teachers don't assign books to torture us and they do it because it may have been something they enjoyed that they want to share with us"—to which I can't resist writing, "Of course we do like to torture you too!" Obviously, I have to be open to the possibility that some students are telling me what they think I want to hear. But when I weigh their remarks against my own daily observations and the reports that come to me through other teachers, I feel entitled to accept much of what they say at face value.

That's especially true in the case of several students who write about the pleasures of learning in an environment of camaraderie and mutual respect, something the teacher certainly intends though sometimes fails to fully appreciate. "I have learned how a class of students could become more like a familly. . . . We can joke around with each other and have fun but we still manage to get all of are work done." One entry that begins "This semester in english has been a blast" goes on to elaborate on "blast" in terms that might surprise adults with little or no acquaintance with young people:

> The class has been very smooth, with no interruptions, everyone's respectful and kind to one another, and we all work as one to always have a productive day in class. That makes learning easier for me and others. Some of my classes are so wild that we never learn anything. That makes tests and quizzes harder because you don't learn anything. With that being said, I learned that a good class with manners, respect, and kindness to one another, you learn more and respect the subject more.

That the reality is somewhat less ideal is noted by another student, whose basis of comparison is several years of being schooled at home:

> I used to want to be a teacher. But now I am not so sure. I realized that teaching is not so simple. Teachers can't just say what they have to say and get on with it. First they have to fight for the class's attention, then they have to tell the class what they need to tell them in a way that relates to teenagers. It's not so easy.

No, it isn't—and it's an indication of how touched I am by some of the paragraphs that this student's frank appraisal of the realities comes to me as a corrective reminder. She's right, I do sometimes have to fight for the students' attention, don't I? But it's easy to gloss over the difficulties when a student who's given you some of your worst times to date, who even acknowledges that he's "been a pain" in his opening sentence, goes on to refer to you as "a real man" who "showed me that with respect and random acts of kindness life is a whole lot better. Also with hard work and someone to guid you, nothing is imposible." We weigh our praises according to their source—according to whether it's Machiavelli who's calling us a prince or Thomas Paine. For this kid, I know, "real man" is the highest accolade, and there is no irony here—at least none coming from him. For my part, I doubt a "real man" would allow himself to be as moved by this as I am, but it is the way his words are proved by his recent behavior that moves me most. That and the fact that this kid sucks up to nobody.

I'm taken down a peg, though, by another of the short-answer sections of the test, which asks students to construct a single formatted note card from a short passage of information. The task ought to be an easy ten points for anyone who's been doing his or her research and noting my comments through successive reviews of the cards the kids have been been handing in, but grading it is like watching artillery mow down a cavalry charge. Few riders emerge from the smoke unscathed.

Exams provide an opportunity for students to reflect more broadly on the literature they've been reading and for the teacher to do the same in regard to what he's been assigning and to what purpose. I don't have many students who ask, "Why do we have to read this?"—in fact, I don't think I have one. Perhaps by this age they've gotten tired of asking. Perhaps they'd be surprised to learn that I haven't.

Young people tend naturally toward a didactic appraisal of literature, and English teachers are supposed to discourage the tendency. Literature has "themes," not morals, we're supposed to tell them, though I find that formulation itself didactic and rather prissy to boot. Ditto for talking ad nauseam about irony. Why shouldn't students—or adults—read literature in the hope of clarifying their own moral understanding? The problem is not that young people search literature for "a moral"; the problem is rather that they come to it with a set of moral preconceptions that impede them in their search. Their approach to James Baldwin's "Sonny's Blues" is typical. Sonny is a heroin addict, drugs are bad, and so the point of the story—almost all of them insist—is that doing drugs will wreck your life. Drugs will surely do that, though Baldwin and his narrator seem to have other concerns.

A similar superimposed reading occurs with another short story on the syllabus, Toni Cade Bambara's "The Lesson," in which a self-appointed neighborhood teacher takes some black children on a tour of the city that concludes at the FAO Schwarz toy store. There they see expensive sailboats and other baubles their parents could never afford. The teacher seems intent on goading her charges—and the author on goading us—toward an awareness of the "savage inequalities" that stack the deck against minorities and the poor. By the close of the story, the recalcitrant young protagonist, Sylvie, outwardly resentful of her day's instruction, shows that she has taken it to heart. We would say her consciousness has been raised. But for many of my students, Bambara's story amounts to a Horatio Alger tale in hip-hop idiom. Rather than see a swindle—a swindle not without implications for poor, working-class, and even middle-class kids growing up in rural America during a period marked by the greatest income disparity since the Great Depression—they perceive "a lesson" on the need to work hard in order to get ahead. Any sense that society may be at fault seems missing from their consciousness.

Even among my older students this seems to be the case. The last reading assignment I give in my Popular Fiction class, which I have decided to center on the theme of young people in search of self-knowledge, is Tim O'Brien's short story "On the Rainy River." After being called up to military duty in Vietnam, a young man comes close to running away to Canada but decides that he is simply not courageous enough to buck the social pressures compelling him to serve. With bitter irony he concludes that he is too cowardly to be a draft dodger, an epiphany my students strongly resist. The girls in class are the most adamant. The narrator needs to be a man, they say. He needs to do his patriotic duty and stop whining about it. Though no one uses the phrase, the implication is that he needs to "get real." Which means what exactly? To bow to the world as it is.

The same resignation informs the majority response to the actions of a black housekeeper named Rosaleen in Sue Monk

Kidd's novel *The Secret Life of Bees*. After swallowing all the degradation she can gag down, Rosaline pours tobacco juice from
her snuff cup on the shoes of some white men who are verbally
abusing her and is beaten and thrown into jail as a result. "Stupid," say more than one of my students, meaning Rosaleen's defiance. This does not mean that the students are racists. In their
eyes they are merely being realists, which is to say, what we're
often urging them to be. Peer pressure we would like them to
resist; aside from that, resistance is seldom held up to them as a
virtue. The essentially political question John Berger raises about
a country doctor in his classic essay *A Fortunate Man* applies to a
teacher too: "How far should one help a patient to accept conditions which are at least as unjust and wrong as the patient is
sick?" More to the point, how far should one help a patient—or a
student—not to accept them? The best I do in the case of Rosaleen
is to turn my students' assertion back to them as a question: "But
is she stupid?"

I know enough not to ask "Is she wrong?" Interestingly
enough, the moralistic preconceptions that students bring to
their reading of literature also include the notion that all morality is relative, or as they would put it, "a person's own opinion."
Their relativism is not confined to morality. At the start of my
Popular Fiction course, which I teach both semesters, I break
the class into groups and ask them to parse the course title by
coming up with a definition of *fiction* and a tentative list of what
ingredients might make a work of fiction *popular*. Though the
students have no problem with making an absolutist assertion
that fiction is "not true," they balk at the notion that popularity
can be analyzed. Popularity, they argue, is purely "a matter of
opinion." It is no such thing. As they, of all people, ought to know,
a person is popular or he isn't; he has friends or he doesn't. Books
sell in the millions or they wind up in remainder bins. The

students are confusing popularity with the right of an individual to his or her tastes, including tastes that are decidedly unpopular. Well, clarifying these sorts of distinctions is what teaching literature is all about. We're "helping kids to think." I know that—but I also suspect that some of the confusions originate in the haphazard teaching of that very subject.

Fortunately, we also read with our hearts, where "what it means to you" has a valid claim. In that category my favorite exam comment comes from a looming giant of a boy who writes that the young protagonist in *The Secret Life of Bees* "has experienced more pain in her little body that I ever have in my life." Not a bad thing for a big man to ponder—the capacities for pain in a little body.

A less sophisticated emotional connection, one based on similarity rather than difference, probably explains the perennial popularity of John Steinbeck's *Of Mice and Men*. I imagine kids are drawn to Lennie for some of the same reasons they were drawn to *Curious George* when they were small. Like them, Lennie and the monkey mean no harm but can't seem to stay out of trouble. Oh, for some Man in a Yellow Hat or someone like Lennie's smarter sidekick, who may not always be nice to Lennie but who sticks by him through the worst, to believe in your good intentions and to make your dreams seem real and, not least of all, to shoot you in the back of the head before you can embarrass yourself to death. I recall from years past one particular student in another teacher's English class, a large boy who raised rabbits, as Lennie dreamed of doing, who became almost obsessed with the story. The book did not necessarily change his life, but it seemed to reflect his life in a powerful way—which in the end may be just as important.

Literature will give my students a larger frame of reference, I keep telling myself, a better understanding of human complexity, of all that shouldn't but often does go wrong in a human life. It may help them to a more compassionate heart. At the least it may give them some diversion from what is going wrong in *their* lives. So can beer—as the poet A. E. Housman put it, "Malt does more than Milton can / To justify God's ways to man"—but knowing some lines from Housman gives you an extra option, something you didn't even know you could order at the bar. That's what I want my students to have: all the options on the menu, all the songs in the catalog, every last word on the privileged side of the 30-million-word gap.

The paltriness of what they do have can be stunning at times. In one of my sophomore classes I'm asked what the word *woo* means. It's a simple enough question, I suppose, but it catches me off guard. I would not need to define *rape* for my students, would I? Or *hick* or *dyke* or *loser*. To woo is to pay court to someone, I say, still short of the mark. It's what you do to win a person's love; it's how you say they're worth the trouble. And so I add one more thing to the list of what I want my students to have along with the 30 million words and a sweet, long life: a sense of themselves as worth the wooing.

It will take more than wooing to get my sophomores to read Edith Wharton. *Ethan Frome* is probably the hardest slog of the year. Vocabulary is a large part of the problem, that and a certain reverse naiveté in sexual matters that is probably best encapsulated in their ignorance of *woo*. Why can't Ethan and Mattie just fuck? The novel is so close to their experience on so many levels—but it also belongs to another universe, another language, a language with all kinds of big words. To say nothing of a lot of little words that I did not realize are big ones to my kids.

I try enticing them with a project I call "The *Ethan Frome* Vocabulary Face-Off." I divide each class into several teams and assign them to master their own customized list of unfamiliar words from the novel. Eventually they'll compete in a three-day bowl for prizes, including grades for their team's performance and bonus "tickets" entitling the bearers to postpone due dates and cut class, plus animal crackers, coconuts, and other edible novelties (a fairly broad term in a region where teenage supermarket cashiers routinely ask me "What are these things?" when ringing up eggplants and Brussels sprouts). Each team member is required to contribute to the team's list and to devise practice exercises for his or her teammates. Homework assignments are to be generated, completed, and corrected by each team.

The project has other intentions besides vocabulary building and honing their cooperative skills. I'm also trying to buy more class time for individual conferences on the second drafts of their research papers. Exams were a brief hiatus; now we're back to the grind, aiming to have papers completed by the beginning of February. I need to have the students working on something while I conference with individuals. The activity needs enough bustle to preserve the confidentiality of the editing sessions and to keep my own whispering from disturbing the class's concentration. The "face-off" seems to fit the bill.

As I ought to have anticipated but didn't, I'm also going to need to stay in close touch with the teams if I want solid results. Even the lists will require some feedback since the words in the text will as often as not be different parts of speech from the forms defined in the dictionary. I'll accept words in any form, I tell the students, so long as some variant appears in the novel and so long as definition, part of speech, and usage align in the materials they prepare. I grumble to myself that students ought to have learned these concepts in middle school—only to imagine some professor saying the same thing about me, several years hence, as she shakes her head over a student's research paper. What were his high school English teachers doing for four years, pray tell?

The difficulties are compounded whenever a student copies a word incorrectly or confuses one word with another. Thus the definition of *intricate* might be given as "a secret or underhand scheme" (the definition of *intrigue*). The last person to claim that he knows the entire English lexicon or the text of *Ethan Frome* by heart, I wonder for a moment if one of my students is teaching me a new word: *malise*, "a piece of hand." In what context would one need to denote a piece of hand? Medicine? It takes a few beats before I realize that I'm missing a piece of definition, "luggage," and the correct spelling of *valise*. Suffice it to say, the vocabulary project does not buy me the time for writing conferences that I hoped it would.

Certainly it would have bought me more if most of my students were willing to consult the meticulous instructions I've written up for them. They'd rather ask me a question as it occurs to them than search for the answer on a printed sheet—or listen carefully when I answer the same question for the third time. My refrain becomes "What does the sheet say?" I wouldn't want to give the impression that my students are too lazy to read the sheets, though some of them are. A better explanation is that they trust what comes straight from the horse's mouth more than what is mediated by the horse's handout sheet, or—to get closer to the crux—more than their ability *to read and comprehend* the horse's handout sheet. Flattering as this might be to a teacher, it is less than reassuring to a teacher who hopes to live out his remaining years in a democracy.

I try to give the matter a political slant. When a rule is written down, I tell the students, then the writer is bound by it no less than the reader. That is why we have a constitution. In an autocratic state the king's whim is the law. Maybe one day he feels like reading a six-hundred-word essay; the next day he feels like a six-line poem. But in this case, I can't hold you accountable for any requirement that isn't spelled out on the sheet. You can wave that sheet in my face as evidence, and I can't win the argument simply by saying "I wrote the sheet." I have to win by referring to what the words actually say. I seem to be getting through— somebody's raising his hand.

"Do you want us to write down the parts of speech?"

They're doing the best they can, I tell myself, and I need to remember they're just kids. Still, it troubles me to think that these kids are only two years away from voting.

I'm similarly troubled by the dubious responsibility students feel toward other members of their teams. Although I allowed optional partnerships for the museum project in the fall, I almost never allow students to form their own groups for in-class assignments where teams are mandatory, competition is expected, and cliquishness is always a risk. I try to mix boys and girls, good students and poor students, strong personalities and more passive personalities, but a class of twenty kids in four or five groups only allows for so many combinations. In spite of my best efforts, some groups jell and others don't. Just getting them to arrange their desks in a propitious formation can be frustrating. As I explain at the start, the best arrangement is a circle or a neat square, with every member having easy access to every other. A few teams get right to it; others have different plans. Some students try to form subgroups within the group, me and my friend versus everyone else. Some isolate themselves by literally turning their backs to their teams. Some cozy up to the borders of other groups in order to facilitate over-the-fence gab. A few seem to find the simple act of moving a desk an inexpressible agony, every inch a station of the cross.

As interesting as they are to observe, the social dynamics fall into predictable types. Familiar to anyone who's ever tried to foster "cooperative learning" is the bossy overachiever, often a girl, who realizes at once that her grade is dependent on the collective efforts of several real or perceived nincompoops and is therefore in serious jeopardy unless she whips them into shape or does all the work herself. Just as often there's someone on her team who recognizes the anxiety and is quite willing to exploit it. Most exasperating are the do-nothing Tobacco Road boys, who lean back in their chairs and grin, so evidently pleased with themselves one would think they'd just invented grinning. Only the most unimaginative teacher would see them as the future failures of America. A fair number of them will go on to own or manage businesses, with a female clerical staff doing most of the work. For the present, I tell them to set all four chair legs on the floor and get busy. I suppose that if I really wanted to "prepare them for the future," I'd urge them to put their feet up on the desks and scratch themselves while holding forth about welfare cheats and all the other deadbeats living off the taxpayer's hard-earned dime.

What's exciting are the groups that manage to come together, calling forth the best qualities of their members. Invariably, they're not only the most productive but also appear to have the most fun. They *socialize* in the deepest sense of the word. The work is fairly divided, with the weaker members doing their best to pull their weight and the more capable doing all they can to enable their more-challenged partners to make a respectable contribution. Occasionally, a notorious slacker surprises everyone by doing yeoman's service on behalf of his group. Sinking yourself and sinking everybody else: two completely different things,

dude. He's praised by his teammates—what's more, he feels entitled to praise them. You see, says the collectivist half of my heart,
cooperation works. To which the other half replies: It certainly
does—in the rarest of cases. Whether it's individual cream or
collective cream, it's still cream that rises to the top.

Sometimes when I'm walking the halls between classes I become
aware of Mr. Messier walking beside me. On certain days and in
certain fragile states of mind, the experience feels almost numi-
nous. I sense I'm not as alone as I've been feeling, and then I see
Mr. Messier alongside me or just to the rear of my shoulder. How
long has he been there? He smiles and asks how my day is going.
The way he puts the question enables me to answer "good" with
honesty. Right now, yes, it's a good day. How could it be otherwise with his support?

I feel it from others as well. I'm not sure I've ever had a stronger sense of being "taken care of" by my coworkers, not even forty
years ago when I found my first full-time job in an accident-ridden
glue factory. Back then I was "the kid" or "the youngblood," as the
foreman liked to call me, and now I'm one of the old-timers, out
of mothballs and quite possibly out of my depth. I wonder sometimes if I look more fragile than I feel, as if I'm a stumble away
from a broken hip or from a more comprehensive breakdown.
The cold I developed over Christmas has proved hard to shake.
Over the years one of my eyelids has dropped down lower than
the other, so I imagine I often look tired. People routinely say that
I do. Certainly no one but the most hyperactive kid could regard
me as less than energetic—my stride is still brisk, and I teach on
my feet with a full dose of adrenaline—but that too might be
cause for concern.

Occasionally I sense a tension in my colleagues between a

wish to warn me and a reluctance to prejudice my perceptions. I can tell they want to say more than they do. Just as the new semester was about to start, for example, a group of junior and senior girls accosted me in the hall, smiling, and informed me that they'd be in the spring section of my Popular Fiction class. A sparkly bunch they were, a flashing feminine constellation of white teeth and diamond studs, with large buckled purses in place of the customary tote bags and backpacks. They asked the usual questions about what we'd be doing in class (Popular Fiction tends to be the default reading elective for midlevel students, who sign up with vaguer expectations than, say, a student might have signing up for Mythology) and whether I was "a hard teacher." They didn't seem to be much worried; in fact, they seemed rather keen. They had heard I was "nice." After I told them not to believe everything they heard and thanked them for introducing themselves, they moved on. A passing teacher offered this cryptic aside: "I see you've met the posse."

FEBRUARY

To expect too much is to have a sentimental view of life and this is a softness that ends in bitterness. Charity is hard and endures.

—Flannery O'Connor, in a letter

I used to say that if anyone asked a new teacher which of the three week-long vacations on the school calendar she could most easily do without—December's, February's, or April's—she would probably choose February, if only by default. Losing December would make short work of Christmas, here today, gone tomorrow, while forfeiting spring break would make the spring seem, well, less like spring, and life depressingly less like college.

In contrast, February break has no nostalgia to recommend it, no holiday to sanctify its claims. It falls too late for Valentine's Day, usually late enough to run through Vermont's annual town meeting on the first Tuesday in March, which is to say, just in time to jog the memory of any voter who may have forgotten how cushy teachers have it. Ask us to jettison one vacation, and anybody in her right mind will toss February over the side.

That is what I used to say, all by way of underscoring the

irony that the February break was always the one that found me in the most enervated state. The closer it got, the more indispensable it seemed. It appeared in my imagination like a lifeboat on the open sea. This year finds me yearning for it no less than before.

The research paper is killing me. With an eye toward teaching the process and leaving no child behind, I've let it go on for too long. In the hopes of allowing for more depth, I've sacrificed too much momentum. Papers are due at the beginning of the month—with all pieces handed in, including notes, drafts, an outline, an e-mailed list of electronic links from students with online sources, and physical books for students who've consulted books—which at the maximum means over fifty papers to correct before the break and countless pieces of documentation to review. A few students have barely started.

As I knew would happen, some students are attempting to catch up by circumventing steps in the process. A teacher insists on such steps in order to keep students from falling through the cracks—they respond by searching with all their might for some cracks. I close every fissure I see opening, if only to remain true to the promise I made at the start of the unit: I'm willing to accept any piece as late as it comes, but I won't accept any piece without the piece that was supposed to precede it.

What ought to be a learning process becomes a chess game, a series of calculated moves. Kids are smart enough to figure out that a teacher is far less likely to cry foul on one of their maneuvers if they use another teaching colleague for a shield. I find a rough draft and note cards for a topic that was never vetted with me, a biography of Winston Churchill, in my office mailbox. This is the first substantial piece of work I see on a paper that was supposed to be about mental telepathy. The student includes a note that he has been working on this paper with one of the tutors in the academic support areas. In short, he has used his tutor to make my requirements of no effect, and he's counting on professional etiquette to sanction an end run around them. That he knows it's an end run is clear from the fact that he won't even put the materials into my hand.

As I will eventually learn when the student and I finally sit down to sort out what happened, he and his father pretty much cobbled together the draft from some books they happened to have lying about the house. The documentation, what there was of it, alternated between inept and fudged. Then he turned to his conscientious, hardworking tutor and had her help him construct the preliminary pieces, in effect walking backward from the finished product, though she had every reason to believe they were moving forward. But all I feel holding the largely bogus materials in my hand is that I've been played a fool. I'm also annoyed that the tutor never thought to keep me in the loop. It's possible I'm also feeling jealous: why didn't the student come to me?

I ought to be happy he turned to someone. He's a palpably unhappy kid with what I've been given to understand is a home life marred by mental instability and parental domination. I've seen him smile only once in almost six months—it was that remarkable, and it lasted but an instant. A research paper is the least of his troubles. Still, I can't help but think that in our zeal to see that failure is not an option, we have unwittingly created an array of options for avoiding *the work assigned*. The ideal is an instructional program tailored to meet student needs; the reality, I fear, often devolves to teachers working at cross-purposes and students working the system to their own (dis)advantage.

The reality also includes the fact that, in spite of its innovations, our school remains a traditional competitive system of grades and rankings, the fair and consistent management of

which falls to classroom teachers like me. Our remedial colleagues can focus on coaching the individual players, but it's left
to us to maintain the decorum of the playing field and the integrity of the scoreboard. Small wonder if we occasionally wind up
butting heads.

At my best, I'm able to see that the friction of competing
interests is as indispensable to an effective school as it is to a via-
ble democracy. God save us from the harmonious operations of a
more totalitarian model. But I'm not at my best right now. I vent
my frustrations over the paper with the tutor. She frustrates me
further by suggesting we look at the episode as a teachable
moment. I offend her by saying how much I'm coming to hate
cant expressions like "teachable moment." That's unfair, and I
apologize. As is typical of her—and fully consistent with her
approach to students—she pays less attention to my apology,
which she accepts warmly and without hesitation, than to the
stress she feels I'm under. She's worried about me.

In fact, the unspoken litany of my daily complaints often
begins with "I'm tired." My wife says that I've gotten into the
habit of exclaiming the words aloud when I'm home. "Why are
you tired?" she asks gently, as much to call me back to the present
moment as to know the reasons. Well, I'm tired of giving instructions to the wind. I'm tired of working with classes when I'd
much prefer to work with individuals. I'm tired of the social and
economic conditions that weigh on some of my students, making
a mockery of my most reasonable expectations. Here is tonight's
homework—which some of my students must try to complete in
what no one but an imbecile would call a home.

At the same time, I'm tired of the constant negotiations
among teachers, tutors, and counselors, of what I sometimes perceive as advocacy run amok. I'm sick of "intervention strategies"
that involve three adults spending up to a half hour on an issue

that would not even exist had one perfectly capable student devoted fifteen minutes to doing a simple assignment. Or fifteen seconds to addressing the issue directly.

A colleague approaches me in the hall. She tells me that one of the students in her study hall came up to my room to hand in a completed late assignment but that when I saw him through the glass beside the closed door of the classroom—I was teaching at the time—I gave him "a dirty look." Or that's what he told her anyway. I have no recollection of seeing this student outside my door, much less of giving him a dirty look. I'm certainly not ungrateful to my colleague for taking the time and energy to nip a grievance in the bud, but I also feel exasperated at having to offer the same explanation twice, once to the colleague and again to the student when, with my full consent, she brings him upstairs (her second trip up, mind you) to meet with me.

First of all, I explain, I have no reason to be giving dirty looks to this boy, whom I happen to like and who often comes to check in with me during my preparation period, never without my giving him a warm welcome and seldom without a word of praise for his shaky efforts at keeping up with his assignments. Couldn't any of that history have figured into his hasty interpretation of my look?

Second, I've gotten into the habit of taking off my glasses when I teach in order to permit my middle-aged eyes to read whatever papers I happen to be holding in my hand, which may explain why I don't recall seeing him outside my classroom. Probably I *couldn't* see him.

And finally, the clincher, which I find both satisfying (because even the student acknowledges it as the clincher) and demoralizing (because after six months in my classroom the clincher ought to go without saying):

"Donald, have you ever once known me to communicate my

displeasure about anything or anyone by any means other than saying exactly what's on my mind? Can you think of a single instance where you had to guess whether I was happy with your performance or dissatisfied with your behavior?"

He can't.

"There's a simple reason for that. I don't speak Dirty Looks, and I don't speak Body Language either. I speak English. As in the following sentences: You are a good kid. I'm happy to accept your assignment. In the future, if ever I seem to be annoyed with you or if you are annoyed with me, come to me right away and we'll straighten it out in five minutes."

But will he come? Always an open question, and not just for the students. I arrive promptly at the announced time and place for a morning meeting between a parent and all of her child's teachers, first scribbling my whereabouts on the blackboard for the benefit of those students who might come to see me before their first class. I discover the meeting's nowhere near ready to begin, dash back to the room for some work to do in the meantime, dash back—still no mom.

When the parent does arrive, I find I'm quickly tired by the sense of charade, what strikes me as dramatic pretense on both sides: *I only want my child to succeed. We only want to help your child reach her full potential.* Such lovely words, so full of virtue and rectitude, but is that really what we want? More than once I sense that the student is asking herself the same question. I used to wonder if my daughter asked it too in the days when her mother and I attended school meetings on her behalf. Is it caring, or projecting the appearance of caring, that matters most to us? Adults are no different from adolescents: what we most desire is the approval of our peers. I include myself in "we." I won't risk this parent's disapproval in order to ask the most pertinent questions. You say that reading comes hard for your daughter. Have you ever given her anything to read? She has a cell phone, a snowmobile, and a horse. Does she have a book? Does she have a place to read where she doesn't hear the blaring of a television set? Does she have a decent place to work?

And if she does, do you think I could come over some morning around second period and borrow it? Because I'm also getting tired of going to the teachers' room and finding it filthy, the sink full of unwashed dishes and floating bits of food, the table grimy and littered with crumbs. Four times now (but who's counting?) I've held my dangling tie to my chest with one hand and wiped that table down with soap and water with the other, just so I could correct papers without picking up grease spots, so I could eat my own midmorning snack without contracting some disease. I want to leave a note of complaint but know I will regret it afterward. Crumbs on the table, teachers on Facebook, Walt Whitman and Willa Cather no longer on the library shelves. Yes, I'm still brooding over the Library of America. You would think that at the least I'd have gotten tired of that.

For any complaints I have, the kids themselves remain my best antidote. The implicit paradox is one that a parent will readily understand: the kids are much of what's driving you crazy and most of what's keeping you sane. Their good humor and almost daily displays of decency buoy my spirits. Still, there are certain patterns of behavior that are beginning to wear my patience thin. Among these are the attention-getting antics of the neediest kids. Antics like interrupting an explanation to ask questions that the explanation will answer in a minute. Raising a hand and then, when acknowledged, saying "No, that's okay." (Translation: You didn't acknowledge me right away so I'm obviously not important.) Like flashbulbs discharged in your face, the interruptions can wreak havoc on your concentration. Sometimes that seems to be their intent.

Finally, after trying private appeals in vain, I call out one of my worst offenders, giving the annoyance its proper name. "This is attention-getting behavior and it needs to stop," I tell her in front of the entire class. Even as I say the words, I feel them cut into her like a knife, because she knows they're true and because we both know why they're true. Attention is exactly what she's starving for. She gets almost none of it at home.

Distracting as they are, attention-getting behaviors do not weary me as much as acts of insolent inattention. My second-semester Popular Fiction class is periodically disturbed by gab, often instigated by but not always restricted to the claque of girls that was identified for me as "the posse." A few zeroes for talking during test periods cool their jets somewhat, but it's a fire I can't entirely put out. I'm told that at least one of my colleagues has given up with this crowd. "I just let them talk in the back of the room and go on teaching." But does such an approach allow the other students, including those most prone to distraction, to go on learning? Often the most neglected kids in a school system are not the so-called troubled children; they're the struggling but mostly cooperative children whom no one troubles to give a second thought.

With just such students in mind, I insist on the decorum of my classroom. But I grow tired of having to repeat myself—and of the strain of keeping my annoyance in check when I do. At an orientation session for new teachers at the beginning of the year, the superintendent told us "Never raise your voice," an equivocal directive given the type of student for whom anything close to a reprimand counts as "yelling." But I hold to the principle that a polite request that can't be heard at conversational volume needs to be repeated at a more audible volume, "audible" to be determined by compliance. Unlike the Temptations, I *am* too proud to beg, but if "yelling" is what it takes to permit a kid with learning disabilities to take a test under the most favorable conditions, I ain't too proud to yell.

In general, though, I'm more amazed than miffed at the amount of communicativeness that saturates the school day, not only among the kids but among adults as well. I'm still not used to it. I'm sure that some of my reaction derives from having worked so many years alone in my house. I try to factor in my own eccentricity. Even so, I find myself wondering if people in past generations felt, or people in other cultures feel, such a compulsive need to gab as I witness all around me. I'm astounded that people have so much to talk about. I sit down with my dearest at the close of the day and find that I'm incapable of more than a few sentences. What exactly is there to say? The food is great. I love your company. I'll be glad when it's February break.

Undoubtedly, some of my students are no less weary of the endless chatter than I. Mostly to give them a leg up on their assignments but also to provide a taste of something different, I devote the last half of a few class periods to silent reading. I'm immediately impressed by the number of students who take to it. One can almost feel them settling into the silence, as into the breathing of deep meditation. I take an empty seat in the middle of the room and read with them. I wish I could hook us all to heart monitors. I can feel the rhythms even out. Perhaps when the February break does come, they'll find occasion to repeat the experience. I certainly intend to.

Hardly a day goes by, no matter how tiring, when I don't feel thankful for my study hall, not a thing many teachers can say. Its sparse population allows me to seat the students at a distance from one another, though we've gotten closer in other ways. I sense a common understanding between us. On more than one occasion a faculty member has walked into my room, paying me no more mind than if I were one of my potted plants, and begun talking aloud—practically yelling!—to one of my study hall students. I'm tempted to protest, but I don't. I assume this must be the way some other study halls work, and I draw satisfaction from the sense that some of the students seem to find these intrusions embarrassing.

This is nothing compared to the satisfaction that comes of an unthinkable request. Unlike freshmen, who are assigned to study halls during any period when they do not have a class or lunch, upperclassmen with acceptable grades are permitted to forgo study halls for what is called earned time. So, in addition to my freshmen regulars, I have a transient population of sophomores, juniors, and seniors who enter and leave as their marking period grades fall and rise. The unthinkable request comes when several of these upperclassmen, newly sprung from study hall for having brought up their grades, ask if they might stay there anyway. They can get their work done, they tell me, and it gives them more free time at night. I find this gratifying, to say the least, including the part about the night.

I have no doubt that some of the attraction of my study hall is the ease with which I grant passes to visit other rooms and especially other teachers. Here too there's an understanding among my regulars: be worthy of the trust. They know that once in a while I'm going to step out of the room and check up on their whereabouts. On one of these forays I find a senior boy hanging out in the school store when he told me he was going to be working in the computer room. I'm pissed, and I tell him as much. Had he asked to go to the school store, I'd have let him. I've long been a believer in a student's need to stretch his legs now and again, a need I exercised quite frequently in my own student days. But there's a matter of accountability here: I need to know where my students are in case of an emergency. If I don't, it's my tail in the wringer, and I don't take kindly to people who take frivolous risks with my livelihood or my reputation.

The boy's contrite. He tells me that he knows we've had a good relationship up until now, and he's loath to think he's ruined it. I tell him he hasn't, though it may be a while before I give him permission to leave my study hall. I know the test will come sooner than I'll find appropriate. And I know what I'll need to do to see that both of us pass. "Do you think you could let me go to the computer room?" he asks, meekly enough, a mere week later. "I do, but we have one piece of unfinished business to settle before I can let that happen."

I peel two dollars from my wallet and tell him to go to the school store and buy two bags of chips, "for me and for thee." When he smiles, I know everything is back where it belongs. Like my earlier dustup with the tutor, the episode ends on a note of reconciliation, though I could also call it rest. To be at odds with anyone right now is simply too exhausting.

Having a wife and daughter working in the public schools saves me from self-pity, though it can add to my sense of weariness. Both women work in special education, a term that supposedly refers to the disabilities of their students though it might just as easily refer to the disabling requirements that go along with "special funding." Every year, for example, they and their colleagues are absorbed in the completion of the "time studies" required of all special education teachers in the state. In its disingenuous zeal for accountability, the Department of Education wants teachers to account for all of their day's activities in fifteen-minute increments. What the department doesn't want, and explicitly states it doesn't want, is any accounting for hours spent before and after the contracted hours of the school day. This strikes me as similar to asking for a description of a centaur that makes no mention of a horse.

Also inadmissible are the daily exigencies—calming a child's tantrum, waiting to meet with a parent who doesn't show up for a scheduled meeting, having a postmeeting heart-to-heart with the parent who does show up only to break down sobbing partway through—anything that can't be assigned a code and logged in with a keystroke.

So if scheduling conflicts (yours or the parent's) compel you to deliver services to a child before the school day begins, you can't count that as service. On the other hand, not counting the morning session as service risks showing you in default of your obligations to the student as spelled out in his or her Individualized Education Program. (An IEP is required for each student served under the umbrella of special ed.) Meetings with parents count only if you schedule them during the times when working parents are least likely to attend. If you work while you eat lunch, you must still indicate that you take a lunch: you can't enter two codes in one space, nor can you show yourself lacking a lunch. (By law every full-time worker in the United States gets a lunch whether she gets one or not.) If you suffer an attack of diarrhea from wolfing down your lunch, you can't note that on the form, since there is no code for using the toilet. You can either fudge the entry or leave the fifteen minutes blank and have the form rejected.

The time study must be recorded on a perpetually revised electronic document that may or may not cooperate in storing your information. (If public education has any current trends, this is at the very top of the list: the rate at which pedagogical conundrums are being replaced by technological ones. A close second is the alarming rate at which educators are losing their ability to tell the two apart.) Needless to say, the time taken to do the time study is not a permissible entry.

In short, under the pretext of wanting to know what its special education teachers are doing, the state wants proof positive that they *are* doing what the state itself inhibits them from getting done.

One might gather from the way I'm carrying on here that I have to do a time study myself or that my wife and daughter are furious at having to do theirs. I don't; they're not. I am alternately touched and amazed by their dedication and resilience—another reason I find the time studies so demeaning. Our daughter comes home for a weekend; she and her mother begin talking shop almost as soon as she gets through the door. I doze off in the living room to the sound of their kitchen-table conspiring—their inexhaustible zeal to find the best approach for this kid and that kid . . . *from each according to his ability, to each according to his need.*

I love them, of course, and they love each other; they also love their work, dispassionately, intellectually—they are no sentimentalists. But another love is at play in their banter, hinted at whenever my daughter says, "I like the bad ones best" or when her mother refers to one of her own baddies as "this little guy," a phrase that tends to dress the three-year-old it summons in a racketeer's necktie and fedora. There was a time when I thought that the weakest reason a person could give for wanting to be a teacher was "I love kids." The declaration of an airhead, I used to think. To some extent I still do—I am no sentimentalist either. But as a primary motivation, I now see it as indispensable, especially if one adds, "I love their parents too." Ditto for any reformist movement in school or out, let alone anything that dares call itself a revolution. "At the risk of sounding ridiculous," Che Guevara said, "let me say that the true revolutionary is guided by a great feeling of love." That goes double for the true teacher. It has become a kind of mantra with me over the past weeks: *I need to love.* I hope my episodic bouts of sickness have not begun to soften my brain. But the greater danger by far is that my midwinter weariness will begin to harden my heart.

For Valentine's Day I buy several bags of bite-sized chocolate hearts and give one to each of my students as Frank Sinatra and Barbra Streisand sing "I've got a crush on you, sweetie pie." With more forethought, I'd have bought some candy that was sugar-free. Childhood diabetes: yet another reason Valentine's Day can be the most depressing day on a kid's calendar. Or morbid obesity. Or you don't have a girlfriend. Or your father just found another one. Or you're the only gay marcher in the dominant culture's annual Straight Pride Parade. I might have done better to ignore the occasion altogether, but for that the school gives too little support. I'd have had an easier time ignoring Christmas.

As in past years the school's business club is selling carnations for a dollar apiece. The purchase price used to include delivery at any time: a knock would come on your classroom door (or else it would fly open minus the knock) and a club member would enter and present the resident sweetie pie with her fifteenth red carnation of the day (or one of less flamboyant hue if the sender was "just a friend"). The deliveries, at least, have become a bit more discreet. But the rest remains as it was. By afternoon the most popular girls are sashaying down the halls like beauty pageant winners while their less-favored sisters clutch a single stem or no stem at all. At least my kids can all clutch a candy, whether they choose to eat it or not. I put the hearts on a plate for the sake of elegance. I walk them up and down the rows in an effort to be courtly. Most of the kids say thanks or no thanks. A few say nothing but still take a heart.

Not long after dispensing the chocolates I have a nightmare in which I'm serving each of my third-period sophomores a splash of red wine. I'm not sure why I'm doing this, but it feels good to pour their allotments into the long-stemmed crystal glasses I must have handed out before the dream began. A teacher passing by my classroom—young and female, but no one I recognize—sticks her head through the doorway and insinuates that I'm violating the separation of church and state. "We're not allowed to give them bread either," she snaps. But I'm not giving them bread, I tell her, or talking about religion; it just happens that our little treat for today is some wine. *Wine!* Christ, I'm giving these kids wine!

"Everybody stop!" I shout. "Everybody put down their glasses right now. Mr. Keizer has made a big mistake." I manage to find a bucket into which I ask the students to empty their glasses. But I'm too late for Stevie, a gentle boy who sometimes comes into my room at the beginning of class and asks if I need any help erasing my boards or passing out papers. His glass is empty, his lolling face as green as a bell pepper. I'm overcome with remorse. *I've killed poor Stevie.*

My wife has an expression: "What would Dr. Freud say?" I wish I knew. Is my subconscious telling me that I need to remember I'm teaching minors? Do I expect too much of my students, discussing subjects or setting them tasks better suited to adults? I do my corrections with a green pen, and the boy who nearly drank himself to death has not had the smoothest sledding with his research paper. Does that explain his green face? Or is my dream symbolic of a deeper frustration, one that comes of acquainting my students with some of the headier delights of literature and culture only to feel thwarted by the constraints of a bell schedule and a grade book? Am I trying to achieve a deeper level of intellectual "communion" than I have a right to expect?

I discount the possible interpretation that my conscience is tender because I digress too often in class. I don't think I do. If anything I may be erring on the other side. In past years I was more likely to share a story, historical or even autobiographical, more willing to get off the subject and circle back around to it. Essentially I was trying to teach my students how to write, or rather how to look at the world like a writer. Then why do I do so little of that now? Is it because I'm overly driven by the various "standards," the Common Core curriculum, the ever-looming NECAPs, the need to hit the ground running because of the precious minutes lost by taking attendance on the computer? In other words, have I been too stingy, rather than too liberal, with the wine?

If I have, then I've been stingiest with my Popular Fiction class, where the omnipresent necessity of keeping order tends to discourage me from digression. I certainly feel the least at my ease with that group, which may mean that I'm keeping everyone at a distance for the sake of a relative few. I decide to strike a different note when my drive to work one morning fills me with an unusual elation. I pull off our dirt road onto the blacktop and look into my rearview mirror just in time to see my wife's red taillights winking at me through her car's exhaust as she turns in the opposite direction. No sooner have I redirected my smile to the road ahead than the biggest full moon I've ever seen begins following me to work, playing hide and seek along a range of mountains. I think I've finally lost it for good, and then it makes one dramatic curtain call just before I enter the village of Barton, so unreal in its diameter that I have to wonder if I'm dreaming.

Lesser lights accost me on the way, things almost as familiar as the moon but transfigured in its glow. An ornamental light-house beaming on the lawn in front of someone's mobile home seems preternaturally gratuitous, dares me to conjure the story behind it—this young working couple manages to get a week on the Maine coast, feels more alive than they have in ages, and decides nothing less than a five-foot lighthouse will do for a souvenir. It's a challenge getting the thing into the car, wiring it to the house. It flashes a warning across their next electric bill—they don't care. To come home to that little lighthouse after a late night out or to wake up to it in the hours before sunrise lifts their spirits out of winter, wafts a smell of saltwater to their brains. A passing snowplow puts me on the same shore, splashing a wave of snowmelt against the side of my car, and I'm suddenly aware of every consolation of the man in the cab, how grand he must feel to ride so high above the road, a lighthouse keeper in his own right, his roof lights turning as he clears the way for milk trucks and school buses, pregnant women rushing to the hospital, bread trucks coming up from the south. On no day can he question the importance of his work: it's as solid as a steering wheel in his hands. There's a thermos of coffee beside him on the seat, the memory of his wife's warm body when he rose at 3:00. He's going to tell her all about this giant moon when he gets home, while she lays on the bacon in her bathrobe and slippers, lighting the day's first cigarette at the stove. Maybe she won't have to go to work this morning, maybe they'll go back to bed after they eat. Maybe they'll make love.

By the time I'm in my Popular Fiction class, I've trimmed my narrative with an eye toward brevity and decorum. I've taken out the wife's warm body and the cigarettes. I don't know if the students are so quiet because I've captivated their imaginations or because they wonder if I've lost my mind. On another day I might have segued from the lunar to the etymology of *lunatic*.

But my lesson today is about art. "I'm a reader of history," I say to them. "I could tell you things that human beings have done to one another that would ruin your sleep for a week. But the world is full of beautiful things as well, and literature exists in part to help us perceive them. Literature helps us open our eyes."

It sounds glib, and I know it's reductive. It ought to have been better planned—what I really meant to say is that there's no way to assign pragmatic value to things of beauty. You can't do a cost-benefit analysis of a moon, a novel, a lighthouse on somebody's front lawn. There's no way to reduce these things to test results or data.

Only much later—now, in fact, as I write—does it occur to me that I may have given the cue, as well as permission, to a boy who decides one day to ignore the topic for that week's journal assignment and write about something else. He was up doing his barn chores on the morning the journal entry was due (but not yet attempted) when he caught sight of a coyote loping across the snow-covered cornfield. He ran for his deer rifle and got back in time to place the varmint in his crosshairs. He fired and saw it drop. He felt "so good" that he decided to write about the episode for his English homework. Did I inspire him to do so? It hardly matters. The important thing is that he was inspired— that he believed I would be capable of appreciating his inspiration. Never mind that a coyote might count as one of the world's beautiful things. Never mind the albatross that Coleridge hangs around the neck of the Ancient Mariner who shot it out of the sky. There's only one person in this room old enough to qualify as an ancient mariner. "Let that boy alone," quoth he.

The due date for the research papers arrives. Right up till the deadline I've been meeting with students both during and outside class to go over drafts, tidy up citations, coach concluding paragraphs. I highlight with a yellow marker any sentences that I suspect have been plagiarized and require students to review them with me before handing in their final drafts. For the few who go limp at the prospect of following the MLA style used by our department, I do the bibliographical citations with them, side by side. I know that in the academic support areas the tutors have been putting in lavish amounts of time to get some of their more challenged charges up to speed. The range of performance runs the full gamut from students who have taken their paper through multiple drafts to students who have still, even now, done nothing beyond choosing their topics. I'm already figuring out terms for a grace period following the due date.

With one eye on those students for whom staying organized is a particular challenge and the other on those adults (parents, tutors, etc.) trying to help them close the gap, I devise a detailed checklist to be handed in with the final product. This is hardly an innovation—I credit the IRS and the Guggenheim Foundation, both of which provided similar kinds of assistance to me— but I'm pleased with it nonetheless. I take pleasure in imagining my students, perhaps with the assistance of their friends, parents, or study hall teachers, methodically putting their various pieces together and checking off each item as it's added. Like packing for a trip, I tell them. I also take comfort from the thought that I'm not going to lose a lot of time or break a lot of hearts (including my own) by having to subtract points for missing pieces.

Grading for major assignments at the school is generally done by means of a rubric, with points awarded for each of a set of criteria and then totaled for the final grade. The way you build mercy into a rubric is to see that there's a "floor" of points awarded simply for coming through with the goods. The main plank in my floor is the last item of the rubric, a criterion labeled "completeness," which allows a student to earn up to twelve points, more than the point spread for a whole letter grade. My hope is that the checklist will enable students to gain a full complement of points for this category, as well as for another called "process," which acknowledges their diligence in following the required steps.

If I devote so much space to discussing the relatively humdrum matter of a checklist, that is because it eventually comes to encapsulate my frustrations and sense of failure. If you like your alliteration to come in threes, you can add a third "f" and say I'm floored by some of the results. Intended to strengthen the connection between my requirements and what the students actually deliver, the checklist comes to stand as the disconnect between us. The old saw about leading a horse to water could not be more apt.

Some students simply do not use the checklist. They lose it, ignore it—don't have it. Granted, if they have all the other pieces listed on the sheet, then for them the document was a superfluous nuisance and its absence of no consequence. Except there is almost no one who has all the items and no checklist. This is simply not how these things work.

Other students supply an accurate but unsatisfactory checklist: that is to say, they check off what they have completed, but what they hand in remains incomplete. The checklist has not prompted them to do anything more than what they would have done without it. Imagine asking your traveling companion, prior to driving to the airport, if he's remembered to bring his photo ID. "No," he says, "but I have all my luggage," and gets into the car. Yeah, but there's still time to go back in the house for the ID. "Nah. Let's go. If anybody asks, I'll say I don't have it." He's honest. He may not make it onto the aircraft, but he's honest.

A more bizarre variation is the student who checks off every item on the list whether he has those items or not. The checklist is a form, you see. You're supposed to fill it out. All those lines need checks; here they are. At the other extreme is the student who hands in the form, duly stapled to the paper, but has not checked off any of the items. The Zen approach. I start fumbling with a mental checklist of my own, some of it straight and some of it bordering on the facetious. Was every kid present when I explained the checklist? Was every kid paying attention? Did I give a quiz to see if they understood? Did I spend three days discussing it? Did I turn filling out the checklist into a lesson in itself?

The checklist business is an irritant, the number of students who hand in a late paper or no paper at all is a discouragement, but the truly demoralizing thing for me is the number of students who completely ignore my edits and suggestions on their rough drafts and hand in a "final" draft identical to the rough one they handed in weeks ago. It's as if *draft* were merely a synonym for *printout*. Had I not assigned other writing units prior to this one I'd be wondering if I've mistakenly assumed an understanding of the meanings of "edit," "rough draft," etc. I'm inclined to wonder anyway. Is it possible I have students who still don't grasp the *reason* one does a rough draft or who think that a final draft exists only for the sake of neatness?

The lack of revision extends to some of the passages I've highlighted as likely plagiarisms. They remain as they were. The students did not come to see me, did not attempt to paraphrase and document what I rightly suspected they'd simply copied verbatim from their sources. The same Internet that put the text at their fingertips makes it easy for me to locate the lifted phrases. I speak privately with the most egregious offender. Did she not understand the sheet on plagiarism, the one that we went over in class and that every student signed? No, she understood it. Why didn't she come to see me about the passages I'd highlighted? She's not sure. "I guess I didn't have time." It's like a bout to see which of the two of us is the more clueless, and I'm the one winning. I simply cannot comprehend why anyone would be so careless of her own welfare.

I shouldn't neglect to say that any disappointments are offset by some wonderful results. Not surprisingly, the paper on Le Chambon is a splendid piece of work, preceded by enough conferencing to allow for no surprises. I'm simply able to enjoy it. Assigning the grade is a mere formality. A paper on the Ashanti people of Africa and another on the traditional clothing worn in India both exhibit not only some of the cross-cultural perspective one hopes to gain through research but also the writers' ability to snap back after a prolonged absence from school. A hockey enthusiast relieves the monotony of statistics that characterizes the typical paper on sports with piquant commentary from members of her hockey-loving clan: Grandma weighs in on this year's prospects for the Maple Leafs and gets a formatted citation for her trouble. My self-described redneck follows through with a respectable paper on John Deere; an art-loving student shows off her new knowledge of Fauvism. The writer on female genital mutilation earns the right to stand on the feminist soapbox of her concluding paragraph and gets some applause in green ink. The boy who wrestled until the very end with the giant squid survives the struggle and emerges with his head just above water, scarred by a few suckers but still glad to be alive. For a midlevel sophomore English class, the unit has hardly been a disaster.

But the results should have been better. I wasn't expecting perfection, but I should have seen a basic competence across the board. I don't. This is especially troublesome given the school administration's repeated reminder that the chief measure of success is not "what got taught" but rather "what got learned." I can hardly find fault with that. Doctors are judged by how many they heal, not by how many drugs they prescribe. But aren't there cases where medicine simply doesn't work, where the doctor's only consolation comes of knowing that he did everything he could?

What else should I have done? In some cases the answer takes the form of a regrettable omission on my part, an error I ought to have flagged on a student's rough draft or note cards but failed to catch in my scramble to return things on time and preserve our momentum. These goofs hurt but at the least I can see they don't hurt the student's grade. Other goofs I can't perceive; probably some of them have to do with the sheer limits of what one teacher can accomplish within the waking hours of a day.

Still others, like the case of plagiarism, have to do with deeply ingrained habits of passive resistance. When asked how he'd attained his mastery of Latin, Dr. Johnson famously replied, "My master whipt me very well. Without that, Sir, I should have done nothing." What a bleak view of human nature, I used to think, but after spending my first Saturday going over research papers, Johnson's reply strikes me as outlandishly optimistic, as if a beating were all it took to teach a kid Latin.

For someone who's spent much of his adult life trying to mine personal experience for "larger," often political implications, it's hard not to feel a stinging challenge to my politics. Most teachers are some variety of centrist liberal, if only because they rightly see their own livelihoods as dependent on a generous social contract. But it is only with a great leap of faith that they achieve even the most lukewarm progressivism, which by its very definition requires the belief that human beings can progress—or want to. It's in making that leap that I lose my footing. I have never doubted that many a disadvantaged kid was saved from the gallows by going to school. But to create a society in which gallows were permanently abolished—how many holdouts would first have to hang? At the risk of sounding impertinent, Comrade Guevara, how many people did your "great feeling of love" inspire you to execute? To reduce ignorance is one thing, but what remedy for inertia—for the tendency in many of us to find the demands of all but the most pedestrian forms of learning or liberation simply *too much work*? The question is way above my pay grade. I can't even find a remedy for plagiarism.

Late in the afternoon of the first Sunday of my February break, I drive up to school to record the research paper grades on Power-School. It has taken me two weeks and two complete weekends of correction to reach this point. It would have taken longer had every student handed in a paper. I'm ashamed at the gratitude I feel toward the kids who've lightened my load.

This semester the administration has enabled the feature that allows students and parents to check their grades online; I've promised to make the research paper grades visible by this date. The scores will make a positive difference for some students, who are my main reason for wanting to get the data into the system. We'll go over the papers themselves after vacation, after my disappointment has had time to mellow. For now it's enough to drive up to the empty school, deactivate the alarm, turn on the lights, and hope the Internet is up and running.

Can it really be no more than a month since I came off midyear exams feeling so elated? I keep asking myself if the results are really as dismal as I think they are or if I'm concentrating too exclusively on what was missing to the neglect of what was not. I know I must never sneeze at the fact that a great bulk of material got handed in. I sneeze all the same. Is it some insipient hypochondria that creates the impression of a disease laying hold of me even as I'm driving home? I was sick for Thanksgiving and sick for Christmas; surely I can't be getting sick for February break as well, not now when I've finally gotten through all those papers. My bottle of water is too cold and I drank from it too fast; probably that's the reason my ears ache when I swallow. A lingering residue of chalk dust might be all that's making me sneeze.

Ice fishing shanties dot the frozen surface of Crystal Lake like a forlorn tundra settlement, smoke rising from their chimneys. The ice will soon be thinning; every year someone waits too long and his shanty, sometimes along with his pickup, breaks through and sinks. Some of my kids took the same sort of risk with their papers. It's the local way, I tell myself, but no, it's the human way, the few degrees that separate any one of us from disaster. I take care not to speed, not to let my wheels hit the salt-softened slush on the shoulders. All I need now is to skid onto the lake and go through the ice. I'm not going to let anything put a crimp in my vacation. That includes obsession with the research papers, my fitful nights of correcting them in my sleep notwithstanding. I did the best I could with the unit. Perhaps with another two years I might have it down pat. *Another two years*—is that really a possibility? No word yet from my predecessor. Contracts will be going out next month, and he'll have to give an answer then. If a position opens up, I may have to give an answer too. I've got my heater blowing hard enough to muffle my music. I can't seem to get warm.

— 9 —

MARCH

The only bearable days I can remember in the course of many years were the few days of a sultry feverish attack of influenza.

—Louis-Ferdinand Céline, *Journey to the End of the Night*

Kathy says she can't remember ever seeing me as sick as I am now. We've been married for thirty-six years. I've had my flu shot—in fact, owing to a glitch in the paperwork at my doctor's office, it seems I've had two—but flu is what I have, what I had throughout the February break, and what has kept me out of school for the first six school days of March. It would have been eight, but school was called off for two days because of snow.

I don't wonder that the disease can be deadly. The spoon in my hand shakes so violently against my soup bowl that I sound like a wedding reception agitating for the newlyweds to kiss. I can't resist a joke about consumptive Russian poets, wheezing out the punch line as my wife looks on in alarm. In bed she holds me tight until I stop trembling. In the morning I wake so drenched that she has to strip the bed. I dream I'm still correcting research papers. I keep making mistakes. I recalibrate my grades only to have them disappear from my computer or float off the screen, curling like ashes above the keyboard. In about as many days I've lost nine pounds.

For as long as we've lived in Vermont I've done my snow removal by hand, a matter of fitness and a point of pride. Within a week I've gone from slow shoveling to being unable to shovel at all. As if the mere sight of me out of doors is a reproach to the neighborhood, men with tractors begin dredging out my driveway even before the sky clears. Kathy insists on shoveling the path to our door. I watch the activity from my window like a child who can't go out to play.

I'm too sick even to attend town meeting. Voting for the school budget is a point of pride more adamant for me than shoveling my own snow. When our daughter was young enough to attend the town elementary school, I acted with obvious self-interest— all the more reason to be a disinterested supporter of younger parents now. And since I don't live in the same school district as I teach, no one can accuse me of trying to pad my own paycheck when I speak in support of teachers. True, I'm not as given to verbal brawling as in years past, and I scarcely have the strength for it this year. Kathy will have to go without me. We're hoping for a quiet meeting. But even a level-funded budget won't pacify the skinflint contingent if they're in an ugly mood.

Past bones in its craw have included an all-school ski program (a "frill," notwithstanding the school's front-yard view of Burke Mountain, whose lodges and condominiums are routinely mucked out by parents who can't afford to buy their own kids a ski pass), a largely state-funded free breakfast program (based on the apparently outrageous proposition that children ought not to be punished for the poverty or neglect of their parents and opposed with the predictable perversity that prides itself on rejecting "state handouts"), and that perennial bugbear, special education. The last of these gripes has always struck me as the most deplorable, especially when the parents of handi-capped students endure the abuse in embarrassed silence. More than once I've had a moist-eyed parent approach me after a meeting and thank me for my remarks.

The air of masquerade can be almost as depressing as the sentiments themselves. Lavishly pensioned retirees step out of immaculate $35,000 pickups to bear witness to the tribulations of living on a "fixed income." Solidly middle-class landowners hold forth on the burdens of minuscule tax increases in the rhetorical overalls of Tom Joad. Countrified transplants who've sent their children to the best private colleges money can buy evoke the Vermont tradition of making do with less.

Not to say that there are no legitimate, or at the least understandable, grievances with the school system. I've had a few of my own. And I've seldom left a town meeting as angry with my neighbors as I am with the social conditions that put us at one another's throats. Especially the people who speak from obvious poverty and even more obvious bitterness—are they wrong to wonder what school ever did for them? Or to assert that school costs are among the very few over which they have any control? Quite correctly they sense that in a class-bound society, education provides much of the basis for despising—and exploiting—those who lack it.

Even the obvious remedy seems to mock them: in a state (and lately a nation) where organized labor is more the exception than the rule, it's hard for unprotected workers not to resent the privileges obtained by unionized teachers, some of whom, I'd be the first to admit, are long on "organized" and short on "labor." Years ago the father of two of my students told me a story about working on the Crown Point bridge connecting Vermont and New York State. There was a crew from each side, and when they met in the middle, the Vermonters discovered they were making a third of the hourly wage of the workers from New York. "They had a union, you see. We didn't." What the father must have felt meeting his unionized counterparts is perhaps not unlike what some of my neighbors feel sitting at town meeting with the likes of me—the difference being that a teacher's union wages come out of their pockets. I try to remember that.

I'm glad to be spared the effort this year. I won't miss the sigh at the microphone or the grumble from the back of the room. I know that a few of my neighbors won't miss me. Vermonters love to speak of "our town meeting tradition" as "democracy in action," which is accurate enough, though not always the most stirring endorsement of democracy. To be the parent of a school-age child whose daily comfort and future prospects are at the mercy of a disgruntled electorate, half of whom are obstinately misinformed and several of whom, at ten in the morning no less, are stinking drunk, is not my idea of a spring tonic. Norman Rockwell does a good job with the tall fellow standing up as the personification of free speech, but he leaves out the demagogues and the dimwits waiting their turns behind him. He's a painter of miniatures, however big his canvas.

Kathy lifts me out of my funk when she returns at lunchtime to say that the budget passed by a good margin with hardly any discussion. Rockwell probably wouldn't have been surprised. I guess I shouldn't be too surprised either. In other words, I shouldn't let the memory of a few benighted decisions make me cynical about democracy. I undermine my own position if I do. To lose all faith in the public's judgment, to forfeit what E. B. White calls "the recurrent suspicion that more than half of the people are right more than half of the time," is as good as conceding that humankind is debased beyond remediation—in which case, why should I care one way or another if the school budget passes? What point is there in teaching those who will "never learn"?

But it's not democracy that gets me down so much as the surly kind of populism that likes to wear democracy's clothes. If in the name of the people we allow public education to be strangled in the tight-fisted mandates of "local control," if we're prepared to put the safety of a school building or the content of its textbooks to popular vote (at least Vermont does not do the latter), then we reduce democracy to what even our most optimistic founders feared it might become: mob rule. If for no other reason than to sharpen our sense that public education and responsible self-government go hand in hand, town meetings are a good idea.

Unlike the towns that make up the Lake Region School District, the town in which Kathy and I live has no designated high school. Most parents opt to send their children to the quasi-private academy in Lyndon, their closest option, though the town will also provide tuition to any other accredited high school at the academy rate. Like its counterparts elsewhere in Vermont, and according to a rationale I've never entirely understood, Lyndon Institute serves as a de facto public high school while retaining several of a private school's prerogatives. Its teachers need not be certified, for instance, and it sets its own tuition without the need for voter approval. For that reason, our discussions at town meeting rarely touch on secondary school expenditures. I have no doubt that the take-it-or-leave-it nature of the academy tuition accounts for the cost-cutting vengeance that some voters bring to the elementary school budget.

Other towns in our county also send their students to the Lyndon high school. Kathy is now working part-time in one of them. She uses what remains of Town Meeting Day, a day off for most teachers in Vermont, to practice further on her new iPad. In two years Lyndon Institute will eliminate all physical texts in favor of digital editions on such a device. That may be part of what's driving its adoption at the elementary school level. In the case of the special needs students Kathy serves, there's also a feeling that smart-book technology will foster the "accommodations" they require.

Kathy shares the hope, not without reservations. It sometimes seems that the accommodations are less to the student and more to the digital device. For example, Kathy fashions "communication boards" that allow nonverbal kids to make their needs and wishes known by pointing to a picture. A glass of water, say, or a favorite game. Up until now she has custommade these boards by hand with an eye to an individual child's skill set; now she's being urged to use a prepackaged app to do the same thing. But some of her students lack the sequencing skills necessary to make the app appear on their screens. When it does, it's likely to feature more pictures than a student is able to comprehend on a single visual field. Never mind, say the state consultants, stick with the iPad. "You can make this work." Kathy intends to do no less, though she has to wonder if putting a kid on an iPad is necessarily the same thing as putting a kid's needs first. In other words, what exactly is the *this* we are trying to make work?

In fairness it should be said that no one is forcing Kathy or her colleagues to go the iPad route, not yet anyway, but there is a definite sense of an imperative in the air. This is not the aberration of a single school system but part of a much wider trend— perhaps wider than most of us care to see. The institute's plan to have all student texts on iPads, for example, will be a blow to the local independent bookstore that has provided the school with texts at substantial discount for decades. It's also an oddly extravagant expenditure given the financial constraints that were cited only the year before to justify laying off a large portion of the school's unionized maintenance staff in order to outsource their responsibilities to a contracted firm.

Decisions such as these underscore the rarely acknowledged fact that all schools operate with at least two curricula: what the school teaches children through its academic programs and what it teaches through its administrative priorities. It may be that the institute is well aware of this. Surely no one can fault the school for failing to prepare the elite sector of its students to assume leadership positions in the "global marketplace." The lessons are apt and unequivocal: technology means everything, loyalty means nothing, local economy and organized labor mean less than nothing. More than any flu, the lessons make me sick.

But figurative sickness remains a luxury in my present state. The real variety is about all I can manage. As confirmed by a chest X-ray and a sample of the sputum I keep coughing up, my flu has become pneumonia. I'm given a strong antibiotic—what I've been asking for from the outset—one level of potency below what would require me to enter the hospital. I'm also given a doctor's note discouraging any quick return to work, not that those colleagues who've heard my voice on the phone would view that prospect with anything but horror.

I'm already at the stage where my lesson plans have shifted from those appropriate to a short-term absence to those appropriate to a last will and testament. I've always done thorough sub plans—to do otherwise is tantamount to throwing a substitute to the lions, even with a class of lambs—but the challenges of doing good plans increase the longer you're out, and there are certain limitations even at the start. Asking a substitute to present new material is at best a risk, at worst a guarantee that you'll have to repeat the presentation at a disadvantage later on. Busy work of the kind that a substitute can be entrusted to correct is immediately, and rightly, perceived by the students as an insult to their intelligence. Assignments that generate lots of material for the recovering teacher to correct might succeed in class but are not likely to work wonders for his recovery. Perhaps the only advantage of being a sick teacher is the chance to catch up on the paper load, an advantage I'm disinclined to surrender. There will be backlog enough without heaping it higher than it already is.

Either the night before an absence or early the next morning I type up my plans for the day, never less than several pages, and e-mail them to Sara and Mr. Messier. The duplication is not their requirement, but I think it's good for both of them to know what's going on in my classes. I suppose there's some display involved: *See, I'm still on the job.* So is poor Sara, who remains my chief mainstay at school, in sickness as in health. She'll print my plans for the sub along with any documents I attach in the form of student assignments. She'll also check in on my classes to see if things are going well. If an uncooperative student is ejected from my room, she's likely to be the first responder. She keeps encouraging me to take what time I need, but her health has not been perfect this year—she's been coughing almost continually since September—and I worry about the added strain I've placed on her.

I set up a relay. Another member of the department, who also commutes from a town outside the district, agrees to bring the sub's comments and any collected papers to the drugstore in Barton, which has agreed to hold the bag until Kathy can drive up after work and retrieve it. Once I resume the normal pace of correction, there's a daily exchange of incoming papers and outgoing papers. By this I hope to accomplish two things. The academic instruction can go forward, and by means of comments on the papers I can maintain some kind of connection to my kids. For my Composition class this exchange takes the form of editorial letters written in response to rough drafts. Were the class larger or on the whole more industrious, this might be too heavy a load. As it is, I can manage.

My greatest fear, the fear of every absent teacher, is that I'm going to lose my classes. The understandings we've forged together will gradually come undone. Nothing is more vulnerable to entropy than the climate of a classroom whose teacher is away— even for a few minutes, let alone three weeks. I'll soon be into my fourth. Every one of my classes has heard my September spiel about the gravity I assign to the mistreatment of a substitute. (I used to work with a teacher who made a point of professing his total indifference to how his classes treated substitutes. That was *their* problem, he used to say. I'm told he eventually became a vet-erinarian. Were he the only one on earth, I'd shoot my sick dog.) Every sub plan I type up includes a space for his or her report on the day. I'll give my classes an opportunity to tell me their version when I return.

The situation is critical with the juniors and seniors in my Popular Fiction class; I've not been with them long enough to bond at the most optimal levels. One of my sophomore classes contains a new student, or rather a return student who left school the previous year trailing an odor of trouble behind him. Even before my illness he was showing his potential as a catalyst for misbehavior with two other boys of a similar bent. I have no difficulty keeping them in line and in fact enjoy a tentative rap-port with all three. The two were actually making some progress until the third arrived. In the cat's absence, however, the mice have begun to play. I hear this from the sub. I also hear it in more general terms from some of the students. "We need you back," writes one girl in her journal. Another sophomore, a poignantly

introverted boy from whom I've scarcely heard ten words since
the year began, writes: "This class is a waste right now."

I send some messages of warning to the frisky ones, and Sara
also gives a few sharp yanks on the reins. There's a certain kind
of boy—often, I suspect, the son of a certain kind of man—who
has a hard time accepting female authority, but Sara's more than
a match for the type, maternal Durga or fearsome Kali as the
case requires. The sub is soon reporting improved behavior. But
I know it is no more stable than the weather in March.

She also reports that my last-period sophomores are treating
her with conspicuous courtesy, as I expected they would. We
can't help enjoying some classes more than others, and these
kids—some of whom gave me the most grief at the start of the
year—have become the apple of my eye. "Do tell the lovies," I
write in my sub plans for eighth period, "that I have received the
news of their exemplary cooperation with particular pleasure,
but no surprise. Tell them I wish I could build them an enormous
beach house in Cancun where they could frolic away the rest of
the winter while I hacked and coughed and read their papers
beneath a distant—but not too distant—palm tree."

For the first time since school began, I find time to write something other than a letter or notes for my journal, a short op-ed
on the Wisconsin governor's bid to deny public sector workers
the right to collective bargaining. As output it's paltry enough,
but when it appears in the *Los Angeles Times* I take it as proof I
can still ring the bell. I do worry, though, about some local
Internet surfer taking it as proof that I'm furthering the cause of
international socialism at taxpayers' expense. Probably sipping a
dry martini while I do it too. But I mustn't give a false impression: when one of the district secretaries routinely asks for the

doctor's note required after a certain number of sick days, the superintendent is reportedly annoyed to learn of the request. It seems my stock remains high, at least as far as integrity goes. I worry about the op-ed all the same, like a monk who's just been caught winking at a milkmaid.

I take notes for another short piece but don't find time to finish. This one is about events closer to home. As part of the same beachhead launched in Wisconsin, the governor of Maine has judged the murals depicting the state's labor history to be anti-business propaganda and has ordered their removal from the statehouse. I have no doubt that if asked to explain himself he would hint at wanting to strike a blow at "socialistic" tendencies, even while ordering erasures of the historical record in the best Soviet tradition.

But governors have no patent on contradiction; we teachers are their equals at least. The Maine governor's initiative reminds me of a quotation I've heard attributed to a former Exeter teacher, according to whom there are only two legitimate "learning disabilities," one curable and the other not. The first is laziness, and the second is stupidity. I'd wager that the teacher was disabled by them both, too lazy to adapt his teaching style to the needs of his students, too stupid to realize why he had to. Like the governor, he became the very thing he hated. I should be careful not to do the same.

These musings and others like them are a feature of my sick days, products of my return to solitude and books. Which is to say that solitude and books are never an unqualified blessing. On some level I miss the unreflective luxury of a day's teaching, though I surely don't miss the need to be reactive. For better or for worse, I have more time for reflection now. It ranges over the usual ground—religion, politics, and literature. Inevitably, most of it comes round to school.

A William Trevor novel I've been reading leads me to consult some of his autobiographical essays, in one of which he
reports that he was an indifferent student. I've already told my
students that Hemingway couldn't spell to save his life; should I
also tell them about Trevor, even though we're not reading him?
More to the point, should I tell them that it was not until I'd
entered graduate school that I began to approach reading assignments with the same conscientiousness that I demand of them? It
comes as something of a jolt for me to remember this. I was not a
conscientious reader. I always read, but I read as and when I felt
moved to read, relying on my listening and writing skills to fudge
my comprehension of assigned texts, including great texts, texts
I was blessed to have put under my nose, *Billy Budd* and *The
Return of the Native*. I was a procrastinator, a daydreamer, a
faker. Well, it's not unusual for a hellion to grow up to be a strict
father, but many is the strict father who bowdlerizes the history
of what a hellion he was. His kids can sometimes read it anyway in his strictness. I wonder what my students are able to
read in mine.

I reach further back into my earliest memories of school, trying to locate when the thought of becoming a teacher might first
have occurred to me. It was probably in second grade, when Mrs.
Davies would let me "teach the class" about my several interests.
Second grade has always seemed like the Garden of Eden in the
Genesis of my school career. I was probably never happier or
more secure in school than I was then. No doubt much of this
had to do with our teacher, though she has survived as a vague
figure in my mind. I think of her as an old woman; it's possible
she was no older than forty. Once she invited our entire class to
a picnic at her house, an enchanted place as I remember, with a
wonderful pile of dirt that I lost no time in excavating. I didn't

take part in the baseball game organized by her sturdy, bald-headed husband, but I've preserved a distinct image of him catching up a classmate as the kid scrambled to first base like a harried piglet and whirling him around in jubilation because he was "safe." The next day Mrs. Davies laughed when she told us how Mr. Davies had fallen fast asleep in his chair that night. So had some of us.

It was also in Mrs. Davies's class that we made the wonderful kid-tall "Big Book" out of painted cardboard pages, each of them holding one of our original handwritten stories. With our teacher's gentle encouragement we read them aloud for our parents and for other classes at the school. Mine was an instant hit. Precocious in my authorial enthusiasm for discussing my work at length, I explained to one audience of admirers how I'd discovered my ingenious story in another book. I assumed that's what you did with stories: you heard them in one place and retold them in another. I can still feel the admiration dissipate like air from a punctured balloon—there may even have been an audible sigh that went with it—and my stomach turning at the sight of Mrs. Davies, so embarrassed and disappointed. Second grade may have been Eden but it was also where I fell from grace. I didn't learn the word *plagiarism* until much later, but it has always carried the implication of original sin.

Perhaps most adults are divided between those who knew the steady ache of never gaining their teachers' approval and those of us who knew the sharp, sudden pain of losing it. I remember accidentally knocking over my friend Tommy Gonzales's science experiment, which went crashing to the floor of our sixth-grade classroom when I opened a window too abruptly after school. Tommy was so knowledgeable in science and so talented in art that our teacher once compared him to Leonardo da

Vinci, which amused Tommy to no end, especially after he found a picture of Leonardo in the encyclopedia, "this wrinkly little geezer with long stringy hair." I still recall the sound of his glass vessels shattering on the floor, the nauseating splash of water. Tommy took it calmly, gifted even in his understanding of what it means to be a friend. As for Mrs. Spitzer, her bitter lamentation as she gathered up the broken glass began to sound as though my offense consisted less of wrecking Tommy's project than of not being Tommy, "such a creative boy, and so talented." I seem to have been some kind of walking disaster at age twelve, though that is probably a common experience of childhood, the sense that we are always, helplessly, screwing up.

It persists for some kids throughout their school careers, and for others till they die, this mysterious and inexhaustible capacity for letting people down. I reread a letter that one of my students handed to me at the beginning of the third quarter, shortly before I took ill:

Dear Mr. Keizer

I wanted to apologize for my lack of accomplishment in my previous term in your class. I started out okey, but then I got lazy and unfortunately it effected your class. I know how much hard work you put into grading my papers along with everyone elses. I know you see potential in maybe a pointless person. You deserve the up most respect. I'm very sorry for my disrespect. My distractions from home effected me in my work. Not that I'm using it as an excuse. Please just know, my work will get better. I will hand it all in. My greatest effort will be put back into your class. Thank you so much for not being upset, and being so kind and thoughtful.

For everything you have done for me.

I'm sorry I disappointed you.
Expect a great comeback
From me.

                                        Thanks always,
                                            [Name]
By the way . . . Im sorry about my misspelling. I am a horrid
speller.

Rereading the letter causes me to wonder if I give my students an exaggerated impression of disappointment, which must
fall especially hard on anyone tempted to see herself as "a maybe
pointless person." I also wonder how much weight I ought to give
to such a letter, how much it grows from genuine remorse, how
much it might be intended to make me feel remorseful. I can't
remember ever writing one like it to any teacher of mine, not to
say I wouldn't do so today if I had the chance. Perhaps to my
seventh-grade teacher, Mr. Keeley, and perhaps only to tell him
that I ought to have appreciated him more than I did. I recall the
afternoon of an especially difficult day, when he dismissed his
students one by one after the final bell and took a long time getting to me. "I'm disappointed in you," he said. The offense was
not accidental. I had openly criticized him that day, almost to
the point of outright defiance, though I can't recall the specific
reason, only the cathartic release when the words left my mouth.
Something he'd done had struck me as intolerably unjust, though
the actual injustice probably had little to do with him. It had
more to do with my emerging indignation at the idea that a
"smart kid" wasn't allowed to rebel, wasn't supposed to get angry,
shouldn't be popular enough to get a girl.

I doubt very much that Mr. Keeley had provoked me; he was
not that sort of teacher. He advised a club for students who liked
to assemble plastic model cars (I belonged) and let Bruce Cazazza

play the Beatles' new *Rubber Soul* album at recess. Mr. Keeley was not married and had a little belly under his waist, proof positive according to one of the boys in class that he was a "fag." What Mr. Keeley was above all else, I think, was sensitive, a considerable liability for a junior high school teacher, so he must also have been brave. He seemed genuinely hurt by my defiance, though it's possible he rejoiced inwardly to see a sensitive boy coming into his own.

For a while now I have been asking my students to do their own reflections in paper journals, an exercise I find especially useful while I'm sick. The assignment keeps them writing and it keeps them and me in touch. Recent topics for my sophomores have included "What Is Something You Would Like to Change about Your World, Your Community, Your School, or Yourself?" and "Which Character Do You More Closely Resemble, Tom Sawyer or Huck Finn?" I also ask them to offer their thoughts on one of three current news stories: the revolution in Libya, the tsunami in Japan, and the union-busting initiative in Wisconsin. Not surprisingly, they are most familiar with the stories farthest from the geographical and political circumstances of their lives. I get a number of entries about Japan, fewer about Libya, none about Wisconsin. The governor of Maine may be wasting his energy: does anyone even remember what those labor murals are about?

The topic of a wished-for change brings the students closer to home. It also shakes my ideologically based tendency to see poverty as the worst thing they face. Though most of my students are not poor in the strictest sense—if I take the census figures for their county as the best indicator, then the label fits only between a tenth and a fifth of those sitting in my classes—I'm most inclined to cite economic disadvantage in any mental argument with an educational theorist or with myself. In the case of student journals, though, the most wrenching entries have to do not with material privation but with ruptures in the writers' families. I get a few like this one:

> If I could change one thing . . . it would probably be my
> parents . . . they are currently split up, and I haven't spoken to
> my mother in 4 weeks and it hurts. They don't get along very
> well anymore like they used to. Our family used to be <u>so</u>
> perfect and happy. We told eachother everything and all of
> ours problems were worked out. No secrets were kept hidden
> at all. It really hurts to know that the perfect couple I know as
> mom and dad, no longer love eacher.

I get only one like this, but it belongs to the type:

> I wish I could be enough of a reason for him [my father] to stay.
> I wish my heart was pure gold and that I couldn't disappoint
> anyone. . . . I wish I had the power to persuade someone who
> was about to jump, their reasons to stay. I wish I was the
> kindest, prettiest, smartest, most unselfish person around.
> Maybe then I wouldn't be such a disappointment.

I have been reading widely in this genre since the year began, regardless of the particular topic. "My Troubled Family"—it cuts across gender, age, and class. Even when students focus on their own social lives, I tend to suspect a domestic subtext. A frequent complaint is "all the drama." Ostensibly the writers are talking about school, the typical cliques and dustups of teenage life, but essentially they are talking about home, where adolescence never dies.

Given my empirically based conviction that a stable home

life is the single most reliable predictor of a student's success in school, I am surprised that the Republican Party, self-appointed champion of family values, takes no pains to press the point. Of course, to do so would undermine its agenda of weakening the very provisions that lend stability to family life, more specifi- cally its agenda of dismantling public education, hamstringing teachers' unions, denying same-sex couples the benefits of mar- riage, preventing employed mothers from achieving income parity, curtailing reproductive rights, outsourcing manufactur- ing jobs, and filling the coffers of the various charlatans who sell education in the form of standardized tests. Not to mention the risk of offending constituents who'd rather harp on family val- ues than value their own families.

But the Republican Party is not the only faction shouting down the question of what it means to be a responsible adult. That precious bourgeois squabble referred to as the "culture wars"—all it means to me now is two different ways of making war on children, two rival sects in the ancient religion of child- devouring Moloch: one that sacrificed and continues to sacrifice working-class children on the altar of American exceptionalism and the other that sacrifices them to the frivolous exceptional- ism of the "transgressive" lifestyle. Winner take all, and chil- dren the losers no matter who wins.

"It has been vivid to me for many years that what we call a race problem here is not a race problem at all," James Baldwin wrote. "The problem is rooted in the question of how one treats one's flesh and blood, especially one's children." The race problem and just about every other problem that crosses a teacher's desk.

My repeated mistake, I've come to believe, is not so much to overemphasize the effects of poverty on my students as to define poverty too narrowly. The mechanisms that cause poverty are largely economic—the evidence for that is more compelling than the fossil record supporting evolution—but the poverty itself is breathtakingly diverse, as varied as the species evolution produced. Returning from a doctor's visit, I get gas next to an SUV at a mini-mart. There's a decal on one side depicting a woman bending over a fender and being fucked from behind above the caption "Only on a Jeep." In the back window is a sticker that reads, "Why should *I* have to press 1 for English?" In the front seat are two passengers, a young man and woman whose dull bloated faces belie any claim they might have as champions of erotic abandon, to say nothing of English. If there's no child car seat in the back it's less likely to mean the couple is childless than that their child rides without a child car seat. I don't bother to look—no more than they have bothered to consider what a child might make of the picture on their hatchback. There is more poverty in this vehicle than in any line at the social welfare office. I refuse either to condemn it or to make peace with it. Where a liberal might see an uneducated slob, where a conservative might see a potential vote (plus an uneducated slob), where certain progressives might see a subculture needing only a little more tolerance for bilingualism to earn an honored place in the Great Rainbow of Cultural Diversity, I see nothing but the waste and degradation of consumer capitalism. True to its progressive cast, the Vermont legislature has recently begun discussing a prohibitive tax on soda in order to prevent childhood obesity. As if soda were the reason children are obese! Who makes the soda? More to the point, what alienating social conditions make the soda—the Coke and the coke—so irresistible?

Once I'm cued in to the concept, this larger poverty dogs me wherever I go. Now some students have taken to complaining in their journals about the "sound quality" of the Ken Burns documentary on Mark Twain they've been watching in class. It's their excuse for not doing the journal assignment that asks them to

respond to the film. On one level, the complaint is valid enough
(the film is a copy and not the best); on another, it's a simple
dodge: most of the kids do the assignment, including the one
who complains most vociferously about the inaudibility of the
film. I'd lay a small fortune that the other with the biggest beef
was mostly impeded by the sound quality of her own incessant
chitchat during the film. On a deeper level, though, I can hardly
blame the kids. This fastidious obsession with visual resolution
and digital sound, irrespective of the quality of the *content
depicted*—what is it but the inevitable result of our gizmo-
hawking market? Vacuity with special effects. We inculcate in
our children the sensibilities of raccoons, a fascination with
shiny objects and an appetite for garbage, and then carp about
"the texting generation" as if thirteen- and fourteen-year-olds
who couldn't boil an egg are capable of creating a culture. They
grow on what we feed them. It has never been otherwise. The
only thing that changes is the food.

On the way back from the doctor's I stop at the state college
library to see if I can get a better copy of the video. I can also test
my strength by walking from the parking lot. I've gotten the red
ball to rise higher in the breath meter though there are still traces
of pneumonia in my lungs. After checking out the film and asking what happened to me, the reference librarian, a brilliant feature of this place for years, tells me of her plan to retire at the end
of the term. She's been helped to her decision by the recent initiatives to shrink the library. She and her colleagues have already
had to sacrifice some of their collection; now they are to lose their
entire periodical wing. The reason is to make room for an endowed
tutorial center just off the library. In a different mind-set I might
see this as a painful but necessary sacrifice; I'd recall the wonderful work done in the academic support areas at the high school.
But it's hard for me today, after six months of teaching and sev-

eral weeks of reflection, not to see the tutorial center and the decimated library as of a piece, not only with each other but with the economic system that contains them both. We sell the disease and we sell the cure, the carcinogenic chemical and the chemotherapy, the high-calorie soda and the exercise bike. We make kids illiterate by shrinking and/or wiring their libraries; then we build wired support centers to teach the illiterates how to read. An iPad for the one and an iPad for the other, twice the profit from the same slick deal. I make it sound more conspiratorial than it is. In fact, it is the absence of conspiracy, of anything approaching a plan or vision, that yields these absurd results. A crapshoot is not a conspiracy, but as social policy it's crap.

I know better than to spend much breath on saying this to the librarian. She doesn't need my homily and she doesn't need my germs, though I've been assured that I'm probably past the point of contagion. The important thing now is regaining my strength, including the physical ability to speak. But I can't stay out forever. I've already used up my fifteen allotted sick days; after using my few remaining personal days, I'll be on unpaid leave. I'm also missing my students, or some of them anyway. The eighth-period class I fantasized about taking to Cancun joins with my seventh-period study hall and sends me an endearing homemade card, a crayon-colored sad sack languishing in bed with an ice bag on his head and a thermometer in his mouth, surrounded by their greetings and signatures. It is possibly an indication of how much I've begun to fade in their memories that one of them can write: "We miss your wonderful face."

Sara includes the card in my relay sack of uncorrected papers. "I think your two morning guys are missing you too," she tells me over the phone. "If he's not back soon," one of them tells her, "we're going to have to go look for him." Perhaps to add emphasis but more probably to discourage her from assuming they've gone soft, his sidekick is quick to add, "Yeah, and we don't even *like* teachers."

Near the end of the month I get my doctor's approval to take my wonderful face back to school. Mr. Messier hires a substitute just the same. If I can't last the day, I'll have coverage; while I'm there, I'll have an aide. His choice of personnel could not be more to my liking: good old Mrs. L., mother of three former students of mine, all grown women now. Well liked by students and staff, she is proof against some bad behaviors, but not all. I've come to her rescue more than once this term when she's been in an adjoining room. My rap is always the same: this is the mother of three former students, and a fine human being, as I'm sure is also true of the students who are giving her a hard time, but they need to let her see their better side. Otherwise, they are going to see my uglier side, because I happen to take any mistreatment of Mrs. L. personally. Now it's her turn to save my bacon, not in the face of misbehavior but as a support to my tentative endurance. She helps me to hand out and collect papers, to monitor small-group discussions, to keep score during the several days of the long-delayed Vocabulary Face-Off. After three days of competition, she helps me tally scores and hand out prizes. I'm also able to do individual writing conferences in a quiet location while she proctors the class.

It's remarkable how much smoother things go with a competent assistant. Some teachers have the benefit of an aide, though strictly speaking the aide is often not the teacher's but a particular kid's. Which is to say that the need for an aide is usually predicated on a handicapping condition in a student, not by the limits of what one human being with two hands and two feet can accomplish in a room full of twenty to thirty kids. It might surprise you, though it shouldn't, that teachers are among the few professionals with no assistants. Think of a doctor without a nurse or a receptionist, a lawyer without a law clerk, a chef without a prep cook, even a clergyperson without an acolyte or deacon. Plumbers and electricians routinely have helpers. Rock musicians have guitar techs. Golfers have caddies. So much for the important professions. A teacher in charge of the educational development of fifty to a hundred diverse and needy human beings is routinely on his or her own.

Oh, to have the offices of a Mrs. L. when I'm running on all eight cylinders! But I know I'm very lucky to have her now. Together we make a whole creature, like the hind and front ends of a horse costume. (Should you be reading this, Mrs. L., be assured that I picture you as the end with ears.) Strictly speaking, a teacher should not leave his or her students unattended; the protocol for an unavoidable bathroom break or a rare summons to the main office is to open the door between adjoining classrooms and ask a neighboring colleague to keep an eye on both classes. With Mrs. L. in the room, I need take no such precautions. I'm able to scurry to the side door of the building, closer than the nearest restroom but still down half a flight of stairs, and spit the fluid I'm still coughing up onto the snow. Hot tea seems to give my voice more mileage (plus another fortifying dose of caffeine), and I can use a lull in the action to walk down the hall and make a cup. Mrs. L. offers to fetch it for me, but I tell her no thanks. I'm a public figure once again; I need to set the right example.

Is it good to be back? In terms of preparation and correction, I've not really been away—I've merely been home, still on the job, submitting my plans and corrected papers by the day. Returning to the bustle of the school day is certainly a shock to the system. But it's good to see the students, and for the most part they seem glad to see me. All but the most hopelessly egocentric make a touching effort not to tax my strength. My Popular Fiction class may prove to be the one exception. The class is too large, too diverse, too restless, too confirmed in habits that are one thing to break in a freshman or sophomore but quite another to break in a junior or senior. Even so, I sense that most of the students are trying to pull with me.

Among my tenth-grade classes, with whom my bonds are stronger, the results of my absence are still palpable. I don't mean that the kids give me grief, only that there is a sense of loss for which *grief* is not an inappropriate word. A parent will understand what I'm getting at; a parent who's lost touch with a child may understand it best. Children are growing all the time. They are not settled civilizations, they are nations coming into their own. The time you miss with them is never entirely recoverable in the way it is with an adult. Grown-ups can catch up; long-lost lovers can get reacquainted after time apart—their bodies may have aged or altered but are mostly the same flesh and fit together in their former ways. This is not to suggest that time lost with a child can't be redeemed; it just can't be recaptured. So I feel a certain sadness at coming back. To be sure, some of this is also about missing the tranquility of my days at home. The books I left unfinished by my living room chair are not likely to be finished any time soon. I pine for them. I'm already pining for the loss of Mrs. L., and she's still here. But mixed with that is the sadness of having missed a small increment of growth in my students' lives. It's like a secret we share, they and I, but are not going to tell each other. Yes, I was truly sick, I didn't cheat, yet somehow it feels as though I betrayed them. I left them in the hands of strangers. I assigned them tasks I couldn't help them do. The reasons are every bit as irrelevant as they are legit. The reasons don't change a thing. I wasn't there.

— 10 —

APRIL

If youth is the season of hope, it is often so only in the sense that our elders are hopeful about us.

—George Eliot, *Middlemarch*

Sara informs me that she's finally heard from my predecessor. He's been traveling in the Far East and touring with his band stateside as part of his unpaid leave of absence. For a while now no one seems to have heard from him, and the silence has generally been taken to mean that he's cut himself loose. Not so, Sara says. He's decided to sign his contract and return next year.

Since the end of August, I've kept his picture taped to the blackboard behind my desk along with my chalked best wishes ("Keep on rockin', Mr. H.") as a way of reminding the students—and me—that the room remains his. No need for such reminders now. There will be no opening in the department, no job for me to apply for on the strength of what I've accomplished this year, no sense of rash impracticality for choosing not to. I consider calling my wife at work to tell her the news, but I already know what she'll say. "You weren't going back there anyway. It was never a question." Maybe not for her.

I feel an extra spring in my step, though I'm still a ways from dancing. There's a quarter of the year yet to go and plenty to negotiate within it. At a department meeting Sara announces that we will be administering the Gates-MacGinitie reading test in our sophomore classes to assess the strengths and weaknesses of our curriculum. Another glitch in my lesson plans. In addition, she's asking that sophomore classes devote some time to practicing for the NECAP (New England Common Assessment Program) tests they'll take next year. Apparently, this has been a strategy for several years running, a preprep preparation for the work juniors will do before their NECAPs in October. The consensus of the department, which to its credit seldom moans about the burden of assessments, or any instructional burden for that matter, is that we ought to do five practice essays based on prompts from past tests. It's been the custom to award students a grade of 100 for every good-faith attempt. This will give my students up to five separate transfusions of fresh blood to their marking period grades, some of which are anemic to say the least. That's the good news.

The bad news, aside from the sudden addition of roughly four hundred pieces of repetitive prose to read and evaluate (everyone writes on the same topic for each practice), is that the NECAP practices amount to a broadside fired at my plans for May and June. I'd planned to finish out the year with a unit on American poetry. Now it seems that Whitman and Dickinson will be competing with such soul-stirring tasks as writing a process analysis paper on "How to Instruct a New Student at School to Use the Cafeteria," with the top scores on the grading rubric reserved for those writers cagey enough to include a "diagram" of the lunch room with their "essay."

I estimate the total liability at around ten days, two per practice: a day to write on each prompt, plus two additional half days apiece for preliminary coaching and postpractice review of the students' performance. I can cut my losses by assigning some of the writings for homework, but that will reduce both my options for assigning other homework and the likelihood that the NECAP work will be completed by all the students. Once again, the demands of standardized testing move to center stage. And once again, we're left to solve a planning puzzle that offers no easy solution.

I keep my complaints to myself. For one thing, my English-teaching colleagues are merely trying to rise to the challenges that originate with powers outside the school. For another, it feels in very poor taste to complain about chores that I am soon not to have. It would be like a prospective parolee grousing about the prison food in front of the lifers. Though I'd be loath to admit it even to myself, I may be relieved to have the formidable task of fostering the comprehension of poetry without ruining its enjoyment tempered by something a bit more flat-footed. Yes, we'd all prefer sitting down in a good restaurant to lining up in the company canteen, but if you're the one doing the cooking, sometimes it's easier just to sling hash.

I won't forgo poetry altogether, though I will have to scrap a tentative unit called "Teach the Geezer." I began working on plans for it over the summer, but I never completed them. The idea was to have students teach me something they knew and I didn't. Units included skills such as fly-casting, dancing, basic sewing, and dressing wild game and subjects such as NASCAR, country-western music, and social networking—all areas in which I have little knowledge or proficiency. Students would have been asked to make lesson plans, practice exercises, and tools for evaluation. Fall probably would have been a good time to try the unit, especially if I wanted to use it as an icebreaker, though a slot in fourth quarter would have made it feel like a culmination, a passing of the instructor's mantle from me to them.

But when I look over the preliminary lesson plans I did for the unit last August, I realize that the kids have already taught the geezer quite a lot. The draft description is wordy, ineffectually humorous, presumptuous (not every student has something he could comfortably teach), and an evaluator's nightmare. I could only have composed such a thing over the summer. There is no time to revise it this April. Still, I think I might have made some form of it work.

As if to confirm April's status as "the cruelest month," three stories appear on the front page of the same local newspaper: a twenty-eight-year-old man drowned after attempting to fly his snowmobile over the Connecticut River in a state of drunken delirium, a two-year-old boy accidentally shot to death by another child with a .22 caliber rifle, and a wretched holdout of a farmer charged with animal cruelty for housing his starving cows in a mire of their own excrement. How the farmer and his family were housed is not mentioned, but I doubt it will produce any arrests.

As far as I know, none of these stories directly involve any student of mine, though I would not be surprised if one did. All of them bespeak what happens to rural communities when small-scale farming and the way of life it supports (the *culture* in *agriculture*) start to fail. If you can imagine Silicon Valley with no silicon you have a fairly good picture of the Northeast Kingdom without a sustainable price for milk.

It has been a little over three years since a fifteen-year-old boy in my town shot and killed his mother's twenty-four-year-old boyfriend in a trailer located on a dirt lane called Freedom Road. The mother suffered from mental illness and her son felt

she was being sexually exploited by the boyfriend. The boy
ordered the man from the house at gunpoint, a struggle ensued,
and the boy shot him. I alluded to the tragedy during a discussion of the school budget at a past town meeting. I said that the
shooter and his victim were "both our sons." Give or take a few
years and miles, they might both have been my students too. It's
impossible that one of them doesn't have at least a distant cousin
in a class of mine.

As the pastures turn emerald and the poplar trees take on
the color that must have inspired Frost to write "Nature's first
green is gold," it's hard to believe that any of these things could
have happened here. If you saw the high school where I teach, its
neat brickwork and parklike grounds, its position atop a hill,
with woods to the west and a view of grazing fields to the east,
you would never imagine the suffering and squalor it conceals.
That is doubtless true of schools all across America, but it is
not supposed to be true of Vermont, a state so evocative of
wholesomeness that its mere name on a bag of potato chips or a
pint of ice cream is what a Catholic cardinal's imprimatur used
to be on a book. Nothing dirty here. But just as one is amazed by
reports of panther scat discovered in woods where it is no longer
possible to get lost, to realize that moose and bear still make their
homes on narrow tracts of land along the interstate, one is repeatedly amazed by glimpses of "the other Vermont" in the newspaper or on the midways of county fairs, even in the aisles of
supermarkets on the days when the assistance checks arrive. I
am capable of believing that such a thing as Bigfoot lurks in the
wilds of Montana or that there are plesiosaurs gliding under the
surface of Loch Ness solely by analogy to the poverty and vio-
lence that lurk behind the deceiving façade of scenic Vermont.

I overhear two girls in my homeroom talking about a fight
between two women in a bar this past weekend. One lost her

husband. The other lost her teeth. An ex-boyfriend brutally beats up the older sister with whom another of my students lives. Moving in with her had seemed a better option than foster care or remaining with her parents, both of them addicts and one on his way to jail. Now the girl is missing school to nurse the battered sister. If I keep coming back to this stuff, it's because it keeps coming back to me.

But not without respite. We get our rations of pride and joy. Word passes like wildfire through the school that Mr. Messier has been selected Vermont's Principal of the Year. No one is surprised by the achievement itself; we are merely surprised to find that the larger world suddenly knows what it's doing. It seems that Mr. Messier's been trying to keep the news under wraps. We're about to unwrap it.

A surprise all-school assembly is organized for the afternoon. A faculty volunteer keeps the principal occupied in his office while over four hundred students and staff members slip as quietly as possible from their classes to the gym. Birnam Wood could not have marched more stealthily to Dunsinane. The happy-birthday mood of conspiracy registers like barometric pressure in the halls. I don't think I've ever seen so many students so expectant as the ones leaning forward from the bleachers. It was here not long ago that Mr. Messier addressed the girls' basketball team during the winter sports awards assembly. They'd come close enough to a state championship to be heartbroken when they didn't take the prize. "You have no reason to be hanging your heads," he had told them, and their heads seemed to lift appreciably as he did. When all the recognitions had been made, he asked the assembled body his familiar question, "Who are we?" There was an unmistakable James Brown vibe when we said it LOUD: "Lake Region!"

So I can anticipate the volume of the ecstatic cry that's coming in another moment, from my own throat as well as everyone else's. My heart sinks just a little when the vice principal calls into his pager—"Mr. Messier, I need you right now in the gym"—because I can imagine the principal's own heart racing as he hurries down from his office, a dozen possible catastrophes scrolling through his mind. He swims before coming to school some mornings and shoots baskets with the kids after lunch, so we can assume his heart is sound. If it survives the next few minutes, it's good for another twenty years at least.

After he has the microphone and the ear of the assembly he loses no time in cutting up his honor, like the slab of cake waiting for him at center court, handing a piece of the credit to every member of his school. *We* are the ones who have made Lake Region an outstanding school; *we* are the ones who put his name in the limelight. Is he also thinking that "we" includes those kids whose deprivations add luster to the school's impressive achievements, though the deprivations remain? That the Cinderella stories of places like ours neglect to mention all the stepchildren who never leave the cinders? "Who are we?"—this time he doesn't pose the question, not aloud, but it has to be on his mind, not least of all today as he sees how much he is loved and is reminded all the more poignantly how much of our welfare is out of his hands.

Mr. Messier is too modest (and, by his own admission, too much of "an emotional guy") to turn his few words of acknowledgment into an acceptance speech, too discreet to start thanking Mom, Dad, and the Virgin Mary (all of whom I imagine he credits), but he would be no more than honest if he offered a word of thanks to his tribe. His surname is generally pronounced like the comparative form of *messy*; other families with the same name say

"MAY-she," but there must have been a time when it was pronounced "May-see-AY," when the bearers, like their descendants
almost to the present day, cut hay and raised cows on well-
managed farms. The best-kept secret about northern New
England is that many of its "old Yankee farmers" were not Yankees at all; they were French Canadians, diaspora cousins of the
Cajuns farther south. But farmers for sure, at least for a time.
There are now fewer dairy farms in the entire state of Vermont
than there used to be in Orleans County alone.

Mr. Messier was raised in that culture of morning chores and
summer fairs, Mass on Sunday and dances on Friday night, once
a kind of norm at Lake Region, now more of an aberration—so
much so that even some kids give voice to agrarian nostalgia,
something you'd scarcely have heard even fifteen years ago.
Teachers are not immune: Not long ago I was talking to a veteran
teacher in northern New Hampshire who told me that his community had lost its last dairy farm several years ago, the final
installment in what he saw as a much greater catastrophe. "When
you had those kids in your class, you could tell them apart from
the others," he said. "Their values were different. The way they
spoke to you was different. You could count on them. And they
were smart too."

I knew what he was talking about, though I also knew enough
not to succumb to romanticism. My resistance is best explained
by the story of a man of my acquaintance, raised on a farm, who
when he was a small boy got it into his head to play an unannounced game of hide-and-seek with his parents. After breakfast
he filched their car keys and locked himself in the trunk of their
car, waiting to be amused by the sound of them calling his name,
anticipating the moment when, after telegraphing his location
through the trunk lid, he'd spring into the sunlight like a jack-
in-the-box. He spent all day in that trunk. He wore his hands

out pounding. No one even noticed he was gone—until it was time for evening chores.

Still, I felt no need to offer my story as a qualification to the New Hampshire teacher's elegy. For the most part my sentiments were in line with his. His words come to mind as I work with my students this year. One of my sophomores gives a talk about his animals. He no longer lives on a farm, but he belongs to a family that farmed for generations, and he has the advantage of a barn for his small menagerie. His unabashed affection for these animals, neither livestock nor pets in any usual sense, is only one vestige of his heritage. Another is his peculiar sense of humor. We've all heard of barnyard humor, but that is merely the subgenre of a broader type, what is commonly called "corny" by people who can't laugh without condescension and know nothing whatsoever about corn. The humor of farm kids grows in part out of working side by side with adults, who like animals have a funny way about them when you study them up close, and in part from the sense of irony derived from dependence on the weather. It's a humor that comes of dropping things and having them kicked over, of getting manure spattered on your clothes. I suppose I could keep it simple and say it's the humor of people who still have contact with the material—as opposed to the virtual—world.

Happily, farm kids are not the only ones who have that contact. I'm refreshed by the range of topics for the process analysis papers my juniors are doing in Composition class, and by the literal hands-on nature of the processes described: how to change the oil in a car, how to bake chocolate chip cookies, how to execute maneuvers in basketball and martial arts, how to sight in a new rifle, as well as how to do a morning round of barn chores. Our young people still know how to "do stuff."

They also know the meaning of work. That was always the

case. The only thing that's changed—a difference very much due to the decline in farms—is the number of kids who travel to their jobs. These days more kids work farther from home, which also means farther from their homework. I have no statistics, but it would not surprise me to learn that more local students are holding down jobs at present than in the heyday of my teaching years in the 1980s. I base my hunch on a tougher economy (albeit one with no shortage of minimum wage service jobs) and a significant increase in "necessities." Now the indispensable vehicle (the preferred term in a region where half the "cars" are trucks) is matched by an equally indispensable cell phone. Since parents are likely to have cell phones too, there are understandable limits on how many "plans" one household can afford. As was always the case with vehicles, if you want one of your own, you're going to have to go out and work for it. To say nothing of households that require an older child's paycheck to make up for a substandard income, a laid-off parent, a missing parent, or some combination of the three.

The idea that a student's main job is *to be a student* is always under stress in a hardscrabble place. It seems to have its best chance when being a student includes being an athlete—a strong argument against the notion that athletics and academics compete for a kid's attention. They often do, but at least the competition is taking place at school. It's probably easier to crack a book in a gym (or a barn) than to smuggle one behind the counter of a Pizza Hut.

I remember sitting at one town meeting next to a father who was clearly proud of his employed son and angry at the elementary school he attended. Not even a teenager, the boy had managed to snag an after-school job for eight dollars an hour, the father told me, which at the time was well above the minimum wage. As for the school and its ever-increasing budget, he had nothing but scorn. The worst of it all, he said, was that "they," the teachers, "teach kids not to work." A strange thing to say. What I think he meant is that the school was teaching his kid that there are things in life that matter at least as much as holding down a job. If that's what he meant, he was right. So was the school.

But I'm not willing to dismiss the father's sentiments out of hand. They come to mind more than once this year, especially when the laudable ideal of "Failure is not an option" begins to make it seem as though futility is. It strikes me that the school often fails to capitalize on the one strength our kids are able to claim in spite of any social and cultural disadvantages that might affect them: they know the meaning of work. Teachers who complain "These kids have no work ethic" couldn't be farther off the mark. The problem is not that these kids lack a work ethic; the problem is that some of them see no connection between a work ethic and school. None of them would think, for example, to say to a customer at the McDonald's drive-up window, "Do you think I could get you those Chicken McNuggets some time tomorrow?" Yet we give sanction to that sort of request when it comes to school assignments. I'm surely not the first teacher to wonder if we might in the long run have cheaper schools *and* higher math scores if we paid students by the hour or at least by the piece. In a society that holds "value" as synonymous with "price," you get what you pay for.

We can't pay, though, so we pander. At a faculty meeting a study hall teacher praises a colleague for hand-delivering duplicate homework assignments to a student who might otherwise fail to bring the originals to his study hall. The voluntary courier then picks up the completed assignments at the end of the period. What is more, the study hall teacher adds, thanks to her colleague's exceptional routine, the student is actually doing his homework in study hall! There's a round of applause such as might occur during an AA meeting, though the teacher sitting next to me rolls her eyes as if to say, "Are these people out of their minds?" The recipient is a decent man and a dedicated teacher; I'd be happy to stand up and applaud him any day of the week. But I have to wonder if his skills are best employed in the capacity of a messenger boy. As for the kid who receives the service, he will undoubtedly go on to be a great success in any field he chooses, so long as its perks include a manservant.

In moments like these I wonder if I've put the wrong spin on the story of the farm boy who locked himself in the trunk of his parents' car. Is it really a tale of parental neglect, of a child with no worth besides his labor? Only if the parents didn't know their son was hiding. What if instead they'd seen him from the kitchen window slip into the car trunk and pull it closed over his head? I happen not to believe they did—but for the sake of argument, what if they had? In that case might they have been trying to impress upon him the kinds of foolishness people living on the edge of subsistence can't afford? Might they have been saying to their son what I have on the tip of my tongue to say at this afternoon's faculty meeting: that a lost sheep and a sheep pretending to be lost are not the same animal? You search for the first one high and low. You're not much of a shepherd if you don't. But if you spend your time running down the pretenders, aren't you telling the rest of your flock that they'd get a sweeter deal if they were lost? Pretty soon lost sheep are the only sheep you've got.

Mark Twain's runaway slave, Jim, expresses something like my indignation when a lost Huckleberry Finn tries to trick him into believing that he was never lost at all. He'd been in a canoe when a combination of fog, swift current, and an unseen island put him some ways from Jim and the raft. But he regains the raft while Jim, exhausted from his frantic attempts to reconnect with his companion, has fallen asleep. When Jim awakes, Huck tries to persuade him that he's dreamed the whole episode.

"I hain't seen no fog, nor no islands, nor no troubles, nor nothing," Huck insists. "I been setting here talking with you all night till you went to sleep about ten minutes ago, and I reckon I done the same. You couldn't a got drunk in that time, so of course you've been dreaming."

To Huck and perhaps to Twain too, Jim is the stereotypically gullible Negro, but reading the episode in my sophomore classes this year, I see him as the archetype of the ever-gullible teacher, or if not gullible then overly prepared to believe that any mistakes must necessarily be his. Jim assumes he must have been dreaming and even begins to interpret the symbolism of his "dream," like a flummoxed teacher searching out the mistakes he must have made in constructing a test that few of his students studied for. But no sooner has Jim succeeded in cloaking Huck's fiction in his own enabling exegesis than Huck points to some very real "leaves and rubbish" on the raft, torn from a tree and gouged from the riverbank during Jim's frantic maneuvers to steer the raft, and slyly asks, "What does *these* things stand for?" What follows is a cri de coeur from Jim—closer than anything I know in literature to the bitterness of a teacher who comes to believe he's been had:

> "What do dey stan' for? I's gwyne to tell you. When I got all wore out wid work, en wid de callin' for you, en went to sleep, my heart wuz mos' broke bekase you wuz los', en I didn' k'yer no mo' what become er me en de raf'. En when I wake up en fine you back agin', all safe en soun', de tears come en I could a got down on my knees en kiss' yo' foot I's so thankful. En all

you wuz thinkin 'bout wuz how you could make a fool uv ole
Jim wid a lie. Dat truck dah is *trash*; en trash is what people is
dat puts dirt on de head er dey fren's en makes 'em ashamed."

Huck was mean; most students who try to trick their teachers are simply lazy, but there are cases when the two overlap. The
first time I felt like Jim was in my rookie year of teaching, when
a senior boy whom I'd painstakingly coaxed along and gener-
ously cut slack for bragged shamelessly in front of me and his
girlfriend, then a freshman of mine, about how he'd bamboozled me the semester before. "Remember when I used to tell you
how I needed more time to write my compositions?" As I recall
he also mocked my praise of work he now boasted of having
slapped together with the least possible effort. I don't regret
helping him and I don't bear him a grudge, though I can't resist
mentioning that he eventually wound up serving on a school
board. I learned some hard lessons that first year, as all fledgling
teachers do, but no teacher learns enough not to get some "dirt
on de head" now and then, and to feel ashamed when she does.

That said, you need to read a whole text to get its full meaning, and the passage about Huck and Jim's reunion is bursting
with further implications. Huck feels bad and apologizes to Jim,
vowing to be a better friend. "I didn't do him no more mean
tricks, and I wouldn't done that one if I'd a knowed it would
make him feel that way." In other words—words that any teacher
does well to adopt as a mantra—Huck is just a kid. He's not yet a
fully formed (or fully moral) human being. He has more growing up to do.

At the same time, Twain reveals the social conditioning that
contributed to Huck's duplicity. Even penitent, Huck remarks,
"It was fifteen minutes before I could work myself up to go and
humble myself to a nigger." Huck is a product of his upbring-

ing, as is the smart aleck raised in the slaphappy folklore of "the teacher we drove nuts," a vein that runs through American literature from Washington Irving to Garrison Keillor. I've known teachers who reminisced fondly in the same vein. *There was this nun . . .*

I'm not sure I ever grasped as fully as I do this year how important it is for an English teacher to see the relevance of a work of literature to his own life. My primary responsibility is to make that connection for my students, but I'll have a hard time making a book come alive for them if it isn't alive for me. *Huckleberry Finn* was never more so.

I begin our class discussions of the novel by asking what questions there were on last night's reading. Invariably we seem to pass from humdrum details of comprehension—not a few caused by Twain's overwrought rendering of dialects, matters best solved by reading the knottier dialogues aloud—to matters more profound: friendship, racism, what it means to be civilized, to be free, to have a conscience. Like Huck and Jim, we let out our fishing lines in the enormous muddy river of this book; every day we pull them in and see what we caught. Some days it's a great bewhiskered lunker, other days something better sized for the pan, but rare is the day we pull up an empty line. I'm sure there must be days when we imitate Huck and Jim in the most wrongheaded ways—they are hardly traveling in the right direction for a runaway slave, down to the Deep South— but I trust the book as they trust their river, notwithstanding the fact that either one can drown you if you're not paying attention.

Resistance to reading continues to dog us; it shows up with the same maddening frequency as those scoundrels the King and the Duke. But it doesn't show up with all the usual kids, so I know that at least a few of them have made a new friend. Others seem not even to try. I break the book into as many bite-sized assignments as the year allows, I set aside class time for reading, and I devise an insurance policy of guaranteed quiz points for every student who gets help with the book in an academic support area. One of the teachers there suggests that my assignments are perhaps heftier than the average of 6 pages per night that I've mentioned to her. In the self-doubting spirit of Jim, I take out my syllabus and break it down with a calculator. It turns out I was wrong about the average. It's 5.8 pages, not 6.

But even in the stagnant, scummy water of self-justification, Jim and Huck don't abandon me. At one point in the novel they come upon a wrecked steamboat and make off with a great trove of books and cigars. They devote several days to smoking the cigars and poring over the books. I needn't be reminded that I am in the hands of an author who made his living from books and spent a hefty portion of it on cigars. Naturally he projected his favorite enthusiasms onto his favorite characters. But Twain was also keen to create characters his readers would find credible—a necessity for any writer who needs to move units to keep himself in smokes—and he doesn't seem to find any lack of verisimilitude in a rough-and-tumble kid and an illiterate slave regarding a salvaged library as real booty. I point this out to my students. I even point it out to the tutor when I tell her, "It's 5.8."

Resistance to reading is hardly my only problem. I have a black student in one of my classes—a minority of one in that section—and I wonder how he'll feel about Jim and the word *nigger*. Before deciding to assign the book, I talk this over with Sara, who says that he needs to confront the issues that have caused the book to be banned in other schools, needs to find his own response, and might as well do that with the help of a teacher who at least realizes the issues are there. As it turns out, the student leaves school before he can see Jim freed. That means he's also spared the nearly unbearable final chapters of the book, when the narrative sinks to the level of sadistic minstrelsy, with Huck and Tom Sawyer subjecting Jim to every conceivable indignity in order to make his emancipation more suitably romantic. Tom has derived these fancies from books, so Twain might be the first person to line up with his critics and say, "Be careful what you read and how you read it."

Even those insufferable chapters speak to my situation as a teacher. If Huck and Jim on the river show us the wonderful possibilities of one-to-one interaction between teacher and student, the reappearance of Tom Sawyer (along with the introduction of Aunt Sally) suggests the fragility of those possibilities when same-age peers begin to exert pressures on the mix. Once Huck has his old playmate back again, Jim doesn't stand a chance.

Poor Jim, but he has made me richer. He reads the water for me, and he tells me where the dangers are. He still castigates himself for striking his little daughter, who he thought was obstinately ignoring him when it turned out she was deaf. Sometimes a kid really can't hear you, Jim reminds me. It isn't the kid's fault. As for the wisdom of Solomon, who'd cut a baby in half just to settle an argument, Jim has no use for it:

> "De 'spute warn't 'bout a half a chile, de 'spute was 'bout a whole chile; en de man dat think he kin settle a 'spute 'bout a whole child wid a half a 'chile, doan' know enough to come in out'n de rain. Doan' talk to me 'bout Sollermun, Huck, I knows him by de back."

Jim has never taught school, but he knows how school policies can take precedence over kids. He's never met my students either, but he knows what they're worth. He'd perform dismally on the Gates-MacGinitie reading test, but he knows the value of books.

Even if he can't read them himself, he knows it's still sweet to hear the stories, sweeter still if you have the company of lively young people, as I do, and the pleasure of a good cigar, as (alas) I don't.

Maybe thanks to Jim, maybe because my limited time in this job has finally been confirmed, and certainly because she has proven herself the most approachable of colleagues, I finally open my heart to the school librarian about the banished Library of America books.

Since their brief farewell appearance in a display window, they've sat like unclaimed luggage in the squat wheeled shelves on which they were ignominiously rolled from the library to the rear of Sara's classroom last September. In grim moments I've thought of soliciting permission to erect shelves in some corner of a stairwell, of adding a lamp and an easy chair to create a makeshift reading room, an alternative library as it were, where passing students could camp out and at least pretend to read the books. I've thought of organizing an extra-credit project in which students would each adopt a volume of the Library of America, familiarize themselves with it, and then in a culminating procession conduct the exiled collection to its new home under the stairwell like the banished Furies being installed under the hill of the Acropolis, only with more of a Mardi Gras flavor. But in addition to being too much work, such measures are likely to be interpreted as an affront to the librarian. Or as evidence that I've gone completely over the edge.

So I tell the librarian what's been weighing on my mind for months, prefacing my remarks with deferential disclaimers about not wishing to presume on her authority or disrespect her good work—needless precautions given that she has done everything short of walking about the school with a suggestion box and a retriever monkey to garner input. But I know I can come on strong, and this is a subject about which I feel passionate. It turns out I do not have the passion all to myself.

"I felt terrible about moving those books from the library," she tells me. "They'd been collected over all those years." But she needed the shelf space for new books, and no one had checked them out or asked their students to consult them. In the end she'd done her triage in the most sensible way, by feeling for a pulse. There wasn't one.

I spare her any condescending spiels about the prerogatives of great literature though I do tell her about the student I had who read Montaigne and Saul Bellow in her free time and went on to write her doctoral dissertation on Keats. I can't resist adding one appeal to the heart by saying that every time I think of those books "not belonging in the library" I feel as though I don't belong there either. I'm not speaking as an author but as an English teacher. In fact, I go on to tell her, every time I remember that several of *my* books remain in the library while these others remain in exile, I feel embarrassed. If it made a difference, I'd be happy to see mine removed in order to make room for a few of the others. A bit melodramatic, that, but I'm about to make my pitch.

"If you were to find a space in the library for a narrow, upright bookcase—and I confess to having a location in mind—I would like to leave as my legacy to the school a bookcase that could be devoted to those Library of America volumes. If you were willing to readmit them. I'd pay for the shelves myself, no purchase order necessary, and you would choose the catalog and the shelf."

She doesn't say she needs time to think about the idea. She wants to do it. I'm relieved she doesn't suggest a brass plaque with my name. I'm even more relieved when she says I won't have to pay for the shelves.

Spring break marks the first school vacation when I have not been ill, and I celebrate with a free-for-all of physical work. I stack firewood. I burn brush. I prune trees, including the crab apple tree my expository writing students gave to me in 1985 as a housewarming gift. It was about twenty inches high then and now stands a good twelve feet, with a span of branches almost as wide. It will be awash with white blossoms by the time of final exams. "Time to plant trees is when you're young," wrote the Vermont poet James Hayford, "So, aging, you can walk in shade / That you and time together made." Several years ago I realized I had heard from no fewer than seven of my former students in a single month: a gay anarchist agitator, a hairdresser, a college professor, a guidance counselor, a dairy farmer, a Web designer, and a felon, three females and four males, all very different but all contributors to the shade that I and time together made. I continue to wonder how much richer my life might have been had I never left teaching. I've met people willing to wonder the same thing on my behalf.

One of the more remarkable and, I think, telling things about the teaching trade is the number of people who need to believe that you love it. Ever since I left the classroom in the midnineties and throughout the past year people have asked if I missed teaching or had plans to take it up again. They didn't want to know; they wanted to hear me say yes. Some didn't bother to ask. "I know the pay is not the greatest, but of course you love it," says a former student, now a thriving local entrepreneur whose income is probably triple mine. The sentiment always puts me in mind of the trope of the happy slave. In fact, our word *peda-*

gogue derives from a Greek word for a type of slave who led children to school. Jim is Huck Finn's teacher not only in spirit but in accordance with an ancient tradition. I am not suggesting that contemporary teachers are slaves or that I was ever treated like one, only that I am inclined to distrust people who expect me to work for love or who need a sentimental mythology to gloss over the impossibilities of teaching and the daily injustices it lays bare.

Mr. Messier never asks me if I love my job. He does often say that he hopes I am enjoying my year at Lake Region. He tells me that I was important to him when he was a high school student and that I am having a similar impact on students this year. He says that he thinks of me as the school's "artist in residence"; apparently he does not think the artisan teacher needs to die. Or that the pastoral principal is a relic of the past. At the close of every day, he walks the students to the buses, his figure unmistakable even with the hood of his windbreaker up. He walks back into the building when the last bus is gone, and I feel that I know exactly what he is thinking, that he has seen his kids off for another day, only wishing he could see every one of them safely home, especially the ones who dread going.

Though my role in his formation is minimal at best, I am unabashedly proud of him, and I would be even if he never got to be Principal of the Year. I can't say with wholehearted conviction that I love teaching. I do love him, and others I have taught who are very different from him. Yet, even with that love and its incomparable satisfactions, I am counting off the days until I can go home for good.

Scores of days and hundreds of "teachable moments" remain before that can happen, however; every week something new. I

almost can't believe what I'm seeing when the door to my classroom opens during my fourth-period Popular Fiction class and
a teaching colleague of mine delivers a small boxed pizza and
several other takeout orders to some girls in my class, including
at least one of the sparkly girls who were identified for me as
"the posse." He does not knock before entering nor does he say a
word to me coming or going. The girls coo their thanks—speaking
his surname as though it were his first, no Mister, no big deal—
and that is that. None of them open up their parcels. No one can
accuse them of eating in class. I let go of my breath and continue
teaching.

After doing a reality check with Sara, who seems more infu-
riated by the incident than I am, I approach the teacher after
school. I see no point in taking up the issue with the girls, who
would only use it as a pretext to foment the collegial tiff I am
hoping to avoid. The teacher has been kind to me in the past; on
several matters of technological difficulty, he's been an invaluable help. I do my best to give the word *disrespectful* a friendly
context. I am careful not to ask if the delivery was his idea or the
girls'. It's a minor point anyway: he is the adult and my colleague,
the one who should have known better.

He apologizes immediately. He says he never meant to show
me any disrespect. He seems surprised that anyone could think
so. No, no, he never intended that. From someone else I might
regard the apology as disingenuous, but from him I can only
regard it as sincere. In other words, I find him almost too naive
to be disingenuous. If he doesn't know how capable his pizza-
eating protégées are of turning on him in an instant, he's a babe
in the woods.

Before that happens, they will turn on me. Or one of them
will. I'm not sure if the pizza incident lit the fuse on a bundle of
tensions or if they'd have exploded anyway, but I think of it as

the ominous sizzle that precedes my worst day of the year. It begins the day after the delivery and in the same class.

We start the period with a Mickey Mouse quiz on the previous night's reading assignment. I have repeatedly asserted in all my classes, both orally and in writing, that I will never, except in cases of sudden illness, negotiate an individual postponement of a quiz or test once a class is in session. Negotiations of that kind should take place in the morning, before school begins, not only out of respect for the student's privacy but also in recognition of the rights of those students who come to class prepared and are entitled to expect something better than auditing someone else's (usually lame) excuses. Nevertheless, I have six students, exactly one third of the class, attempt to talk me out of taking their quiz. It is the last week of April. They have had three and a half months to learn the rule about in-class negotiations, three and a half months to adjust to my bizarre expectation that students taking a "reading elective" are actually going to read. Those with better than spotty attendance have also heard me say that I consider preparedness a matter of social responsibility. Students who don't read the assignments don't just lower their grades; they deprive their classmates of their insights. I know I wasn't dreaming when I said this, but I wonder for a moment if I'm dreaming now.

Only a sadist would subject the reader to an account of all half dozen excuses; I will confine myself to the prize. One of my students has spent her April break and another week besides vacationing with her family in Jamaica. Prior to beginning her extended absence she had all her teachers sign the official sheet indicating that she had received the assignments she would miss, a school requirement for any student with a planned absence. I signed her sheet, gave her the homework, and told her to have a good time. I never raise an eyebrow at absences like these, though some teachers do and perhaps I should. But I can't help seeing them against the background of mortality. Years ago a boy approached me and asked what I thought about his taking some days off from school to go duck hunting with his father. I told him that I hoped his father would live to a ripe old age, but given the tendency of fathers to check out of this world unexpectedly, he probably ought to go hunting with his father while he could. "Get yourself some ducks, and when it's too dark to shoot, read your book." He did both.

In this case, though, the girl appears dumbfounded that I would have expected her to read. "I was in Jamaica!" she whispers wide-eyed. (Later in the day she will vent to another teacher: "How can you expect somebody to read in Jamaica!") For a moment we must resemble one of those cartoon encounters between an alien and an earthling. We don't scream and our hair doesn't stand on end, but it's a similar instance of mutual incredulity. A reader possessed of no more than the very crudest class consciousness probably pictures some spoiled rich girl scowling as she twists the ends of her hundred-dollar haircut with her manicured fingers. In fact, this girl is neither spoiled nor rich nor given to scowling, though I suppose that if her family can spend two weeks in Jamaica she hardly qualifies for the lumpen proletariat. Still and all, I wonder if any spoiled rich girl would stoop to such an excuse. A trip to Jamaica would be no big deal to such a kid. She'd have no sense of a once-in-a-lifetime opportunity profaned by a teacher's reading assignment. It flashes through my mind that, once again, I'm dealing with poverty even when I'm not, strictly speaking, dealing with poverty.

For the most part, though, what flashes through my mind with the numbing repetitiveness of a strobe light is that I'm dealing with farce. I have a class full of high school juniors and seniors for whom *required* reading remains a novel idea. I have at least some students for whom placing a fast food order with a

teacher is a perfectly tenable idea. I have a colleague ready, willing, and able to deliver the order piping hot to their desks. Worst
of all, I have a class full of students who, in spite of all kinds of
cooperative learning exercises, not to mention the most ostenta-
tious displays of "school spirit," seem not to have much care for
one another's welfare. Time and again I break them into heterogeneous groups to tackle some task, urging them to leave no one
out, *rewarding* them for leaving no one out, only to watch as the
strongest show the least regard for the weak, isolating them not
only from the work at hand but from any part in the shenanigans that enliven the work. And now two of my brightest are
talking with the quiz still in progress. And now you are going to
see me not at my best.

I start out well enough, though I'd have done better merely
to make note of the infraction, collect the quizzes, and give
each student the zero she knows is the consequence for talking
during a test. Instead—call this mistake number one—I ask the
two to speak to me outside the room. I'm concerned by what I
perceive as the brazenness of the infraction; it wasn't something
I "caught" so much as something I felt I was meant to see. Need
I say that none of this has to do with cheating? Both students
had turned their quizzes face down on their desks when they
began to talk. Neither was among the six who tried to excuse
themselves from the evaluation. What this has to do with is the
common courtesy that I expect even the smartest kid to show
and even the slowest kid to enjoy. In a feeble attempt to make the
concept of mutuality better understood, I try putting it on a different footing.

"Have I ever disrespected either of you?" I ask. "Because if I
have, I want you to tell me when and how so I can apologize."
Both say no. Why then have they broken a rule that they know is
important to me? One girl, who broke the silence merely to

answer the question put to her by the other, is obviously regretful, maybe for my sake, probably for the sake of her grade. (And I wonder later if she was thinking to herself: He tolerated the effrontery of having hot food delivered to certain special characters during a class discussion without a single word of protest, and now he's lecturing me about disrespect?) The other girl is of a more explosive temperament. "Go ahead and give me the friggin' zero," she says. As I ought to surmise, her ire probably has very little to do with me. More likely it has to do with whatever set of intolerable conditions prevented her from reading her assignment, perhaps with the fact she is *never* one to make excuses or ask for a break. Possibly she is also losing patience with a man she perceives as a tiresome pedant, utterly oblivious to the world outside his precious books.

In any case she goes on to say, "I'm the type of person who when she wants to say something she just says it." In other words, I counter, the type of person who makes her own rules. "Yes," she says. Before I can check the impulse to sarcasm, I say, "Then I wish you luck in the world as it is." "Oh," she says, "I imagine I'm going to be pretty lucky." Does she really? I'm not sarcastic when I say, "I hope you truly are."

That's the end of the discussion, during which I'm sure there have been further, much more egregious interruptions of the testing session—to say nothing of the tension I've added by stepping out of the room. (As an aside, I'll note that Mr. Messier is out of the building today, and though the school always runs smoothly on the rare occasions when he's absent, I sense a psychic ripple in the building when he's gone.) Even here, I have the opportunity to cut my losses if I'll take it, but I don't. Part of my problem is that I'm not sure there's all that much to lose. Respect? Good will? I'm granting requests from the sublime to the ridiculous from the minute I step into this building until the minute I go home; is it too much to ask that a couple of mine could also be granted?

I've not been keeping count, but by this point we must be up to my fourth or fifth mistake, which consists of turning from my hallway conference to vent my frustrations (not a mistake unless you do it *while you're frustrated*) by telling the entire class I've just about had it with the lack of preparation, the constant excuses, the flouting of a few simple rules, and not least of all the smug attitudes of people who either can work faster than their peers or else are beyond caring one way or another about their own academic performance. Is this what our much-touted school spirit comes down to, yelling at pep rallies and then treating our classmates as though they're beneath contempt?

"You're judging us!" a student calls out, though I suspect she has already judged herself in the light of what I've said and is not happy with what she sees. "You don't know what we're thinking!" She's right, I say. I am judging, and I don't know what other people are thinking. But I'm not judging *people* or attempting to read their minds. I'm judging the only thing I can judge. I write two words on the blackboard, rapidly and in large letters: THOUGHTS and ACTIONS. In the process my chalk breaks in my hand. I pick up another piece and finish. I point to the second word and say, "This is all anybody can judge. Listen: all your life you're going to meet people who *think* they're not racists—'Don't get me wrong, I've got nothing against black people'—but if their actions say otherwise, what are you left to conclude?"

Mistake number whatever-we're-up-to-now: using analogies with people who almost always see them as literal comparisons. Add to that the mistake—perhaps the worst of the bunch—of addressing an entire class on matters that do not, in all particulars, refer to every member of the class. The problem with the mind-set that would seek the one lost sheep at the expense of the ninety-nine is the real risk of haranguing the ninety-nine for always getting lost. And if that happens to be accurate, as is close to being the case here, it's a piss-poor way to say thanks to the one or two sheep who've never once given you a lick of trouble.

I might be able to acknowledge these exceptions, but nothing I have to say is permitted development, qualification, half a chance. For one thing, I'm still susceptible to bouts of coughing. For another, I'm being challenged before I can complete my thoughts. Finally, one of the students—the one who's the type of person to say what's on her mind no matter what—becomes so abrasive that I ask her to go to the principal's office, something I've not done with any student since the beginning of the year. On her way out she refers to my breaking of a piece of chalk as evidence that I am "out of control." When a friend gets up to go with her, I remind her that I've not given her permission to leave. She doesn't care. Sensing the potential for momentum, a third girl stands up from her desk—one of the pizza recipients from yesterday—walks to the door, and exhorts the entire class to follow her to the office. "Come on, guys," she says. She has no takers. When the other girl who'd been talking during the quiz meekly asks if she can go to the guidance office, a request I never refuse, the number of exiles grows to four.

Suddenly the room feels eerily quiet. The silence is broken by a young man who sits near the back of the room, not my best student but possibly my most mature and without a doubt my volunteer fireman of choice (he has a beeper on his belt and the insignia of his town squad tattooed on his shoulder) should I ever be so out of control as to yell "Fire!" when I'm burning alive. "Well, now that they've left," he says dryly, "we can get something done."

Everything in our brief history leads me to believe he is saying this in support, though it might also be his politic way of saying that I have allowed a few students and a few of my frustrations to waste a lot of our time. I will pay for that mistake in kind. So will other students, who will lack my full attention in the classes that follow. First, I need to find time to speak to my department head. I can always count on her to be in my corner, but I never want her blindsided by any action of mine. She sizes up the incident even before I can finish my account. It's part of a larger pattern, she says, and I'm relieved to discover she doesn't mean any pattern of mine. By her count this is the third time one of these girls has attempted to stage a mass walkout and the first time it didn't succeed. In one instance the walkout accompanied— Sara does not say it caused—a teacher's termination partway through the year.

I'm glad she tells me this. Without that information I might be even more stunned than I am when a girl from the class asks me later in the day if I'm "going to be fired." "Why on earth would you think I was going to be fired?" I ask. "I don't know. I just don't want you to be." I'm also glad when a teacher from another department sticks his head in my door and says, "You're not the first to have a run-in with this crew. Hold the line."

But there is no line to hold, not really. I give my account to the vice principal, who has already heard my defectors' version, in which the broken piece of chalk figures prominently. I'm momentarily stunned when he says he's randomly asked other students in the class for an account of what happened. Sara later tells me that given the individuals involved this was a prudent move on his part. For now, I can't help but feel hurt that my word is not enough. "And what did the other students tell you?" I ask. "Exactly what you told me," he says, adding that he is not surprised. He's already decided on his course of action. The students who left class without permission will be given a "cut" and disciplined accordingly. The student sent to the office for rudeness will serve a detention or face further consequences. Parents will be notified of the actions taken, as will Mr. Messier when he returns to school.

In my account of what happened I felt I should mention the pizza incident of the day before. The vice principal is keen to know the name of the teacher who delivered the goods—adding that "Mr. Messier would very much want to know this"—but I say I can't tell him. The teacher apologized to me when I approached him, and it would be disgraceful to name him now. I only brought up the incident, I say, to describe the climate in which these events occurred.

No doubt I also brought it up to look as sympathetic as possible. The matter has been settled so definitively, and so clearly in my favor—but with a cool objectivity, too—that I'm feeling uneasy. Any teacher might, and any person who thinks that schools will always take a teacher's side (or should) has never worked in a school. Some years ago in a school very close to mine, a teacher's aide went to her principal to report that she'd seen one of the eighth-grade boys exposing himself and urinating outside the school. She hoped to report her observation anonymously but the principal would have none of that. An accomplished practitioner of "conflict resolution," he told the aide to remain right where she was while he called the boy down to the office to confront his accuser.

"Mrs. Miller says she saw you expose yourself and urinate in front of the school. Did you do that?"

"Nope."

"Then why did Mrs. Miller say that's what you were doing?"

"Dunno."

"Do you think it's possible," the principal offered in complete seriousness, appealing to Mrs. Miller as well as the boy, "that you were holding a bottle of soda and spilled some of it accidentally in a way that made it look like you were doing what Mrs. Miller thinks you were doing?"

"That's it!" said the boy. "That's what happened." Problem solved, though that is not the punch line. Mrs. Miller happens to have a husband and four sons, which, though it hardly qualifies her to sit on the Supreme Court, does give her impeccable credentials as an expert witness in any case involving the difference between a urinating penis and a spilling bottle of soda. I don't take it for granted that I've fared much better than Mrs. Miller.

And still I'm uneasy. In the course of our conversation, as he's giving me all the support any teacher could want, the vice principal makes an observation that takes me aback no less than "I was in Jamaica!" and "Are you going to be fired?" Conceding that the students who came to the office were exaggerating for effect, he notes: "Now if you'd broken a piece of chalk deliberately because you were upset, I could understand how they might be afraid."

Really? Not if I'd thrown the chalk across the room or aimed it at one of them, or forced the chalk into one of their hands, or chalked an insult on their desks or persons, but if I broke a piece of chalk deliberately, in my own hand, in my own frustration at being ignored, provoked, and then defied, that might give a person pause? *A piece of chalk?*

Well, I know I did not break the piece of chalk deliberately, and none of my students would be frightened if I did. I'm actually more prone to break chalk in a good mood than in a bad one. I teach with fervor, I write with vigor, and I write my words large. I'm as likely to drop my chalk into the tray as to place it there when I'm done. I'm breaking chalk all the time. My classroom floor is littered with it. Most days my clothes are covered with dust. The ghost of my scrawl remains on the blackboard even after I've erased the words.

And yet, like Twain's Jim, who's ready to believe that he dreamed his separation from Huck until he sees the condition of the raft, I actually go to the chalk tray in my classroom to see if it looks as I remember it. I examine its contents like a cancer candidate checking his stools for blood. It is full of white and yellow nubs of chalk, many of them worn to uselessness. But is there broken chalk? Yes, there is a quantity of broken chalk—not a single accusatory piece, implicating me in a trauma, but the humdrum litter of fragments I expect to find. I am not an evil teacher. I do not deliberately break chalk.

At the close of what feels like the longest day of the school year, I stand outside my classroom as the students make their way down the hall to the buses. It's my customary place at this time of day, as is true for a number of my colleagues, who use the opportunity for an extra word of cheer, a final reminder, the swooping up of an assignment that was due "no later than three this afternoon." It feels like a good day to remain at my desk, I've had enough interactions to last me a month, but I'm determined to show I'm still here, still spiffy and shameless in my chalk-dusted jacket and tie.

As the last stragglers begin to pick up their pace to a slow run, a girl halts in front of me and blurts out, "You're the greatest, Mr. Keizer!" That's all. The final stun-gun moment in a day full of them. I don't ask why she would say this, though I might well wonder. She's not in any of my classes. I'm not even sure I know her name. We've had a few friendly exchanges, many of them outside the door of the special education classroom where she spends a good part of each day, nothing beyond a few words.

But I bet I know what she's trying to tell me. In fact, I'm in the mood this afternoon to place all kinds of bets. I bet, for example, that she heard about my little set-to less than an hour after it happened. I bet she knows all the key players by name. I bet she knows them better than I do, and I bet she knows at least one of them better than she wishes she did. Oh, but these are all bets I could lose. Best put my money on surer things. I bet nobody ever fetched this kid a pizza in the middle of her fourth-period class.

— 11 —

MAY

"Think about something cheerful, old man," he said. "Every minute now you are closer to home."

—Ernest Hemingway, *The Old Man and the Sea*

Osama bin Laden is killed on the second day of the month. I'm expecting a barrage of comments, in anticipation of which I decide to let Homer speak my piece. From top to bottom on my blackboard I write a dozen lines from *The Odyssey*, what Odysseus says after he has slain the suitors and his faithful servant Eurykleia is about to rejoice. "No crowing aloud," he tells her, though he's willing to add that the suitors got what they deserved. "To glory over slain men is no piety."

The last time I did something like this was back in September, when two soldiers from a Northeast Kingdom town were killed in Afghanistan. I chose the Who for my spokespersons, writing the names of the soldiers on the blackboard "in memoriam" before playing the song "Young Man Blues" (the live version from Leeds). That was a matter of five minutes between classes, just enough time to permit Roger Daltry a few feral repetitions of the "nuthin" that is a young man's allotted portion "these days." I leave the lines from Homer up for the better part of a week.

Still, no one asks me what they mean or what they are doing on my blackboard. As nearly as I can tell, no one reads them. For that matter, no one mentions Osama bin Laden. At the close of the third day there is nothing left for me to do but erase the lines and go for a haircut, which in my case involves reducing a half inch of salt-and-pepper thatch to a maintenance-free quarter and which I know will infallibly arouse keen interest and lively comment (all of it sweet) the next day.

On other fronts, the written word is holding its own. We're doing drama now and soon to start poetry. I wish I hadn't put them off until late spring. I discover how much the students enjoy reading aloud—especially what was always meant to be read that way. Girls vie for the part of Emily in *Our Town*; the unlikeliest boys take a shot at Whitman's *Song of Myself.* I come to suspect that it is not reading my students hate so much as reading in isolation. The same radical privacy that I seek in books, my mind's way of eating its lunch alone, is what turns their stomachs. I learn of two girls in my tenth-grade classes who got through *Ethan Frome* by reading aloud to each other over Skype, not unlike George Gibbs and Emily Webb chatting between their upstairs bedroom windows, just with different kinds of windows. They are acutely *social* creatures, these kids, and it is a slow learner indeed who fails to grasp that fact even as he prattles on about building a more social democracy.

The relative brevity of the genres, as well as the empty spaces on the page between poetic stanzas and lines of dramatic dialogue, works in our favor too. For several years now (perhaps as my closeted answer to the question "Do you miss teaching?") I've kept a notebook for a reading curriculum I hope to develop someday. It would be aimed at the most marginal teenage readers and incorporate some of the world's most venerated texts. The linchpin of the program would be the use of radically short genres: the aphorism, the slogan, the haiku, the epigram, the epitaph, the joke, etc. The twin objectives would be to put the noses of nonreaders in books for part of each day and to lift their chins the rest of the time. When college-bound peers turned aside from their SparkNotes summaries of *Beowulf* long enough to ask, "So what're you reading, Rodney," Rodney could answer, "Nothing much. Just Pindar and Lao-tzu and them guys." A mere three lines of text could easily inspire as many pages of prose and as many periods of class discussion. Instead of giving remedial readers baby bottles of formula fiction you'd be giving them shot glasses of 100-proof insight. This week "Awake and sing, all ye who dwell in dust," next week "Workers of the world unite!" As I said, someday. Right now I have gems aplenty with Emily Dickinson's packed quatrains and the more imagistic pieces of William Carlos Williams, who also gives us plums "so sweet / and so cold."

Reading poetry with my sophomores reminds me of reading it when I was a sophomore myself, when a twenty-two-year-old raven-haired beauty named Miss Pombo inspired me to raze "electrical engineer" from my future horizon and write "poet" in its place. I can hardly hope to have the same impact. Her enthusiasm for her students and for what she taught was irrepressible; even my skeptical father was prompted to say to her after a parent-teacher conference, "You were born to teach." And he hadn't even had the experience of listening to her read from Lawrence Ferlinghetti's *A Coney Island of the Mind* as she dangled her dusky legs from the edge of her desk. I wasn't the only boy who took a keen interest in all things literary that year. Ferlinghetti marked the beginning of my lifelong love affair with New Directions paperbacks, and I suppose that for a time I also

had a crush on my teacher. Perhaps it showed; a female classmate rubbed my back consolingly after we saw Miss Pombo take
the arm of the business education teacher one night after the
showing of a film in the school auditorium. "Poor Garret," she
sighed, seeming to hint that I might consider paying more attention to women my age. Eventually I would come under the wing
of the business teacher too, who lent me Sartre's *Nausea* to read,
another New Directions paperback, and who made the administration itchy by growing a beard. When the couple married a
few years later, they invited me to write a poem for their wedding. I was out of high school by then and publishing poetry in
little magazines, but I owed my initiation to Miss Pombo, who'd
also set me up for Sartre by writing the word *existentialism* on
her blackboard.

In past years this would be around the time I'd be introducing the same word to my Advanced Placement English class, a
bonus lecture as we worked our way through Beckett, Kafka,
and Camus. I have no hankering to do such a thing this year, no
more than I have to be teaching AP, but the lecture comes to
mind with the scent of cut grass wafting through my classroom
window. Most of my seniors were less than enamored with the
Continental authors, less impressed than I thought they'd be by
Gregor Samsa's metamorphosis, but they loved the existential
stuff. It wasn't unusual to have a few of them claim to have
found, at long last, an identifier they could live with. Their
fathers were hippies or Republicans; they were existentialists. At
the time I construed their enthusiasm as of a piece with their
enjoyment of Anne Rice and Stephen King, their counterpart to
my classmates' fascination with the Hell's Angels and the Doors.
It was scary and dark, this stuff about a godless universe
(Kierkegaard never impresses an adolescent imagination so well
as Nietzsche) and radical free will, the imperative to make one's

own meaning in the face of death, the decision to stay in bed on a school day clarified as the destiny of creatures *condemned to choose*. This year, though, I find myself wondering if the existential leanings of those AP kids had more to do with the similarities between their daily routine as students and the notion that existence is absurd. What better title for an anthology that included *The Myth of Sisyphus, The Penal Colony,* and *Waiting for Godot* than *Three Ways to Look at High School*?

Such thoughts as these come with the season. May can be an absurd month, fraught with seemingly meaningless interruptions, a feckless teacher's windfall but a conscientious teacher's nightmare come true. No upended cockroach ever felt so immobilized; all my little legs are going at once, but I'm going nowhere. A guidance counselor informs me that over half my third-period sophomores will be fifteen minutes late for class in order to complete their course sign-ups for next year. The day before that, a science class canoe trip—the rivers are finally iced out—took a quarter of my first-period Composition class. Other field trips dependent on spring weather and clear roads are sure to follow. Next week classes have been shortened to accommodate AP exams. The NECAP practice essays remain an ongoing part of the English regimen, and I'm still arranging makeups for the kids who missed all or part of the Gates-MacGinitie reading test we gave in April. Graduation practice, the prom, and "senior skip day" (as hallowed as it is unauthorized) are still a ways off, but preparations are already in the air.

For all that, I take a particular pleasure in this May, and I think it owes to more than balmy weather and the realization that—to paraphrase Shelley—if May is here, June can't be far behind. I've accomplished most of what I hoped to, and I have enough experience under my belt to know that "most" is the best a teacher (or any other mortal) dares hope for. I also know from past experience to approach the end of the year with diminished expectations—to plan for it as though it contained fewer days than the calendar indicates, which in point of fact it does.

The Popular Fiction class I feared I might have lost has pretty much come around. I've approached the "mopping up" of last month's debacle with the best strategic combination I know: scrupulous preparedness, a touch more formality, zero tolerance for the slightest testing of the rules, unflappable calmness when meting out the consequences, and unconditional acceptance of every step taken toward reconciliation. I've not adjusted a single one of my classroom requirements, nor would I consider doing so—first, because I continue to believe they're right, and second, because any retreat now would be disastrous. That said, I try to remember what I have too often forgotten to my peril: as far as teaching goes, when all you are is right, what you really are is in trouble. As the Israeli poet Yehuda Amichai wrote: "From the place where we are right / flowers will never grow." Had I managed to be just a little more than right when things started blowing up in my face, perhaps nothing more than a bit humorous, I might have had a few flowers to pick for consolation.

As it turns out, I get the flowers anyway. They arrive in May, when the other north country flowers begin to bloom. One of them comes from a private conversation with one of my former mutineers, whom I discover walking the halls one day with tearstained cheeks and bloody knuckles. I have nothing to do with the reason she punched the girls' room wall, but perhaps she's able to see me as someone who might understand how a person could. I am, after all, a man who writes with enough passion to break chalk. I try to help her put her troubles in perspective. I recall (but do not quote) a school bus driver who told me once that the reason young people commit suicide is that they haven't lived long enough to realize that most situations improve if we wait another day. That sounded wise, though not all of us will manage to live as long as the driver did. I hope this young woman will. I praise what I've observed of her integrity, her intelligence and fierce heart—what I wish I'd expressed more emphatically before now. I also coax her to let me escort her to the nurse's office. I wish her luck as I take my leave, but not aloud. I wouldn't want to sound sarcastic or give the impression that the best thing she has going for her is luck. It isn't.

Other flowers come from the same rocky May schedule in which it seems nothing will grow. A combination of absences, some of them prom-related, reduces the Popular Fiction class to a motley handful, including some of my poorest-performing students and some of my brightest. Not all of them will skip the prom but apparently none of them feel any need to skip school the day before. We're in the midst of discussing Jon Krakauer's *Into the Wild*. (As it's been taught in recent years, Popular Fiction includes popular nonfiction whose authors have taken discernible imaginative liberties.) Suddenly what I've thought of as my weakest class yields one of the best discussions of the year. Almost everyone participates. No one seems cowed by anyone else, and some of the questions raised are as good as anything I used to get in AP. It's like watching a pickup game of basketball where the only object is to keep the ball in motion and to see it swish through the net as often as the laws of physics allow. The students pass ideas from one to another; they're quick to lift any player who falls. "This is what I think Justin might be trying to say." Dribbling faster than anyone on the court, taking the longest shots, snatching one another's rebounds almost as soon as they're off the rim are the two girls who zeroed out for talking during last month's quiz. They're not vying for points, merely showing what they can do, perhaps seeing if they can make me smile. They can. And laugh for joy.

My cough is back, not that it ever went away. It's become more noticeable, though. An X-ray is ordered but my lungs are clear. I'm told to "keep an eye on it," words that some malign power seems to take as an invitation for a practical joke. I come down with conjunctivitis, pink eye, first in one eye and then in both. After everything else I've caught, it's almost amusing. I look like a rabbit on a bender.

Always finicky where my eyes are concerned, I'm hopeless at using my prescribed eye drops. Kathy does her best to put them in at night and recommends I get help with the daylight dose from the school nurses. There are two of them, Joannie, who does the review of blood-borne pathogens at the start of the year, and Jeannette. They draw a curtain around me, instructing me to lie down on the couch. They give me a spot on the ceiling to watch as they sneak in the drops. They dab at the missed shots, a hint of how they must dab tears and disinfect bruised knuckles. I don't wonder that some of my students are constantly asking to see the nurse. I never refuse them permission, though I always call down to the nurse's office in advance of their arrival, just in case they pass out on the way or, as is far more likely, are tempted to go on walkabout for the next half hour. But the nurse's office is the main draw, and I get requests backed by explanations that I'd have thought would embarrass most high school kids: a Band-Aid for an invisible paper cut, a checkup for a stubbed toe, each but a notch or two below a kiss on a boo-boo. I'm grateful they have the option.

In later life my students will seek the same consolations from

masseuses and hairdressers, bartenders and truck-stop wait-
resses, always at their own cost and on their own time and often
without that gentle affirmative nudge to "go back to work because
you're just fine, really." Something we can all stand to hear now
and then. In my version of the perfect world, every workplace
would have, in addition to basketball hoops and a marching
band, the equivalent of a school nurse. And every school would
have a cosmetologist and an athletic trainer; I couldn't begin to
guess how many "discipline problems" originate in a student's
hatred of his or her appearance. But at the moment not all schools
even have nurses. Their elimination for the sake of fiscal auster-
ity, along with that of art and music teachers and guidance counselors, evokes a world very different from the one I conjure, a
world in which any attempt at loveliness is suspect and every
form of meanness is the rule.

For now, at least, Lake Region and its "extras" seem relatively
safe, its sports programs safer still. I'm glad. On my way to the
faculty parking lot I pass the boys' baseball team doing a fielding
drill on the grass. It's a balmy day; the side doors have been
propped open to take advantage of the breeze. I don't know for
sure, but it's possible the diamond on the upper campus is still
soggy from snowmelt or a recent shower. Or maybe the JV squad
has it today—I'm the last person who would know. These are the
varsity players in any case, some of them students of mine. One
by one their coach smacks each of them a ground ball, the player
on deck catches or retrieves it, throwing it to the captain, who
stands, glove at the ready, beside the coach. The rhythm is brisk
but unhurried, punctuated by the crack of ball on bat, the slap of
ball on glove, and short exclamations, mostly of praise and mostly
from the coach.

In these after-school hours, "Coach" is what he's called, but
he also happens to be the school's vice principal. Not that many

years ago he was an outstanding player for Sacred Heart High School, one of our two rivals to the north. He was captain of his team and also its catcher, details I've gathered as the year's progressed. So I understand now, as I didn't understand last August, that when he appeared before the faculty in his catcher's outfit on that second dreadful staff development day, he was not in costume so much as in his most familiar second skin. It's possible he was needing as much armor that day as I was. "This is who I really am," he might have been telling us, not the school's hatchet man down in the office but a player on your team whose job it is to catch anything thrown at him, sometimes one of your pissed-off students and sometimes the assignment of coming up with a staff development exercise that's bound to piss at least one of you off.

I shouldn't be putting words in his mouth. But I know from our conversations that he lives for these afternoons. They're part of what keeps him sane, perhaps the better part of what entitles him to still think of himself as a teacher. I'm glad he has this reward at the end of the day. It lifts my spirits to see him enjoying it.

I envy him too, as I do coaches in general. They work long hours for little pay, and they get more scrutiny and flak in several months than many teachers get in as many years—especially in seasons when losses outnumber wins—but they can count on their players' motivation. They don't have to hawk their wares. They set up their booths and the customers come, all of them willing and most of them able. Coaches save some of the most endangered kids and make heroes out of the most gifted. Yes, and some coaches are perfect jerks. But the ones who know what they're doing, who keep their eye on what's most important as zealously as they want their players to keep their eyes on the ball, can be magnificent. If gifted teachers are the great prose authors of a school, its novelists, orators, and essayists, gifted coaches are its poets.

Once I'm to my car it occurs to me that I haven't taken a single photograph all year that wasn't connected to a project or a field trip. Most of the time, I've been too focused on doing a good job and keeping things straight to take in the sights, much less to catch any with a camera. Still, I'm glad I have no camera with me this afternoon. That would make it too easy to lose a picture I intend to keep. I fix my pink eyes on the image and snap a mental photograph of "Coach" and his "men" before backing out of my space, a memento of May days at Lake Region, and as good as any yearbook to me.

By popular demand and for several of my own reasons, not the least of which is to give as many students as possible the chance of a strong finish, I do a reprise of the museum project I did the previous fall. I gave the assignment in March, with a preapproval date of April 1 and a completion date of May 11—plenty of time for the more conscientious students to peck away at the task, but also, as I know only too well, plenty of time for the others to procrastinate. Whether we ought to spend time doing something like this again is another question altogether.

The impetus to repeat an assignment that went reasonably well the first time around is at once risky and irresistible. Risky, because it's likely to go less well the second time, after the novelty is gone. Irresistible, because one wants the chance to make a good thing better. In a different situation, I could say, "Next year, I'm going to do the 'museum' this way," but there is no next year for me. I want my students to have a second try as well, the importance of which I'm not sure I grasped fully as a younger teacher. If students who fell down on their first attempt because of poor time management, shoddy workmanship, or an ill-conceived partnership take a better tack this time, then their sense of success will be doubled. They'll have the good grade and the satisfaction of having risen above their deficiencies.

With all of this in mind, I try to devise the widest possible array of project suggestions. I retain the options for students to engage with the literature in a hands-on way by doing paintings, sculptures, dioramas, board games, needlepoint or, in a more literary way, by composing fiction, poetry, a dramatic monologue, or a screenplay based on the novels we've read. As in the fall, I appeal to special interests with options to create a computer game, a scrapbook (a popular hobby of late, at least in the hinterlands), or a song. New to the list are a 4-H-style project connected to Lennie's rabbits in *Of Mice and Men*, a lecture (for example, "The Influence of *Huckleberry Finn* on American Literature"), a debate ("Is *Huckleberry Finn* a racist novel?") based on research, and a full-scale model of a Mississippi river raft, also based on some research. Obviously, I'm hoping for a few second tries in that area as well.

The results, when they come in, are on the whole a level above the ones I received in October. The enthusiasm is at least as strong, no small achievement given the lateness in the year. It doesn't surprise me that I get no lectures or debates; nor does it surprise me that I do get rabbits, or one rabbit anyway, so for several days my classroom has some of the earthy sensations of a kindergarten or a biology lab. (Has there been any research, I wonder, comparable to what's been done in nursing homes and prisons, on the stress-reducing effects of having animals in a school environment?) Two boys undertake to build a life-sized raft and truck it to school, upping the ante by using hand axes to fell and shape the trees for the sake of authenticity. "Huck wouldn't have had a chainsaw," they tell me. The raft includes a wigwam made of evergreen branches and a sand-bottomed fire pit. The boys park their replica outside the side door of the building with a sign on the wall of the stairwell inviting passersby to step out for a look. It feels like the perfect symbol of our mission: to get away from the prim Widow Douglas and float free for a while.

Even so, we are no farther from the riverbank and its cruelties than Huck and Jim are. Not all the students have adults to help them with their projects. One of the boys who builds the raft tells me he still plans to join the marines after he graduates. Another student turns to one of the school custodians for help in restoring an old sleigh that he identifies as Ethan Frome's for our museum and will give to his little sister when he takes it home. Perhaps there's a marine sergeant who'll take a custodial interest in his classmate, moved by the *Semper Fi* already tattooed on his arm.

We get a steady stream of visitors. Some come merely for the refreshments, but most seem impressed by the handiwork and leave their compliments in our guest book. We have sprawling dioramas of the dream farm that George conjures for Lennie, a homemade DVD abridgment of *Ethan Frome*, and a cut-paper mosaic of the sun rising over the old man and the sea that arrests the attention of nearly every visitor who enters the room and proves for anybody who ever doubted it that inexpensive materials combined with care and talent can produce marvelous results.

The museum takes up several days. It fortifies grades, as do the dreary NECAP practice essays, five in all. I'm surprised that most of the students do not seem to mind the latter. They brainstorm the one about how to instruct a new student to use the cafeteria as enthusiastically as if we were engaged in writing a recipe for success in love. I suppose I shouldn't be so amazed. If they are anything, my sophomores are good sports. And sports may provide the best metaphors for explaining their enthusiasm. The trouble with school is that we divide too much of a student's work between tests that "count" and practices that don't—not unlike the way we regulate athletics. Granted, it would be absurd to do the reverse, to grade students when they're still at the practice stage or to give exams that are "just for fun." But occasionally to combine the carefree intensity of practice with a guaranteed high score for good-faith effort has definite benefits. The kids are secure in their spontaneity and secure that it will bring them some reward.

I confess I'm not completely comfortable with the custom of giving an automatic 100 to every student who addresses the prompt and fills the space in a more or less satisfactory fashion. I don't begrudge the students their 100s, but I resent the overall implications. You can blow off Mark Twain so long as you play ball for us on the standardized tests, the reason being that while the first has to do only with your progress toward becoming an educated human being, the latter has to do with your teachers' ability to remain gainfully employed at an accredited school. Surely the matter is not so cynical as that, but it comes close. I take care not to let my cynicism show. I return each set of practices with a few comments on each paper—the volume permits little more—and a more substantial set of general comments (printed on a handout for everyone), all derived from repeated strengths or mistakes I've observed on the papers. I tell students that they should study these sheets for their final exam. No automatic 100s for that.

For the most part, their efforts on the NECAP practices are not depressing. Since the writings are done by hand, the word processor is not able to give the false impression of a finished product or enable speed of composition to outstrip careful thought. Predictably, some students do not complete all five practices. Not even the promise of an automatic 100 is enough to entice them. If you can get such a high grade for one paper, maybe you only need to write three. That Exeter teacher who said that laziness was the curable learning disability and stupidity the incurable may have erred not so much in his taxonomy as in his prognosis. If stupidity and laziness are truly all we have to contend with, then I'll take the task of curing stupidity. Only a less lazy man than I would try to find a cure for the other.

As if in homage to the season, babies in carry-on car seats begin to appear in the hallways, life-sized baby dolls, as it turns out, a project for a class in parenting. I recall a similar assignment from my previous teaching stint, though then it was done with a swaddled egg in a cigar box. The symbolism was obvious, emphasizing the fragility of a newborn. In the updated, higher-tech version, the students, all girls as far as I can tell, are expected to attend to the artificial infant's simulated needs, responding promptly whenever it cries and keeping close watch over it, though the dolls don't break as easily as the eggs did.

The parenting class is offered only to juniors and seniors but lo and behold a sophomore girl shows up in my last-period class with baby in hand. It seems the "mother" has absented herself from school for a day or two in order to handle her prodigious prom arrangements and has left the baby with a round-the-clock sitter, teasing out the simulation, to say nothing of the irony, more than she probably knows. But I have to say, her choice of a sitter is impeccable, a girl I'd surely have chosen were I needing one for any child of mine. Meredith already has the experience, for one thing, routinely caring for her little niece, who lives with her on the family farm. She also works part-time at McDonald's, competes as an amateur wrestler (a pursuit I find hard to reconcile with her diminutive height and demure behavior, though I've been told she can "beat the shit out of any boy in this school"), reads her drowsy big brother's English assignments aloud to him as he drives her to school in his truck (he's up at 2:00 a.m. doing barn chores and occasionally nods off in my first-period class), and can always be counted on to bring a pan of home-baked cookies for an after-school study session (even when she herself can't stay) and to deliver A+ speaking assignments, like the one on historical infatuation entitled "How I Stalked J.F.K." A pearl of a girl, in other words, so I'm glad she has charge of the "baby," not only because she'll see it gets the right care but also because I hope she'll see, if she hasn't already, that this is a responsibility she doesn't need for a while.

Midway through the period the doll erupts in a fit of wailing. My first thought is to ask who has their blasted cell phone on and whatever possessed them to choose such a perverse ringtone. Then I notice Meredith, clearly mortified by the outburst—this is a kid who waits patiently until everyone has finished speaking before putting her pencil into the noisy electric sharpener. Smiling, I offer to rock the doll for her while I teach. "No," she says, "I'll take care of it," and hurries from the room.

Five minutes later I am still doing my teach-at-Armageddon routine and the baby is still screaming out in the hall. Finally, one of the students says, "Mr. Keizer, I think maybe you better go out there."

When I do, I find Meredith frantically trying to turn a black plastic key into the control box at the back of the doll. She is visibly distressed. I feel a bit rattled myself at this point—the cry is "fake" but up close it arouses a very real and even primal response. I also try the key to no avail, noticing that there are written directions (and we know how much good they do) to turn the key clockwise. What I also discover is that the lady wrestler or some caretaker before her has succeeded in twisting the key into a worthless corkscrew of plastic. It turns only on itself. Can you get in touch with the student who gave this to you? I ask, raising my voice to be heard. She can't. She adds that if the crying is deactivated by any other method than turning the key it could compromise the other student's grade. I couldn't give a fig, I want to say, but instead ask if she knows the teacher in charge of the parenting class. No, she's somebody up at the career center ten miles to the north.

The doll keeps wailing, louder, it seems. I am indignant on behalf of Meredith and on my own behalf as well. We have been handed "a situation" for which we have not been prepared. Somewhat beyond what the assignment intends, we are feeling what every parent feels at one time or another: overwhelmed, clueless, and (needlessly) alone.

I tell Meredith what I think we should do and reluctantly she nods her head. I pop the voice box from the doll's plastic back. Like something out of Poe, the box continues wailing in my hand as I stare at it dumbfounded. Wanting to stomp the thing under my boot, I pull the ribbon that expels the batteries and the noise finally stops.

But the simulation continues, at least for one deathly moment. In real life, in a predicament not too far removed from the experience of many of my students, I would not have been this girl's teacher. I would have been her boyfriend, perhaps the baby's father, perhaps not. I couldn't have pulled out the batteries, because there wouldn't have been any batteries to pull out. Instead, I would have taken up the infant in a fit of frustration and shaken it until it either died or became permanently eligible for special services. I, in turn, would have become eligible to have my deer-in-the-headlights mug shot appear in the police blotter of the local paper. Another stupid redneck loser gets his. Or, if you prefer, another shaken, stunned, and stunted baby boy comes of age in the richest nation in the world.

I do not have to wonder if any of my students are thinking these same thoughts. I do not have to wonder because, when I step back into the classroom, I tell them exactly what I think.

JUNE

> Our school was not the worst. It certainly did teach me a few
> things: elementary knowledge, the habit of methodical work,
> and outward discipline.... The same school, however, sowed
> in me, contrary to its direct purpose, the seeds of enmity
> for the existing order. These seeds... did not fall on barren
> ground.
>
> —Leon Trotsky, *My Life*

June is the accordion month of the school calendar: its final day
remains tentative almost till the end, when the total number of
unanticipated school closing days is finally known along with
the number that will have to be made up to finish out the contracted year. Beyond that, teachers will each have their own
informal ending dates, depending on their ability to put their
affairs in order prior to the summer recess. Especially for heads
of departments, the last day of the term can fall late in the month
or even early in July. I remember those extra days from my own
tenure as a department head, when it seemed I'd never get out.

I have determined that whatever it requires, the official last
day will be *my* last day. In this I have both Sara's and Mr. Messier's support. I'm also determined that nothing will cause me to
leave under a cloud. I feel like a soldier counting down the days
remaining in his tour of duty: lucky up till now, he waits for the
bullet to come out of the blue, the street to explode under his

feet. I try not to be superstitious. More than that, I try not to be careless. This is especially important at this time of year, not only because it finds me tired but because there's a type of student whose last-ditch attempt to earn credit for a course he's failing is to discredit its teacher. I don't have many of that ilk, but I know from the bad experiences of other teachers that I have at least one or two.

I did my best to see that, at least in terms of new material and major grades, the marking period effectively ended at Memorial Day. I use the rest of the time for review, for enrichment, and for catching up those students with a few missing assignments—though I deliver repeated, strenuous warnings that I'm taking no deathbed confessions, answering no question like "What assignments am I missing?" two minutes before I'm out the door. I tell myself and I tell the kids that this is my due for a year of diligence. I go directly to "my old job," not the beach, the day after school lets out, and I intend to go unencumbered.

Say what I will, I know the boundaries are going to be pressed. More than a week after I've closed the gate on journal assignments, on an afternoon when a rare tornado is predicted for northeastern Vermont and an announcement has come over the intercom giving teachers permission to leave at three, two girls come up from one of the academic support areas to see "if you can tell us what journal assignments we're missing" (something I've been doing for weeks, both by way of general announcements to my classes and by written invitation to individuals who've fallen behind) and "if it might be possible for us to make them up" and "if you can tell us if we'd pass if we did" and "if we could do a few others for extra credit if we won't."

Without the predicted tornado, I might simply be irritated, but in this case I'm flabbergasted almost to the point of laughing aloud, which I'd surely do but for fear of seeming to mock the girls. Instead I say yes to their first two requests and no to the others. Admittedly, I'm eating some of my words and lowering some of my standards; admittedly, these girls are almost sublime in their fecklessness, but I remember what Huck's friend Jim had to say about the wisdom of cutting a child in half just to prove a point.

These aren't my last or best surprises. They'll continue, good and bad, until the year ends. The drudgery of completing the agreed-upon five NECAP practice essays is lightened by a few surprises beyond the jolt that comes when I learn at a department meeting that the very teachers who set the bar at five during a previous meeting have decided to interpret the number figuratively. I've held to the five in what I thought was a spirit of colleagueship. I swallow hard but say nothing; I sometimes wonder if, after nine months of bridling my tongue, I will spend the last weeks of June standing in my backyard screaming. But, as I said, the practice essays are not all a waste, especially the installment for the "reflective essay." Recalling the prompt on last October's NECAP, I ask students to write an essay based on a quotation. I ask them to do it at home and invite them to take their time with it. Hoping to make the assignment do double duty, I choose a quotation from *Our Town*: "Wherever you come near the human race, there's layers and layers of nonsense." I'm not casting aspersions on my students when I choose it—though I do expect that it will set some of them thinking about school.

It does, but not exclusively. One girl does some research (after having done virtually none for her research paper) and comes upon the example of a perfectly grammatical but utterly nonsensical sentence constructed by a man she identifies as Noam Chromsky. "I bet I'm the only teacher in the state who got a reference to the famous linguist Noam Chomsky on a <u>NECAP practice essay</u>," I write on her paper. It so happens I've recently purchased a black-and-white postcard of the very same Noam, looking skeptical and a tad cadaverous, and I attach it to her paper in lieu of a gold star. Another girl writes about the way she's been mocked for preferring to hang out with boys, many of whom are Future Farmers of America like her. She has little patience, she writes, for the "layers and layers of nonsense" that attend social interactions among more "typical" girls, and she could do without their snide remarks. Still another student writes of the loss of her cell phone, followed by the awesome discovery in the weeks thereafter that she enjoys her life more without it. She says she probably won't bother to get another. I wonder if Thornton Wilder could have anticipated the layers and layers of sense in these papers.

I have my sophomores do the last practice essay as part of their final exam, noting that I'll evaluate it by how well they've incorporated my feedback on the previous four. I give them the question ahead of time, as I do with essay questions for all my exams, and allow them to bring notes and an outline. Some of the best performances on the final exam are from students under the special ed umbrella, a credit to their aides and teachers but no less a credit to their own grim diligence. (Anybody who believes that special education is about coddling underachievers needs to get his ass into a school.) The highest exam grade in my sophomore classes goes to a boy who's repeating the course. I'm not surprised. He's a bright kid. I suspect many of his difficulties have to do with factors outside school. He shines when we do our review for the exam, often supplying the correct answer no one else seems to have. There and on the exam itself I suspect he wants to give me one last proof that I've been right in my overall assessment of his abilities. I'll miss him, a soft-spoken boy who never passes me in the hall without a kind word.

It's a truism that exams evaluate the teacher as much as the students, and on that score I pass as almost all of them do, though I hardly pass with distinction. "Patriotism is abstract, but a flag is _____," reads one of my sentence-completion items, drawing on the illustration I've used repeatedly throughout the year to clarify the distinction between abstract and concrete. One girl writes *cement.* As was sometimes true for her teacher, she got heartbreakingly close to the right answer but not quite close enough for it to count.

Except for an imaginative question or two, my exams are pretty much the traditional written deal. My colleague who teaches Advanced Placement Language and Literature has his students write essays and give a reading in the library after school, either as part of their final exam or as a major project for the last quarter, I'm not sure. But I attend, always interested in what a student can do, especially under the guidance of a master teacher like my colleague. Notwithstanding one father who attends the occasion in a muscle shirt, I'm struck by the visible difference between these college-bound seniors and many of the upperclassmen I teach. Part of it is clothing, part of it is poise; much of it is a greater tendency toward slenderness. Not all of what I see can be attributed to class—the ability levels don't sort themselves out that neatly—though I suspect some of it can.

What also impresses me, in the awkward schmoozing that takes place before and after the reading, is the reticence of some of the students as I attempt to make conversation. They hardly know me, of course; they're young, they're shy, and some of them have to be a little nervous—but there is something else I recognize, remember actually, from the days when I taught the upper track and could count on greater attentiveness to my overtures. Many students, especially grade-conscious students and "top-level students" most of all, are quick to discriminate between adults who matter and those who don't. On the one hand are teachers who might conceivably have something to say to them, by way of instruction, or for them, by way of a letter of reference; on the other hand, those less deserving of notice. I may be overstating the case, but I'm not the first teacher to do so. Even at this age one detects in certain ambitious students the first traces of a subtle snobbery. One need go no further than to remember that the courses they take are referred to as "honors level" to figure out where they're getting it.

This is not an observation I feel free to share. I confine my remarks to praising the essays, which are praiseworthy to say the least, and praising the teacher. He is highly dedicated and opinionated in what he does, but I've never found him pompous or vain. I suspect his students trust him, and they should. My private observations go to Kathy, as hers come to me. Her transitional year has gone reasonably well. She likes her colleagues at the elementary school and at Dartmouth, though she misses working in a preschool setting, and the systemic intransigence of elementary school is thrown into increasingly sharper relief by the colleagueship she experiences at the hospital. If she needs something at the latter, be it materials or a day off to attend a professional conference, it's assumed she's working to improve the program. If she expresses the same needs at the elementary school, it's assumed—or at least responded to as if—she may be trying to pull a fast one.

"I'm not sure I can let you go for this," says a since-departed principal when Kathy asks permission to attend a two-day workshop in order to maintain her professional license. "If I allow you to take the time, our students will be without speech services for two days." And if she doesn't take the time, the students will be without a licensed speech pathologist—but this requires further explanation from Kathy and a day or two of additional contemplation on the part of the principal before the imprimatur is granted. One of the administrators at the hospital is a former school speech pathologist and explains her change of careers by dryly noting that she got tired of working in an environment "where nothing gets done." Kathy tires of that too, though she's quick to add that many of her colleagues have it worse. At present they're straining to develop alternative NECAP examinations, as required by law, for special education students, some of whom are nonverbal and lack the most basic social skills—yet another example of taking time away from teaching in order to test what you lack the time to teach.

Probably the year's big story for her was the adoption of the iPad. By the end of the year, her colleagues remain more sold on it than she. As she predicted, the needs of the children are as likely to be reinterpreted in relation to the machinery as the format of the machinery adapted to them, assuming their needs are even noticeable beside the glare of the digital bling. On the positive side, the devices are powerful motivators for some kids and status symbols too, something cool in the hands of an "uncool" kid. Not that this is allowed to stand without comment. In one class a substitute teacher sees a special ed student working on an iPad and quips to the student's aide—in the presence of the student—"So that's why our taxes went up, so these kids can have their daily schedules written on an iPad."

There are probably more implications about the nature of public schools packed into Kathy's experience with the iPad than there are apps. But, unlike technology, human ingenuity has no limits. A technical consultant tells one of Kathy's colleagues that dish drainers make ideal storage racks for classroom sets of iPads. So, one afternoon, while the tech crews are once again reconfiguring the school's computers—and probably nullifying most of Kathy's downloads and creations in the process—she and her sidekick head down to the Dollar General to look for dish drainers. Soon I'll be saying good-bye to the world of schools, not only to the frustrations contained in the story of the iPad but also to enchanted mornings where teachers get out of their cars like a theophany of peddler goddesses, dressed up and cheerful in spite of bulging sacks on both shoulders, sections of varicolored foam rubber tubing (for what, God knows) waving from their sacks, snowmen on their sweaters for winter and pumpkins on their stockings for Halloween, and—as if this weren't vision enough—a dish drainer tucked under each arm.

Graduation occurs before the last official day of school, a bow to the special needs of seniors, who've already made plans around the unrevised calendar. I'll attend in spite of my temporary status and the load of work I still have to complete if I want to graduate too. I consider staying away but then learn that Mr. Messier plans to quote from my first book in his remarks. (He asks me ahead of time if I'd mind.) I probably ought to be there in case he has anything else up his sleeve. I also feel an obligation to the handful of seniors I taught. On the most basic level, I feel that I don't deserve to stay away.

As in the past, I view commencement exercises as an act of penance for the sins of the teaching year. Not a full expiation, for sure, but at least an act of contrition. The lengthy monotony of the proceedings, the stifling heat of a gymnasium in mid-June, the oxygen deprivation that comes of sitting with hundreds of spectators in a scarcely ventilated space—what else besides a guilty conscience could keep a person coming year after year? Add to these the inevitable if unintended insult that comes of being publicly "thanked" for an education whose quality is thrown into doubt by every other sentence accompanying the thanks, the self-congratulatory tone and smug insider jokes of the valedictory speakers, the steady deflation of making the rounds afterward to congratulate students in whose eyes it's clear that anything you might have meant to them or they to you is dissolving like a mirage. Most of all, the oppressive loneliness that is relieved only by remembering that any number of the students up on the dais are feeling lonelier still. At the conclusion of what many of them have repeatedly been assured are the best years of their lives—which in some cases will prove sadly true, the relative crappiness of those years notwithstanding—small wonder that more than a few of them will be stone drunk by nightfall.

Of course, there's plenty to move even a jaded heart: the sight of kids who are the first in their families to graduate high school or the first to be going on for further study, the pride in their eyes and in the eyes fixed on them. The kids overcome with more emotion than the occasion would seem to warrant, as if this were their first encounter with transience. The kids who unashamedly give flowers to their mothers, embracing the only individuals in the world besides themselves who truly know how hard it was to get to this day and how close they came to not making it. The uncanny self-possession of those students who put their high school years in perspective a long time ago, who will go on to do the quiet useful work they've set their sights on all along, who will keep their yearbooks but not open them often, who have instinctively understood that life gives a person several true friends at most and who will remain true to their friends all their lives. One imagines them looking beyond the few graduation parties they'll attend this weekend to a road trip planned for November or a year's stint on an uncle's fishing boat somewhere in Washington State. They will give only a little time to finding themselves because they've never felt any great need to go looking for someone they already know.

I don't take a seat but stand near the door, at the edge of the bleachers, where few people will notice if I duck out to the men's room or drop to my haunches at the mention of my name. The sight of Mr. Messier at the podium moves me, as does his decision to quote from my book, though the passage he chooses and the question with which he introduces it amount to a conundrum. He reads my opening description of the region, as seen through the eyes of a new teacher, its natural beauty and stultifying poverty, its isolation and heartache, and asks the graduates to think how much has changed at the school and in their community since the book appeared in 1988. I'm almost certain the answer he's implying is "a lot." I'm less sure that everyone in the audience would give the same answer. To the degree that he himself represents a positive change at the school, he is fully entitled to his optimism. The author of the passage, though, has his doubts.

My mind begins to wander during the other speeches. It slips outside the gymnasium and drifts downhill to the underpass where senior art students have recently painted the mural that each successive graduating class leaves for a legacy until a new one requires the space. During the week I watched it take shape in the form of a rural landscape, with an image of Lake Region High School atop a green hill and the words RANGER PRIDE written in the blue sky above it. Then, when I drove up to school over the weekend to retrieve my misplaced grade book, I noticed in alarm that someone had painted an enormous fist breaking through the center of the cement "canvas," its knuckles aimed at the viewer and the background torn into stylized shreds around it.

My first thought was that a group of talented graffiti guerrillas, perhaps kids from the rival high school to the north of us, had stolen down one night and defaced our mural, symbolically punching us out on our own turf. There will be consequences for this! The fists won't be symbolic either. I considered calling the principal in the hopes of averting an incident. Was it possible no one else had noticed what the vandals did? Well, it was a Sunday and they could have made their raid in the wee hours of that same morning. Several minutes passed before I understood that the fist was part of the design, a realization that felt like a fist punching through me. Why put a fist through the landscape that supposedly inspires your pride? I suppose that, taken as a paradox, it made a kind of sense: a senior wants to punch his way free of the place he also loves.

Come Monday, praise for the completed mural was widespread and fulsome, especially among the faculty. There was no attempt and apparently no felt need to give it any interpretation. My uneasiness was my problem. This is how students must have felt in my classes some days: What on earth is he talking about? Am I the only person who doesn't get it? Why do Ethan and Mattie run their sleigh into a tree? Why do people call things tragic that are just plain stupid? Or is the stupid one me?

I return my attention to the order of ceremonies on my program; I do a visual count of the rows remaining to receive their diplomas. My faults are more than I can number, but my penance is about two-thirds done.

Had I been invited to speak at graduation, as teachers sometimes are, and had I accepted, what might I have said? Probably nothing too heavy. High school graduations are not the place for diatribes or manifestos. Neither are high school classrooms. I have always believed it is a teacher's duty to teach the curriculum and not to pontificate, to inspire debates and not to settle doctrines. I did on one or two occasions tell my students that the society they were living in valued people of their age, region, and class primarily as cannon fodder, cheap labor, and gullible consumers and that education could give them some of the weapons necessary to fight back. Those things I did say, and I might have ventured at least that far in a graduation speech. I find myself wishing, though, that I had had a simple refrain, some terse slogan I could have repeated to my classes day after day, like the Roman senator Cato, who is supposed to have ended every speech by saying "Carthage must be destroyed."

In fact, Cato's refrain might have done nicely. As it happens, the people of Carthage worshipped the same god their Phoenician ancestors had, a Canaanite deity they called Moloch, whose signature burnt offering was the dearest thing his worshippers had. When the Romans eventually took Cato's advice, they found within the walls of the doomed city a multitude of clay urns containing the tiny charred bones of children. The Romans worshipped their own version of Moloch, needless to say, as do we if our poets are to be believed. "Moloch whose love is endless oil and stone! Moloch whose soul is electricity and banks!" So wrote Allen Ginsberg when I was a mere three years old, half a century before the financial meltdown of 2007–08, an unknown number of years before the last American soldier leaves Afghanistan.

Carthago delenda est. I couldn't say that to kids without more explanation than I had time for and more trouble than my long-suffering hosts deserved, but at least I can say it to you. The sentimental hypocrisy that holds children to be our most precious resource even as every indicator from the conduct of foreign policy to the debate over guns puts them several notches down in value from the availability of cheap oil and the goodwill of the NRA—*delenda est.* The fatuous assurance that children are happiest when their parents behave as if no happiness matters so much as their own and that of their live-in lovers—*delenda est.* The two-headed effrontery of believing that equal opportunity in the society at large can be promoted merely by reforming schools and that schools can be reformed without radically transforming the structures of society—*delenda est,* both heads at a single stroke.

And who better suited to wield the sword than we who are charged with giving our students a "head start" only so that—as one civil rights worker put it years ago—the most disadvantaged of them can run sooner into a brick wall? Who better than us to demand the wall's destruction? May I live to see the day when a teachers' strike is at the vanguard of a general strike.

Till then, I have a room to straighten and grades to turn in. I have an inventory to complete. I have one last installment of my productivity rubric to enter on PowerSchool. I have a few scattered opportunities to tell a few drop-by visitors that I hope they'll have a safe and happy summer.

On my last day, Mr. Messier takes me to breakfast and the English department takes me to lunch. The breakfast is at the same café in Barton where I've been meeting my lone student for months. He and I have already had our year-end breakfast and agreed to have at least one encore after he starts at a local college this fall. I trust Mr. Messier knows what I've asked Sara to pass on to anyone who suggests marking my departure in some special way—"no party, no presents, no fuss"—and he has chosen this quiet way to say good-bye and thanks. I can hardly imagine one better. Though we've had many occasions to chat throughout the year, most have had some agenda, and all were subject to the interruptions that come at a principal like a barrage of driving snow. Now we're able to relax, take stock of the year, and look to our respective futures. I know how much of his heart and sense of vocation are involved in Lake Region and so it comes as more than a pat on the shoulder when he tells me that I have been good for the school. He hopes my time there has also been good for me. I'm not lying when I tell him that it has.

In addition to picking up the tab for my coffee and double portion of bacon, the principal hands me two gifts. One is the library's hardbound copy of my first book—"We'll replace it," he says—with yearbook-style farewells and accolades from a handful of my students written inside the covers. It would seem he has tried to seek out the kids who've meant most to me during the year or to whom I've meant the most, though both of us know those categories can never be better than an educated guess. He includes himself among them, repeating something he'd said to me early in the term when I gave him my diagnosis of a troubled young man in one of my classes: "You may have been away for fifteen years, but you still have it!" There on the dust jacket is my author photo from over twenty years ago, unsmiling, earnest, with darker, longer hair and beard, someone I would not recognize if I passed him on the street.

The other present is a letter to the principal from a colleague with whom I've had the most perplexing relationship, a person who will greet me affably on some days and hardly acknowledge me on others. Though of late there have been unexpected compliments about the good preparation I've given to the students we share, I have always assumed that my mercurial colleague regarded me with suspicion at first, perhaps even with distaste. I note from the date on the letter that it was written early in the term. It nominates me for the school's Teacher of the Year. The honor rightfully went to someone else and probably ought never to go to someone passing through a school system on a temporary gig. But the letter gets my nomination for Surprise of the Year, yet another example of how easily we misjudge others—and, let's face it, how easily they misjudge us.

My lunch with the English department is at the restaurant at the Orleans Country Club, already in operation when Kathy and I first came to the Kingdom, though I often forget it's there. Perched invisibly above the town and the furniture factory, the greens lie close to the houses built at the crest of what some people call Snob Hill. It is hardly Beverly Hills, nor is life in the valley altogether desolate, though several months from now the local paper will report the arrest of one of our citizens for the theft of "some sausages and a ham."

Once everyone is seated—the guidance counselors have come too—I receive my cordially inscribed card and perfect gift: a small shrub with varicolored leaves that I'd like to set in my garden straightaway. I'm impressed for one last time by the dedication of my peers, still inclined to talk shop on this rare chance to be away from it, and by the sobering recognition that all of us have already moved beyond our temporary partnership. I have been among these people for no more than a year, never a permanent fixture, and the year is effectively over. Any messes I've made will be theirs to clean up. Any improvements I made were built on their prior successes and will need their further efforts to maintain. I wonder how many of them are as anxious as I am for the food to get eaten and the check to come, how many feel forgivably resentful at this added obligation, one more thing to stall their passage to the well-earned summer break. School is like this: awards and citations, trophies and send-offs, wave upon wave, lest anyone feel unacknowledged—but how restless one can feel at the banquet.

I'm glad that most of my good-byes to my students are behind me. I said a formal good-bye to all of my classes before handing out their final exams. I told them that I had hoped to leave with some words of wisdom but that I could come up with none that suited me beyond a simple statement of their own preciousness as human beings. I thanked them for their overall kindness and told them that any stray thing they might regret having done or said to me was already forgiven. I hoped they'd find the wherewithal to extend the same forgiveness to me.

Then I reminded them not to talk until all the exams were concluded and wished them luck. I could not tell if they were saddened by what I said or mildly offended by its terseness—already it felt as if there was distance opening between us. Less formally, I shook hands with the bearish freshman in my teaching roommate's class, who'd made a point of saying good morning to me nearly every second period as he was coming into the room and I was gathering up my stuff to leave. I wished him luck too, not knowing he'd be killed in a car accident before the end of the year. To one of his reticent classmates, a long-haired boy I'd made stay after school for covering his desk with graffiti, I gave an inexpensive sketchpad. No hard feelings, I meant to say, and your graffiti shows promise.

With those of my own students who came back to see their corrected exams or dropped in to say their good-byes on the day of their last exam there was more to say, some of it poignant. I'll draw a curtain on those, but I can't resist sharing one brief exchange that happened near the end, a little thing, though it left me with a sense of benediction.

On the final day of exams—a half day for students with the afternoon reserved for makeups—an announcement came over the intercom a few minutes after the buses left that there was Chinese food in the upstairs faculty workroom for any teachers who wanted some. I happened not to and continued my correcting. Within the minute two boys poked their heads into my room, one of them the boy I chewed out for tailgating me that November afternoon when I was going to see my daughter in Burlington.

"Hey, Mr. Keizer," he said, "did you hear that announcement about the Chinese food?" I did, I said, touched by their concern that no teacher miss out on a free lunch. I added that I wasn't hungry.

"Do you think you could snag some for us?"

I was touched even more that they judged me fit for such buccaneering—though apparently they'd spoken in jest. "You're going to do it?" the other asked incredulously as I sprang up from my desk. "Are you kidding? This is the best idea I've heard in a month."

I filled a plate with some of every entrée, nuked it in the faculty microwave, and made off with the booty and two clean forks. My guys were waiting at my classroom door like spectators at a finish line. They could bring the dirty plate to me, I told them, not so much out of kindness as out of fear that a colleague of mine might wind up poisoned if they gave it too Platonic a wash. They were back in what seemed like a minute. "That was so good!" they said, handing me the dirty plate and thanking me, though I might as well have thanked them. Funny thing about Chinese food: ever notice that an hour after you steal some for a couple of hungry rascals your heart still feels full?

My last chore after grades are done is to put my room in order. I place my exams and practice NECAP essays in neat, sorted piles. I empty the desk of everything but the office supplies and stationery that were left for me when I arrived, with a few additions: a new stapler, fresher felt-tip markers, butterfly paperclips in assorted boxes, the remote control and instruction booklet for the computer projector. I take my tin of mints, my jar of ocean pebbles, my framed photographs of patrons scanning the stacks of a blitzed London bookstore and the Rose Room at the New York Public Library. Between the pages of an art book, I tuck a mixed CD of Japanese "noise music," a parting gift from a once-sour young poet, lately turned sweet. I bequeath my daughter's lime tree, which she bequeathed to me after college and which has thrived remarkably in the close air of my classroom, to Sara along with my poster of Eleanor Roosevelt. They would have been fast friends, Eleanor and Sara; they've been something like my patron saints this year, two smiles I could always count on during the toughest days. Malcolm X doesn't smile, so he's going home with me. Sara comes by to ask if there is anything she can do—besides the hundred and one things she's already done—to help me leave on time. If there is anyone at the school I will miss, anyone who I think will genuinely miss me, it is Sara. I believe we both know that when we assure each other that we're not really saying good-bye.

It takes me several trips to get my crates of books and decorations to my car, along with my new plant and several of my old ones. I fold forward my backseats and fill my hatchback to the ceiling. When everything is loaded, I close the car and head back toward the school. I have one last thing to do before I can leave. I took away the doorstop on my last trip to the car, and I turned my keys in to the main office half an hour ago, but there's no need for me to get inside. I need only stand within arm's length of the building. Even under hands as callused as mine, the bricks are warm.

So I'm free. I head home past the Crystal Saloon and along Crystal Lake, not for the last time but very probably for my last time as a teacher going home from school. My windows are open, my music is loud. Though I'm driving the same car I've driven all term and for six years prior to that, I feel as though it's been returned to me after a year's impoundment. I can drive it wherever I want to now and at any hour. Better still, I can keep it parked in the dooryard below my office windows, its inertness the visible sign of every blessed moment I can stay put. I hope I'll never have to take another job besides writing, but I know I'll never regret the teaching I did this year.

The Sunday after our last day of school Kathy and I head down the interstate for a celebratory outing, an early Eucharist (from the Greek for "thanksgiving") in Littleton, New Hampshire, followed by breakfast at the diner there, a stroll around town to walk off the pancakes and take in the farmers' market, and anywhere our hearts fancy after that. There are no papers to grade, no lessons to plan. The day's a beauty—"so cool, so calm, so bright," to quote George Herbert, "the bridall of the earth and skie." But apparently not perfect. For a quarter mile or so I worry I'm going to have car trouble or some kind of roadside altercation—why else is the driver behind me gesticulating so wildly at seven o'clock on a Sunday morning? As he pulls hard to my right to take the third St. Johnsbury exit, I slow down to get a look at his face and a sense of his meaning if I can. If my tailpipe's sagging, if he flips me the bird, I'm not going to let it wreck my day.

He turns out to be one of my former sophomores, a newly minted junior, his learner's permit exchanged for a license. He's at the wheel of the used car that I know from an early composition to be his pride and joy. For reasons I could never learn, the final draft never got handed in. He did manage to finish his research paper, though, in spite of his bid to stack my firewood instead. It was a fine piece of work for which he earned an A. He's beaming at us now, still waving as his car turns down the ramp and away from our direction. He must have noticed me a ways back and only wanted to be sure I noticed him.

ACKNOWLEDGMENTS

I owe a great debt to those students and staff members at Lake Region Union High School whose kindness sustained me during the year recounted in this book. I wish especially to thank Erikka Adams, Timothy Chamberlin, Danielle Conley, Eric Degre, Michelle Hubert, Sara McKenny, Andre Messier, Cathy Sargent, and Chastity Urie, lacking whose frequent ministrations I might not have survived to "tell the tale." That said, the tale is mine, written entirely without the aid, knowledge, or permission of anyone in the Lake Region community. It amounts to one small slice of one man's experience at an extraordinary school. Any faults in the telling belong to me alone.

I also wish to thank Ellen Rosenbush, my longtime editor at *Harper's Magazine*, who shepherded the essay on which this book is based, and my agent Jim Rutman, for his representation of that project. To his colleague Peter Matson I owe much of my good fortune in having Sara Bershtel as my relentless, astute, and ever-gracious editor at Metropolitan Books. Her assistant, Connor Guy, and my copy editor, Roslyn Schloss, also made invaluable contributions to the text, as did Christopher O'Connell to the book's production. Not least of all, I'm grateful to Kathy Keizer and Howard Frank Mosher, my first readers for this and every other book I've written.

I dedicate *Getting Schooled* to teachers, thinking particularly of my own, a list that includes the individuals mentioned above, as well as many former mentors, teaching colleagues, and students. Foremost in their company are my wife, Kathy, and my daughter, Sarah, both dedicated teachers in our public schools and constant teachers to me.

ABOUT THE AUTHOR

GARRET KEIZER is the author, most recently, of *Privacy* and *The Unwanted Sound of Everything We Want*. A contributing editor at *Harper's Magazine* and a former Guggenheim Fellow, he has written for *The New York Times*, the *Los Angeles Times*, *Lapham's Quarterly*, *The Village Voice*, *Mother Jones*, and *Virginia Quarterly Review*, among other publications. He lives with his wife in Vermont.

Learning
in Action

Learning
in Action

A GUIDE TO PUTTING
THE LEARNING ORGANIZATION
TO WORK

David A. Garvin

HARVARD BUSINESS SCHOOL PRESS
Boston, Massachusetts

Library of Congress Cataloging-in-Publication Data

Garvin, David A.
Learning in action : a guide to putting the learning organization to work /
David A. Garvin.
p. cm.
Includes bibliographical references and index.
ISBN 1–57851–251–4 (alk. paper)
1. Organizational learning. 2. Organizational learning—Case studies. I. Title.
HD58.82 .G37 2000
658.4′06—dc21   99–048911

The paper used in this publication meets the requirements of the American National
Standard for Permanence of Paper for Publications and Documents in Libraries and
Archives Z39.48–1992.

*To my parents,
who taught me to love learning,
and to my wife and daughters,
who keep me learning every day*

Contents

Preface

By now the value of organizational learning is widely recognized. Managers view knowledge as a key corporate asset, to be leveraged and exploited for competitive purposes. They see best practices as sources of superior productivity and growth, to be disseminated as quickly as possible. They consider creative ideas and innovative thinking essential to success in emerging, rapidly changing markets. For all of these reasons, it is hard to find a manager today who does not give at least lip service to the importance of building a learning organization.

Yet despite this apparent acceptance, progress has been slow. Learning organizations have been embraced in theory but are still surprisingly rare. Managers find them easy to imagine but hard to create and sustain. The reason, in large part, is the lack of guidelines for practice. Past discussions of the subject have paid little or no attention to the gritty details of implementation. They have presented a compelling case for learning and painted a tempting picture of the desired endpoint but have left many questions unanswered. Most are operational and action-oriented: How do I, as a manager, get started? What tools and techniques must I master? What processes must be in place? When and how is each approach best used? What do I need to do personally to lead the learning process? And how will I know when my company has truly become a learning organization?

The aim of this book is to provide answers to these questions and, in the process, to help managers build more effective learning organizations. The analysis that follows has four distinguishing features. First, it is comprehensive and synthetic. In exploring the landscape of learning, I have drawn on research from many fields, including anthropology, cognitive science, economics, education, engineering, management, organization theory, philosophy, political science, and psychology. My goal is to provide a broad, integrated view of the topic that is grounded in scholarship. Much of the evidence I cite has deep practical importance yet has never before been assembled in one place or translated into terms that are accessible to managers. Together, the findings from these studies present a compelling picture of the drivers of organizational learning, the practices that contribute to success and failure, and the behaviors required of managers and employees.

Second, the book is filled with a wealth of examples. They take two forms: detailed case studies and brief snapshots. The case studies provide in-depth profiles of successful learning processes at organizations such as Xerox, L.L. Bean, the U.S. Army, GE, Timken, and Allegheny Ludlum Steel. They are based on extensive field research and include a wide range of quotations, tips and techniques, instructions, and lists of dos and don'ts. Each is a complete, composite picture of learning in action. The snapshots are more tightly focused; each singles out a particularly effective program or policy or else highlights an error that could be easily avoided. They do not attempt to present a complete learning story. But they do broaden the range of companies covered and show how learning can be applied in extremely diverse settings. Among the companies featured are Banc One, Boeing, British Petroleum, Corning, Disney, Emerson Electric, Intel, Microsoft, Motorola, Nike, Pepsi, Target, Time Life, and Wal-Mart, as well as a host of lesser-known firms.

Third, the book has a distinctive point of view. I argue that at the heart of organizational learning lies a set of processes that can be designed, deployed, and led. These processes need not be left to chance. They can—and, according to the main argument of the book, should—be managed. This is not to suggest that learning always arrives through planning or systematic analysis. Serendipity—in the form of unexpected connections or unanticipated events—clearly plays a role. The focus here, however, is on increasing the odds of success and improving the breadth, depth, and speed of learning by following well-crafted processes and procedures. Learning will always remain something of an art, but even the best artists can improve their technique.

Fourth, and perhaps most important, the book has a strong practical bent. Many managers remain uncomfortable with the soaring, high-minded prose of past discussions of organizational learning. They are driven by far more immediate concerns. Their focus—and the one that I have adopted in this book—is getting things done. Whenever a critical learning process is described, it is accompanied by a concrete discussion of the policies, programs, and procedures that are required for success. Whenever a tool or technique is featured, it is accompanied by a set of instructions for applying it in real organizations. Whenever a mind-set or environment is cited as conducive to learning, it is accompanied by a list of supporting steps and activities. And whenever the challenge of leading learning is discussed, it is accompanied by specific suggestions for creating opportunities, sharing knowledge, setting the proper tone, and shaping the discussion process.

The book is divided into three broad sections. The first, which consists of chapters 1 and 2, is introductory and provides the foundation for all that follows. It describes the basic elements of learning organizations as well as the primary processes. Chapter 1 begins by contrasting individual and organizational learning, then offers a precise definition of learning organizations, several litmus tests for evaluating progress, and a few simple questions that managers can ask to help them get started in raising learning higher on the corporate agenda. Chapter 2 describes the basic steps in every learning process—acquiring, interpreting, and applying knowledge—and examines the challenges posed by each one. It also introduces the notion of learning disabilities—common biases and errors that impede effective learning—and suggests ways that they can best be overcome. The chapter concludes with a discussion of the defining characteristics of supportive learning environments and presents examples of policies and programs that encourage them.

The second section, which consists of chapters 3, 4, and 5, examines different modes or processes of learning. Each involves the same basic steps of acquiring, interpreting, and applying information, but applies them in different ways. Each draws data from different sources and involves a different set of challenges. Chapter 3 discusses intelligence, the collection and interpretation of information that exists outside the organization. Interviewing and observational techniques are examples. Chapter 4 discusses experience, the accumulation of knowledge through action. Postproject reviews and action learning programs are examples. Chapter 5 discusses experimentation, the manipulation of variables or changing of conditions to draw inferences. Prototypes, exploratory designs, and tests of competing theories are examples. In each chapter, the basic characteristics of that mode of learning are first described, the necessary supporting conditions and essential steps for success are then discussed, and several variations or alternative approaches are examined. Each major alternative is accompanied by an extended case study that shows the process in action.

Together, these three chapters present a set of processes that collectively provide companies with virtually all they need to know to create a learning organization. The processes fit together neatly, since each has a different orientation. Intelligence gathering is aimed at the present; it ensures that organizations attend to currently available information. Experiential learning is aimed at the past; it ensures that organizations draw lessons from activities that have already taken place. Experimentation is aimed at the future; it ensures that organizations look ahead, trying out new designs or theories to test their validity. Present, past, and future—the coverage is comprehensive and complete.

The final section of the book, which consists of chapter 6, shifts the focus from organizations to individuals. It explores the leadership challenge that confronts executives wishing to build learning organizations. How can they personally stimulate inquiry, prompt debate, and encourage deeper thinking among subordinates? The chapter provides several answers. It begins by describing learning forums—settings and events, such as systems audits and meetings with customers, whose primary purpose is fostering learning—and shows how managers can create and support them. It then discusses the importance of setting the proper atmosphere and tone—a mix of challenge and testing on the one hand, and collegiality, collaboration, and security on the other—and highlights the ways that executives can maintain this delicate balance. Special attention is paid to the most effective use of questioning, listening, and responding, for they are the primary tools that leaders have for shaping discussions. The chapter concludes with a discussion of how executives can become better learners themselves. If they hope to build learning organizations, they too must become more open to divergent views, more aware of their personal biases, and more comfortable with raw, unfiltered data. Otherwise, they will never be able to lead others in learning.

Throughout, the book is guided by a simple premise: learning organizations are built from the gritty details of practice. Sweeping metaphors and grand themes are far less helpful than the knowledge of how individuals and organizations learn on a daily basis. The key to success is mastery of the details, coupled with a command of the levers that shape behavior. This book shows managers how they can use that understanding to create learning organizations that work.

David A. Garvin
December 1999

Acknowledgments

I have learned a great deal writing this book and have had the benefit of many teachers. I would like to offer my thanks.

First and foremost, I wish to thank the managers and military leaders who consented to interviews, provided explanations, contributed data, and otherwise generated the raw material that lies at the heart of this book. They are the true heroes of the project, for they serve as inspirations and models, offering living proof that learning organizations do in fact exist. All of the people I spoke with were candid and cooperative, committed to telling their stories accurately and completely. Without their help, this book would not exist.

Equally helpful were my academic colleagues, who provided insightful comments on an earlier draft of the manuscript. I would like to thank Robert Burgelman, Roland Christensen, Michael Cusumano, Donald Hambrick, Morten Hansen, Gary Klein, Michael Roberto, and Michael Tushman for adding so much to my understanding of learning organizations. They posed penetrating questions, made me think hard about the underlying concepts and frameworks, suggested relevant literature and examples, and ensured that my arguments were tight and easy to follow. The final manuscript is vastly improved as a result.

Many of the detailed examples in this book first appeared in two Harvard Business School Video series, *Putting the Learning Organization to Work* and *Working Smarter*. Many people participated in their development, and I have drawn heavily on our work together. I am especially grateful to William Brennan and Jane Heifetz of Harvard Business School Video, Ed Gray of David Grubin Productions, Joe Blatt of River-Run Media, and the directors Thomas Ott and Eric Stange for their many contributions.

A number of others helped move the project along. My editor, Marjorie Williams, was a source of endless good advice; her suggestions and support have been invaluable. My research associates, Artemis March, Janet Simpson, Donald Sull, and Jonathan West, helped research and write the case studies that appear as examples throughout the book; they were active, insightful collaborators. My secretary, Andrea Truax, typed and retyped endless charts and tables; she also ensured that the final manuscript was polished and error free. Aimee Hamel of the Word Processing Center saved the day several times, finding ways to make my word processing program behave as requested.

But, as always, the greatest contributions came from my family. My parents taught me to cherish and love learning; they pointed me toward many of my current pursuits. My wife, Lynn, listened and led in equal measure; she has been and continues to be my source of inspiration. My daughters, Diana and Cynthia, showed me the true meaning of learning; they keep me grounded while teaching me something new every day. These five special people represent the very best of learning in action, and I dedicate this book to them.

I

FOUNDATIONS

1

From Individual to Organizational Learning

Learning is the most natural of activities. It is an essential part of the human experience, and something that we as individuals do throughout our lives. Yet more often than not, our progress as learners goes unrecognized or unheeded. It happens as if by magic: one day we are ignorant, then time passes and suddenly we possess a wealth of new knowledge.

Children provide the most obvious example, for they are instinctive, intuitive learners. Much of childhood is spent expanding one's horizons and acquiring new perspectives, abilities, and skills. But the work of development does not end in childhood. Countless studies have shown that individuals continue to adapt and grow as they age.[1] Self-directed learning projects, for example, are quite common. According to pioneering research conducted in the early 1970s, the average adult engages in approximately eight learning projects per year, and roughly 90 percent of adults can cite at least one such project that they pursued in the previous year.[2] Typically, adults devote one hundred hours annually to each learning project, even though fewer than 1 percent are undertaken for credit.

Moreover, these projects are extremely diverse, ranging from general occupational skills, such as accounting, shorthand, and tool design, to specific job knowledge, such as advertising strategy and the needs of disadvantaged adolescents, to personal interests and home-related
responsibilities, such as cooking skills, child and baby care, and playing a
musical instrument. Most projects are motivated by a major life transition either at home or on the job, are problem-focused, and are intimately
linked to a desire for self-renewal and personal growth.

Today, corporations face similar needs. They too are in the midst of
massive transformations requiring renewal and growth; for this reason,
many have jumped on the learning bandwagon. The most obvious mani-
festation of their commitment is company-sponsored education and
training. In the U.S. alone, spending on corporate education has grown at
5 percent a year for the past decade; it now totals nearly $60 billion
annually.[3] A number of leading companies, including Motorola, General
Electric, and McDonald's, have established their own corporate "universities," offering a wide range of technical, business, and remedial courses.
Others, such as Intel and Andersen Consulting, now spend as much as
6 percent of payroll on education and training, while requiring two weeks
of class time per year for all employees.[4]

Yet even with these commitments, most managers remain surprisingly ambivalent about learning. Many give lip service to its importance,
voicing strong public support for efforts to broaden employees' knowledge and skills. But when pressed, they usually express very different
feelings. For all too many managers, learning is of questionable value
because it diverts employees' attention from "real work."

Executives are action-oriented, and their goal is to get things done.
Any activity that does not produce immediate, tangible results is therefore viewed with a certain degree of suspicion. Programs to stimulate
learning frequently fall into this category, especially if they require time
for reflection, synthesis, and review. The result is a clash of values, as a
leading proponent of learning has observed:

> The most difficult challenge is developing a culture that values . . .
> learning. A colleague once . . . told me of a dialogue with a loading
> dock foreman who, in great frustration, finally said to him, "Look, I

can either ship product or talk about it. Which do you want me to do?" The correct answer can only be "Both," but it is hard to make that answer a reality.[5]

The implicit analogy is to academic scholarship, with its overtones of bookishness, ivory-tower impracticality, and leisurely reflection. Professors are devoted to the life of the mind; they have chosen lives that give them ample opportunity to hone their arguments to a razor's edge. Managers see themselves at the opposite end of the spectrum: doers rather than thinkers, pressured for time and thus willing to rely on workable rather than ideal solutions. This view is well represented by a story that Charles Handy, the British futurist, tells about a presentation he made sketching out the organization of the future, which stressed the importance of intelligence, information, and ideas. "Increasingly," he said to a group of chief executives, "your corporations will come to resemble universities or colleges." "Then God help us all," one of them replied.[6]

In the same spirit, learning is seen by many managers as a New Age phenomenon, whose goal is releasing human potential rather than improving the bottom line. Here, scholars are partly to blame, for their discussions of learning organizations have often been reverential and utopian. Peter Senge, who popularized learning organizations in his book *The Fifth Discipline,* describes them as places "where people continually expand their capacity to create the results they truly desire, where new and expansive patterns of thinking are nurtured, where collective aspiration is set free, and where people are continually learning how to learn together."[7] Ikujiro Nonaka, a Japanese scholar, uses similar language, characterizing knowledge-creating companies as places where "inventing new knowledge is not a specialized activity . . . it is a way of behaving, indeed, a way of being, in which everyone is a knowledge worker."[8] These descriptions, while uplifting, lack a framework for action, and thus provide little comfort to practical-minded managers.

An additional source of unease comes from managers' quest for stability and predictability. At most companies, efficiency is a hallowed goal, best served by well-established routines. Yet learning demands constant questioning and repeated reevaluations of established practice. Skepticism and open-mindedness are essential. But because many managers "cannot bear to have their cherished beliefs challenged . . . on a continuing basis . . . evaluation and organization . . . are to some extent contradictory terms."[9]

For all these reasons, learning has yet to establish a secure beachhead at many corporations. It occurs, of course, but more often through benign neglect than active support. All too many managers continue to regard time spent learning as a necessary but unproductive evil. Such views are unfortunate because they reflect an extraordinarily narrow conception of the potential impact of learning. Nor do they recognize the many guises in which new knowledge appears. Far from being academic, philosophical, and inefficient, corporate learning is much more likely to be practical, applied, and intimately linked to the bottom line.

LEARNING IN ACTION

Consider the following examples:

- Thirty continuous casters, all designed by the same supplier but installed at different steel makers, took widely varying times to reach anticipated production levels. Start-up periods—the elapsed time from the first pouring of steel through a caster until the unit was producing at full capacity—varied from 7.5 months to over 6 years. The median start-up took 24 months. A rough calculation suggested that the lost contribution from these delays totaled $137 million, primarily because of slow and inadequate learning.[10]

- In industries as varied as banking, computers, health care, and oil, the typical intrafirm transfer of a best practice—from first identification of the practice to successful performance at the receiving unit— took nearly three years. The primary barriers were not motivational (a bias against ideas "not-invented here") but knowledge-related: limited understanding of the elements of successful practice and difficulty in absorbing new knowledge and insights.[11] The associated costs were significant. A study of intrafirm transfers of manufacturing technology found that over 50 percent experienced severe productivity problems. The initial productivity loss at the receiving plants averaged 34 percent, with a low of 4 percent and a high of 150 percent. The time to recover the lost productivity ranged from 1 to 13 months; at 20 percent of the facilities, the original levels were never regained.[12]

- When radical or disruptive technologies are involved, conventional marketing research is of little help. This is especially true if current customers are the primary sources of information. The disk-drive industry provides a telling example. As the industry shifted from 14-inch to 8-inch to 5.25-inch to 3.5-inch drives, virtually all of the leading firms were displaced. Each time, they failed to shift to the next-generation technology, largely because their current customers were expressing satisfaction with existing products while demand was coming from newer organizations that they were neither serving nor surveying. The failure was one of learning, not technological prowess.[13] Much the same displacement occurred in the semiconductor industry as it shifted from vacuum tubes to semiconductors to microprocessors.[14]

- In late 1994 Intel discovered a flaw in its Pentium processor. The problem, due to a design error in the chip, caused a rounding error in division once every nine billion calculations. The company knew of the problem early, considered it to be minor, and developed a policy of reassurance and occasional replacement. But it vastly underestimated the ensuing public reaction. Once the problem was publicized, the press was highly critical, as were customers and industry experts. After several months of analysis, reflection, and review—in other words, intensive learning—Intel announced a completely new policy: it would replace the offending part for anyone who wanted it changed. The cost? A $475 million write-off.[15]

At first glance, these examples involve seemingly unrelated challenges: installing new equipment, transferring best practices, responding to technological changes, and interpreting customer feedback. But at a deeper level, they are remarkably similar. Each illustrates the difficulties of effective implementation and, by implication, the power and potential of improved organizational learning.

There are several common denominators. First, in each of these cases success requires additional knowledge. Whether the task is operating an unfamiliar piece of equipment or understanding an emerging market, learning is essential to achieving desired results. Sometimes the knowledge is new and has to be created from scratch; at other times it already exists and has to be transferred elsewhere in the organization. Either way, the required insights are practical, applied, and focused on the task at hand. Learning is not desired for learning's sake, or for abstract, academic purposes. It is needed to get the job done.

Second, in each case improved learning has direct links to the bottom line. Both costs and revenues are affected. On the cost side, smoother transfers of best practices yield impressive gains in productivity. A sense for the size of the payoffs can be obtained by comparing the best and worst transferrers of manufacturing technology, whose productivity losses differed by a factor of 40. On the revenue side, better processing of customer and market information would undoubtedly improve the odds of succeeding with next-generation products, leading to more accurate market positioning and increased sales. The continuous caster example shows that where capacity is a constraint, more rapid ramp-ups to full production yield large increases in sales and contribution. Again, a sense for the payoffs can be gained by comparing the best and worst performers; their startup periods differed by a factor of 10.

Third and perhaps most important, managers seldom use the term learning when describing these situations. Typically, they reserve it for other purposes, primarily discussions of education and training programs or workshops where knowledge sharing is the stated goal. When learning is embedded in real work, managers normally use other language; frequently, they overlook learning's role completely. Yet situations like these—where learning is essential for completing a task, yet is neither recognized nor publicly acknowledged—are extraordinarily common. Entrepreneurship, for example, invariably involves new skills and behaviors, as do most business development projects. Effective mergers and acquisitions demand learning on both sides of the table. The same is true of most cost-reduction and quality-improvement programs, where process and operating knowledge must be deepened and expanded.

Because these situations arise so frequently, all organizations learn at some point in their lives. A few learn repeatedly but largely by happenstance. Long-successful companies, however, such as IBM and Johnson & Johnson, are invariably committed, conscientious learners.[16] In fact, it is almost a truism to say that such organizations learn, for they have prospered for decades while facing diverse and varied conditions. Revolutionary technologies, shifting markets, and unanticipated competitors have all required innovative responses. How else would these companies have survived if they were not continually learning something new?

One implication of this argument is that we need to view organizational effectiveness through a different lens. Corporate success is best judged by adaptability and flexibility, not the usual short-term measures of profitability and productivity. The latter present mere snapshots in time; a more appropriate metric would take into account long-term survival and growth:

> If we view organizations as adaptive, problem-solving, organic structures, then inferences about effectiveness have to be made, not from static measures of output, but on the basis of the processes through which the organization approaches problems. . . . The measure of health is flexibility, the freedom to learn through experience, the freedom to change with changing internal and external circumstances. . . .[17]

Examples include Microsoft's 1995 shift from operating systems and applications software to Internet offerings, which required a wholly new strategy as well as the broadening of programming and software skills, and 3M's continued outpouring of new products, often far removed from its base in adhesives and abrasives. Such adaptability is common in learning organizations.

LEARNING ORGANIZATIONS

Surprisingly, a clear definition of learning organizations has proved to be elusive over the years. Organizational theorists have studied learning for a long time, but as the quotations in Table 1-1 suggest, there is still considerable disagreement.[18] Most scholars agree that learning is a process that unfolds over time and link it with knowledge acquisition, deeper understanding, and improved performance. But they differ on other important matters.

Some, for example, believe that behavioral change is required for

---

TABLE 1-1

DEFINITIONS OF ORGANIZATIONAL LEARNING

Organizational learning means the process of improving actions through better knowledge and understanding.[a]

Organizational learning is defined as increasing an organization's capacity to take effective action.[b]

An entity learns if, through its processing of information, the range of potential behaviors is increased.[c]

Organizational learning is a process of detecting and correcting error.[d]

Organizational learning is defined as the process by which knowledge about action-outcome relationships between the organization and the environment is developed.[e]

Organizations are seen as learning by encoding inferences from history into routines that guide behavior.[f]

Organizational learning occurs through shared insights, knowledge, and mental models . . . [and] builds on past knowledge and experience—that is, on memory.[g]

---

a C. Marlene Fiol and Marjorie A. Lyles, "Organizational Learning," *Academy of Management Review* 10 (1985): 803.

b Daniel H. Kim, "The Link between Individual and Organizational Learning," *Sloan Management Review* (fall 1993): 43.

c George P. Huber, "Organizational Learning: The Contributing Processes and the Literatures," *Organization Science* 2 (1991): 89.

d Chris Argyris, "Double Loop Learning in Organizations," *Harvard Business Review* 55 (September/October 1977): 116.

e Richard L. Daft and Karl E. Weick, "Toward a Model of Organizations as Interpretation Systems," *Academy of Management Review* 9 (1984): 286.

f Barbara Levitt and James G. March, "Organizational Learning," *Annual Review of Sociology* 14 (1991): 319.

g Ray Stata, "Organizational Learning—The Key to Management Innovation," *Sloan Management Review* (spring 1989): 64.

---

learning; others insist that new ways of thinking are enough. Some cite information processing as the mechanism through which learning takes place; others propose shared insights, organizational routines, even memory. Some see the interpretative process as central to effective learning; others focus on the detection and correction of errors. And some think that organizational learning is common, while others believe that flawed, self-serving assessments are the norm.

Practitioners, of course, are less interested in academic fine points than in having a definition that is clear, compelling, and actionable. How, then, can we distinguish between these competing voices, yet build on the insights of other scholars? As a first step, consider the following definition:

A learning organization is an organization skilled at creating, acquiring, interpreting, transferring, and retaining knowledge, and at purposefully modifying its behavior to reflect new knowledge and insights.

This definition begins with a simple truth: new ideas are essential if learning is to take place. Sometimes they are created through flashes of insight and creativity; that is frequently the job of research centers such as Bell Laboratories and Xerox PARC. At other times they arrive from outside the organization, gleaned from technical articles, knowledgeable experts, or tracking studies. But even an abundance of new knowledge does not ensure that a learning organization exists. As the story of the Pentium processor makes clear, raw unfiltered information is of limited value. Managers must also be skilled at giving meaning to the data they have assembled. Without the ability to interpret unfamiliar knowledge accurately, even the best ideas will remain unutilized.

Nor does the process end with interpretation. Knowledge must also be shared collectively, rather than limited to a privileged few. New ideas must diffuse rapidly throughout the organization, extending from person to person, department to department, and division to division. Eventually, they must become embedded in organizational "memory," appearing as policies, procedures, and norms to ensure that they are retained over time. Purely local knowledge is valuable, but it does not mark the existence of an organization that has learned.

These activities provide the foundation for learning organizations. But they are no guarantee of success. Without accompanying changes in the way that work gets done, only the potential for improvement exists. According to this definition, learning requires action. But that action cannot be uninformed; it must be tied in some way to prior reflection. For this reason, neither book knowledge alone—collecting facts, without putting them into practice—nor spur-of-the-moment activity—doing something, without a clear rationale—meets the standard.

This is a surprisingly stringent test, for it rules out a number of obvious candidates for learning organizations. Many universities fail to qualify, as do many consulting firms. Even such a diligent student of modern management as General Motors is found wanting. All of these organizations have been effective at creating, acquiring, and interpreting knowledge but notably less successful in applying that knowledge to their own activities. Total quality management, for example, is now taught at many business schools, but the number using it to guide their own decision making is very small. Organizational consultants advise clients on social dynamics and small-group behavior but are notorious for their own infighting and factionalism. And GM, with a few exceptions such as New United Motors Manufacturing, Inc. (NUMMI), its highly productive assembly plant in Fremont, California, has had great difficulty mimicking the manufacturing practices of industry leaders like Toyota, even though its managers have carefully studied just-in-time production methods.

Organizations that do pass the definitional test—Xerox, L.L. Bean, and the many other examples cited in later chapters—have, by contrast, become adept at translating new knowledge into new ways of behaving. These organizations actively manage the learning process so that it is focused and purposeful. Learning occurs by design and in pursuit of clearly defined needs, rather than for its own sake. GE provides an instructive example. In 1989 Jack Welch, the company's CEO, launched Work-Out, a problem-solving process modeled after a New England town meeting. Welch was determined to improve productivity while streamlining the company's slow, cumbersome decision-making process. His learning agenda was quite explicit:

> Work-Out has a practical and an intellectual goal. The practical goal is to get rid of thousands of bad habits accumulated since the creation of General Electric. . . . [T]he intellectual part begins by putting the leaders of each business in front of a hundred or so of their people, eight to ten times a year, to let them hear what their people think. . . . Ultimately, we're talking about redefining the relationship between boss and subordinate. I want to get to the point where people challenge their bosses every day.[19]

To that end, Work-Out combined three days of off-site discussion by groups of thirty to one hundred hourly and salaried employees, aimed at fleshing out departmental or divisional problems and developing possible solutions, with a final intense session, at which the boss returned, was bombarded by the group's proposals, and was forced to make instant, on-the-spot decisions. For each recommendation, his or her only alternatives were to say yes, no, or I need more data. Welch made this process a virtual requirement at GE and personally pressed managers to get involved—he was determined to share the learning widely and retain it in organizational memory—and by mid-1993 over 85 percent of the work force had participated. By all accounts, the process was a huge success; not only did productivity improve, but managers' responsiveness increased as well. For these reasons, Work-Out provides a perfect example of a learning organization in action, for it shows how the creation, interpretation, and retention of knowledge can be coupled with changes in behavior to produce meaningful results.

LITMUS TESTS

By this point readers will be wondering, How will I know if mine is a learning organization? Are there any obvious clues? There are, in fact, a few simple litmus tests that can be applied to determine whether or not a company qualifies.[20] Each is framed as a question that probes for evidence of distinctive behaviors. The presence of these traits does not guarantee the existence of a learning organization—specific practices and processes are also required—but their absence certainly raises grave doubts.

> *Does the organization have a defined learning agenda?* Learning organizations have a clear picture of their future knowledge requirements. They know what they need to know, whether the subject is customers, competitors, markets, technologies, or production processes, and are actively pursuing the desired information. Even in industries that are changing as rapidly as telecommunications, computers, and financial services, broad areas of needed learning can usually be mapped with some precision. Once they have been identified, these topics are pursued through multiple approaches, including experiments, simulations, research studies, post-audits, and benchmarking visits, rather than education and training alone.

> *Is the organization open to discordant information?* If an organization regularly "shoots the messenger" who brings forward unexpected or bad news, the environment is clearly hostile to learning.

Behavior change is extremely difficult in such settings, for there are few challenges to the status quo. Sensitive topics—dissension in the ranks, unhappy customers, preemptive moves by competitors, problems with new technologies—are considered to be off limits, and messages are filtered, massaged, and watered down as they make their way up the chain of command. Senior managers are likely to remain out of touch because they will be confronted with little of the conflict and contrast that are so essential to effective learning.

Does the organization avoid repeated mistakes? Learning organizations reflect on their past experience, distill it into useful lessons, share the knowledge internally, and ensure that errors are not repeated elsewhere. Databases, intranets, training sessions, and workshops can all be used for this purpose. Even more critical, however, "is a mind-set that . . . enables companies to recognize the value of productive failure as contrasted with unproductive success. A productive failure is one that leads to insights, understanding, and thus an addition to the commonly held wisdom of the organization. An unproductive success occurs when something goes well, but nobody knows how or why."[21] There is a peculiar logic at work here: to avoid repeating mistakes, managers must learn to accept them the first time around. They must adopt the philosophy of John McCoy, the chairman of Banc One, who observed: "I don't remember my successes. It's the mistakes that I . . . learned from."[22] This mind-set is rare in corporate America, because it requires a tolerance for error and a willingness to view failures as a necessary by-product of experimentation and risk taking.

Does the organization lose critical knowledge when key people leave? The story is all too common: a talented engineer (or marketer or production supervisor) leaves the company, and critical skills disappear as well. Tasks that were previously routine become impossible, for the required know-how can no longer be found. Why? Because crucial knowledge was tacit, unarticulated, and unshared, locked in the head of a single person. Learning organizations avoid this problem by institutionalizing essential knowledge. Whenever possible, they codify it in policies or procedures, retain it in reports or memos, disperse it to large groups of people, and build it into the company's values, norms, and operating practices. Knowledge becomes common property, rather than the province of individuals or small groups.

Does the organization act on what it knows? Learning organizations are not simply repositories of knowledge. They take advantage of their new learnings and adapt their behavior accordingly. Information is to be used; if it languishes or is ignored, its impact is certain to be minimal. By this test, an organization that discovers an unmet market need but fails to fill it does not qualify as a learning organization, nor does a company that identifies its own best practices but is unable to transfer them across departments or divisions.

FIRST STEPS

Learning organizations are not built overnight. As later chapters will show, most successful examples are the products of carefully cultivated attitudes, commitments, and management processes that have accrued slowly and steadily over time. Still, some changes can be made immediately. Any company that wishes to become a learning organization can begin by answering three simple questions.

- What are our most pressing business challenges and greatest business opportunities?

- What do we need to learn to meet the challenges and take advantage of the opportunities?

- How should the necessary knowledge and skills be acquired?

The first of these questions is the most common. In most companies the answer already exists in the output of annual retreats, monthly review meetings, and strategic planning exercises. At some point, virtually all companies require that their managers identify the unit's strengths and weaknesses and develop an associated list of opportunities and threats (SWOTs). These SWOTs typically provide the basis for the company's annual plan, as well as the goals for individual managers.

The second question is much rarer. Most managers move immediately from identifying an opportunity or problem to developing an action plan; they seldom pause to ask what needs to be learned if they are to proceed in an informed fashion. Yet new knowledge is invariably required if real progress is to be made. Consider, for example, a consumer goods company that has decided to begin selling its products in China. To succeed, it must develop knowledge on several fronts: an understanding of the role of government officials, the nature of existing supply networks, how to distribute products effectively, the required adaptations of designs and formulations to local needs, and how to advertise and price competitively. Such information is crucial to moving forward but is unlikely to be readily available and on tap. It must be actively assembled and acquired.

Alternatively, consider a steelmaker experiencing problems with a new generation of materials. Yields are low, and defects are multiplying. Again, the company's learning needs can be clearly specified: deeper knowledge of the cause-and-effect relationships governing the production process, and identification of the critical process variables (temperature, pressure, time) that must be controlled for superior performance. Without this knowledge, improvement is likely to be impeded by false starts and misdirected efforts. Or consider an airline planning to upgrade its fleet by acquiring more modern planes. Its learning needs cover a broad sweep: new approaches to routing and scheduling to accommodate the faster, more flexible jets, and new skills for those pilots, mechanics, and flight attendants who will service and use the new equipment. Here too learning is an essential intermediate step on the road to effective action.

The explicit identification of learning needs leads naturally to the third question, which is rarer still. New ideas do not materialize of their own accord; they must be actively pursued. Managers must learn to ask, What is the best way to acquire the necessary knowledge and skills? Organizations have a wide range of learning tools at their disposal; in any given situation, some are likely to provide more leverage than others.

The consumer goods company, for example, could learn more about the Chinese market by relying on a consulting firm with expertise in the region, forming a joint venture with a Chinese partner, hiring a manager from another company who has already built a successful Chinese subsidiary, sending benchmarking teams and study missions to China, or establishing a small-scale pilot operation to gain practical knowledge firsthand. The steel maker could conduct shop-floor experiments to identify critical operating variables, send metallurgists back to the library or the laboratory to carry out further investigative research, or collaborate with academic scientists to diagnose and solve the problem. The airline could develop software programs to optimize routing and scheduling, collect competitive intelligence to identify the scheduling practices used by airlines that had modernized earlier, purchase simulators as part of its own education and training program, or send employees to outside vendors or established flight academies to acquire needed skills.

In each case, the most effective learning strategy depends on the situation. There is no stock answer, nor is there a single best approach. But by asking these questions, managers are taking an important first step: they are agreeing that learning can be managed. New knowledge need not materialize by magic, nor through sweeping metaphors or grand themes. The roots of learning organizations lie in the gritty realities of practice.

2

The Learning Process

Organizational learning demands inquisitiveness and openness—a willingness by managers to challenge assumptions and tackle conventional wisdom. Otherwise, behavior will continue to be ruled by habit, and the status quo will remain undisturbed.

Unfortunately, most organizations have been designed with the status quo firmly in mind. They accomplish their work through what scholars call "routines," commonly accepted practices and procedures that are uniform, unvarying, and performed without thinking.[1] Repetition and consistency, rather than new insights, are the primary goals. Examples include McDonald's strict standards for cooking burgers and fries, timed tasks on an assembly line, and rules for processing travel vouchers in a busy office. In most cases, the associated activities are programmed and automatic, and soon become accepted as "the way we do things around here."

Managers are equally vulnerable to habit, especially when processing information and interpreting events. They are continually bombarded by facts, opinions, and forecasts; to avoid overload, many rely on time-tested categories and filters.[2] Often, these categories are implicit and unstated; like most routines, they are invoked without conscious thought. Examples include assumptions about market boundaries—who is a potential competitor, and who is not—and the underlying economics of a business. Even when industry environments are changing rapidly, these assumptions continue to influence the way that managers think about customers, competitors, and required competencies.

The goal of these routines is laudable: improved efficiency through standardization. Time is saved in both operations and information processing because the same approach is used repeatedly—and often unconsciously. Unfortunately, the side effects can be severe. Learning requires new knowledge and approaches—as a pioneering scientist has put it, "discovery consists of seeing what everybody has seen and thinking what nobody has thought"—and habitual, preset responses leave little room for fresh perspectives or innovative ways of thinking.[3] In the presence of routines, the wonder of organizational learning is that it occurs at all. To ensure that it does, managers first need to develop a better understanding of the learning process—the stages through which learning unfolds, the biases and disabilities that so often stand in the way, and the enablers and supporting conditions that allow new ideas to flourish. Only then will they be able to combat ingrained routines and actively cultivate learning.

STAGES OF LEARNING

Virtually all studies of organizational learning divide the process into three or four stages. The terminology varies, but the same basic steps appear again and again.[4] For learning to occur, organizations must first *acquire* information, assembling facts, observations, and data. At this stage, the raw material of learning is gathered, and the crucial questions include, What information should we collect? From where? How should it be obtained, and by whom? Next, organizations *interpret* information, producing perspectives, positions, and refined understanding. At this point, the raw material is processed and reviewed, and the crucial questions include, What does the information mean? What categories should we apply? What cause-and-effect relationships are at work? Finally, organizations *use* or *apply* information, engaging in tasks, activities, and new behaviors. At this time, analysis is translated into action, and the crucial questions include, What new activities are appropriate? What behaviors must be modified? How do we generate a collective response by the organization? Not surprisingly, each of these stages brings its own distinctive tasks and challenges.

Acquiring Information

It is easy for managers to be overwhelmed in today's information-rich economy. The number of business books, journals, conferences, and Web sites with up-to-the-minute insights continues to grow at an alarming rate. Is it any wonder that most organizations find themselves drowning in data? In such settings, acquiring information is easy—too easy, in fact. The real challenge for managers is to distinguish relevant from irrelevant information, while remaining open to unexpected, and occasionally un-welcome, surprises.

In technical terms, the first task involves separating "signals" from "noise." Both terms are drawn from modern information theory but have commonsense definitions. A signal is the true impact or evidence associated with an activity or event; noise is any contradictory, confusing, or random information that obscures the message.[5] Effective organizational learning demands clear signals and minimal noise, as well as the ability to share critical insights so that they do not remain isolated or unacknowledged. Unfortunately, in many settings, especially those involving rapid change and multiple sources of data, the combination is rare. Low signal-to-noise ratios are a pervasive problem, as the following examples suggest:

- The Japanese raid on Pearl Harbor was preceded by a number of clear signals, including the famous message "East Wind Rain," drawn from the top-secret code MAGIC, suggesting that an attack was imminent. As a leading historian has observed: "Our decisionmakers had at hand an impressive amount of information on the enemy."[6] Yet at the same time, there was a welter of conflicting evidence, especially from European sources, that pointed to different conclusions. No single analyst had a complete, integrated picture because critical intelligence information was not widely shared. The Japanese were also maintaining strict secrecy about the attack, while announcing a number of false targets. All told, the noise in the system was simply too great for a clear message to get through. According to the same historian: "We failed to anticipate Pearl Harbor not for want of the relevant materials, but because of a plethora of irrelevant ones . . . [I]t is much easier *after* the event to sort the relevant from the irrelevant signals . . . Signals that are characterized today as absolutely unequivocal warnings of a surprise air attack on Pearl Harbor become, on analysis, not merely ambiguous but occasionally inconsistent with such an attack."[7]

- The explosion of the space shuttle *Challenger* is often cited as a preventable disaster resulting from failure to heed clear signals of potential danger prior to launch. But those signals were extremely difficult to read in real time; many of them, on careful analysis, were mixed, weak, or routine. "A mixed signal was one where a signal of potential danger was followed by signals that all was well, convincing engineers that the problem had been successfully diagnosed [and] corrected . . . A weak signal was one that was unclear, or one that, after analysis, seemed such an improbable event that working engineers believed there was little probability of it recurring . . . Routine signals are those that occur frequently. The frequent event . . . loses some of its seriousness as similar events occur."[8] In particular, damage to the *Challenger*'s O-rings, which sealed the solid rocket booster joints and were later implicated in the disaster, had been found on a number of previous flights but were not regarded as a serious concern. Why? Because the known sources of the problem had already been fixed; cold temperatures, which produced much of the deterioration, were rare in Florida and not expected to recur; and previous flights had weathered the damage without problems. Here, too, fuzzy signals resulted in critical problems being overlooked.

- Semiconductor manufacturing is a business where rapid learning is essential for commercial success. Manufacturing yields are typically quite low when a new semiconductor is introduced; they must be raised quickly if the product is to become profitable. Experimentation is therefore common during the first few months of production; the goals are to identify critical operating parameters and setpoints, to better understand the underlying manufacturing process, and to increase yields. Unfortunately, these experiments do not always produce the desired learning. Studies of VLSI (very large scale integration) integrated circuit fabrication have found extremely high levels of process noise, making improvements difficult to identify. In most cases, there was so much variability within and across production lots that experiments were of limited value. For example, in four of the five plants studied the "probability of overlooking a three percent yield improvement was over twenty percent." At times, noise levels were so high that the likelihood of identifying critical variables was "little better than pure chance."[9]

These examples suggest that acquiring information is surprisingly difficult. Valuable signals are frequently accompanied by worthless noise. Critical insights remain in isolated pockets and are not always connected or pulled together. Even when all the necessary data have been obtained, the underlying message often remains obscure. The implications for managers are obvious. To enhance learning, they must improve signal-to-noise ratios, develop mechanisms for pooling information, and work to craft an integrated, unbiased picture of events.

As if these challenges were not enough, there is a further complication. Unlike instruments or electronic equipment, which are programmed to record all incoming data, managers are more selective. They do not attend to all information but instead rely on "processes that amplify some stimuli and attenuate others, thus distorting the raw data and focusing attention."[10] A hypothesis is first formed, or a perspective established; information is then collected with these frameworks in mind.[11] As social psychologists have observed, the results are predictable: "much of what people would label as information only reaffirms old news."[12]

In fact, it is extremely difficult—and, at times, impossible—for organizations to assemble pure, unvarnished facts, especially if they are unexpected. Most people are drawn to the familiar, and managers are no exception. Market research provides a good example. Studies show that managers typically use market research for confirmatory purposes—to reduce uncertainties, fill information gaps, and generate support for decisions that have already been made—rather than as a source of new insights.[13] Open-minded inquiry is seldom the goal. Instead, data collection is normally limited to current customers, known competitors, and a narrow set of questions. Surprises are shunned, and unforeseen or counterintuitive findings, which could produce deep learning, usually have the opposite effect: they upset managers and receive little attention. Here, as in many other settings, effective organizational learning requires a more open and accepting process for acquiring information.

Interpreting Information

Even if organizations were able to acquire all essential information, they would still have to interpret it. Industry environments are seldom tidy or orderly; most are in constant flux. Unadorned facts and opinions are therefore of limited value. They become useful only after they have been classified, grouped, or placed within a larger context. For this reason, scholars have observed:

> Organizations must make interpretations. Managers must literally wade into the swarm of events that constitute and surround the organization and actively try to impose some order. . . . Interpretation is the process of translating these events, of developing models for understanding, of bringing out meaning, and of assembling conceptual schemes.[14]

To evaluate the impact of a new product, for example, managers must first make assumptions about industry rivalry and customer needs; the same is true when assessing the consequences of a complex, cross-border alliance. In both situations, they rely heavily on what cognitive scientists call "schemas," deeply rooted mental structures that organize knowledge and give it form and meaning. At an abstract level, schemas consist of categories, models, classification schemes, and assumed cause-and-effect relationships that together give shape and texture to independent, unconnected observations. They play a variety of roles: organizing and classifying new information, filling in missing data, assigning probabilities to events, and providing rationales and explanations for behavior. To the extent that the underlying frameworks are shared, members of an organization will think along similar lines.[15]

Peter Drucker, for example, has observed that all companies have an implicit "theory of the business," a set of shared assumptions about markets, customers, competitors, technology, and the organization's mission and competencies.[16] These theories provide consistent, cohesive frameworks for interpreting events and guiding behavior. Unfortunately, they also have a critical weakness: they eventually become obsolete. The theory on which a business was built does not always accord with current realities; when the two diverge, problems are inevitable. IBM's fall from grace in the 1980s is representative. At the time, managers were unable to harmonize the company's long-standing theory of the business, which was based on a dominant presence in mainframe computers, with the growing demand for PCs, which required a very different competitive logic.

Interpretative frameworks thus present two challenges for managers. First, as the IBM example illustrates, they must be tested and updated continually. Without active scanning of the environment and an openness to contradictory information, frameworks can quickly become irrelevant. Second, managers must recognize that their frameworks are invariably sketchy and incomplete; they are approximations of reality that are "reasonable rather than right."[17] In most cases, the underlying cause-and-effect relationships are difficult to specify, and data can be viewed in more than one light. Supporting evidence is often fragmentary. The same facts may well produce conflicting interpretations, with considerable room for disagreement and debate. Do a competitor's price cuts, for example, imply that a price war is imminent, or are they an innocuous attempt to reduce excess inventory? When does rising demand signal a turnaround in the economy, and when is it a mere seasonal correction? Are the latest technologies fads that will soon disappear, or do they signify fundamental shifts in product requirements?

Each of these questions lacks an obvious, factual answer, and each can be addressed only by invoking an interpretative framework. For this reason, interpretation lies at the heart of decision making. As Dean Stanley Teele of the Harvard Business School was fond of telling students: "The art of management is the art of making meaningful generalizations out of inadequate facts." But which generalizations should managers use? And on what basis should they choose? The goal, of course, is to select the most accurate interpretation, the one whose categories, constructs, and cause-and-effect relationships best match reality. But because accuracy can be determined only after the fact, managers must rely on proxies when making comparisons, judging competing frameworks by their richness and degree of detail. In general, more effective frameworks are better grounded in concrete data, include more comprehensive taxonomies, are tied together by stronger, more fine-grained causal linkages, and are more widely shared by key actors.[18] Xerox, for example, was far more successful in marketing its copiers after it expanded its original two broad categories of customers—large and small accounts—to six—large- and small-customer major accounts, large and small named accounts, general markets, and government/education. Predictive power improved because the new categories were more differentiated and better able to discriminate between actors and their needs.[19]

Applying Information

Because learning is usually associated with thinking rather than doing, this stage is not always considered to be part of the learning process. But according to the definition and litmus tests of chapter 1, action is essential; if an entity does not purposefully modify its behavior to reflect new knowledge and insights, it does not qualify as a learning organization. Two steps are required. Managers must translate their interpretations into concrete behaviors and must then ensure that a critical mass of the organization adopts the new activities.

The first task is often difficult. Interpretative frameworks classify and organize data; they do not always have obvious implications for action. Agreeing on the meaning of events still leaves open the question of what to do about them. Recall, for example, Intel's difficulties with the flawed Pentium processor. Even after managers recognized that their "Intel Inside" advertising campaign, coupled with the company's vast size, had transformed the firm into a highly visible consumer marketer, they remained unsure how to respond. According to Andy Grove, Intel's chairman and CEO:

> the old rules of business no longer worked. New rules prevailed. . . .
> The trouble was, not only didn't we realize that the rules had
> changed—what was worse, we didn't know what rules we now had
> to abide by. . . .

It's like sailing a boat when the wind shifts on you. . . . [T]he boat suddenly heels over. What worked before doesn't work anymore; you need to steer the boat in a different direction quickly before you are in trouble, yet you have to get a feel of the new direction and the strength of the wind before you can hope to right the boat and set a new course.[20]

Even when the behavioral implications of a new interpretation are obvious, employees may still not take the required steps. Habits and routines are difficult to dislodge. To overcome inertia, managers must first send clear signals but, even more important, must offer opportunities to practice new behaviors. Hands-on experience is usually the best teacher, and managers must make the time for employees to learn new behaviors: "If you really want people to spend time doing something new, give them the time to do it. Take away old activities, provide released time, ask them to work overtime—somehow demonstrate that time allocation patterns are to change."[21]

It is essential to eliminate unnecessary or outdated tasks at the same time that new ones are added. Otherwise, overload is inevitable. Most companies, unfortunately, only understand the concept of addition; they are much weaker when it comes to subtracting work. Continental Airlines is a notable exception. In the mid-1990s, it studied a competitor, Southwest Airlines, to learn how to cross-utilize personnel (to have the same people perform multiple tasks such as loading baggage and boarding customers at the gate). Initially, employees objected to cross-utilization, fearing that workloads would increase. But they were soon persuaded, after management asked them to list all the "dumb, non-value-added things" they did each day and then eliminated many of these useless chores. The result was a much speedier adoption of cross-utilization because time was now available for learning.[22]

Time to practice, however, is seldom sufficient by itself, especially if new competencies are required and members of the organization must broaden or alter their skills. Then, resistance is likely to reflect deeper forces—personal values, a sense of identity, preferred work styles—and forceful action is often necessary if behavior is to change. Software providers, for example, have long preached the gospel of customer service. But their help lines still suffer from technical jargon and poor communication because employees continue to identify with the technology, rather than with unskilled users. To overcome the problem, a new breed of customer service representatives may be needed, and financial incentives may have to be tied directly to customer satisfaction scores. Only then will a critical mass of the organization make the desired behavioral shifts.

LEARNING DISABILITIES

At first glance, the acquire-interpret-apply process is a model of simplicity. Each of the three stages brings challenges, but they appear to be predictable and easy to identify. With attention and forethought, managers would seem to face few difficulties in cultivating learning.

Unfortunately, a wide range of learning disabilities impede the process. They are a common and often unavoidable by-product of the way people think and act, and occur at every stage in the learning process. Acquisition problems arise from oversights, omissions, and errors in the way information is collected; they result in slanted or incomplete data. Interpretation problems arise from distortions in the way that information is processed by preexisting frameworks; a large number occur because managers are imperfect statisticians and make flawed judgments about the likelihood and probability of events. Application and use problems arise from corporate risk aversion and the difficulties people have in recognizing that their actual behavior often deviates markedly from their espoused behavior. Together, these problems conspire to undermine learning and reduce its effectiveness. Managers must tackle them aggressively if they want accurate inferences and appropriate action to result from new information.

Biased Information

When acquiring information, organizations suffer from three primary disabilities: blind spots, filtering, and lack of information sharing. Blind spots arise when scanning and search activities are narrow or misdirected, resulting in areas where managers "will . . . not see the significance of events . . . at all, will perceive them incorrectly, or will perceive them very slowly."[23] They normally reflect mistaken or incomplete assumptions. A common error is misjudging industry boundaries and expecting that competition will continue to come from traditional sources. Newspapers, for example, long underestimated the threat posed by cable TV and the Internet, as did the major networks. Only after audiences declined steadily did both groups begin to reexamine their definitions of the industry. The rise of biotechnology had a similar impact on pharmaceutical firms, who initially overlooked chemical companies as likely competitors because they failed to see the similarities between the requirements for success in biotechnology and chemical companies' long-established competencies and skills.[24]

Blind spots are especially likely to arise during times of crisis. Stress and anxiety typically lead to restrictions in the amount and type of information that managers process, as well as a tendency to search for data that confirm preexisting views.[25] The result is a narrowing of focus and attention. Nike, for example, after a decade of extraordinarily rapid growth, faced slowing sales in the early 1980s. Reebok had entered the market with an innovative new design, a soft, comfortable aerobics shoe made of garment leather that required no break-in period. Sales quickly took off. Yet managers at Nike were slow to respond, largely because of their traditional focus on athletes and performance-oriented shoes. Many, in fact, found it so difficult to accept customers' changing preferences that they deemed the first prototype, made of soft leather, as "simply unsuitable" for a Nike product. According to a senior executive: "We could still be purists and talk about shoes that were for runners and athletes. And anybody who didn't make it the way we made it was a fool. We also had the idea that everything we sold . . . was used by an athlete to perform, which was absolute bull."[26]

Nike's difficulties are closely related to another bias in acquiring information: filtering. Filtering occurs when critical data are downplayed or ignored because they do not accord with preexisting schemas or frameworks.[27] In a revealing set of experiments, psychologists found that exposing supporters and opponents of capital punishment to *identical* evidence led them to diametrically opposed conclusions.[28] Polarization actually increased, and established positions became more entrenched. Why?

Because each group read the findings selectively, allowing assumptions to drown out facts. They discounted surprises and minimized the importance of contrary evidence. Such problems are especially likely to occur under stress, when expectations are high, existing hypotheses or interpretations serve as a defense against anxiety or threats, attention is focused elsewhere, and attentiveness decreases because a period of intense concentration has come to an end. In the Tenerife air disaster, for example, two jumbo jets collided on takeoff with a loss of 583 lives. Among the causes were a series of miscommunications in which pilots heard distorted messages yet did not raise questions, filled in missing information in ways that confirmed their assumptions about clearances and lack of obstructions, were preoccupied with flying their planes rather than monitoring radio traffic, and relaxed momentarily after completing difficult maneuvers.[29] The parallels to management are painfully clear. Like the pilots at Tenerife, managers under pressure often hear what they want to hear.

Lack of information sharing only compounds the problem. Undiffused, local knowledge is of limited use, for it is seldom available when needed. To ensure effectiveness, critical incoming data must quickly become common property, woven into the organization's collective consciousness. Otherwise, as the attack on Pearl Harbor illustrates, it will remain unheeded, without the visibility needed to impact decision making.

Unfortunately, such sharing is easier said than done. Information hoarding is a fact of organizational life, especially in political settings or where information is highly valued.[30] Functional fiefdoms contribute to the problem, as do departmental loyalties and narrow, issue-oriented coalitions. But even when the problem has been recognized and independent competitive intelligence or environmental analysis groups have been established, difficulties remain. Especially when they are freestanding, these groups often find themselves isolated and unable to tie into the decision-making process. They remain vulnerable because they lack well-defined roles and power bases and are not tightly integrated into the line organization. As one director of environmental analysis described the problem: "It doesn't help to have a 16 cylinder engine, if it isn't connected to the wheels."[31]

Flawed Interpretation

Disabilities are common during interpretation because the underlying processes are complex and poorly understood. Interpretation involves judgment and a certain amount of inspired guesswork; both are easily swayed by factors other than logic or reason. In particular, human beings are subject to a wide range of interpretative errors because they are notoriously poor statisticians. Few people understand the strict requirements for inferring causation; fewer still are well versed in the laws and limits of probabilistic reasoning.[32] Even the most sophisticated managers make these mistakes.[33] Despite the best of intentions, they routinely develop interpretations, causal connections, and probability estimates that are seriously biased.

Scholars have identified a number of distinctive problems. The best known include the following:

- *illusory correlation:* viewing events as related simply because they have appeared together;
- *illusory causation:* ascribing causality to events that occur in sequence and seem to be linked;
- *the illusion of validity:* increasing confidence in one's judgment, especially with larger and larger amounts of information, even though the accuracy of judgment remains unchanged;
- *framing effects:* different responses to identical, uncertain payoffs that have been framed as potential gains rather than potential losses;
- *categorical bias:* the use and persistence of stereotypical categories for classifying people and events, even when faced with conflicting information;
- *availability bias:* assessing the probability of events by the ease with which examples come to mind, rather than their actual frequencies or likelihoods;
- *regression artifacts:* ascribing causality to actions that change a variable from an extreme (high or low) level to an average level, even though the change is really due to chance (i.e., the greater likelihood

that an average score will be obtained rather than an extreme value); and

- **hindsight bias:** the systematic biasing of probability estimates toward actual outcomes.[34]

At first glance, many of these errors seem esoteric and even irrelevant to the task of management. But they have very real implications. Consider two examples: the illusion of validity and hindsight bias. The former is simply a fancy way of describing an age-old problem: *hubris,* or excessive confidence in one's ability to form accurate judgments. Unfortunately, such confidence is seldom warranted, especially when information is incomplete or ambiguous. A study of clinical psychologists, for example, found that their ability to answer questions about a subject's personality type changed relatively little as they received more data, increasing from being 26 percent to 28 percent correct. But their confidence in their accuracy rose far more dramatically. Initially, psychologists estimated that they would answer 33 percent of the questions correctly; once they had complete background information, they estimated that they would be 53 percent correct. As the author of the study concluded: "The judges' confidence ratings showed that *they become convinced of their own increasing understanding of the case* . . . entirely out of proportion to the actual correctness of those decisions."[35] Is it at all difficult to imagine managers reacting similarly to increasing amounts of information about customers, competitors, or employees? Is there any reason to believe that their self-assessments will be any more accurate than psychologists'?

Hindsight bias is an equally pervasive problem. It too describes a familiar phenomenon: the tendency to look back on events and assume that one "knew it all along." When presented with information about historical situations and asked to judge the probability of different outcomes, individuals systematically bias their estimates in the direction of the outcomes that actually occurred. They appear, on reflection, to have been inevitable. The process works unconsciously and is difficult to overcome, even when subjects have been warned in advance. Retrospective assessments are therefore quite different from those made in real time.

In a revealing experiment, M.B.A. students were divided into groups and asked to analyze a complex investment proposal. Each group was provided with identical facts about the project but was given different information about outcomes. "When told, but then asked to ignore, the results . . . they were unable to do so. . . . [T]hose who were told of favorable outcomes rated the project as more promising, less risky, more likely to succeed, and more attractive for a personal investment than did others told of less favorable results; subjects given no outcome information fell in between."[36] The implications for managers are disturbing. Because of hindsight bias, it is extremely difficult to judge the appropriateness of past decisions and draw inferences for the future. To learn from experience, managers must be able to evaluate situations as they appeared at the time that choices were made. They must ask, "Considering what I knew then, how likely did the event seem?"[37] Unfortunately, because of biases in remembered or reconstructed evaluations, the answers that emerge are seldom accurate.

Inaction

At the third stage of the learning process, the primary problem is passivity—an inability or unwillingness to act on new interpretations. Inertia is partly to blame, as are continued efforts to justify the past. Most individuals and organizations are also risk averse; they do not like to experiment with unfamiliar, untested approaches. In part, this is a problem of incentives and the frequent lack of support for new initiatives. As Jack Welch of GE put it: "Change has no constituency."[38] At times, however, the problem runs deeper and reflects the very human tendency to overlook personal shortcomings.

A certain level of self-awareness is essential if changes are to be made. Current practice must be clearly understood; only then is it possible to take remedial action. Yet all too often, the required understanding is lacking. People are surprisingly unaware of their own behavior; they do not always act the way they think they do. In technical terms, the problem is one of distinguishing "espoused theories" from "theories-in-use":

> When someone is asked how he would behave under certain circumstances, the answer he usually gives is his espoused theory of action for that situation. This is the theory of action to which he gives allegiance and which, upon request, he communicates to others. However, the theory that actually governs his actions is his

theory-in-use, which may or may not be compatible with his espoused theory; furthermore, the individual may or may not be aware
of the incompatibility of the two theories.[39]

The examples are legion: the autocratic manager who claims that he is
already using participative approaches, the surly saleswoman who asserts
that she is only responding to customer needs, the arrogant consultant
who insists that he avoids dictating to clients. All firmly believe that
they are acting in the manner described and are usually unaware of any
discrepancies. Learning is extremely unlikely in such settings because
people remain unconvinced that changes in behavior are actually
required.

SUPPORTIVE LEARNING ENVIRONMENTS

Learning disabilities are common and predictable. Like competition, they
are a fact of organizational life. But that does not mean they have to be
paralyzing. Companies can take a number of steps to minimize these
disabilities and cultivate more accurate, effective learning. To begin, they
need to create supportive, stimulating environments. Four conditions are
essential if learning is to flourish: the recognition and acceptance of
differences; the provision of timely, unvarnished feedback; the pursuit of
new ways of thinking and untapped sources of information; and the
acceptance of errors, mistakes, and occasional failures as the price of
improvement.

Recognize and Accept Differences

Differences are crucial to learning because they provide energy and motivation. Without them, lethargy and drift are likely, and prevailing schemas and frameworks are almost certain to remain in place. Questions
arise only when we become aware of inconsistencies, contradictions, and
competing perspectives; the resulting tensions produce discomfort and
lead to a search for solutions. In business settings, inconsistencies frequently take the form of gaps or unfilled promises—gulfs between aspira-

tions and reality or expected and actual performance. Divergent opinions, especially among powerful managers, are an equally strong force for change. But these differences must first be acknowledged and brought into close proximity if learning is to occur.[40] In many organizations, the difficulty lies not in creating differences—they are invariably widespread and deeply rooted—but in ensuring that processes exist for bringing divergent points of view together, airing them fully, and resolving the resulting tensions productively.

Boeing, for example, has developed a system of checks and balances that serves precisely this purpose. The development of a new airframe is a several-billion-dollar bet, and the task is dauntingly complex. A typical 767 contains over three million parts and eighty-five miles of wiring. Because the potential for error is so great, Boeing has long used audit teams to inject diverse views into the design process. When the 767 was still on the drawing board, teams of experienced managers were asked to review every significant element of the program, including technology, finance, manufacturing, and management. Teams acted as devil's advocates, introducing competing perspectives and questioning all aspects of the work. A typical audit took three months. To preserve autonomy, all teams were isolated organizationally and given a direct reporting line to the chairman.[41]

Emerson Electric has used a similar approach in strategic planning. Each fiscal year, senior corporate officers meet with the management of every division to discuss their plans. A few basic charts are presented summarizing historical trends, financial targets, sales goals, and expected sources of growth and cost savings, but the real focus is the discussion that follows. Differences are highlighted and even created when necessary. According to Charles (Chuck) Knight, the company's long-term CEO:

> The mood is confrontational—by design. Though we're not trying to put anyone on the spot, we do want to challenge assumptions and conventional thinking. . . . Often, a manager will give a logical presentation on why we should approve a plan. We may challenge that logic by questioning underlying assumptions illogically. The people

who know their strategies in detail are the ones who, after going through that, are able to stand up for the merits of their proposal.[42]

Although the settings differ, both Boeing and Emerson Electric are pursuing the same goal: encouraging learning by battling complacency. Conflict and debate are invaluable for this purpose; both result from differences that have been brought into close contact. The same ends can be achieved by other means. Heterogeneous management teams, made up of individuals of diverse ages, genders, functional backgrounds, and industry experiences, are helpful, as are attempts to develop multiple alternatives, options, and scenarios before settling on a single course of action.[43] Occasionally, the decision-making process itself can be re-designed. Techniques for introducing differences include "dialectical inquiry" and "devil's advocacy"; the former breaks teams into subgroups to develop competing positions, while the latter institutionalizes criticism by assigning the responsibility and role to an individual or subgroup.[44] Both approaches have been judged to produce superior outcomes in a wide range of experimental settings. Both have also proven themselves under fire. After his disastrous experience with the Bay of Pigs, President Kennedy redesigned the process of national security decision making to explicitly include these techniques and used them to great effect in the Cuban Missile Crisis.[45]

Provide Timely Feedback

Timely, accurate feedback is equally important in encouraging learning.[46] By compressing the learning cycle into a brief period and then coupling it with revised, updated information, organizations can more quickly as-similate new observations; can more easily compare predicted and actual behaviors; and can more readily identify problems and disabilities. Com-panies can obtain these benefits even with simple feedback processes. Skilled managers, for example, often float trial balloons to get a quick reading on their organizations' receptiveness to new proposals. Effective product developers rely heavily on prototypes—small models, mock-ups, or simulations, built quickly and inexpensively—to uncover potential design conflicts and manufacturing problems. Shop-floor employees calibrate their skills by visiting customers' factories and discussing their work.

More elaborate systems can have even greater impact, especially if they introduce detailed, comparative data. Such systems create immediate pressures to learn because the facts are difficult to deny. Flawed interpretations are far more likely to be questioned, as are inertia and failure to act. Banc One, for example, a large bank-holding company, for many years used its financial reporting system for this purpose. After a new bank was acquired, it was immediately converted to a standard IT system to ensure apples-to-apples comparisons. All banks then received a monthly "peer report," based on asset size, which compared their performance to comparable banks on measures of revenue, income, balance sheet quality, productivity, and liquidity. The culture was one of "share and compare," and both were expected. As the chairman observed at the time: "[E]veryone has access to everyone else's numbers. They can see who is the best, who is the worst. If you see you're the worst, you pick a better bank and see what's happening there. It's friendly peer competition, but not deadly . . . [because you're] . . . not competing in the same market."[47] The result? Banc One consistently increased the return on assets of acquired banks by a spectacular 62 percent, well above industry norms.[48]

Other companies rely more heavily on external feedback. Both Wal-Mart and GE use a process called Quick Market Intelligence (QMI) to stay in close touch with the field. The typical cycle is one week. From Monday to Thursday, Wal-Mart's regional managers fan out to collect information on competitors' stores, as well as their own. On Friday, they reconvene, accompanied by buyers, functional heads, and vice presidents, to discuss their findings about prices, merchandise, and sales. Decisions are made on the spot and are then communicated immediately to store managers through video.[49] GE Appliances devotes equal attention to staying in touch with the market. Weekly teleconferences and video conferences link top executives with their counterparts in Europe, Asia, and South America; the same process is used to connect field salespeople with headquarters and plant personnel. The goal, according to a vice president, is real-time learning and responsiveness: "QMI . . . circumvents layers of bureaucracy. . . . [Salespeople] get on the phone for an hour and talk about what happened that week, what are the big opportunities they can go after, and people pick up assignments then and there. The following week they go through it again, so the most they can be off on anything is a week."[50]

Stimulate New Ideas

Such feedback is powerful but has an important limitation. It is primarily corrective, a way of resetting a wayward course rather than generating fresh insights. Effective learning also requires a steady flow of new ideas. Some companies focus externally; their approach, like Milliken's, is to "steal ideas shamelessly." Chaparral Steel, one of the world's most productive minimills, sends its first-line supervisors on sabbaticals around the globe, where they visit academic and industry leaders, develop an understanding of new work practices and technologies, and then bring what they have learned back to the company and apply it to daily operations.[51] GE's Impact Program originally sent manufacturing managers to Japan to study factory innovations, such as quality circles and kanban cards; later, Europe was the destination, and productivity improvement practices were the target.

Other companies focus internally. Their goal is to foster creative cultures by introducing forums and processes that ferret out ideas, incentives that encourage risk taking, and targets that spur employees. Disney, for example, believes that ideas for successful animated films are everywhere in the organization; they need only be drawn out and developed. Three times a year senior managers, including the chairman, vice chairman, and president of feature animation, attend a Gong Show, at which any employee, from secretary to senior executive, is permitted to pitch concepts and story lines. Pitches are limited to five minutes, and managers respond immediately—and bluntly—to all proposals. If the pitch is accepted, the presenter gets the normal fee for a first treatment, usually $20,000. The results? An extraordinary esprit de corps, not to mention the central concepts for *Hercules* and other animated features.[52]

Disney's approach works well when ideas are already bubbling and prodding is unnecessary. At times, however, more aggressive approaches are required. Toshio Okuno, the plant manager of Higashimaru Shoyu, a Japanese soy sauce manufacturer, devised one of the most unusual: the *hangen* (cutting in half) game. To improve productivity, Okuno repeatedly cut work groups in half, then asked the remaining workers, including those observing the process, to identify any unnecessary or noncritical tasks that could be eliminated. Based on their suggestions, work flows were redesigned, and extraneous employees were reassigned elsewhere in the plant. The most spectacular results were achieved on the bottling line, where a twenty-five-person group was quickly reduced to thirteen line workers, plus three roving troubleshooters. Okuno's explanation? "[T]o become more efficient, it is necessary to continuously review one's job to ensure that every task is absolutely necessary. Unfortunately, it is impossible to do so under normal conditions. There simply isn't enough pressure to allow creative thinking to occur."[53] The *hangen* game's bold targets stretched employees by providing the stimulus to pursue breakthroughs rather than the usual marginal improvements.

Tolerate Errors and Mistakes

Pressure alone, of course, will not produce bold thinking. The environment must also encourage risk taking. Employees must feel that the benefits of pursuing new approaches exceed the costs; otherwise, they will not contribute. Such settings are termed "psychologically safe." They have five distinguishing features: "(1) opportunities for training and practice, (2) support and encouragement to overcome fear and shame associated with making errors, (3) coaching and rewards for efforts in the right direction, (4) norms that legitimize the making of errors, and (5) norms that reward innovative thinking and experimentation."[54] Both culture and incentives play pivotal roles. IDEO, for example, the largest product design consulting firm in the United States, has built its entire culture around brainstorming. Sessions occur daily, and freewheeling discussions are the norm. Civility and praise are encouraged; interruptions and criticism are not. Designers are urged to treat the process as a game; the goal is to generate "wild ideas" and "defer judgment" as long as possible. The result, according to a careful anthropological study, is that at IDEO "there is little cost for suggesting a bad idea as long as a person occasionally comes up with a good one."[55] A sense of psychological safety has clearly been built into the culture.

3M has long worked to create similarly supportive settings for its scientists. Resources are clearly part of the story. Funds are readily available for experiments, and researchers are encouraged to invest 15 percent of their time on projects of their own choosing. But even more important are deliberate attempts to create an atmosphere that encourages fresh thinking. Early in their career, new employees attend a class on risk taking. They come with their supervisors and are regaled with stories about products that survived despite the opposition of bosses. Thinsulate, the wildly successful insulating material, is featured prominently; the project was killed five times by the CEO, only to rise phoenixlike on each occasion. Students then participate in an exercise in which they are given real money to wager. They first walk a long plank laid on the floor to collect a small amount of money at the other side. Then, they are asked if they would cross the same plank for a larger payoff, but under slightly different conditions—the plank is now seven stories high, stretched between 3M's headquarters buildings. Most immediately complain of the risk, at which point instructors respond, "What risk? You already proved you could do it."[56] The message is clear—risk is in the eyes of the beholder.

Yet even with a supportive culture, employees will resist new ideas if they believe that they will be penalized for anything less than perfection. Errors, mistakes, and occasional failures must be accepted—embraced even—if learning is to occur. Especially when flawed information, biased interpretations, or differences between espoused and actual behavior exist, corrections will be suggested only if employees are certain that managers will not "shoot the messenger" bringing unwanted news. This is perhaps the most important condition supporting learning and the most difficult to implement. The problem is human nature: the fact that "everyone wants to learn, but nobody wants to be wrong."[57] Unfortunately, it is seldom possible to have one without the other.

Organizations thus face a difficult dilemma. Candor is needed on precisely those topics that people prefer to avoid. Moreover, the problem must be met head on, for there is no way around it: "You cannot solve your problems until you know what they are. And you will not know what they are unless you create an environment where people feel free to tell you."[58] Three conditions are essential: a culture that does not demand infallibility and perfection; freedom to fail without punishment or penalty; and systems or incentives that encourage the identification, analysis, and review of errors. IBM's legendary founder, Thomas Watson Sr., apparently understood the first condition well. Company lore has it that a young manager, after losing $10 million in a risky venture, was called into Watson's office. The young man, thoroughly intimidated, began by saying: "I guess you want my resignation." Watson replied: "You can't be serious. We just spent $10 million educating you."[59]

As Watson recognized, demanding infallibility is a prescription for paralysis. Business environments are inherently uncertain; it is the rare manager who makes all calls correctly. Those who do are invariably risk averse and plodding. They collect excessive amounts of data, eschew innovation, and stick to the party line. Learning is seldom high on their, or their subordinates', agendas. Freedom to fail creates a different mindset. It opens up possibilities and creates opportunities to improve. In such settings, there may be mistakes, but they will be acknowledged and discussed—and seldom repeated. A recent study of errors in administering drugs in hospitals, in fact, found higher *reported* error rates in units with greater openness and more sympathetic management. When environments were less supportive and errors were associated with blame or discipline—a search for the guilty, rather than a search for solutions—errors were much more likely to be hidden or suppressed.[60] Fear does little to encourage learning.

At times, supportive cultures must be coupled with changed incentives if mistakes are to surface. Employees who see themselves at risk must occasionally be granted anonymity and immunity. The Federal Aviation Administration (FAA), for example, established the Aviation Safety Reporting System (ASRS) to ensure that pilots voluntarily report "incidents" or "near misses"—deviations from required altitudes, headings, or spacing between planes that might constitute FAA violations. As long as pilots file safety reports—confidentially—with the ASRS within ten days of an incident's occurrence, they are granted partial immunity by the FAA.[61] Within hospitals, weekly morbidity and mortality conferences serve a similar purpose, allowing doctors to debrief confidentially, discussing errors or problems they encountered without fear of liability.[62] The same approach could easily be applied to safety violations in a factory, refinery, mine, or nuclear power plant or data processing errors in a back office.

Some readers may find this argument disturbing, for it appears to

TABLE 2-1

LEARNING BARRIERS AND FACILITATORS

Stage of Learning	Barriers to Learning	Facilitators of Learning	Tools and Techniques
Acquiring	Reliance on a few, traditional data sources Difficulty separating signals from noise Biased, filtered data collection Limited pooling of available information	A broad base of contributors and data sources A process for sharing diverse perspectives and points of view A willingness to embrace contradictory, unexpected findings	Forums for brainstorming, generating new ideas, and stimulating creative thinking Regular benchmarking and peer comparisons Quick feedback and market intelligence
Interpreting	Biased, incorrect estimates Improper attribution of cause and effect Overconfidence in judgment	A process of conflict and debate that tests prevailing views The provision of timely, accurate feedback	Probing, challenging review sessions Dialectical inquiry, devil's advocacy processes Audit teams
Applying	Unwillingness to change behavior Lack of time to practice new skills Fear of failure	Incentives that encourage new approaches The creation of space for learning A sense of psychological safety	Linking promotion, pay, and status to the development of new ideas and skills Eliminating unnecessary, obsolete work when new tasks are added Acceptance of mistakes due to systems problems, unanticipated events, or inexperience Partial immunity when reporting errors

encourage permissiveness and a lack of accountability. But there is an important distinction. Freedom to fail should not be confused with a license to commit foolish mistakes. Accountability remains essential for effective performance, and no organization should embrace fuzzy or wrongheaded thinking. At GE, the difference is well understood. According to the head of leadership development: "If your decision made sense, given the database you had at the time, you won't be hanged for it. If you made a bad decision and anyone could have foreseen it, nobody's very forgiving at GE. We don't tolerate mediocrity."[63] Other organizations would be wise to follow the same rule. Safety nets are no excuse for low standards.

But they remain essential. Learning, after all, is a delicate and difficult undertaking. There are many barriers to overcome, and stimulating environments must be consciously created (see Table 2-1). Routines are ever present, and it is far easier to accept current practice than to question prevailing views or experiment with untried approaches. Disabilities frequently impede the process. If learning is to occur, individuals must feel comfortable taking on the status quo. They must be encouraged and supported, especially when events do not turn out as planned. Mistakes and errors are humbling, but they are also extraordinarily effective teachers. As the old saying goes: "Good decisions come from wisdom, knowledge, and experience. And wisdom, knowledge, and experience come from bad decisions."

II

TYPES OF LEARNING

3

Intelligence

There is no single best approach to learning. Successful managers possess a portfolio of skills and apply them selectively, based on the information available and issues to be addressed. They are pragmatists, not purists, who share the scientist's goal of solving problems "by finding ways of getting at [them]."[1]

The choices are seldom easy or obvious. Managers may glean information on product requirements through focus groups or field observations, may improve work processes through hands-on experience or designed experiments, and may monitor competitive moves through press clippings or private databases. Each of these methods employs the same basic steps of acquiring, interpreting, and applying information. Each suffers from similar disabilities and responds to similar supporting conditions. Each also has distinctive strengths and weaknesses and requires vastly different sensitivities, systems, and skills. The challenge for managers is to become more knowledgeable about the range of techniques available, so that they can tailor their learning strategies to the tasks at hand.

This chapter addresses the first of these methods: the collection and interpretation of information that exists outside the organization. Chapters 4 and 5 discuss the accumulation of knowledge through experience and the manipulation of variables and experimental conditions to draw inferences. In general, the progression is from less to more active modes, from techniques that accept the environment as given to those that engage or alter it to create insights. The discussion thus begins in this chapter with incremental learning and small-scale improvements and moves gradually to radical changes, including breakthroughs and dramatic innovations, in chapter 5.[2]

GATHERING INTELLIGENCE

Few companies could survive today without accurate, up-to-date information on the external environment. Competitors, customers, technologies, regulations, and social and demographic trends must all be understood for effective decision making. This, in the broadest sense, is the purpose of intelligence: "the selection, collection, interpretation and distribution of . . . information that has strategic importance."[3] Typically, the emphasis is on publicly available data, information that can be collected directly—and legally—from individuals or organizations. But there are disagreements on whether other approaches to intelligence gathering are acceptable, and managers vary in their openness to less direct methods and their willingness to pursue confidential material.

In part, the reasons for these disagreements are historical. The concept of intelligence has both military and diplomatic roots.[4] The Chinese were early proponents, as were the Swedes and Prussians; all viewed espionage as an instrument of statecraft and the primary tool of intelligence. These approaches came later to the English-speaking world. The British Army created a formal intelligence branch in 1873; the U.S. Army followed suit twelve years later but long lacked uniform standards of operation. Sporadic efforts to standardize methods of intelligence gathering followed, but it was not until World War II that the process was centralized and consolidated in this country. In fact, for many years leaders resisted covert intelligence activities because they felt that they violated standards of fair play. During World War I, for example, the War Department established a cryptanalysis section, called the Black Chamber, to decipher critical codes. It later served the State Department, intercepting and decoding messages from other countries to their ambassadors.[5] But when Harry Stimson, the secretary of state, learned of the unit in 1929, he ordered it dismantled, noting that "gentlemen do not read other gentlemen's mail."[6]

The surprise attack on Pearl Harbor, widely regarded as a failure of intelligence, led to more intensive efforts. In its aftermath, the Office of Strategic Services was created; in 1947 its successor, the Central Intelligence Agency, was formed. Both groups were charged with collecting information on the enemy through a variety of means, ranging from library research to reconnaissance flights to agents dropped behind enemy lines. Later, the National Security Agency was formed and engaged in even more clandestine activities.

Because of this history, intelligence gathering has long had unsavory, and often unethical, overtones. Especially during the Cold War, spying and subterfuge were accepted parts of the game, regarded as necessary because of the issues at stake. All too often, business intelligence has been viewed as little more than a commercial version of the same cloak-and-dagger activities. The titles of two recent reviews in the popular press—"I Spy, You Spy" and "They Snoop to Conquer"—are representative.[7] But there is no necessary connection between these activities and the illicit or covert. The primary goal of intelligence is securing salient, current information about the environment; in most cases, the necessary data are readily available or there for the asking.

Data can be gathered in three ways: through search, inquiry, or observation. Search relies on public sources or documents; the primary skills are careful analysis and research. Inquiry relies on interviews or surveys; the primary skills are framing and asking insightful questions. Observation relies on direct contact with users; the primary skills are attentive looking and listening. Surprisingly, the underlying process of intelligence gathering remains the same. In each case, managers decide what information to look for, figure out where to look, assemble the raw material, determine its meaning and implications, and then disseminate their findings to relevant parties.

SEARCH

For most managers, this form of learning is part of the daily routine. Their success, after all, requires staying a step ahead of competitors; to do so, they must remain current and well informed. The credo of Frederick the Great—"it is pardonable to be defeated, but never to be surprised"—is as pertinent to managers as it is to statesmen.[8]

Much of the resulting activity, which scholars call "viewing" or "monitoring," is virtually automatic.[9] Managers collect and process information in a steady, unbroken stream, drawing on a host of formal and informal sources. Strategic planners, for example, regularly read the Wall Street Journal, skim the trade press, and surf company Web sites to gain insights about competitors. Brand managers routinely track product sales, pricing, and market shares through Nielsen and SAMI audits. R&D scientists stay abreast of the latest technologies by studying patent filings and attending specialized conferences and symposia. All also rely heavily on "soft" information gained through personal contacts—hearsay and tidbits plucked from conversations with insiders and outsiders—to ensure ready access to late-breaking news.[10]

At times, however, the desired information is complex, difficult to access, or squirreled away in assorted nooks and crannies. Then, automatic approaches are unlikely to be effective, and more active search is required. Managers must seek out specialized reports or comb through databases to produce a complete, coherent story. Both primary and secondary sources are helpful.[11] They range from the obvious—annual reports, SEC 10-Ks, newspaper and magazine articles, trade shows, and databases such as DIALOG, INVESTEXT, and NEXIS—to the obscure. Environmental Protection Agency (EPA) and Uniform Commercial Code (UCC) filings, for example, are little known but surprisingly comprehensive sources of basic operating information, especially when combined with creative judgment. Coors used Anheuser-Busch's reports of wastewater discharges to determine its brewing capacity in the Denver area, while a food-packaging company used UCC filings, which are posted by lenders and list all goods that have been purchased, leased, or pledged as collateral, to estimate the equipment in a competitor's facility and the associated depreciation charges.[12]

A particularly effective technique is to draw on knowledge that has already been accumulated internally. Salespeople are an obvious source, but there are many others, including managers themselves. The trick is to organize an orderly collection process. Motorola, for example, assigns one member of its intelligence unit to debrief company executives after they have returned from overseas, and occasionally domestic, trips. The resulting information is then collated, distilled, and mined for insights.[13] AT&T has benefited from similar discipline. In the mid-1980s it established a program called "Access to AT&T Analysts" that put company experts on-line, allowing employees to pose questions directly to those in the know. The program came with a unique feature, a flagging system that routinely tracked the ten companies attracting the most attention from employees. Most of the time, the list included the same set of suspects; on one occasion, however, a new name appeared. Further research showed that the company had just entered one of AT&T's lines of business, providing an early warning that would not otherwise have been available.[14]

Approaches to Search

Whatever the sources of data, competition and the market are the primary topics of interest. Regulatory and technical issues rank a distant second and third. A summary of studies of search activity in several U.S. industries—chemicals, farm equipment, financial services, meat packing, and diverse multinationals—found that managers devoted 49 percent of their total search time to securing market information, 19 percent to regulatory information, 16 percent to technical information, 11 percent to resource-related information, 8 percent to broad environmental conditions, and 7 percent to acquisition leads. The proportions for Korean managers were strikingly similar. Both groups also relied more heavily on external sources (at least 55 percent of total search time) but varied considerably by industry in their use of passive and active modes of search.[15] Other studies have found that viewing and monitoring are more likely to be used when the industry is predictable and relatively homogeneous, while active, directed modes of search are more effective when the environment is unpredictable, turbulent, or complex.[16] Even in those settings, however, few organizations have full-fledged intelligence units; those that do, an estimated 10 percent of all large corporations, are often firms like Kodak and Merck with an obvious, established set of competitors.[17]

Guidelines for Effective Search

There are a number of guidelines for effective search. Companies should collect information from diverse sources, cross-check their findings to ensure reliability, shift smoothly between passive and active modes, devote considerable effort to analysis and interpretation, and connect intelligence gathering directly with decision making. The first two tasks are necessary because much intelligence is of questionable validity. Internet sites, for example, are notorious for mixing facts, opinions, and hearsay without attempting to differentiate one from the other; the same is true of unconfirmed rumors and late-breaking news. As the president of a medium-sized chemical company observed: "I can usually find more than enough information on questions of importance. The real problem is whether I can believe it."[18] Comparisons and cross-checks are vital for guaranteeing that collected data are accurate.

The next two tasks are needed because intelligence is rarely self-explanatory or obvious. Signals are difficult to distinguish from noise, and critical insights often spring from barely noticeable differences. In most cases, routine monitoring provides an effective early warning but not a complete picture of events. Follow up is needed to flesh out and broaden the story, and some mechanism must be available for triggering the shift from automatic to targeted search. Effectiveness is often closely linked with the ability to "switch cognitive gears" and probe further once a novel event or unanticipated discrepancy has been recognized.[19] This is precisely what happened at AT&T when the top-ten list generated an unexpected company name. Analysts must also take care to develop the business implications of their findings. Managers are action-oriented; they view data without recommendations as unhelpful and incomplete. Many environmental analysis units, for example, devote far more time and attention to collecting information than to interpreting it. Even at firms with highly regarded units, senior executives were sharply critical: "The straight reporting of environmental 'facts' by staff, without connection to plans or policies, was often seen as worthless."[20]

Interpretation, however, does not complete the learning process. If search activities are to have real impact, executives must internalize the information they receive and apply it where appropriate. Eventually, they must move from analysis to action, the second to the third step in the acquire-interpret-apply cycle. Yet all too often, critical intelligence is communicated to the top of the organization, only to remain unacknowledged or ignored. Effective search processes overcome the problem by linking important insights directly to decision making, ensuring that they will have an immediate impact.

XEROX'S SEARCH PROCESSES: SPURRING STRATEGIC CHANGE

Xerox provides a dramatic example of effective intelligence gathering.[21] In the 1980s and 1990s the company engaged in a series of intelligence exercises: Xerox '92, Xerox '95, Xerox 2000, and Xerox 2005. Each was designed to scan the environment, predict trends a decade ahead, and provide a foundation for long-term strategy.[22] Xerox '92, conducted over a seven-month period, was the most traditional study, a high-level "strategic reconnaissance" prepared by the corporate strategy staff. It was designed to answer a single, broad question using the techniques of systems and environmental analysis: How might Xerox's revenues grow over the coming decade?

The assessment was based on six factors—economics (e.g., expected growth of the global economy, on a region-by-region basis), demographics (e.g., expected number of factory versus office workers), social forces (e.g., the proportion of employees working at home versus the office), technology (e.g., trends in miniaturization and digital versus analog technology), government policy (e.g., public regulation and trade policy), and competition (e.g., profiles of key competitors and their expected behavior)—and information was collected largely from public sources. The data were then combined using a simple conceptual model to derive estimates of Xerox's likely revenues and market share.[23] The resulting 300-page report was highly visible; it was presented to the company's top 250 managers in a half-day session and was even made "required reading." Yet the results were discouraging. According to Roger

Levien, vice president of corporate strategy and the initiator of the project: "Xerox '92 was widely recognized as an excellent piece of work. But it had zero impact on the strategic direction of the company."

There were two basic problems. First, Xerox '92 was a staff exercise; there was little direct involvement of senior managers and limited incentive for them to apply the results. The search process was careful and complete but was not driven by a compelling business need or linked to an upcoming decision. Second, the conclusions remained distant and abstract; while the data were carefully massaged by analysts, they were not processed firsthand by senior managers nor tested against their personal theories and experiences. Not surprisingly, few managers identified with the study's findings or drew on them for insights.

Xerox '95 differed in both method and impact. It was a far more participative process, involving the top fifteen corporate managers as well as the strategy office, again over a seven-month period. Intelligence gathering now had a clear purpose; the goal, set by David Kearns, the CEO, was to determine a broad strategic direction for the company. Most important, the process included a heavy hands-on component, with senior managers actively weighing in at critical junctures with their own observations, experiences, and opinions.

To begin, members of the strategy office conducted lengthy interviews with participating managers. Each time, they asked the same broad questions:

- What is the desired future state for Xerox (including size, financial performance, the way we work, worldwide/geographical presence, staff/people, and reputation)?

- What are expected trends in technology, economics, politics, competition, and emerging opportunities/threats?

- What are the business implications (including current businesses, extensions of current businesses, and new areas)?

- What are the required competencies?

- What are current weaknesses? Current strengths?

- What are the imperatives for Xerox?

- What are the desired outputs of the Xerox '95 process?

The strategy office then collated the answers and fed them back to participants; they provided the foundation for a day-long discussion of the company's long-term goals and critical success factors. The results were disappointing. Both the interviews and discussion revealed huge differences in perspective, so much so that at the end of the session a frustrated Kearns concluded: "It's absolutely clear to me that we don't even agree on what business we're in."

Members of the strategy office were therefore assigned responsibility for collecting further information and imposing order. They developed questionnaires, with more detailed questions about competitive positioning, customer segments, company size, and functional strategies, and distributed them to all participants. After reviewing the responses, analysts identified four alternative strategies. Each was framed as a "pure tone," a distinctive, differentiated strategy that was easy to describe and discuss. Together, the tones mapped out the entire "strategy space" and covered the spectrum of possibilities. Each was given a code name, based on a representative company that followed a similar approach, and was described in a single brief sentence, using the Hollywood notion of a "high concept." The choices included:

- *Boeing:* "sticking to the knitting" and remaining a first-class copier and printer business;

- *Chrysler:* facing off against IBM in the systems business and becoming a strong number two or three;

- *Sears:* focusing on distribution and expanding the company's offerings to include as many products as possible;

- *BMW:* focusing on financial performance and exiting businesses that did not provide superior short-term returns.[24]

These alternatives were discussed by senior managers at a second day-long meeting. Participants were assigned to small groups and asked to develop a single strategy in detail; each group included at least one supporter and one critic. The full team then reconvened to discuss the alternatives; again, there were sharp disagreements. For the most part, the disputes hinged on different underlying assumptions—the likely role of paper in the office of the future, the expected growth of Asian versus

North American markets, the anticipated moves of key competitors—rather than disagreements about the strategies themselves. As Levien observed: "Where you stood on a strategy was determined by your view of the world."

The strategy office was asked to resolve the differences. It began by conducting further economic and political research. Within a month, analysts produced a list of forty major trends that might impact Xerox's future; each was framed as a "view-of-the-world" assumption about the expected social or competitive environment. At the next off-site meeting, senior managers spent three days reviewing the assumptions and assessing alternative strategies. Initially, they were assigned to small groups to discuss the forty trends and select the ten that they felt were most important to Xerox. Then, the full team reconvened to discuss the pared down list. Using a Consensor, an electronic device that allows individuals to vote anonymously by entering their preferences on a keypad or numbered dials, participants rated each assumption in turn, eventually reducing the list to fourteen. These assumptions were then used as a filter for reviewing the four pure strategies. At the end of the discussion, Kearns asked each participant for a recommendation; this time, votes could be cast for mixed strategies. Kearns reviewed the comments overnight and announced his decision the next morning, a "modified Boeing" strategy that eventually led to Xerox's becoming "the document company."

Xerox '95 was a major advance over its predecessor. Throughout the process, senior managers were actively engaged in evaluating intelligence, testing it against their personal schemas and experiences. The resulting frameworks became theirs, not the staff's, and insights were that much more likely to be internalized and accepted. Search activities were linked directly to decision making, providing additional motivation and momentum. Moreover, the four pure tones ensured that the interpretative process was both disciplined and broad. The tones provided a lens for screening data, yet kept the group from settling prematurely on an easy solution, improving both clarity and differentiation.

But Xerox '95 was not without weaknesses. Much of the initial intelligence was drawn solely from internal sources. External search was limited, and at no time did senior managers directly confront the environment. The critical view-of-the-world assumptions were generated independently by the strategy office, with little input from line managers. They appeared relatively late in the process and were based on quick, cursory research. Activities were also poorly timed and sequenced, with considerable meandering up front and a rush to judgment at the end.

Xerox 2000 was designed to overcome these weaknesses. Unlike its predecessors, it stretched over a full year and included eleven meetings, each roughly a month apart. Eight of the meetings were designed to assess the environment and develop view-of-the-world assumptions; the remaining three were to set strategic direction. The process was initiated by Paul Allaire, Kearns's successor as CEO, who had participated in Xerox '95 and believed that a similar exercise would be useful in generating a shared vision of the company's future. A core group of Allaire plus four senior managers, handpicked for their strategic skills, participated in the entire exercise; they were joined by five operating officers during the later stages of decision making. The corporate strategy office again provided staff support, supplemented by outside consultants and subject matter experts.

This time, senior managers participated personally in intelligence gathering. The group also paid far more attention to external search. View-of-the-world meetings, for example, drew heavily on firsthand information—unfiltered, unprocessed, and occasionally contradictory—so that managers could assess trends and critical assumptions directly. Each meeting was a full-day affair, with required reading prior to the meeting—a twenty-page white paper, prepared by the strategy office or outside consultants, that reviewed the most current published research. Discussions were videotaped and transcribed, and topics were carefully sequenced. They became increasingly focused over time, moving from broad trends in the economy and society to specialized information about the industry and key competitors. All, however, drew on a wide range of experts, sources, and sites (see Table 3-1).

After each topic was covered, members of the strategy office met to review the discussion and write up view-of-the-world assumptions. They produced sixty in all, approximately fifteen per topic. Each assumption was stated as succinctly as possible and included, when appropriate, implications for action. For example, a critical assumption in the area of

TABLE 3-1
XEROX 2000: VIEW-OF-THE-WORLD MEETINGS

Economy and Society

    1. Discuss Europe 2000 and Asia 2000 with an expert presenter for each topic; held at the Japan House.

    2. Discuss the global corporation with a leading academic expert and the chief editorial writer of the *Financial Times;* held at the New York Stock Exchange.

Technology and Organization

    3. Explore advances in computer science with experts in the field; held at the MIT Media Laboratory.

    4. Explore imaging and documentation technology with experts in the field; held at the Association of Image and Information Management trade show.

Markets and Customers

    5. Discuss customers' needs after hearing presentations by the IT directors of four major customers.

    6. Explore diverse channels and customer needs after attending COMDEX (the computer trade show), visiting a local CompUSA store, and meeting with a systems integrator.

Industry and Competition

    7. Discuss industry trends after hearing presentations by industry association consultants.

    8. Discuss competitors after hearing presentations by an academic expert and the IT director of Fuji-Xerox, who provided data on Canon, the company's chief competitor.

economy and society was that "trends will continue toward increased globalization, simultaneously with increased regionalization and localization; successful global competitors will combine global integration with 'insider status' in each major market."

Once the complete list was in hand, senior managers were asked to rank all sixty assumptions by their level of agreement and perceived strategic importance. Questionnaires were used for the purpose; they were distributed, collected, and summarized by the strategy office prior to the first direction-setting meeting. The senior team then met to discuss the rankings; eventually, after extensive debate and voting, they reduced the list to twenty-eight shared assumptions. These assumptions, plus prior work on the strengths and weaknesses of the organization, led to a series of "strategic imperatives." Each flagged an important area for development, using the phrase "Xerox must . . . " The group then used these imperatives, plus prior work on the company's strengths and weaknesses, to analyze and assess alternative strategies, businesses, and organizational architectures before selecting a final proposal. It was implemented a year later and led to dramatic improvements in performance, including sharp gains in profitability and stock price.

Xerox 2000 represents intelligence gathering at its best. Because senior managers engaged directly in search activities, vital information was processed without screening or filtering by intermediaries. Because research reports were combined with firsthand exposure to customers, technologies, and subject matter experts, biases were minimized and a wide range of perspectives were explored. Because meetings were spread over an extended period, time was available for careful and complete analysis—before choices were made. And because interpretation was followed immediately by decision making, new understandings were incorporated into action.

Xerox 2000 also built on the lessons of its predecessors (see Table 3-2). The major categories for collecting and presenting information—economics and society, technology and organization, markets and customers, industry and competition—were elaborations of those first used in Xerox '92. The process of articulating and ranking view-of-the-world assumptions was a refinement of the methods pioneered in Xerox '95. Those methods, in fact, were vital to the success of the entire effort.

Unresolved debates can frequently be traced to unstated perceptions or beliefs that lie just below the surface. Without a common, articulated foundation—a conscious effort to bring these differences into the open—groups often find it difficult to move forward.[25] Xerox 2000 tackled the problem directly by devoting the entire front end of the process to debating and clarifying assumptions. As Levien observed, the stimulus was Xerox '95: "We discovered that the more time you invest at the senior management level in agreeing on where the world is going, the more likely you are to get agreement on strategy."[26]

There was another associated learning. In the early stages of Xerox 2000, managers cast their nets widely, generating and debating a long list

TABLE 3-2

THE EVOLUTION OF INTELLIGENCE GATHERING AT XEROX

	Xerox '92	Xerox '95	Xerox 2000
Purpose	Estimate the company's revenue growth over the next decade	Determine a broad strategic direction for the company	Develop a shared vision of the company's future
Participants	Corporate strategy staff	15 top managers, including the CEO, supported by the corporate strategy staff	5 top managers with strategic skills, including the CEO, later joined by 5 top operating officers, supported by the corporate strategy staff and outside experts
Duration	7 months	7 months	1 year
Process	All analysis performed by staff, final report presented to top 250 managers	Alternating periods of interviewing and surveying of managers by staff, followed by discussion of findings; strategic alternatives and lists of underlying assumptions created by managers before final decision by the CEO	Intense focus up front on developing a shared set of assumptions about the external environment, drawing on firsthand experience, white papers, and meetings with experts; divergence to develop a broad set of perspectives before narrowing the list; only at the end consider strategic imperatives, alternatives, and organization design

TABLE 3-2 (CONTINUED)

THE EVOLUTION OF INTELLIGENCE GATHERING AT XEROX

Critical tasks	Data collection from primary and secondary sources; trend analysis; modeling and estimation	Interviewing and surveying managers; creating "pure tone" strategies and "view-of-the-world" assumptions	Collecting market intelligence through visits, discussions, and external search; interpreting findings and applying them to strategic choices
Strengths	Careful, systematic analysis	Complete airing and comparison of differing views; open discussion of assumptions and strategic alternatives; high involvement of top managers	Direct involvement of top managers in intelligence gathering; systematic development and review of assumptions
Weaknesses	Little or no impact on decision making	Little external intelligence; too much reliance on staff for analysis; poor sequencing of activities	Time-consuming

of alternative assumptions. They strove for breadth, seeking out multiple possibilities rather than gravitating immediately to the most likely prospects. Diversity of this sort avoids the common trap of premature closure—settling too quickly on an easy, obvious solution. Only after they had developed a complete set of assumptions did managers vote to narrow the list and establish priorities. This approach—first "diverging" to create multiple alternatives, then "converging" on a smaller set—has long been associated with effective problem solving, intelligence gathering, and decision making.[27] Unfortunately, far too many groups are content to pursue the second step without the first.

Xerox's search for intelligence did not end with Xerox 2000. Five years later, Allaire launched a follow-on exercise, Xerox 2005, using many of the same techniques. Seventeen managers participated; they ranged from young high-potentials to senior officers. The goal was to identify, by businesses and geographical regions, the areas of greatest opportunity for Xerox; once again, the process began with a critical evaluation of underlying assumptions. This time, however, the strategy office had already prepared an overview of thirty major competitors, as well as an assessment of the company's strengths and weaknesses. Discussion was therefore highly focused, and the process moved quickly to action. After briefly reviewing likely competitive scenarios, participants decided on a number of concrete steps, most of them extensions of existing businesses. Xerox 2005 thus continued the company's tradition of using search to spur strategic change.

INQUIRY

Despite its appeal, search has an important limitation: the required data must already exist. Information is collected, not constructed or created, and there is little effort to generate new raw material. At times, a more probing process is required, for certain information cannot be found through search alone. How often, for example, do families buy a new car? How long is the average business trip? What activities are most in demand at health clubs? Because published information is sketchy or incomplete, questions of this sort must usually be answered through inquiry, using interviews or questionnaires to draw data directly from users. This approach is common in market research, where it has long been used to acquire information about consumers' behavior and preferences.

Guidelines for Effective Inquiry

Since we all use questions on a daily basis, inquiry would seem to demand few special skills. But the process can easily derail, and careful planning is required. The choice of respondents is crucial; even small changes in mix can produce vastly different results. Predictions are especially sensitive to these choices. In 1936 the editors of *Literary Digest* tried to predict the outcome of the upcoming presidential election by using a sample of voters drawn from telephone books and club memberships, groups that tended to be far more Republican than the population at large. Not surprisingly, their projection—a victory for Alf Landon, the Republican candidate—was way off the mark. Franklin Roosevelt, the Democratic incumbent, won in a landslide.[28]

Questions must also be carefully framed, since subtle, almost indistinguishable, differences in wording can cause wide swings in responses. Perceptual data must be treated with caution, since most individuals lack the self-awareness needed to articulate latent feelings and needs. Even when people are able to respond to a proposal or concept, their stated views may not be accurate harbingers of the future. When asked during market tests for their reactions to the concept of a film about "a professor who fights Nazis to rescue a sacred relic," consumers were uniformly negative. Yet *Raiders of the Lost Ark* went on to become one of the biggest moneymakers in Hollywood history.[29] Test groups were equally unenthusiastic about the proposed title of *Star Wars,* noting that they had little interest in either science fiction or war movies.[30]

Stories like these suggest that inquiry remains very much an art. Nevertheless, there are a few broad guidelines. Respondents must be representative and appropriate; otherwise, the results will be meaningless. It makes little sense, for example, to ask baby boomers about the latest rock bands, or seniors about snowboarding. Refusal rates must be carefully monitored; if certain groups cooperate while others do not, there will undoubtedly be biases.[31] Sampling procedures and research methods must be rigorous, with sound, thoughtfully constructed designs.

Perhaps most important, questions must be worded to avoid slanting results. Common errors include leading the witness ("Do you prefer our brand for its taste, or for some other reason?"), loading the dice ("Do you believe that preschool children should be allowed to learn at their own rates?"), false precision ("Exactly how many mail-order catalogs did you receive in the last six months?"), and fuzzy language ("Are you a strong or weak supporter of the proposed amendment?").[32]

Forms of Inquiry

There are two basic approaches to inquiry: descriptive and exploratory.[33] Descriptive approaches are the most traditional; they involve precise, focused questions and targeted information collection. Usually, the goal is to determine frequencies or patterns of use, or to compare one's products and services with competitors'. Most surveys and questionnaires employ this approach, as do focus groups and structured conversations with users. There are obvious advantages, including well-defined methodologies, easy-to-summarize results, and little ambiguity in interpretation. Marketers have used these techniques to generate facts of dizzying detail. Coca-Cola knows how many ice cubes we put in a glass, Frito-Lay knows whether we eat broken or whole pretzels first, and Timex knows when we received our first watches.[34] Yet despite these insights, the approach has several limitations. With targeted questions, it is extremely difficult to generate unexpected ideas, tease out unmet needs, or discover something fundamentally new about consumers' likes and dislikes.[35]

Exploratory approaches overcome many of these problems. They use open-ended questions to elicit users' perceptions and needs. Frequently, stories and firsthand experiences are sought because they are thought to embody larger truths.[36] Clinical and ethnographic techniques therefore play important roles, and interpretation becomes a more challenging task. Among the required skills are the ability to conduct unstructured, far-reaching interviews (beginning with what anthropologists call "grand-tour questions"), follow up and probe discretely, suspend judgment, keep an open mind, and listen empathically.[37] These techniques are designed to ensure that respondents say what is really on their minds, rather than answering well-meaning but possibly irrelevant questions. Robert Galvin, the CEO of Motorola, used this approach to great effect in the 1980s when he launched the company's quality process. Galvin insisted that all members of the Operating and Policy Committee—including himself—personally visit customers and ask a single question: "What do you like about doing business with Motorola, and what don't you like?" The result, he observed, was invariably a sobering conversation and at least fifteen pages of notes.

Occasionally, questions must be framed less directly. Latent needs are difficult to extract; when sensitive subjects are involved, even open-ended questions may fail to produce the desired insights. The underlying feelings may be hard to identify; at times, they are recognized but kept from view because they are "socially unacceptable."[38] In a classic study published in 1950, people were asked if they used Nescafé, an instant coffee. Those who did not were asked why; most responded that they did not like the flavor. But when projective techniques were used instead, a different picture emerged. Such techniques present subjects with ambiguous or unclear material and then ask for interpretations. Rorschach tests are a well-known example. In the Nescafé case, people were shown two hypothetical shopping lists and asked to characterize the women who made the purchases. The lists were identical, except that one included Nescafé while the other included Maxwell House. The responses, however, were dramatically different. Forty-eight percent of respondents described the woman who purchased Nescafé as lazy, 48 percent described her as failing to plan household purchases and schedules well, and 16 percent described her as not a good wife; the corresponding percentages for the woman who bought Maxwell House were 4 percent, 12 percent, and 0 percent.[39] In the 1950s, at least, instant coffee triggered deep feelings about a woman's responsibility for home and hearth that could be unearthed only through indirect techniques.

To be successful, these techniques must be accompanied by attentive listening. Inquiry, after all, is a two-way street. There is little learning if questions are posed but answers fail to register. Unfortunately, sensitive, supportive listening is extremely hard work.

> It requires, first, that the listener focus carefully on what is being said—and *how*. . . . The tone and music of the speaker's voice, the perspective from which she speaks, the degree of authority or confidence invoked or projected, the speaker's emotional attach-

ment to the ideas, and the emotional force of the ideas on the listener—all these elements are integral to the full meaning of a message.[40]

In addition, most managers view the task as thankless, with little personal payoff. Talking is vastly preferred to listening because it offers visibility and exposure. Those who talk hold onto the spotlight; listeners remain largely offstage. The results are predictable but hardly conducive to learning. As a leading executive has observed, only partly in jest: "One often hears the remark 'He talks too much,' but when did anyone last hear the criticism 'He listens too much?'"[41]

L.L. BEAN'S CREATIVE INQUIRY: CONVERSING WITH CUSTOMERS

L.L. Bean, the direct-mail marketer of outdoor clothing and equipment, has long relied on inquiry as a source of learning.[42] The process can be traced to the company's earliest years. Legend has it that the original L.L. sold one hundred pairs of his first product, the Maine hunting boot, only to have them all returned as defective. He talked with customers and listened carefully to their complaints, fixed each and every boot without charge, and created a sense of commitment and responsiveness that pervades the company even today. L.L. Bean continues to draw on this legacy, deepening its understanding of customer needs by combining its own creative techniques with traditional methods of inquiry.

Field testers, for example, are used extensively as a source of descriptive information. Rather than collecting impressions second- or thirdhand, L.L. Bean goes to those in the know—experienced users who have lived with the product, often under demanding conditions. Over time, it has developed a database of more than 1,200 testers. The selection process is rigorous—the original model was the Yale Medical School application—and applicants must submit a series of essays, profiles, and product evaluations before they are accepted. After testers have evaluated several products, they are assigned to one of three categories, allowing Bean to select the right mix of testers for any project. *Lead users* are those who spend enormous amounts of time researching their purchases; typically, after taking them home, they personally modify and improve them. These users have two identifying characteristics: they "face needs that will be general in the marketplace—but face them months or years before [others] . . . and . . . are positioned to benefit significantly by obtaining a solution to those needs."[43] Frequently, their livelihood or safety depends on the products they buy. At L.L. Bean, lead users include mountaineering guides, Outward Bound instructors, and park rangers; at a software firm, they might be computer-savvy telecommuters or road warriors. *Demanding users* are as informed and committed to an activity as lead users but do not modify products or make a living from them. Examples would be dedicated hunters and hikers, who spend much of their spare time in the woods. *Happy customers* are satisfied but intermittent users, the once-per-season backpacker or the family that camps out every other summer.

Testers are selected not only for their experience, but also for their articulateness and candor. The combination is rare, and Bean goes to great lengths to cultivate the individuals it finds. Many have developed close, multiyear relationships with developers. Trust is essential. Testers must feel free to call them as they see them, without concern for repercussions or hurt feelings; at the same time, they must have faith in the company that has supplied them with products. Bean is well aware of this delicate line. According to David Bennell, manager of research and testing:

> We don't ask them to do more than is appropriate. We don't put them in dangerous situations. We don't send them products that we know will fail. We encourage them not to use a product if they're going to be out for three months in Antarctica, and they have to absolutely rely on it. We want them to be safe.

Normally, testers are sent several samples, one from L.L. Bean and at least one from a competitor, to use for three months. These side-by-side comparisons are considered essential to stimulate learning. As Tom Armstrong Jr., director of outerwear and footwear, observed: "It's hard to test something in a void. What we're really interested in is the Bean, but the foil of a competitor seems to elicit more ideas from our testers."

Often, testers will be asked for their assessments of particular attributes—the fit of a garment, the traction of a boot, the durability of a fly rod—as well as general impressions.

To maximize learning, Bean requests extensive feedback. Communication is encouraged in all forms, including telephone, letters, and e-mail. Testers are provided with data logs for recording information and are asked to complete a number of surveys. But the process is flexible, and feedback sometimes comes in unexpected packages. One tester traveled the Australian outback for several months, camping out each night in an L.L. Bean tent. Rather than carrying logs or rating forms, which would have added weight to an already overburdened pack, he simply scrawled his observations on the ceiling and walls. When the trip was over, he sent the annotated tent back to the company for all to read.

Bean solicits formal feedback at three points: when the product is first received (to assess first impressions, "out-of-box quality," and initial fit), at the midpoint of the test (to identify design opportunities and obvious problems), and at the end of the test (to collect a comprehensive, comparative assessment, including recommended changes). This format keeps cycles short and ensures that little learning is lost. Midpoint evaluations are often especially revealing because of the creative approach that the company employs. Typically, Bean structures these sessions as group conversations and builds them around an outdoor activity such as hiking or cross-country skiing. Fifteen to thirty field testers attend, as well as developers, marketers, and occasionally vendors and manufacturers.

Perhaps the best example of this process is the Cresta Hiker. Bean introduced the boot in 1987; for many years, it was a best-seller. In the early 1990s, however, sales began to decline because of advances in competitive boots. After extensive interviewing and testing, Bean developed an upgraded version of the Hiker, using new designs and materials, and sent it to a broad mix of testers for evaluation. Two months into the process, the group was invited to Pinkham Notch, New Hampshire, at the base of Mt. Washington, to discuss their experiences. But first they went for a hike—not just any hike but one artfully designed to stimulate learning.

To begin, participants were divided into groups by foot size. One group consisted only of men who wore size nine; another consisted only of women who wore size seven. Each participant was given two or three pairs of boots—the new Cresta Hiker, as well as the very best competitive offerings—and was instructed to hike for one and a half hours in one pair, then to switch to another brand, continuing the process up and down the trail. Hikers were urged to take notes, share observations, and trade boots. One group waded through streams to check the boots' water resistance; another briefly wore mismatched pairs to assess comfort and fit. As Bennell observed, this approach was dramatically different—and far more effective in eliciting insights—than traditional modes of inquiry:

> The old way would have been to bring a group of customers together in a focus group and ask them what are their likes, dislikes, and experiences. The problem is that what they say and what they do could be very different, not because they're trying to lie to us but just because it's difficult in a focus group environment to clearly understand the customer.
>
> We decided to go out into the end use environment. We wanted to bring the vendor/manufacturer in. We wanted to bring product developers together, and we wanted to really see customers behaving with hiking boots. About every hour, we'd switch footwear products. Meanwhile, developers are watching all of this happen, and they're doing the switch as well, so everybody, including the manufacturer, is evaluating footwear in the place where people hike.
>
> We're also very, very much interacting with each other. Developers are asking customers questions. Manufacturers are asking customers questions. Testers are asking each other questions. It's very different from a focus group. This is behavior in the making and in the watching.

The next day, the entire group reconvened to reflect on the process and craft recommendations. In addition to obvious design changes, developers sought information on preferences and trade-offs: "If we made these design changes, would you be happy? Suppose we could only make two changes—which should they be? Suppose these changes added $x to the price, would you still buy the boot?" After returning to Bean, the design team immediately debriefed and extracted key learnings. They used the insights they had collected to make further changes in the boot's sole, toe, and side panels. Prototypes were quickly developed and sent to testers for their reactions. They approved, and the new Cresta Hiker was launched in 1996. The learning process was given top billing and became a potent marketing tool. According to Pat Murtagh, product developer for active footwear:

> We actually introduced the boot by talking about the process—the fact that changes came directly from the customer. In the catalog we've been able to tell that story, using photography from our testing days up at Mt. Washington, and pointing to some of the specific requirements that customers brought to us and saying this is how they translate into the changes that are built into the shoe.

The results were stunning. Sales rose 85 percent over the previous year, and the initial shipment sold out within weeks.

Bean's approach to the Cresta Hiker offers several lessons for effective inquiry (see Table 3-3). They include the power of conducting conversations in context rather than in artificial settings; the importance of conversing with users while they are carrying out activities rather than sedentary or bored; the benefits of conducting comparative tests rather than assessments in isolation; the usefulness of side-by-side comparisons and short feedback cycles rather than drawn out, extended processes; the importance of cultivating long-term associations with users rather than holding brief, once-and-for-all meetings; the benefits of categorizing users by type rather than mixing them indiscriminately; and the value of employing a diversity of methods rather than a single, unvarying technique. The last point is particularly important.[44] Traditional methods of inquiry, such as focus groups, surveys, and laboratory tests, have much to offer, and Bean uses them extensively to collect information on products and customers. The Cresta Hiker was no exception. But by combining these techniques with its own innovative approaches, the company generated much richer insights and vastly increased its learning.

TABLE 3-3

TECHNIQUES FOR DESCRIPTIVE INQUIRY:
LESSONS FROM THE CRESTA HIKER

---

1. Rely on experienced field testers.

- Use a rigorous screening and selection process.
- Categorize by type and intensity of experience (e.g., lead users, demanding users, happy customers).
- Cultivate long-term relationships based on trust.
- Encourage candor and honest feedback.

2. Collect information at multiple points and in multiple ways.

- Include first impressions, midpoint evaluations, and overall assessments.
- Encourage communication by phone, letters, and e-mail.
- Keep cycles short so that information is not lost.
- Combine qualitative and quantitative data.

3. Encourage conversations that maximize learning.

- Group users with similar characteristics.
- Conduct conversations in the settings of use.
- Mingle users with designers, marketers, and suppliers.
- Provide competitive products as a basis for comparison.

4. Validate all findings.

- Conduct a systematic debriefing process.
- Probe for trade-offs and value judgments.
- Check back with users to ensure that new designs accurately reflect their recommendations.
- Use large-scale surveys to confirm initial qualitative results.

This same spirit of innovation can be found in the company's exploratory methods. To generate radical redesigns or develop deep knowledge about a product category, Bean now uses a technique called "concept engineering."[45] It has three basic elements, which mirror the stages of learning: open-ended interviewing to acquire data, collaborative interpretation and synthesis to define user needs, and unfettered brainstorming to generate prototypes and new designs. The process begins with the formation of a cross-functional team, consisting of product developers, marketing managers, and product testing assistants. At their first meeting, the team establishes a learning agenda by defining the scope of the project. In some cases, the task is obvious—for example, to develop a new hunting boot or an innovative "sleeping system"—and discussion is relatively brief. In other cases, the mission is unclear, and a complex scope statement is required. After considerable wrangling, the parka and outerwear team eventually decided that its goal was "to develop a complete, compatible apparel layering system for a variety of active, outdoor, four-season activities with components suitable for everyday use."

Once the scope has been determined, the team develops interview questions. Typically, no more than five or six questions are involved; all are broad and reflective. Wording is crucial because the team is seeking windows into the customer's world. They are looking for ways to get people to tell their stories and relate personal experiences. As one developer put it, the goal is to "find questions that will prompt people to speak." The hunting boot team, for example, created the following list:

- In what kinds of conditions do you find yourself hunting? Can you describe a situation in the field where your hunting footwear let you down?

- Where do you store your hunting equipment? If you were to show me your sporting goods closet/storage area, what would I see? What footwear equipment do you have there?

- Describe what went through your mind when you purchased your last pair of boots. Please describe the experience.

- If you could build your own custom hunting boots, what would they look like? What features of other footwear or sporting products would you like to incorporate into your current hunting footwear?

- What haven't I asked you about your footwear that you'd like to discuss?

Such questions are designed to elicit "thick descriptions"—rich, nuanced pictures of the environment that allow researchers "to draw large conclusions from small, but very densely textured facts."[46]

At the same time, the team is selecting interviewees, drawing on the company's database of field testers. They strive for a mix of characteristics, combining lead users, demanding customers, and happy customers, men and women, young and old, and people from different parts of the country. In addition, a small number of noncustomers are included; usually, they are former Bean customers culled from the company's master file, or experts known to prefer other brands. Novices or first-time users are deliberately excluded because they lack needed experience. As one developer put it: "It's an empathy thing; they have to have suffered." The final list is small, with approximately fifteen to eighteen names, but broadly representative, giving the team confidence that the results will be meaningful.

All interviews take place at users' homes or workplaces. Typically, they last for 1¼ hours and are conducted by two people, an interviewer and a scribe. The interviewer poses questions, asks for clarification, follows up on topics of interest, listens attentively, and generally keeps the process moving. The scribe serves as a human tape recorder. According to Bennell:

> That person is just writing as quickly as they can exactly what the customer says—and I mean *exactly*. The metaphor we use is that the customer's voice goes in your ear. It bypasses your brain. It goes right to your pen or your pencil, and you get it down. You're not trying to filter. You're not trying to guess at what they said. You're trying to capture their words verbatim.

Both roles require practice, and team members generally simulate interviews before heading out to the field. The process is quite different from the usual, targeted interviewing (see Table 3-4).

Immediately after completing an interview, the interviewer and scribe meet to debrief. First, they reconstruct the interview and fill in gaps in their notes; then, using yellow Post-Its, they write up a long list of "voices" and "images," one item per Post-It. A *voice* is a verbatim quote—in Armstrong's words, a "sound bite"—taken directly from the interview (e.g., "at the end of a day of hiking, I come into camp and strip off my jacket"); an *image* is an evocative picture or scene that may or may not have been stated directly (e.g., "dripping with sweat"). Together,

TABLE 3-4
L.L. BEAN'S GUIDELINES FOR EXPLORATORY INTERVIEWING

1. Go to the user's environment; do not use an interview room or focus group facility.

2. Conduct the interviews yourself; do not farm them out to a market research firm.

3. Be as open-minded as possible; do not begin with specific hypotheses in mind.

4. Let users tell their stories; do not interrupt.

5. Listen for understanding; do not judge.

6. Ask "why" and "how" questions for clarification; do not rely on unstated assumptions.

7. Follow the interviewee's lead; do not rush from topic to topic.

8. Take down all comments verbatim; do not summarize or paraphrase.

these vignettes produce an almost visceral identification with the environment and a deep understanding of the activity or experience. They also signify a subtle shift in perspective. According to Pete Gilmour, product manager for footwear: "We're looked to be the experts on our products. We develop them, we come up with the concepts, and we have this kind of expert opinion about everything we do. And what this process is all about is throwing that out the window, and letting the customer be the expert."

After all interviews have been completed, the interpretative process begins. At this stage, the goal is to develop a shared understanding of the customer's world, as well as agreement on the most important product requirements. Because the team is seeking common ground, intense concentration is required, and meetings are often difficult and drawn out. The first project team spent five days in discussion and named the process "Hell Week"; meetings have since been reduced to three days, but the nickname remains.

To begin, the entire group meets to share voices and images. Each interviewing team, after all, has talked with different users and has developed a slightly different picture of the customer's world. They exchange Post-Its and listen to one another's findings. Then, the team engages in several rounds of voting, reducing the number of images from several hundred to thirty-five or forty. By grouping, categorizing, and connecting the Post-Its that remain, they develop a single, composite diagram that presents an integrated picture of the activity and the environment in which it takes place.

The process involves two distinctive steps. First, all Post-Its are placed on the wall, and team members silently arrange and rearrange them to form categories. Individuals are not permitted to speak; they simply move Post-Its in a silent dance, creating their own connections as others do the same.[47] The goal is to force synthetic thinking and broaden perspectives. According to Murtagh:

> There are some connections that are very clear, very linear, and very easy for everyone to see. Part of the exercise is getting past them, expanding connections so that we walk away with some significant insight. The process of moving things around without speaking forces us to think about connections that we would not make individually, connections that other people are making that are not obvious to us. So there's a great learning that goes on, and it forces you to learn in your own world because there's no discussion about it.

Once consensus has been reached—the team can tell because the Post-Its remain in place and are no longer being moved—discussion resumes. The team tries to summarize succinctly each cluster of images, taking great care to distinguish and clarify categories. This step is called "scrubbing the stickies"; the goal, according to Murtagh, is to ensure that there is genuine agreement and understanding:

> We have to be clear as a group that these little Post-It notes are capturing exactly the things we think they are, that the language within them is accurate. Often, we're in our own worlds, and we write things down and think that everybody else understands them. The scrubbing process gives us the opportunity to be precise with our language. It gives us the opportunity to discuss what each one means. Ultimately, it allows us all to agree on what is up on the wall.

A similar process is used to define customer requirements. The team combines concrete voices and images to create more general ideas, translating them into explicit needs. The process is one of progressive abstraction. The apparel team, for example, generated one of its requirements by moving from voice ("I walk into camp and strip off my jacket") to image ("dripping with sweat") to driving idea ("need two shirts") to requirement statement ("layer next to the skin that can dry within ten minutes"). After producing a lengthy list, the team distills, synthesizes, and "scrubs" the requirements. They reduce the number by voting, then group the remaining items into categories. Again, they silently arrange and rearrange Post-Its, then discuss appropriate category headings or titles. Because the ranking of requirements is crucial, the final list is carefully validated. To ensure representativeness, the team develops a written questionnaire and sends it to one thousand customers.

With these rankings in hand, team members begin the search for solutions. Brainstorming and wild ideas are encouraged, and no proposal is out of bounds. A particularly effective technique is borrowing—taking a technology or feature from one product category and applying it to another. Gaiters, for example, are used to keep snow out of boots when cross-country skiing. Why not use the same approach to seal the tops of hunting or fishing footwear? Analogies like these stimulate creativity; they also ensure that the group has fun. Eventually, however, the team applies a rigorous test: how well do the new ideas match up against customer requirements? At times, there are disagreements. The sleeping system team generated seven potential designs, then narrowed the list to two. Each had zealous supporters. To resolve the debate, the team divided itself in half; each group took one option and assessed it against the best competitive offerings. When the groups reconvened, the solution was obvious: the "Burrito Bag," so named because it came with multiple layers of fleece that could be wrapped and unwrapped to regulate temperature. It was a nearly perfect match with the top customer requirements. But to be certain, the team sent prototypes to five of its original interviewees, asking "Does this solve the problems you told us about?" The answer was a resounding yes, and the bag was launched in spring 1997. Within weeks, sales were 200 percent above forecast, and vendors were struggling to keep up with demand.

This approach to product development puts a premium on learning. Inquiry takes center stage, interpretation is carefully structured, and solutions are deferred until the very end. As one developer put it, the goal is to "bubble up deep knowledge to the point where it is actionable." The resulting process is unusual in two respects: the amount of direct contact between designers and customers, and the time spent developing a shared understanding of customer needs. At times, the payoff is a single "Aha" like the Burrito Bag; more often, the insights are applied in bits and pieces over the years. According to Armstrong:

> There are usually some twenty to twenty-four customer requirements that get adopted at the end of a project and provide learnings that go on season after season. Ultimately, that's the real power of this approach. Individual products come and go, but if you can leverage those requirements against all of your future developments—using them as a touchstone—chances are you're going to be on track with the customer.

OBSERVATION

At times, even the most thoughtful questions will be ineffective. When knowledge is tacit or unarticulated, known only at a subconscious or nonverbal level, individuals are likely to have trouble communicating clearly. Examples include latent, untapped feelings or needs; processes or practices that have been internalized and are performed without thinking; and shortcuts, workarounds, and rules of thumb that are the product of years of experience.[48] In such cases, a leading philosopher has observed, "we can know more than we can tell."[49] The resulting knowledge is difficult to extract, even if questions are artfully and sensitively framed. Companies seeking this kind of information often have only one option: direct observation.

Designers of office equipment, for example, must first understand the realities of white-collar work. Yet formal office procedures often bear little resemblance to employees' actual behavior. When researchers at Xerox asked accounting clerks to describe their jobs, they received answers that corresponded reasonably well with the formal procedures described in the company's job manual. But when they observed clerks in action, they found that they were behaving quite differently:

> [T]hey relied on a rich variety of informal practices that weren't in the manual but turned out to be crucial to getting the work done. In fact, the clerks were constantly improvising, inventing new methods to deal with unexpected difficulties and to solve immediate problems. Without being aware of it, they were far more innovative and creative than anybody who heard them describe their "routine" jobs ever would have thought.[50]

The problem is particularly acute when new or unfamiliar technologies are involved. Then, all learnings unfold in real time, and adaptations are often subtle and difficult to identify. Designers must usually observe users directly to ensure that important insights are not lost. Steelcase has used this approach to collect data on its new office system, Personal Harbors, which was designed to encourage collaboration and group work.[51] The system combines innovative, adjustable personal work spaces, equipped with a full array of computer and communication technologies, with a large, open commons area. To better understand the resulting interactions and flows, researchers conducted field tests at three companies. Each firm agreed to use Personal Harbors for at least several months and to share its experiences with Steelcase. To collect information, researchers used traditional methods of inquiry, such as questionnaires, focus groups, and user journals, plus time-lapsed videotape. By mounting cameras unobtrusively at each site, they developed an objective visual record, ensuring that users' perceptions were supplemented by observed patterns of behavior.

Guidelines for Effective Observation

Anthropologists and sociologists have long relied on these techniques to conduct field work.[52] Together with the Xerox and Steelcase examples, their experiences suggest several guidelines for practice. Observation should be carried out in context, in real rather than artificial settings.

Observers should immerse themselves in the local scene, watching individuals and groups as they conduct their daily work. At times, this may require that they become "participant observers," simultaneously involved in and detached from the activity at hand. Yet even then they should remain as unobtrusive as possible—the proverbial flies on the wall—to preserve natural patterns of behavior and avoid distortions due to their presence. Learning is most effective when observers blend into the background and others are onstage. But observation must still be public and aboveboard. To avoid breaches of trust, observers should identify themselves and explain their goals, especially when lengthy periods of immersion are required to obtain sensitive information. Deeply rooted ways of thinking, feeling, and acting should not be discovered through subterfuge or disguise.

Several skills are essential. Surprisingly, the initial requirement is political savvy and negotiating ability. Every observer, after all, must first obtain access and acceptance. In most organizations, permission is required to videotape or observe individuals or groups. Tact and persuasiveness are essential for gaining entrée, and anonymity and confidentiality must usually be guaranteed. But all too often, inexperienced observers assume that this stage has been completed once guarantees have been made and a senior member of the organization has agreed to serve as host or has signed off on the project. In fact, "entrée is a *continuous* process of establishing and developing relationships, not only with a chief host but with a variety of less powerful persons. . . . [T]here are many doorways that must be negotiated."[53] The deepest learnings often occur only after observers have been fully accepted by the local community and people feel free to behave naturally.

Once entrée has been obtained, the most important skills are attentive looking and listening. In the immortal words of Yogi Berra: "You can observe a lot by watching."[54] The best observers keep detailed records and are scrupulous in pursuing accuracy and fidelity. They work hard to keep personal biases and preconceptions at bay, while constantly seeking out anomalies, exceptions, and contradictory evidence. This is more difficult than it first appears, for "not only do observers frequently miss seemingly obvious things . . . they often invent quite false observations."[55] Charles Darwin, the father of evolutionary theory and one of the finest observers of all time, went so far as to keep a separate record of all observations that contradicted his theory "because he knew they had a way of slipping out of the memory more readily than the welcome facts."[56]

Skilled observers also suspend judgment and postpone analysis as long as possible; they strive to do more "'sponging up' (of sights and sounds) than 'spewing out' (of interpretations)."[57] Curiosity and receptivity are essential to success, as is the ability to retain and muse on information without immediately sorting or classifying it. According to a prominent scientist:

> Novices . . . worry too soon about developing salient categories for final analysis, about developing brilliant concepts, and about establishing "patterns of interaction." . . . Not so our model researcher; he is quite content to experience the ambiance of the scene. He has great patience, as well as a tolerance for ambiguity and for his own ignorance. . . . [H]e is genuinely busy being a learner.[58]

This is especially important during the initial minutes, hours, and days of observation. First impressions are usually the most powerful teachers; they come at a time when observers are most sensitive to subtle distinctions and cues. As familiarity and exposure increase, most people find it more and more difficult to separate themselves from the environment and make fine discriminations.

In most cases, observation involves listening as well as watching. Sometimes, the required skill is nothing more than a well-tuned ear, for conversations are often within earshot or accompany videotapes. On other occasions, information must be elicited, through either casual, incidental questioning or formal interviewing. Both techniques demand sensitivity and restraint. As a sociologist investigating inner-city behavior discovered after his blunt questions about illegal gambling stopped a promising discussion cold: "One has to learn when to question and when not to question as well as what questions to ask."[59] It is equally essential to use the language of participants when posing questions, both to create comfort and to avoid forcing responses into artificial categories.

Eventually, researchers must couple observation with interpretation to form meaningful insights and connections. One approach is to begin early to develop collection plans to target observations and provide focus.

The alternative is open-minded immersion, with sorting and sifting performed after the fact. In general, the choice depends on the clarity of goals and on how precisely the learning agenda can be defined before the process begins. Either way, however, it is essential to have a classification scheme that is broad enough to encompass the full range of observed behaviors and experiences.

Approaches to Observation

Approaches to observation are distinguished primarily by the degree of involvement or participation required.[60] Passive observation lies at one extreme. Observers are silent and unobtrusive; there is no interaction, and the goal is simply to record experiences for later review. The advantages of this approach are ready access to users and limited difficulty securing permission; the disadvantages are an inability to pose follow-up questions and clarify meaning. The process can be performed by unacknowledged or identified observers, and in natural or constructed settings.

Honda, for example, sent a floundering design team to Disneyland, where they spent the entire day in the parking lot, "watching how people in the United States used their cars, what they put in their trunks, and noting which design features made each activity easier or more difficult."[61] U.S. designers, by contrast, frequently invite users to staged clinics, where they interact with mock-ups and prototypes. Appliance manufacturers use test kitchens for similar purposes, while computer firms employ usability laboratories. Occasionally, the process can be conducted remotely, using cameras, recording equipment, or other instrumentation. Hoover became suspicious when it found, in response to surveys, that people claimed to be vacuuming their homes one hour per week. To be certain, the company attached timers to a few models and exchanged them with users' current machines. They showed that people spent a little more than half the stated time actually vacuuming.[62]

Observation becomes more probing when it is coupled with modest amounts of participation and interaction. Observers are no longer mute but limit their discussions with users to clarifications and on-the-spot attempts to refine understanding. Critical skills include the ability to convey interest, probe discretely, and intervene without disruption. The advantage of this approach is that it often leads to deeper insights than passive observation; the disadvantage is that observers' questions will distort, to some degree, the natural flow of activities. Questions may be informal or scripted, and interventions may be more or less structured.

Milliken, for example, has created "first-delivery teams" that accompany the first shipment of products; team members follow the product through the customer's production process to see how it is used, pose occasional questions along the way, and then develop ideas for further improvement. Digital Equipment, by contrast, developed a structured, interactive process that was used by software engineers to observe users of new technologies as they went about their work.[63] Called "contextual inquiry," it included a defined learning agenda, planned interviews, and targeted questions. Still, most interventions were broad and general, designed to keep users focused on the task and technology at hand. Sample questions included: What are you doing? Why are you doing that? Is that what you expected? Tell me about the problem you just encountered? How do you work around it?

Participant observation lies at the other end of the spectrum from passive techniques. Observers are fully engaged in activities and are accepted as insiders. Marketers at Serengeti Eyewear, a division of Corning that manufactured and sold sunglasses, for example, stayed in touch with consumers by spending at least some time every few months selling sunglasses from behind the counter of different retail outlets.[64] Here, crucial skills include gaining trust and acceptance, performing required tasks competently, "being constantly on stage . . . without dropping your guard,"[65] and, perhaps most important, maintaining bifocal vision—simultaneously participating in events while remaining a detached, objective observer. The advantages of this approach are deep, empathic understanding and insights, often in the language and categories of users, plus the opportunity to observe natural interactions and patterns. The disadvantages are difficulties in obtaining access, long periods of data collection, and observers who occasionally "go native" and lose objectivity. For these reasons, businesses have often been slow to employ this mode of learning, despite its enormous power.

Observation, it should be clear, is an invaluable technique for collecting first-hand, unfiltered information. But it is not inherently superior to search or inquiry. The three techniques are complementary. Each provides a window on the world that is best used under certain circumstances. Search is well suited to settings where needed information has already been published or is there for the taking. Inquiry is well suited to settings where facts or insights have yet to be collected but key sources can be readily identified and questioned. Observation is well suited to settings where questions are likely to produce incomplete or misleading responses but insights can be gained by watching people at work or at play. Independently, these three techniques have much to offer; in combination, they provide intelligence of the highest order.

THE U.S. ARMY'S CENTER FOR ARMY LESSONS LEARNED: NOT MAKING THE SAME MISTAKE TWICE

The U.S. Army's Center for Army Lessons Learned (CALL), based at Fort Leavenworth, Kansas, is a leader in participant observation.[66] CALL was founded in 1985; its initial role was to capture lessons from the National Training Centers, where troops engage in long, simulated battles to test their readiness and skills. Later, as the Army's mission broadened to include "operations other than war"—interventions in Somalia, Bosnia, and Haiti, plus fire fighting, flood control, and other forms of disaster relief at home—CALL was charged with learning from these experiences as well. Today, CALL observation teams are among the first troops on the ground in any Army operation. They collect on-the-spot information about new practices and techniques, identify problems and trouble spots, distinguish approaches that work from those that do not, and share their findings with others. According to Colonel Orin A. Nagel, director of CALL from 1994 to 1996:

> CALL stands at the crossroads of knowledge in the United States Army. We are both a provider of information and a collector of information. We like to think of ourselves as a conduit between what's going on in a thousand locations in the Army and what you need to know in your location.

CALL is the Army's institutional memory—the guy who's been around forever, the bottom drawer of your oldest employee. We are a knowledge repository, with three customers: the unit that's on the ground today, the unit that's training to replace them tomorrow, and the rest of the Army, who can use these lessons next year or whenever we have something similar going on.

Despite this broad mandate, the center is relatively small. It is divided into several divisions: a Lessons Learned Division, which develops and disseminates lessons from actual operations, major exercises, and the Combat Training Centers; an Information Systems Division, which supports CALL's hardware and software; a Research Division, which designs and maintains CALL's database and document storage and retrieval systems; the Foreign Military Studies Office, which produces high-quality military security assessments; and the University After Next Division, which provides the best practices and technologies from public, academic, private, and military sectors to the Army.

The heart of the center's activities is real-time observation and data collection. All steps are carefully planned in advance, beginning with a clear statement of learning needs. To determine "critical information requirements," the director of CALL meets quarterly with the chief of staff of the Army and even more frequently with brigade and battalion commanders. Among his questions: What do you need to know to be more effective in the future? What operations are pending that will impose new demands on soldiers? What kinds of decisions will commanders face that they have not faced before?

With the answers in hand, CALL leaders identify appropriate missions and form collection teams. Teams are of varying size, depending on the task. For small assignments, there may be as few as eight to ten participants; on large operations, there are as many as forty or fifty. In Bosnia, the observation team consisted of thirty-eight people; only six were CALL observers. For obvious reasons, every team relies heavily on borrowed manpower. Teams are headed by a line officer from an outside unit, selected for his or her rank, credibility, and access to the group being observed. A second supporting leader, skilled in observation and collection, is drawn from CALL. Several members of CALL's Lessons

Learned Division are assigned to the team; they are often supplemented by combat camera crews. Additional experts are then recruited from the various military schools to contribute their knowledge of communications, logistics, and other relevant fields. Occasionally, even more specialized skills are required. In Haiti, because of the distinctive culture, the observation team included both a minister and a linguist.

This approach has several advantages. By designating a line officer with connections to the unit being observed as leader, it overcomes the problem of access that so often plagues participant observation. By drawing on CALL's skilled observers and designating one member of CALL as coleader of the team, it ensures that the process of observation will be disciplined and accurate and that appropriate methodologies will be used. By involving camera crews, it provides for a detailed visual record that will supplement and support written observations. And by drawing on subject matter experts, it keeps CALL's staff small while introducing diverse perspectives and a cross-fertilization of ideas. The last point is particularly important, as Nagel observed:

> If you have the same people looking at the same things all of the time, you're going to get the same perspectives back. But if you have twenty different people looking at twenty different issues, then you get twenty different perspectives. And that starts to give credibility to your knowledge base. You begin to feel comfortable that what you are observing is in fact what is going on.

Specialized experts are also able to contribute immediately to units in the field. Because they are a help rather than a hindrance, with valuable knowledge to impart, they are able to overcome the natural suspicion that so often prevents observers from becoming insiders. Assimilation is quick and easy, knowledge sharing becomes a two-way street, and observers and participants become almost indistinguishable. But why would specialized experts participate in the first place? Because they are able to obtain information and insights that would not otherwise be available. Those members of the engineer school who were part of CALL's team in Bosnia were among the first to observe the crossing of the Sava River. They were able to bring critical new knowledge back to their colleagues, for study and subsequent inclusion in curriculum, training, and doctrine.

All teams begin with a collection plan, a formal document that guides the observation process. Plans are structured hierarchically, with a few overarching themes at the top and a large group of focused topics below. They begin with *issues,* which are broad areas that Army leaders have identified as targets of learning; proceed to *subissues,* which are functions and tasks that fall under a broader theme and map directly into the categories of the Army's Blueprint of the Battlefield, a generic process model that fits all operations; and conclude with detailed sets of *questions,* which specify the precise areas where data must be collected and observations must be made. All plans are constructed with the advice and input of subject matter experts, who know where current knowledge is thin and additional information is required. In Haiti, for example, an aircraft carrier, the U.S.S. Eisenhower, was used for the first time to deploy troops. Because carriers are designed for pilots and planes, not soldiers and troop-carrying helicopters, the logistics, staging, and loading of troops all presented unique problems. Questions were developed in each area to ensure that lessons were learned for use in future operations.

Occasionally, collection plans must be prepared before teams are formed. This is necessary because certain missions can be anticipated but still arrive without warning. The date of deployment is unknown. More often, time is available before operations are scheduled to begin, and teams develop their own collection plans. Subject matter experts first canvas their peers to develop an initial set of issues, subissues, and questions; then, the team assembles at CALL headquarters for a three- to five-day workshop. During the workshop, members develop and refine the collection plan, learn how to observe unobtrusively, and are taught the CALL methodology for extracting and distilling lessons.

To ensure continuity, the process begins even before troops are sent to the field. According to Nagel:

Today, when you see the Army deploying on an operation, CALL is not only there with the lead soldier, it has already been there for weeks. We work with the unit from the day they are notified, helping them in their final training, passing on the lessons learned from the last similar operation, and sorting out the information and knowledge that they're going to need as they go into that theater. Then we're right with them from the time that the first soldier goes in until the last soldier comes out.

Once units are in the field, data collection begins in earnest. Whenever possible, members of the collection team try to observe events on the spot and in real time; they supplement their observations with interviews, briefings, photographs, videotapes, and written reports. In addition to questions identified in the collection plan, they focus on emerging problems and unexpected difficulties. The team in Haiti, for example, discovered that cargo containers were arriving with their content lists inside, making routing impossible without first opening the container. The team in Bosnia discovered that untracked, snow-covered roads were especially dangerous because they were likely to be mined. At times, teams have trouble tracing problems to their source—a process called "threading the needle"—and must tap additional sources of information. Anonymity, however, is always guaranteed, and individuals are never singled out or identified by name. Quick fixes and warnings are then developed and disseminated, often at evening briefings. This rapid information sharing is an important part of CALL's role; it both enhances credibility and provides an immediate payoff to units in the field. As Nagel put it: "It would be a shame if a soldier in one battalion made the same mistake tomorrow that was made in a different battalion today."

Teams are urged to develop their observations as quickly as possible. Each day, their notes are sent electronically to CALL headquarters for review. Every team has its own dedicated analyst, who serves as editor, interpreter, and librarian. Observation is thus separated, to the extent possible, from interpretation and the development of formal lessons. But the process is highly interactive, as Nagel observed:

The analyst's job is to look at all information coming from the team and sort and evaluate it. Is it complete? Does it make any sense? Does it pass the "so-what" test? He'll make some notes and then ship that observation back to the team for more information. "Tell me a little more about this. Tell me a little more about that. I don't quite understand how this fits with what you told me yesterday." The team will then collect more information, make some changes, and send the observation back. The analyst will clean it up and begin loading it into the computer.

All observations, as well as supporting documents, photographs, and videotapes, are coded in the categories of the Blueprint of the Battlefield. Coding is relatively rapid because collection plans are designed with these categories in mind. New lessons can often be accessed through CALL's Web site within days. Moreover, because the Blueprint is a standardized indexing and retrieval system, field units know precisely where to look for needed information.

At the end of their assignment, collection teams return to CALL headquarters to prepare an Initial Impressions report. That document summarizes the most important lessons; it is immediately sent to replacement units. Later, additional bulletins, newsletters, and handbooks are developed for dissemination throughout the Army. Videotapes are prepared as well; they are valued for their immediacy and fidelity and because they provide a feel for the local setting. In addition, CALL observers participate personally in knowledge transfer. They temporarily join up with replacement units, communicate lessons directly, and contribute to training scenarios developed from observations in the field. The latter are especially powerful. Based on its observations of the 10th Mountain Division, the first group in Haiti, CALL developed twenty-four training vignettes. They covered such topics as crowd control and weapons searches. The follow-on unit built its training around these vignettes; when it returned from the field six months later, the division commander observed that he had actually executed twenty-three of the twenty-four scenarios. The only one he had not encountered was reacting to a terrorist attack.

CALL's approach is a model of effective learning (see Table 3-5). Observation is targeted and carefully planned, observers are knowledgeable and well trained, and acceptance by field units is assured through networking, added value, and assurances of anonymity. All data are col-

TABLE 3-5
REAL-TIME OBSERVATION: LESSONS FROM CALL

1. *Keep the unit small.*

- Combine dedicated employees with borrowed manpower.
- Focus on a limited number of strategically important operations or initiatives.

2. *Develop a plan for collecting information.*

- Establish learning needs in advance.
- Solicit input from subject matter experts.
- Proceed from broad issues to narrow, targeted questions.

3. *Form collection teams with well-defined responsibilities.*

- Assign dual leaders: a line manager and a member of the collection unit.
- Combine trained observers with subject matter experts.
- Add specialized skills (e.g., language experts, translators) when necessary.

4. *Employ a disciplined process of observation.*

- Assign collection teams to operating units before they are sent to the field.
- Ensure that collection teams are among the first individuals on-site.
- Combine observation with written reports, interviews, and on-the-spot debriefings.
- Do not attribute observations (especially mistakes) to particular individuals or units.
- Use video and still cameras to compile an objective visual record.
- Separate observation from analysis: assign the roles to different people, and ensure continuing dialogue between them.

5. *Actively disseminate results.*

- Relay critical, pertinent information to members of field units as soon as possible.
- Summarize findings in written and oral reports and send them to follow-on units.
- Participate personally in knowledge transfer by temporarily joining up with follow-on units.
- Capture and communicate lessons using vivid, easy-to-follow formats such as training scenarios.

lected on the spot, drawing on multiple sources and perspectives, and accuracy and reliability are relentlessly pursued. Objective analysts provide additional checks and balances; they also keep interpretation separate from observation. Feedback cycles are short, so that critical information becomes available while it is still useful. Diverse formats are used to package knowledge and communicate lessons, ensuring widespread dissemination.

The entire system rests on norms of reciprocity and on a collective commitment to learn from others. According to Nagel:

> When I talk to a soldier about CALL, I say, "You have an unlimited credit card. You can come to my data warehouse and have access to all the knowledge that I have. But one day I am going to come knocking on your door and say, 'Hey, it's Nagel. I'm here to collect. It's your turn to pay in. You've been drawing on your account, on the tens of thousands of others who have input data, knowledge, and information, and now it's time to return the favor.'"
>
> He's been using this information for years. He knows that he can't figure out where it came from, so it's pretty safe to let CALL come in and look at his operation. He knows that we've got credibility, we produce pretty good stuff, and we make sure that anonymity is preserved so that nobody else is going to be able to figure out that he's the only guy that managed to screw things up. And we always go out of our way to give credit to the people who first crack a problem.
>
> Besides, he knows we're going to be helpful. As I used to tell my kids, "You don't have to make every mistake personally. I've made plenty of them, and if you just let me tell you what they were and how you can avoid them, there's still plenty of mistakes for you to make."

As chapter 1 pointed out, one of the litmus tests of a learning organization is that it seldom makes the same mistake twice. CALL ensures that the U.S. Army passes this test.

4

Experience

Practice makes perfect. Experience is the best teacher. Trained at the school of hard knocks. This mode of learning is so widely recognized it even has its own proverbs. All suggest that certain types of knowledge come only from participation and personal involvement—from doing things rather than studying or talking about them. We undertake new projects, carry out challenging tasks, and immerse ourselves in unfamiliar environments; then, we repeat the process, usually with considerably more success. These cycles of activity generate rich veins of information; when those veins are tapped, we learn from experience. The mining process may be unconscious or reflective, individual or organizational, spontaneous or planned; the goals, however, remain deeper understanding, increased skill, and superior performance.

This mode of learning has been studied by a wide range of scholars. Philosophers, for example, have been debating its importance for hundreds of years. Two schools have occupied center stage. Rationalists, represented by Descartes and Leibniz, argued that knowledge was based on innate ideas and principles known independently of experience, while empiricists, represented by Locke, Berkeley, and Hume, disagreed, arguing that knowledge came only from perceptions and sensory data.[1]

In the early 1900s, John Dewey, the American pragmatist, added a practical spin to this long-running debate. As an empiricist as well as a stern critic of traditional schooling, he argued that "all genuine education comes about through experience" and proposed a curriculum that drew on a steady stream of hands-on projects rather than the usual lectures and tests.[2] Practical, applied problems ensured that there was no separation of subject matter and method; they gave students "something to do, not something to learn; and the doing is of such nature as to demand thinking, or the intentional noting of connections; learning naturally results."[3] Business scholars soon adopted this same approach, coining the phrase "action learning" to describe the immersion of students in complex, multifunctional workplace problems rather than theory alone.[4]

Today psychologists have joined the chorus. Many now define learning as changes in behavior brought about by experience, with trial and error the primary mechanism at work.[5] Like Dewey, they believe that the process is most effective when it is situated and grounded, linked closely with concrete activities and past experience.[6] Unanchored ideas and concepts—techniques without a home—are difficult to grasp. They are far more likely to be understood when they are taught in familiar contexts, settings, and environments.

Problem solving, for example, can seldom be mastered as an abstract art. It must first be coupled with focused experiential knowledge—a deep understanding of relevant areas of practice, such as business, politics, science, or law—if deep learning is to occur. According to a study by the National Research Council:

> General skills such as breaking down a problem into simpler problems or checking to see whether one has captured the main idea of a passage may be impossible to apply if one does not have a store of knowledge about similar problems—or know enough about the topic to recognize its central ideas.[7]

The dilemma should be obvious. Novices lack experience, which is why they are engaged in learning. But to learn most effectively, they must already have sufficient prior knowledge. Otherwise, they will be slow to process and retain new facts and concepts because of a lack of what scholars call "absorptive capacity"—the ability to interpret and classify information based on preexisting schemas and frameworks.[8]

Practice therefore plays a large role in explaining expert performance. Elite chess players, musicians, and athletes are distinguished less by their innate talents and abilities than by the accumulated amount of time they have spent in deliberate, supervised practice.[9] Far from being naturally superior, the most accomplished performers have simply dedicated themselves to working harder and longer at mastering their craft. Typically, they begin practicing two to five years earlier than their less accomplished peers and then remain focused, capturing the benefits of experience. The process has a certain natural rhythm and cannot be rushed. Studies in a wide range of fields show that world-class performance is achieved only after ten years of effort.[10] But that superiority comes at a price. The associated mental and physical skills are highly specialized and do not transfer easily across fields.

Managers are no different. They too take years to perfect their craft and learn best from practice and hands-on experiences. But to be effective, those experiences must be diverse. When it comes to leadership, more of the same seldom produces superior results. Instead, the best teachers are varied assignments (working in a start-up, a turnaround, an international subsidiary, and a large successful domestic business); hardships and difficulties (overcoming business failures, missed opportunities, and demotions); and serving bosses with different strengths and styles (both positive and negative role models).[11] As an expert on management development has observed: "[T]he potential lessons in each kind of experience are determined by the overlap between what the experience demands and what a person does not yet know how to do. . . . [D]evelopment results from doing something *different* from one's current strengths."[12]

These arguments suggest that we learn from experience in two distinct ways: by repetition and by exposure. Repetition ensures that the same tasks are performed more efficiently over time. Skills are honed through repeated use, and the goal is refinement and depth. The adage "practice makes perfect" is as true of swinging a golf club as it is of conducting a performance review or fitting parts on an assembly line. Exposure, on the other hand, ensures that a new set of talents is devel-

oped. Skills are added through the exploration of unfamiliar environments or the assumption of new responsibilities; when coupled with
personal involvement, the results are commitment and change. The target may be musical composition or management skills, but the rationale
for doing something different is always breadth and expanded understanding.

LEARNING AND EXPERIENCE CURVES

The impact of these processes is difficult to measure directly. Both repetition and exposure operate in the background; their lessons are often
implicit and automatic. In fact, much learning from experience occurs
without conscious thought or control. Many of the resulting rules, tasks,
and procedures emerge without our awareness and cannot easily be articulated or retrieved.[13] For these reasons, engineers and economists have
turned to more concrete, accessible measures of experience. Rather than
trying to disentangle and evaluate the distinctive contributions of repetition and exposure, they have bundled them under a single, comprehensive umbrella: the learning curve.[14]

   The concept dates back to the discovery in the 1920s and 1930s that
the costs of airframe manufacturing fell predictably with increases in
cumulative volume.[15] These increases were viewed as proxies for greater
skill and knowledge, and most early studies examined their impact on the
costs of direct labor. Later studies expanded the focus, looking at total
manufacturing costs and the impact of experience in other industries,
including automobile assembly, shipbuilding, oil refining, and consumer
electronics. Learning rates were highly variable but tended to cluster in
the 75 to 85 percent range (meaning that with a doubling of cumulative
production from one to two units, two to four units, four to eight units,
and so on, costs fell to 75 to 85 percent of their previous level).[16] The
combined effect of these improvements could be staggering. In 1906 and
1907 Ford introduced several automobiles priced at more than $5,000.
Two years later the company settled on a single, standardized design, the
Model T, bringing the price down to $3,000. By 1923, after eight million
units of the Model T had been produced and an 85 percent learning
curve was firmly in place, the price had fallen to $900 (see Figure 4-1).[17]

FIGURE 4-1

PRICE OF MODEL T, 1909–1923

(AVERAGE LIST PRICE IN 1958 DOLLARS)

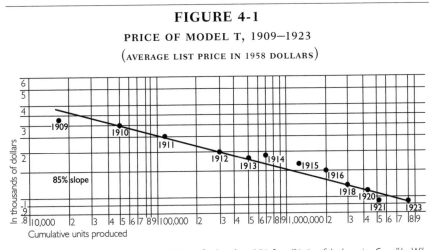

Cumulative units produced

These effects are not confined to manufacturing but apply to almost any repetitive activity. Accident rates fall steadily with cumulative experience, as does the time required for parts replacement and maintenance. There is an additional, associated effect that scholars call "learning by using."[18] Often, the reliability and repair needs of complex capital goods—turbines, generators, boiler vessels, and the like—can be established only through experience. Failure rates are difficult to predict in advance; since safety may be at stake, engineers' initial estimates are usually conservative. The result is a steady expansion of knowledge through use, as well as increased efficiency. Airlines experienced this effect when they shifted from piston to jet engines. Initially, they had little idea of the proper timing of overhauls. The new engines were assumed to be more durable, but there were many unknowns. To avoid problems, engineers scheduled overhauls every 2,000 hours, just as they had with piston engines. With experience, however, their confidence in the reliability of jet engines increased, and they raised the time between overhauls to as long as 8,000 hours.

Firms like the Boston Consulting Group took these ideas to a higher level in the 1970s.[19] Drawing on the logic of learning curves, they argued that industries as a whole faced experience curves, predictable decreases in costs and prices as industries grew and their total production increased. Again, improvement rates were highly variable but tended to fall in roughly the same range as learning curves: 75 to 90 percent.[20] With these figures, consultants suggested, came an iron law of competition. To profit from experience, companies had to rapidly increase their production ahead of competitors, thereby lowering prices and gaining market share. Texas Instruments applied this approach with great success in pocket calculators, as did DuPont in titanium dioxide.

Both learning and experience curves are still widely used, especially in the aerospace, defense, and electronics industries. Boeing, for example, has established learning curves for every workstation in its assembly plant; they assist in monitoring productivity, determining work flows and staffing levels, and setting prices and profit margins on new airplanes. But other companies have floundered when they have applied these techniques. The problem, in large part, is the vast mythology that now surrounds learning and experience curves and impedes their thoughtful use.

Consider these popular but misguided views:

- *Labor learning is the primary engine driving improvement.* This assumption dates back to the original work on learning curves, which examined complex products and time-consuming assembly operations. Because parts were fitted by hand, improved labor rates were usually the target. But the lessons of experience come in many other guises. While production and service workers certainly become more skilled and efficient with practice, additional savings result from simplified processes, rationalized layouts, superior tooling, standardized products, and new forms of organization. Exposure and insight bring new ideas; with them come a wide range of improvements. According to an experienced observer: "The industrial learning curve thus embraces more than the increasing skill of an individual by repetition of a simple operation. Instead, it describes a more complex organism—the collective efforts of many people, some in line and others in staff positions, but all aiming to accomplish a common task progressively more efficiently."[21]

- *Learning rates are uniform across products, processes, firms, and industries.* Early researchers, drawing on data from the airframe industry, reported an 80 percent learning rate. That figure soon became accepted as a universal phenomenon, with great predictability.

Yet subsequent studies have uncovered widely varying learning rates and surprisingly little uniformity. Even within a single industry, there is considerable dispersion. In airframe manufacturing, curves differ by type of airplane, as well as by facility. During World War II, bombers, fighters, and trainers each had strikingly different learning rates. Moreover, the difference between the average industry learning rate for any one of those categories and the experience of a particular manufacturing facility was typically 25 percent.[22] Similar differences have been observed in other industries such as chemical processing, suggesting the danger of projecting individual learning curves from industry averages.[23] Some products, processes, and plants simply have more potential for experience-based improvements than others. They involve less customization, more frequent repetition, and greater transparency in equipment and techniques.

- *Learning curves are stable over time.* For many years, learning curves were thought to have great predictive power. Existing improvement rates were expected to remain steady, with little or no change over time. Unfortunately, such stability requires that both inputs and outputs remain constant and undisturbed; otherwise, there will be large errors. Knowledge, after all, normally depreciates with time and is easily lost. Both Lockheed and Douglas Aircraft suffered the consequences. Lockheed introduced the L-1011 TriStar in 1972, basing its price on steady and predictable cost reductions. A year later the company announced that profits would begin to flow by mid-1974. But because of widely varying production rates, learning was far less rapid than anticipated. In late 1975 managers reported that production costs were still above selling prices; they remained at that level for the remainder of the program.[24] Douglas encountered similar problems. It set prices for the DC-9 based on an anticipated 85 percent learning curve. But a few years into production, the economy boomed, and a large number of experienced workers left for other employers. Because they took their knowledge with them, the 85 percent learning rate was never obtained. Despite a massive hiring program, large losses ensued.[25]

- *Knowledge gained through experience is easily retained and transferred.* Learning curves measure the accumulation of knowledge, not its retention. But the usual assumption is that gains will be maintained over time, either because they become embodied in techniques and procedures or because they pass fluidly from one group of production workers to the next. Studies of shipbuilding and truck manufacturing suggest that both arguments are flawed.[26] During World War II, the construction of Liberty Ships was accompanied by rapid depreciation of knowledge. Continuing production was essential to learning; without it, only 3.2 percent of the stock of knowledge at the beginning of the year was available twelve months later. In truck manufacturing, knowledge was also difficult to retain and communicate. It did not transfer fully between workers on a company's first and second shifts, despite significant investments in training. These findings suggest that experience may be a wise teacher, but that its lessons are easily forgotten.

- *Learning and experience curves are universal sources of competitive advantage.* Consultants have long extolled the virtuous cycle of increasing output, reaping the benefits of experience, reducing prices, seizing market share, and then repeating the process until an unassailable competitive position has been established. There is indeed value to this approach but only if the environment is ripe. When industries are early in their life cycles and output doubles rapidly, when technologies are stable and unlikely to change, and when customers are sensitive to price changes, riding the experience curve is often an effective strategy.[27] But when cost leadership comes from sources other than experience (minimills in steel, just-in-time production in autos) or when the primary basis for competition is product or service differentiation (applications programs in software, the fit and features of running shoes), strategies based on learning or experience curves are far less likely to be successful. In fact, when it comes to acquisitions, increases in experience often lead, at least in the short run, to poorer financial performance. Why? Because "[a]cquisitions are a complex practice and lessons from one acquisition simply cannot be extrapolated to another."[28] Managers tend to generalize inappropriately from earlier efforts, drawing parallels that are incorrect and misleading.[29]

These findings have a number of practical implications. Operationally, they suggest that managers should pursue learning opportunities with indirect as well as direct labor; use experience as a catalyst for considering new methods, as well as as a form of repetitive practice; be wary of estimated learning rates, especially when drawn from other products, processes, or facilities; maintain steady, unvarying production levels rather than responding to sudden surges in demand; minimize employee turnover to capture the lessons of experience; and institutionalize and retain knowledge through training and explicit procedures. Strategically, they suggest that managers should match their use of learning and experience curves to the demands of the environment. These curves are not an all-purpose solution to competitive problems. But under the right circumstances they can provide an edge. How does one tell? By asking the following questions: Does the industry exhibit a significant experience curve? Do some facilities learn more rapidly than others? Can the sources of advantage be kept proprietary? Will price reductions lead to increased sales? Are new technologies or products likely to undermine these advantages, or will they persist over time?[30]

Perhaps most important, these findings suggests that learning from experience is an active process. Improvements must be carefully and consciously managed. There is nothing automatic about the resulting gains, and "merely expecting progress does not bring it about."[31] Quite the opposite, in fact:

> Costs do not fall by natural inclination—they rise. Almost all cost reductions are the result of concerted, and often substantial, effort. . . . Without . . . steady, significant pressure . . . the experience effect will rarely be obtained. In other words, accumulated experience does not *cause* cost reductions but rather provides an opportunity which alert managements can exploit.[32]

REFLECTION AND REVIEW

Surprisingly, few companies take the time to reflect on their experiences and develop lessons for the future. With the repeated activities that are captured by learning curves, the task can sometimes be avoided, since efficiencies and practical guidelines often emerge as a by-product of getting things done. But when activities are episodic or rare—new product launches, geographical expansions, the introduction of unfamiliar technologies or processes—conscious reflection is usually necessary if lessons are to be learned. Managers must carefully review past efforts to distinguish effective from ineffective practice; they must then record their findings in an accessible form and disseminate the results to employees. One expert has called this process the "Santayana Review," citing the famous philosopher George Santayana, who coined the phrase "Those who cannot remember the past are condemned to repeat it."[33]

Unfortunately, a wide range of barriers stand in the way. The most obvious are time pressures. Most businesses operate with little or no slack. Tasks are tightly sequenced, and milestones pass all too quickly. As a harried computer engineer observed about his company's design process: "There was no question of deadlines. You'd already missed it, whatever it was."[34] In such settings, tomorrow's tasks are far more important than yesterday's. Reflection becomes an avoidable luxury because it adds an additional step, with uncertain payoff, to an already compressed schedule. Moreover, employees seldom welcome reviews of past projects. Rather than serving as opportunities for learning, they frequently become searches for the guilty, an excuse to scapegoat. In all too many companies, there are good reasons to believe that mistakes are best kept hidden.

Yet even when the environment is supportive, reflection can be problematic. Cause-and-effect relationships are difficult to disentangle when samples are small.[35] A complex project often involves hundreds of participants and thousands of steps; how does one isolate the critical variables and determine their relative contribution? Here, failures play a vital role, especially when compared with prior expectations or successes. Failures focus attention, simplify diagnosis, help discriminate among alternatives, and provide essential operating and design information.[36] A study of more than 150 new products concluded that "the knowledge gained from failures [is] often instrumental in achieving subsequent successes. . . . [P]roducts that fail act as important probes into user space about what it would take to make a brand new effort successful. . . . In the simplest terms, failure is the ultimate teacher."[37] IBM's 360 computer series, for example, one of the most popular and profitable ever built, was based on the technology of the failed Stretch computer that preceded it. The lessons learned from the initial, unsuccessful launch were used to modify and enhance the next generation of products.

Single Case or Comparison Reviews

Lessons may be drawn from single cases or comparisons. The former, usually written up as narratives or institutional histories, attempt to tease out insights and practical advice by combining diverse recollections and commentaries.[38] Microsoft, for example, now follows virtually every new software release with a detailed postmortem.[39] The majority involve written reports and require three to six months of work. Groups review their time together, zero in on problems, distinguish effective from ineffective processes, and make recommendations for the future. Over time, postmortems have become steadily more comprehensive and now include separate discussions of program management, development, testing, product management, and user education. They are usually sharply self-critical and "read like the recountings of disasters. If all product names were removed . . . readers would assume they were investigations of failed projects. [Yet] nearly all . . . proved to be among the best-sellers in their category."[40]

Comparisons involve side-by-side assessments of successes and failures or contrasts of superior and average performers. The presence of multiple cases highlights differences, isolates causal factors, and reduces interpretative errors. Boeing used this approach immediately after experiencing difficulties with its 737 and 747 plane programs. Both planes were introduced with much fanfare—as well as serious problems. To ensure that the problems were not repeated, senior managers commissioned a high-level employee group, called Project Homework, to compare the development processes of the 737 and 747 with those of the 707 and 727, two of the company's most profitable planes. The group was asked to develop a set of "lessons learned" that could be used on future projects. After working for three years, they produced hundreds of recommendations and an inch-thick booklet. Several members of the team were then transferred to the 757 and 767 start-ups. Guided by experience, they produced the most successful, error-free launches in Boeing's history.[41]

Whether single cases or comparisons are used, the required conditions remain the same. Reviews must be conducted immediately, while memories are fresh and data can still be verified. They must be accepted as "real work" rather than avoidable frills and consciously scheduled into work plans and projects. A disciplined, structured process is essential, as are trained facilitators; both keep discussions focused, emotions under control, and finger-pointing to a minimum. Reviews should be as objective as possible, with considerable time and effort devoted to verifying the nature and sequence of events. Facts must be clearly separated from opinions; otherwise, interpretation is certain to be difficult and divisive. Here, helpful steps include the involvement of neutral third-party observers and analysts, as well as the use of internal control groups.

Perhaps most important, the climate must be right. A supportive, tolerant culture is essential if reviews are to flourish. Most employees will cooperate only if they believe that self-assessment and critical thinking are truly valued by management. There must be room for mistakes, as well as improvement. For this reason, perfectionist cultures seldom produce active, honest reflection. Their evaluation and control systems are intolerant of error, leading employees to associate mistakes with career risk rather than learning.

Individual, Group, or Organizational Reviews

Reviews may also focus on individuals, groups, or organizations. At the individual level, the goal is to distill and disseminate the elements of effective practice. Skilled managers, engineers, marketers, and salespeople normally employ a distinctive bag of tricks—a set of tools and techniques, learned through experience, that their less successful counterparts have yet to adopt. They also possess distinctive patterns of thought, feeling, and behavior.[42] By putting the most effective performers under a microscope, companies can identify these essential attitudes and approaches and ensure that they are shared. The resulting profiles have two primary uses: screening potential employees and developing existing talent.

AT&T's Bell Laboratories, for example, studied its own software engineers to determine why some were more productive than others.[43] Managers and engineers were first asked to identify star performers; since there was only a 50 percent overlap in the nominations of the two groups, the stars were identified as those ranked highly by both camps. They were then interviewed in depth about how they went about their work and, specifically, what they did to be more productive. To weed out spurious explanations, a control group of average performers was asked the same questions; a number of obvious answers, such as superior cognitive skills or advanced technical knowledge, were quickly eliminated. Instead, researchers zeroed in on the striking differences in the two groups' descriptions of "taking initiative." To the stars, the phrase meant networking widely, pursuing tasks that went beyond stated job requirements, pretesting ideas, and seeking out constructive criticism. Middling performers put far more weight on self-promotion, glitzy presentations, and impression management. Using these insights, the Bell Labs team designed an innovative, hands-on training program, which the star performers then delivered to a subset of their peers. The results were immediate and impressive. Participants reported a quick 10 percent productivity improvement, rising to 25 percent a year later. There were equally striking gains in managers' evaluations of their ability to spot problems, conduct high-quality work, keep their bosses informed, work across organizational boundaries, and attend to customer and competitive needs.

At the group level, reviews often focus on complex, expensive capital projects.[44] Typically, the goal is to identify a few critical "rules of the road"—processes and procedures that keep quality high, schedules on track, and costs under control. Usually, the review process is ad hoc, conducted by participants themselves (as at Microsoft) or by a specially assigned group (as at Boeing). Occasionally, however, reviews are more structured, with standardized approaches and a dedicated, experienced team. For many years, British Petroleum had a small, five-person group, the Post-Project Appraisal unit (PPA), that collected information on major investment projects, wrote up case studies, and derived lessons for planners that were then incorporated in the annual revisions of the company's planning guidelines.[45] The group reviewed only six projects annually and presented their findings directly to the board, giving them high visibility as well as autonomy and clout. The bulk of their time was spent in the field, interviewing an average of forty individuals per project. All reviews covered the period from project conception, beginning before the submission of a formal proposal, through the first few years of operation. Members of the appraisal unit then synthesized the lessons in three separate booklets—one each for acquisitions, joint ventures, and project development and control—and distributed the findings to all project planners.

From the company's point of view, the value of this process is obvious. But why would individual managers or employees provide information for case studies that were certain to identify their flaws? Because the process was designed to be as objective and even-handed as possible. The appraisal unit was staffed with experienced, credible experts, without functional or divisional loyalties; case studies were sent to interviewees before submission to the board, ensuring that their comments and corrections were incorporated in final drafts; and individual cases, with their occasionally pointed critiques, were not circulated throughout the company but were abstracted and presented to a wider audience in the less threatening form of broad, generic recommendations. Today, the PPA no longer exists as an independent unit, but British Petroleum continues to conduct regular reviews at the project level.

Organizational reviews typically take one of two forms: studies of ongoing operations or assessments of change programs. The former normally focus on "best practices"—those structures, systems, and processes that have generated superior performance at one site or division and thus deserve rapid dissemination. There are often substantial opportunities for improvement. Even at well-managed companies, quality and productivity differences of 2:1 are commonly found when similar operations are compared.[46] Because these differences normally result from a bundle of mutually reinforcing practices, reviews should always be comprehensive and multifunctional. But they may involve different levels of management. In general, senior managers should be the focus when large-scale systems are involved, while middle- and lower-level managers should be the focus when daily operations are of interest.

Consider the contrasting approaches taken by Chrysler and Toyota. Chrysler's top executives asked outside experts to develop a case study featuring Diamond-Star Motors, its joint venture with Mitsubishi, and then to lead five hundred senior managers in small-group discussions of the implications for the company's current design, manufacturing, and purchasing systems. The highly successful LH cars were the result. Toyota, by contrast, rotated nearly three hundred middle- and lower-level managers and production coordinators, in groups of thirty to sixty, through three-month stints at New United Motors Manufacturing, Inc. (NUMMI), its joint venture with General Motors. Many went through multiple rotations: three months at the joint venture, observing production methods, charting quality performance, meeting with government officials, and developing an understanding of American employees; then three months back at Toyota City, reflecting on their experiences and developing lessons. Eventually, a large number of these employees transferred to Toyota's new plants in Kentucky and Ontario, where they were able to apply their new learnings firsthand.[47]

Reviews of change programs have a different focus. Rather than targeting best practices, they zero in on critical missteps and needed midcourse corrections. The goal is to "capture reality in flight," uncovering difficulties before they become sizable or entrenched.[48] Xerox, in an unusually thoughtful and well-designed process (called a Presidential Review because it was sponsored and led by Paul Allaire, the company's president and CEO), revisited its newly designed organization in 1993, one year after introduction. The process began with extensive interviews with more than thirty senior managers, who were asked to describe the transition from the old to the new organization, point out unexpected problems and difficulties, and highlight differences they had observed between Xerox's "design intent" (the stated goals of the redesign) and actual results. To ensure objectivity, all interviews were conducted by outside consultants, who then summarized their findings in a brief report. The consultants also developed a workbook to stimulate further reflection and sent it to all participants a month before the scheduled review meeting. The workbook included descriptions of Xerox's newly developed strategy, structure, processes, and culture, followed by diagnostic questions in each area designed to assess progress to date and evaluate the change management process. Among the questions: What has changed? What still needs to be done in this area? Where are the largest gaps between what is intended and what is currently true? If you were to outline the barriers that need to be dealt with, what comes to mind? What would you have done differently? What should we do now? Forty-five senior managers then assembled for a day-long meeting, where they pooled their reflections, identified major trouble spots, and developed recommendations and action plans.

All of these review processes are designed to avoid recurrent mistakes while reproducing successes. They are necessary because management, like many other professions, is more art than science. The right choices are not always obvious in the heat of the moment. Sometimes, plans are little more than inspired guesswork, and effective strategies and practices can be identified only after the fact. As the philosopher Kierkegaard put it: "Life is lived forward, but understood backward." To move ahead, one must often first look behind.

THE U.S. ARMY'S AFTER ACTION REVIEWS: SEIZING THE CHANCE TO LEARN

The U.S. Army is one of the few organizations to have institutionalized these reflection and review processes, especially at the group level. After Action Reviews (AARs) are now standard Army procedure.[49] They were introduced in the mid-1970s and were originally designed to capture lessons from the simulated battles of the National Training Centers. The technique diffused slowly—according to the Army's chief of staff, it was a decade before the process was fully accepted by line officers and embedded in the culture—and only in recent years have AARs become common practice. The turning point was the Gulf War. AARs sprang up spontaneously as small groups of soldiers gathered together, in foxholes or around vehicles in the middle of the desert, to review their most recent missions and identify possible improvements. Haiti marked a further step forward. There, for the first time, AARs were incorporated into all phases of the operation and were used extensively to capture and disseminate critical organizational knowledge.

The technique is relatively straightforward. It bears a striking resemblance to "chalk talks" in sports, where players and coaches gather around a blackboard shortly after a game to discuss the team's performance. Both chalk talks and AARs are designed to make learning routine, to create, as one commander put it, "a state of mind where everybody is continuously assessing themselves, their units, and their organizations and asking how they can improve." In practice, this means that all participants meet immediately after an important activity or event to review their assignments, identify successes and failures, and look for ways to perform better the next time around. The process may be formal or informal, may involve large or small groups, and may last for minutes, hours, or days. But discussion always revolves around the same four questions:

- What did we set out to do?
- What actually happened?
- Why did it happen?
- What are we going to do next time?

According to Army guidelines, roughly 25 percent of the time should be devoted to the first two questions, 25 percent to the third, and 50 percent to the fourth.

The first question is deceptively simple. Group members must agree on the purpose of their mission and the definition of success. Otherwise, there will be no basis for evaluating performance or comparing plans with results. In the Army, objectives are normally defined with great precision. They include three elements: "the key *tasks* involved, the *conditions* under which each task may need to be performed, and the acceptable *standards* for success. (For example, at a range of 2,000 yards, hit an enemy tank moving at 20 miles per hour over uneven terrain at night with an 80% success rate.)"[50] With objectives like these, there is little ambiguity, and it is easy to determine whether a job has been done well or poorly. Such clarity also avoids confused, inconclusive reviews. According to an experienced AAR facilitator:

> Unsuccessful AARs are often those where the boss has the attitude, "I don't know what I want, so I can't tell you exactly what to do. But I'll recognize it when I see it. So just go out there and do good things." That's not helpful. We insist that our leadership, from the very top officer to those in charge of three to five men, give soldiers clear guidance. They must have a standard.[51]

The second question requires that participants agree on what actually happened during a mission. This too is more difficult than it first appears. Facts can be slippery, especially when stress is high and events move rapidly. All too often, memories are flawed, leading to competing or inconsistent stories. Reality—what soldiers call "ground truth"—becomes difficult to pin down, resulting in gridlock and AARs that progress slowly if at all. But these problems can be overcome. At the National Training Centers, facts are verified by pooling information from three diverse, objective sources: observer-controllers, instrumentation, and taping.

Observer-controllers are skilled, experienced soldiers who shadow individual officers throughout their training exercises. They also provide on-the-spot coaching and lead AARs. (Not surprisingly, many later do a tour of duty at the Center for Army Lessons Learned [CALL], where they are assigned to the Lessons Learned Division.) A training exercise for three thousand to four thousand people normally involves approximately six hundred observer-controllers. Typically, their time in service makes them a bit senior to the officers they are observing, providing both credibility and clout. And because they have complete access to battle plans, are intimately familiar with the terrain, and are constantly present during maneuvers, they can effectively arbitrate debates when facts are in dispute.

Technology, in the form of instrumentation and taping, provides an additional source of objective information. The resulting record is extremely detailed and leaves little room for argument. Onboard microprocessors track the exact position and movement of vehicles over time, while sophisticated, laser-based technologies note when and where weapons were fired as well as the resulting hits and misses. Video cameras, mounted at critical locations throughout the training centers, record troop movements. These films provide vivid, compelling testimony, with extraordinary fidelity. As one officer put it: "If a picture is worth a thousand words, a motion picture must be worth a million." Audiotapes round out the story, conveying the exact timing and content of communications both within and across units.

Together, these tools and approaches ensure that facts are reconstructed with considerable accuracy. During AARs at the National Training Centers, soldiers have little problem answering the question, What actually happened? Unfortunately, they face many more difficulties in the field, where observer-controllers and recording technologies are not always available. Occasionally, CALL teams and combat video crews will be on hand to provide objective data. But in most cases, accurate reconstruction depends on pooling multiple perspectives in a process that resembles "majority rules." Then, immediacy is crucial to success, as is wide participation. To minimize memory losses, AARs must be conducted as soon after the event as practical—preferably, the very same day. They should include, whenever possible, all key participants, as well as unbiased, third-party observers, members of staff and supporting units, and even senior commanders. Participants should agree on some mechanism to resolve disagreements and ensure that discussion does not grind to a halt when differences emerge.

Once the facts are established, diagnosis can begin. Outside the Army, many groups start their reviews at this stage, assuming that prior steps can be omitted without problems. But agreement on both the standards to be met (question one) as well as actual performance (question two) is essential to avoiding endless debates. The Army's insistence that the first 25 percent of every AAR be devoted to these topics is a critical insight. And the benefits are hardly confined to the military. Companies can also gain by devoting time up front to clarifying goals and targets and setting unambiguous standards—expected levels of customer satisfaction, milestones for project completion, penetration rates for new products—and then comparing them with results during the review process. By deferring diagnosis, these two steps vastly improve the odds that ensuing discussions will be grounded and productive.

The third question begins the process of analysis by asking for an examination of cause and effect. At this stage, the goal is to tease out the underlying reasons for success or failure. A tank unit expected to reach a critical checkpoint at a certain hour but was twenty minutes late; what caused the discrepancy? A scout set out to inspect a position to the north but ended up five miles east; how did he become lost? A commander planned to coordinate artillery attacks with two other battalions but never communicated his intentions; what caused the breakdown? Answering these questions requires problem-solving skills, as well as a willingness to accept responsibility. Groups must brainstorm possible explanations and then find ways to choose among several plausible alternatives, often in the face of limited and conflicting data. They must also be ruthlessly honest. Individuals need to face up to their own deficiencies, avoiding the all-too-common tendency to turn a deaf ear when personal errors or weaknesses are uncovered. This is particularly true of leaders. As one commander observed: "If you're not willing to hear criticism, you probably shouldn't be doing an AAR."

At times, analysis is simple, and cause and effect are easy to untangle. Missed opportunities or roads not taken are usually obvious to both individuals and groups. In Haiti, a sergeant responsible for convoying soldiers to the beach returned several hours late because one of his trucks became stuck in the sand. The ensuing AAR was brief and to the point: he had failed to pack a tow bar. The first units entering Port-au-Prince were startled to discover that delivering babies was an important part of their mission. They quickly wrote an AAR to ensure that all medics received at least rudimentary obstetrics training.

On other occasions, challenges are more complex, and a series of AARs may be required to home in on the problem. Then, a process of progressive refinement is useful for teasing out explanations and developing possible solutions. Units assigned the task of clearing guns from suspected rebel strongholds in Haiti initially had little success. Their first AAR examined the current process, the resulting resistance, and how it might be overcome. Soldiers noted the absence of dogs in the area and the locals' frightened response to the German shepherds used by the military police. Perhaps, they suggested, the dogs should be more visible. In the next town, they were placed up front, and cooperation immediately improved. Soon after, during another AAR, soldiers noted that they had encountered no women in their sweeps through the towns. Perhaps they could be encouraged to assist in the collection effort if they had a woman soldier to identify with. In the next village, one unit assigned a female commander as leader and visibly acknowledged her authority. The result was further gains in cooperation. Finally, during a third AAR, soldiers noted that they faced far more resistance when confronting people in the streets than when they approached them in their homes. The unit shifted its modus operandi to house-to-house searches, and even more guns were secured.

This last example suggests that the final step in an AAR—deciding what to do next time—is often inseparable from diagnosis. Participants are usually eager to propose solutions, and many arise naturally once problems are well understood. It is particularly important that participants focus on things they can fix, rather than external forces outside their control. Otherwise, the process is likely to have little immediate impact. This stage has another goal as well: identifying areas where groups are performing well and should stay the course. In Army lingo, these are activities to be "sustained." Surprisingly, they are often difficult to identify. When standards are met, variation is limited and there are few obvious clues to the sources of superior performance. Failures are far easier to diagnose.[52] Yet if successes are to be repeated, the underlying causes must be clearly articulated.

Identifying activities to be sustained was one of the assignments of the first unit in Haiti. Because soldiers faced a host of unfamiliar challenges—keeping the peace, delivering food, overseeing elections, even collecting trash—they were asked to review virtually all of their missions and develop a set of standard operating procedures for follow-on units. AARs were the primary tool. As one participant recalled: "We AAR'd everything." Small squads conducted them daily, debriefing orally and informally; larger sections conducted them after every critical mission, presenting the results in formal reports; and platoon leaders conducted them weekly, submitting their findings to commanders for further distillation and review. Quick feedback led to quick implementation, sharply increasing the rate of learning.

Initially, soldiers found many areas for improvement and strove only to make each effort better than its predecessor. But with experience, there were fewer and fewer problems, and attention shifted to sustaining successes. Eventually, the unit developed a series of "cookbook recipes" that captured their own best practices, wrote them up, and submitted them for review. Frequently the practices were set in Army doctrine and used by both CALL and the National Training Centers to prepare follow-on units for their upcoming assignments.

Together, these examples show that AARs are a powerful, appealing tool. They have many advantages. The concept is easy to grasp and inexpensive to apply, amounting to little more than organized reflection. The four questions provide a simple roadmap, appropriate for any situation. The process demands few skills other than careful observation and systematic problem solving. Even so, success is not guaranteed. A number of conditions must first be met.

To begin, reviews must be framed as dialogues, not lectures or debates. Army experts suggest that participants speak as much as 75 percent of the time. The process must also be as egalitarian as possible: the broader and more even the participation, the better. Under no circumstances should leaders dominate discussions or seize control. They should also refrain from posing their own problems for analysis or lobbying for preferred solutions. Such actions undermine AARs by suggesting that they exist for the leader's benefit rather than the group's.

Skilled facilitation is essential. Facilitators guide the discussion from beginning to end, ensuring that participants stay on track. They introduce the topic, keep the group focused, establish and enforce ground rules, monitor and maintain the schedule, transition from one question to the next, and summarize the resulting action plans. Even more important, they personally set the tone. AARs require openness and candor, a willingness to set aside traditional lines of authority. There must be honest interchange between superiors and subordinates, a recognition, in the words of the Army's chief of staff, that "disagreement is not disrespect." Because this attitude seldom comes naturally to hierarchical organizations, it must be carefully and consciously cultivated. According to a facilitator at one of the National Training Centers:

> We preface our AARs by saying, "We're not judges, and we're not evaluators. We're not going to talk—you are. But to be successful, we have to have an information exchange between the lowest soldier in the ranks and the highest, because the highest ranking officer doesn't see everything that's going on. This is his opportunity to get feedback."

Of course, feedback will be forthcoming only if commanders are willing to publicly acknowledge their flaws. Such statements have enormous symbolic value, and skilled facilitators try to draw them out early in AARs. As one facilitator observed:

When leaders admit up front that they did some things right and some things wrong, it really opens up the whole group. They understand that this isn't a "Who shot John?" type of review. It's "Let's figure out what's best so that we can do better next time."

Straight talk must also be supported by the larger organization. Incentives and rewards must reinforce the openness required by AARs; otherwise, mistakes will never be discussed and the process will continue to be viewed with suspicion. Here, actions speak louder than words. According to a mid-level officer:

I think one of the reasons why we are able to talk so frankly in AARs is that our superiors have set the conditions that they want to know what is truly the problem and what you are really thinking—not just the answer they want to hear. If they find out that you are hiding a fact or are less than completely honest, recently that has been death to your career. People who have lacked integrity or candor are leaving the service because they are not getting promoted.

Yet even with the proper incentives, discussions can still derail. Candor comes in many forms, not all of them constructive. For this reason, the Army has developed ground rules for AARs that are enforced by facilitators. Tact and civility are required, and personal attacks are forbidden. There will be no searches for the guilty. As one facilitator put it: "We don't use the 'b' or the 'f' word. We don't place blame, and we don't find fault." Plain speaking, however, is essential, and facilitators normally suggest to participants that they enter AARs with "no thin skins." They are also told that "discussions will stay in house." There will be no report cards and no relaying of information to bosses. Mistakes admitted in an AAR cannot be held against soldiers later on. They are opportunities for learning, not blemishes on one's record, and are excluded from personnel evaluations. Reprisals—either during AARs or after the fact—are not allowed.

Some structure is necessary to ensure coherence and avoid random, rambling discussions. The best AARs therefore follow a well-defined path. They normally begin shortly after the activity was completed but not so soon that there is no opportunity to plan carefully or identify likely learning opportunities. To begin, facilitators usually write the topic of discussion on a flip chart in front of the group and suggest that speakers confine their comments to that topic. The group then marches through events in sequence, using the timeline of the mission to guide them. At each step, the facilitator pauses to ask participants the four basic questions. Occasionally, when tasks are complex, the group will break the chronology of events down further, using additional categories, such as intelligence and maneuver, drawn from the Army's Blueprint of the Battlefield, to organize discussion. Many facilitators anticipate factual disputes before they arise and have videotapes or other documentation on hand for resolving them. During wrap-ups, the entire group generates two lists, one of activities to be sustained and another of activities to be improved. To ensure that these learnings are not lost, one member is assigned the role of secretary and recorder.

As discussion unfolds, facilitators ask questions. This is a high art, for AARs must be tough and probing without causing defensiveness. Facilitators must therefore choose their words carefully, pressing for honest self-assessments without directing criticism at specific individuals. They must keep the spotlight on the group, asking, for example, how a platoon could have done better escorting a convoy, rather than questioning the platoon officer about his personal failings and lack of direction. At the same time, facilitators must remain attuned to differing points of view. They must ensure that disagreements surface and conflicts are ironed out; both are essential to learning. Not surprisingly, many facilitators have become experts at reading body language and drawing people into discussions at just the right moment, using subtle cues: "I see you shaking your head over there; do you see the situation differently?" Poor AARs can often be traced to facilitators who have misunderstood their roles and use the occasion to tell personal war stories and anecdotes.

Clearly, facilitators require a multitude of skills. They must be sensitive observers and artful discussion leaders. They must be knowledgeable about the subject at hand. And they must be respected by subordinates and peers. This combination is hard to find in one person, so the

Army draws on diverse sources. At the National Training Centers, all facilitators are observer-controllers. They are considered to be ideal for the task because they combine intimate, objective knowledge of operations with extensive experience leading discussions. But because they are seldom available in the field, line officers must at times lead their own AARs. This presents few problems for small, intimate groups like squads or sections, which have close working relationships. Difficulties increase, however, as units become larger. Then, one mid-level officer observed, "too often, the person in charge is intimidating." A few commanders still insist on leading their own AARs because they consider themselves capable of encouraging openness and debate. But most Army experts agree that the task is best left to individuals with less at stake, either staff members outside the chain of command or higher ranking officers with a broader perspective. Commanders, they believe, are more likely to benefit from AARs by listening attentively and contributing selectively, rather than assuming their customary positions of leadership.

AARs, then, have a number of strict requirements (see Table 4-1). Among the most critical are immediacy, broad participation, a structured process, the availability of objective data, skilled facilitation, attention to recording and dissemination, and a climate of openness and candor. Even more important, however, is simple repetition. Unless reviews are carried out routinely at all levels of the organization, they will never be viewed as more than an interesting diversion. Consistency breeds comfort and acceptance. It is for this reason that most Army training exercises now include daily AARs and that AARs were used so extensively in Haiti. It is also why General Gordon Sullivan, the Army's former chief of staff, did not exempt himself from the process. He too engaged in regular AARs. For example, early in his tenure, he and his staff reviewed responses to difficult questions from the House Appropriations Committee; later, they focused on major policy initiatives. Such practices ensure that AARs become second nature. Eventually, a new mind-set develops in the organization, a recognition that no activity is truly complete until participants have reflected on their experiences and understood the reasons for success or failure. Then, and only then, has learning been incorporated into daily work.

TABLE 4-1

CONDUCTING AFTER ACTION REVIEWS

Do	Don't
Schedule AARs shortly after the completion of an activity.	Conduct AARs without planning.
Make reviews routine.	Conduct reviews infrequently or irregularly.
Collect objective data whenever possible.	Allow debates to bog down when establishing the facts.
Use trained facilitators.	Allow dominating leaders to run AARs.
Establish clear ground rules: encourage candor and openness; focus on things that can be fixed; keep all discussions confidential.	Base performance evaluations or promotions on mistakes admitted in AARs.
Proceed systematically: What did we set out to do? What actually happened? Why did it happen? What are we going to do next time?	Permit unstructured, meandering, disorganized discussions.
Involve all participants in discussions.	Allow senior managers or facilitators to dominate discussions.
Probe for underlying cause-and-effect relationships.	Criticize or fault individual behavior or performance.
Identify activities to be sustained as well as errors to be avoided.	Conclude without a list of learnings to be applied in the future.

EXPERIENTIAL LEARNING

For all their power, reflection and review processes have an important weakness: they take place after the fact. Because reviews are the final step in a long chain of events, learning occurs with a lag. Reflection, after all, does not begin until all tasks have been completed. Most errors are therefore discovered relatively late in the game. This presents few problems for repetitive activities like convoys and patrols, service calls, or tasks on an assembly line, where second chances come quickly. But when assignments are drawn out or challenges recur infrequently, the process is far less efficient. Immediate applications are often hard to find, and opportunities for practice are limited. In such settings, the lessons of experience are easily lost.

They can be found with the help of a well-designed educational process. The goal remains the same—to develop practical, applied knowledge by drawing on experience—but with an important twist. Reflection and action are now intimately intertwined. After-the-fact reviews are replaced by alternating periods of learning and doing. Work-related tasks remain the focus, since most studies suggest that adults absorb new ideas best when they are linked directly to everyday challenges.[53] But learning is more proactive than in the typical review process, combining three elements: an introduction to relevant concepts, theories, and tools; a carefully selected problem or simulation to test and apply new knowledge; and a process that includes pauses along the way to evaluate progress, share learnings, and make midcourse corrections. The approach goes by various names—action learning, experiential learning, problem-centered learning—but all can be traced to the writings of John Dewey and his insistence on the "intimate and necessary relation between the processes of actual experience and education."[54]

Today, most corporations seem to agree. Theories and abstract discussions are out; tangible, results-oriented programs are in. Their goal is to mimic or reproduce experience, while providing practice in essential skills. Management development executives for example, clearly prefer classes that are active, anchored, and applied. They cite workshops as the most popular—and by far the most effective—instructional approach.[55] Traditional methods, such as lectures, are still widely used, but primarily for conveying facts, principles, and basic techniques. Because they are one step removed from application, they are less likely to produce lasting change. As one educator archly observed: "All too often, information flows from the notes of the professor into the notebooks of students without passing through the minds of either."[56]

A Focus on Problems

Experiential learning programs are completely different. They are built around problems and concrete challenges that ensure active participation. The problems may be real or simulated. Real problems have the advantage of immediacy and fidelity; simulated problems can be tailored to specific learning needs.

Real Problems. When real problems are used, they typically involve pressing, high-visibility projects, with measurable results that matter to important people in the organization. If solved, they are likely to produce substantial payoffs. The best projects are multifunctional; require face-to-face contact with customers, competitors, or suppliers; and lack obvious, easy solutions. Today, they often include an international component to increase global exposure. A group at GE was asked to develop a consumer-lighting strategy for western Europe; a team at Whirlpool was chartered with recovering overpaid duty on compressors that the company was importing from a Brazilian affiliate; and a group at Motorola was assigned the task of assessing the company's opportunities in the Latin American market.[57] In each case, the problem was nominated by top managers, with the assistance of training experts. At times, teams will select their own problems. When Xerox introduced quality training in the 1980s, all work groups were required to apply the new techniques to a problem of their choosing. The senior executive team, for example, tackled operations reviews, which were frustrating and time-consuming, and completely redesigned the process.[58]

Real problems clearly motivate learners by putting them on the firing line. With few boundaries between the classroom and the workplace, students focus on the "here and now," not the "there and then."[59] But there is a downside as well. Programs built around real problems have two limitations: failure is highly visible, and innovative ideas are hard to teach. Significant problems, almost by definition, command the interest and attention of senior managers. Proposed solutions are certain to receive careful scrutiny, especially if they challenge the status quo. At GE, all action-learning projects conclude with a presentation to division presidents or other business leaders. Tough, occasionally hostile, questions are the norm. This is by design. According to the former head of GE's executive training center: "The key to action learning . . . is . . . to create performance anxiety [with] the illusion of pretty high risk. . . . [If] you did a crummy report, you're not going to lose your job, but you're going to be professionally embarrassed."[60] While these conditions are certain to stimulate intensive work, they are less likely to encourage risk taking. New ideas and techniques are difficult to apply; participants are understandingly reluctant to experiment when the results will be displayed in an open forum. The exposure is too great, and a crucial ingredient is missing: psychological safety. The result, according to a leading cognitive scientist, is limited learning: "[W]hen people who have made mistakes or taken risks that didn't pan out receive public tongue-lashings from the boss . . . it's difficult to learn . . . rather than admitting an error and seeking help, employees prefer to cover it up and avoid public humiliation."[61] For these reasons, the use of real problems is likely to be most effective in settings where tough, trial-by-fire cultures are already in place or where critical feedback can be provided in ways that minimize public embarrassment.

Real problems have another disadvantage: they are seldom designed for learning. Top managers usually select problems for their importance and potential payoff, not their ability to illustrate critical concepts or techniques. The goal, of course, is to identify problems that are broad and representative, requiring the application of knowledge that will be useful in other settings. But they are difficult to find, and the resulting activities are often more valuable for the generic process skills they impart—teamwork and negotiation, for example—rather than the associated frameworks, principles, or tools.

Simulated Problems. Simulated problems offer a solution. They are designed with specific skills in mind and come in many forms, ranging from simple to dauntingly complex. The associated learnings may be physical, social, or cognitive. A manufacturer training employees to pack boxes of biscuits has them practice with wooden cutouts so that they learn how different sizes and shapes fit together.[62] Flight crews fly complete trips in high-fidelity simulators, where they face instrument malfunctions, engine failures, and other unexpected emergencies "that *require* the coordinated actions of all crewmembers for success."[63] Wal-Mart trains new managers with its Always Store, a simulated version of a real store that includes in-basket exercises, customer service problems, and the strategic challenge of stealing market share from a tough local competitor.[64] Despite their differences, all of these programs share the same goal: providing the lessons of experience at a fraction of the cost.

The best simulations combine realism, variety, and low risk. Failure is acceptable because real catastrophes are avoided. Critical variables are easily manipulated, producing new wrinkles and variations. Conflict and difficulty are ever-present, ensuring that learners are drawn in and treat exercises seriously. Immersion is seldom a problem because participants identify closely with the challenges at hand. In fact, most simulations are tailored to the needs of specific groups. Pilots, for example, have long been selected for their technical proficiency and self-reliance—the elusive "right stuff." Yet over the past twenty years, air carrier accidents and incidents have consistently been traced "to inadequacies in leadership qualities, communication skills, crew coordination, or decision making."[65] Today's Line-Oriented Flight Training (LOFT) presents pilots and crews with complex, simulated problems that demand precisely these talents. LOFT also provides the opportunity to experience, in advance, such rare but important events as equipment failures. The result is a compression of actual experience and vastly accelerated learning.

Simulations must be as realistic as possible. If participants view them as a game or can easily anticipate outcomes, the lessons are unlikely to stick. Some element of surprise is usually essential. Typically, it takes one of two forms: an expected success fails to materialize or a sudden, emotional identification occurs. Unexpected failures lead to reflection and new approaches; emotional reactions produce deeply etched imprints on our minds.[66] BARNGA, an exercise designed to show the difficulties of cross-cultural communication, is representative. Groups sit at different tables and learn to play a simple card game. They believe that they are all playing the same game. But without their knowledge, each table has been given slightly different rules. After five minutes, participants are instructed to play silently and resolve any disagreements with gestures and hand signals. Then, two members of each group rotate to another table. Again, silence is enforced. Problems soon arise because participants are in fact playing by different rules. Newcomers to the table fail to relate to established players. Neither's moves make sense to the other. Yet because of the limits on communication, the resulting disagreements can seldom be resolved. During debriefing, the real-world parallels quickly become clear: people in different cultures work under different, often unspoken rules. Because participants have experienced the associated disagreements, this lesson is understood at a visceral rather than an academic level. As one participant observed: "The anger and confusion that BARNGA produces in 10 minutes is worth 10 hours of lecture from an anthropologist."[67]

Verisimilitude and fidelity are equally important to successful simulations. Role plays, for example, are often used to teach employees how to handle performance appraisals, negotiations, and other stressful situations.[68] Most exercises use interpersonal conflict and easily recognized characters to create involvement and identification. Bad Mouth Betty, Hysterical Harold, and other "customers from hell" are featured in the role plays used by Target Stores to teach new salesclerks the basics of customer service.[69] Here, the primary risks are poor casting and unconvincing acting. Without truly believable characters, participants will play along, but there will be little deep learning. Diamond Technology Partners, a strategy and technology consulting firm, found a creative solution. It asked a retired CEO, rather than an employee, to be the client in a simulated reengineering assignment. He played his part to perfection. When a trainee criticized his company's strategy and called him incompetent, he fired the team on the spot, even though the exercise was only partially completed. His decision, while not in the script, was perfectly in character. It also provided participants with a vivid, unforgettable lesson.[70]

Management games are even truer to life. They focus on competitive interactions, with outcomes that are difficult to predict in advance. Teams develop strategies, commit resources, and struggle for advantage as events unfold in real time. Because most games are built around a complete business or industry model, they are usually more comprehensive than simple exercises.[71] Polaroid's Graphic Imaging (PGI) division drew valuable lessons from a game that had participants competing to pitch their company's products at a fictitious industry trade show. Several teams were assigned the roles of competitors such as Kodak and Fuji, one played PGI, and another, the Wild Ducks, was instructed to come up with an unexpected technology that might blindside the market. All teams drew from the same two-hundred-page preparation book, which was filled with market data and competitive intelligence, including complete descriptions of competitors and their products. Teams then made presentations to a panel of judges, primarily peers but with a few real customers sprinkled in. The results were a much deeper understanding of the market and several quick changes in product positioning.[72]

Program Design

These arguments suggest that well-chosen problems, whether real or simulated, share several characteristics, including complexity, scope, and unexpected surprises (see Table 4-2). Effective experiential programs share other traits as well. Concepts and tools are introduced only when needed. They are tightly coupled to problems, delivered "just-in-time" rather than days or weeks in advance. Most managers, after all, when faced with a new approach, will use it or lose it. The best tools are therefore accessible and easy to apply; they map neatly onto the task at hand. GE learned this lesson early in its Work-Out program. After introducing complex techniques with little success, trainers developed the RAMMPP Matrix. Named for the most common sources of unnecessary work—reports, approvals, meetings, measures, policies, and practices—it was immediately and enthusiastically embraced by employees, who saw it as a mirror of their own experiences. The result was quick acceptance and a steady stream of productivity improvements.[73]

Time is another ingredient in successful experiential programs. Skill builds slowly, and alternating periods of teaching, discussion, application, and reflection are usually needed for cementing critical lessons. Inaction is an obvious concern, but it can be overcome with the proper incentives. GTE's Quality: The Competitive Edge program was offered to teams of business-unit presidents and the managers reporting to them. Each president was allowed to bring as many people as desired, with no limits on the composition or size of teams. After assembling for the three-day

---

TABLE 4-2
PROBLEMS THAT STIMULATE LEARNING

---

1. They are significant (the issues matter to people in the organization).

2. They are complex (the solution is not obvious).

3. They are multifunctional (participants must work across boundaries).

4. They involve difficult people issues (the problems are organizational as well as technical).

5. They are action-oriented (the goal is to do something, not simply analyze a situation).

6. They are ill-structured (participants must frame and define problems as well as solve them).

7. They involve surprises (neither the data nor the results are completely predictable).

---

course, participants received a notebook of materials, together with a personalized covering letter from the sector head who oversaw their unit. The letter came as something of a shock: it explained that the team was expected to deliver a complete quality plan, based on the course concepts, within sixty days. Motivation was no longer an issue; now the problem was execution. Two-to-three-hour discussion periods were spread throughout the program so that teams could internalize lessons and begin working on their plans. Work continued when they returned to their units, and all plans were soon submitted to the relevant sector heads for evaluation. They were then reviewed, revised, and implemented with considerable success.

As this example suggests, senior managers are an essential part of experiential learning programs. They wear many hats. As sponsors, they bestow attention, resources, and rewards, keeping learning high on the agenda. As evaluators and clients, they help select projects and judge proposals, offering feedback and advice to participants. As role models, they provide examples to emulate, allowing others to benefit from their personal experiences. The action-learning programs at GE and GTE illustrate the first two roles; the China Accelerated Management Program (CAMP) at Motorola illustrates the third. CAMP was designed to rapidly develop local Chinese management talent and includes a six-week assignment in which participants live in another part of Asia and "shadow" a higher-level manager in order to gain experience.[74] Such senior management involvement is often critical to program success. At Motorola, training in quality tools and process skills had a negative return when there was no management support. But when the same training was actively reinforced by senior managers through sponsorship, evaluation, and conscious modeling, every dollar invested produced a $33 return.[75]

Teams also play a pivotal role in the learning process. They provide opportunities for pooling complementary skills, exploring new frameworks, and sharing tacit, experiential knowledge. Depending on the project, teams take one of three forms. *Natural teams,* like those at Xerox and GTE, already exist; typically, they consist of a boss and his or her direct reports, or a group of functional experts who work together frequently. Their primary advantage is the ease with which projects can be transported back to the workplace; their primary disadvantage is the persistence of existing stereotypes and roles.

Peer teams, like those at Motorola and GE, consist of individuals at roughly the same level who have been assembled, on a one-time basis, for a particular program. Normally, they lack any previous affiliation. The primary advantage of peer teams is freedom of thought and action; the primary disadvantage is the difficulty participants often have reforming their home organizations. The problem is particularly acute in traditional action-learning projects, which meet regularly in "sets," small groups of four to eight led by a facilitator.[76] Each individual works on a separate project that continues for months, and the group's role is to provide counseling, support, and room for reflection. The focus is on personal growth rather than new factual knowledge, and participants are often deeply changed by the experience. Their organizations, however, have seldom moved as far. Reentry is invariably a difficult process.

Alternatively, *diagonal-slice teams* consist of a cross-section of individuals drawn from a single organization. As the name implies, trainers form these teams by taking a deep, diagonal cut across levels and functions. Their primary advantage is the presence of a wide range of skills and perspectives; their primary disadvantages are a lack of shared experience and occasional difficulties overcoming hierarchical and functional barriers.

Experiential programs, then, involve a multitude of choices. Problems must be chosen with care; sessions must include a mix of concepts, applications, and pauses for reflection; incentives must encourage action;

senior managers must be assigned appropriate roles; and teams must contain the right set of participants. The process is time-consuming, but the payoff is worth the price. Experience is a wise teacher, with lessons that are often best discovered by combining learning with doing.

GE'S CHANGE ACCELERATION PROCESS: MAKING CHANGE STICK

One of the most effective experiential learning programs is GE's Change Acceleration Process (CAP), taught at Crotonville, the company's education and training center.[77] Crotonville was founded in 1956 by Ralph Cordiner, the CEO, to develop a cadre of general managers to support GE's shift to decentralized business units. Initially, a single comprehensive advanced management program was offered. Later, Crotonville was used by subsequent CEOs to introduce a broad range of concepts and tools: strategic planning, which GE pioneered, as well as improved cash management and advanced accounting methods. Programs bore a striking resemblance to those at leading business schools. The goals were virtually identical—to convey the latest knowledge to up-and-coming managers—and most courses were straightforward and conventional, a combination of lectures, case studies, and in-depth technical discussions.

All this changed in 1981 when Jack Welch became CEO. Welch had a radically new vision of the company and saw Crotonville as one of his primary levers for change. GE, he believed, was slow, stodgy, and plagued by bad habits: "parochialism, turf battles, status, 'functionalitis,' and, most important, the biggest sin of a bureaucracy, the focus on itself and its inner workings."[78] Managers and employees were separated by a vast gulf; teamwork was poor to nonexistent; and applied problem-solving skills were lacking. Welch therefore gave Crotonville a new mandate: to open up dialogue, instill corporate values, and stimulate cultural change. As Steve Kerr, vice president of corporate leadership development and current head of Crotonville, observed, learning was redefined as "a change in behavior. If people don't act differently, we feel that we've wasted the shareholder's money. So it was logical to connect learning and doing."

The resulting courses fall into three distinct categories. Management development programs, geared to critical career transitions such as the shift into first-line management, business-unit leadership, and control of a global business, are offered on a regular schedule to help managers gain the skills required for their new responsibilities. Focused workshops, aimed at companywide initiatives such as cycle-time reduction and quality management, are offered on an ad hoc basis to introduce managers to best practices both within and outside GE. Broad-based improvement programs, designed to produce fundamental changes in work practices and behaviors, are offered continuously to ensure that significant cultural changes occur simultaneously in all parts of the organization. Work-Out, described in chapter 1, was Crotonville's first large-scale improvement program; CAP was its successor.[79]

CAP grew from Welch's realization that the future was inherently uncertain—and was likely to stay that way. Surprises were inevitable, and it was impossible to anticipate upcoming events. But it was possible to manage the change process more effectively. What was needed was a set of concepts, tools, and techniques for making rapid adjustments and adaptations—in Kerr's terms, "a generalized coping mechanism." Welch assigned the task to four well-known consultants, asking them to review the literature and develop a state-of-the-art model. Kerr, who was one of the four, recalled:

> We studied and studied and studied and brought forth a mouse—a very pedestrian model of change. It was the old unfreezing, changing, refreezing. Lewin had it in the 1940s, Schein had it in the 1970s, and Beckhardt had it in the 1980s. We were kind of embarrassed.
>
> But this was a case where the client made the consultants feel good. Welch said to us: "The trouble with you academics is that you value creativity. If you've done something once, you don't like to do the same thing again. We don't have that hang up. I have only two questions for you: Is what you found true?" We said yeah. "And

are my people doing it now?" We said not consistently. So he said: "Stop apologizing and start teaching."

The resulting program, with its seven-step model of change, was launched in 1992. To ensure acceptance, Welch paid for all of the initial training; in return, he insisted that the top managers at GE, including every company president, corporate officer, and senior executive, commit to seven days of classes spread over a ninety-day period. Attendance was mandatory. A year later, nearly 750 managers had participated, and the program was firmly established.

All participants come to CAP in teams, and each team brings a problem of its own to solve. At Welch's insistence, the problems are "need to do, not nice to do"; they are competitive necessities. At GE Supply, the task was rolling out a quality improvement program to 120 geographically dispersed sites; at GE Plastics Japan, the task was turning around a business that had been unprofitable for five straight years; at GE Aircraft Engines, the task was reducing the cycle time from engine order to remittance; and at GE Lighting, the task was integrating separate technology groups into a single, global organization. Typically, problems are selected by business-unit presidents or leaders; if corporate services are involved, they are selected by department or function heads. As a further check on the process, in the early days Welch personally received lists of all current projects. This had the great advantage of ensuring that problems were of sufficient scale to warrant sustained commitment and attention. According to Jacquie Vierling, manager of Work-Out, Best Practices, and Change Acceleration:

> People were always complaining, "I don't have time to go away to Crotonville and learn." So we said, "If it's a strategic issue and you have to do it anyway, then coming to Crotonville is not time away from your work. It's time away to work on your work."

Participants seem to agree. As one member of the GE Supply team put it:

The nice thing about CAP is that it's relevant. You can relate the theory to something that's really practical, that's actually real. It has a hell of a lot more meaning. We were working on our project in a very structured fashion, but it didn't feel as though we were in a class.

Projects must meet several tests. They must involve cultural and organizational dilemmas, must require work beyond the few days devoted to CAP classes, and must have a significant payoff for both the business and the corporation as a whole. The first requirement ensures that CAP's tools and techniques are relevant and helpful, since they are designed to tackle people problems rather than technical or financial barriers to change. The second requirement ensures that participants do not see the course as a bounded, one-time event, demanding only a few days of class time, but as a learning experience that continues well beyond Crotonville. It also highlights the program's twin goals: solving a pressing problem and learning broader, more generic change management skills. The third requirement ensures that CAP's limited training slots are allocated in ways that are likely to provide the greatest value. Because classes are time consuming and expensive, projects must have an acceptable return if the company's investment is to be recouped.

Each project is officially sponsored by a senior manager, who provides oversight and support. Sponsors must have the authority to act on the recommendations of CAP teams, as well as overcome the political barriers that so often derail change projects. As Kerr observed, these roles are crucial to success:

> We have had cases where the project was important, the team was bright, and the content of the program was good, but all we did was frustrate participants because they didn't have the high level entrée and air cover that were needed to make the project work.

Sponsors serve several other important functions as well. They select program participants, set goals and expectations, receive and review progress reports, and hold groups accountable for meeting milestones and results.

Because success normally requires a concerted, collective effort, CAP training is offered only to teams. Otherwise, critical mass is lacking, and little is accomplished. According to Kerr:

> The golden rule of organizational development is, "Never send a changed person back to an unchanged environment." Yet 99% of training breaks that rule. People go off to Harvard or Stanford or Michigan or Crotonville in ones and twos, and they're not united in any way. Even if they get excited, they come back to a full desk and a boss who doesn't understand their passion. Most of the time, no learning occurs, since we define learning as a change in behavior. But when people come in teams with a "need-to-do" project, it's much more successful.

Typically, teams consist of eight to twelve people, who represent a diagonal slice of the organization. But there is considerable flexibility, depending on the project and the sponsor's preferences. Peer teams, for example, are used when necessary, as they were on a project that assembled a large number of the company's environmental health and safety officers to tackle a common policy challenge. In all cases, selection is guided by the same two criteria: team members must have credibility within their organizations and must represent a variety of critical stakeholders. Both are considered essential because they increase the odds of effective implementation. Membership is also carefully tailored to the problem at hand. Successful CAP teams have included, when necessary, union members and factory workers as well as vice presidents. At GE Plastics Japan, where unquestioning acceptance of the status quo had produced a string of financial losses, participants were selected in large part for their independence and willingness to consider radically new directions.

All teams have their own coaches. Most have been through special training or have been involved in earlier projects as participants. Coaches are educators and facilitators, process experts who are knowledgeable about change and skilled in applying CAP concepts and tools. Their primary responsibility is to maintain the order and discipline of the change process. Because teams work under intense pressure, coaches also arbitrate disagreements and ensure that destructive conflict is avoided. Surprisingly, most have limited knowledge of the problem at hand. Teams are assumed to possess all necessary content knowledge; they own the problem and remain responsible for devising solutions.

Initially, all coaches were provided by Crotonville; today, they come from the divisions. There are now dozens in every GE business, working with teams before, during, and after CAP classes. Coaches are constantly present—at the home site, as teams frame their projects; at Crotonville, as teams learn and then apply unfamiliar concepts; and again at the home site, as teams carry their work to completion. They provide seamlessness and continuity, linking the various stages of the learning process. The best coaches are also objective and open-minded; they are able to serve as disinterested guides rather than impassioned advocates. According to Vierling:

> If the coach feels that he or she has the answer or wants to drive the team in a certain direction, they will not be successful. You need someone who doesn't have a vested interest in the project. In fact, we've had coaches say: "Take me off this team because I know what I want. I can't be objective. I can't pull the best ideas out of the team because I have my own ideas."

All CAP courses are organized around a common framework and set of tools. The framework is straightforward and easy to apply. It divides the change process into seven steps: leading change, creating a shared need, shaping a vision, mobilizing commitment, making change last, monitoring progress, and changing systems and structures (see Table 4-3). As Kerr observed, this framework has several appealing features. It is simple, "not rocket science but a parsimonious list that people can get their arms around." It is concrete, not "esoteric and metaphysical but puzzles and structural questions that people can deal with." It is credible, "probably 90% common sense." And it is complete, a comprehensive series of steps that managers use as a "pilot's checklist."

The pilot's checklist analogy came originally from Welch; it is now used in all CAP sessions. Checklists are employed by even the most

---

TABLE 4-3
THE CHANGE ACCELERATION PROCESS (CAP)

---

1. Leading Change
   Having a leader who owns and champions the change and commits his or her personal time and attention

2. Creating a Shared Need
   Ensuring that employees throughout the organization understand the reason for change

3. Shaping a Vision
   Ensuring that employees see the desired outcome of change in concrete behavioral terms

4. Mobilizing Commitment
   Understanding the interests of diverse stakeholders, identifying key constituents, and building a coalition of supporters

5. Making Change Last
   Taking the initial steps to get change started and developing longer-term plans to ensure that change persists

6. Monitoring Progress
   Creating and installing metrics to assess the success of change, including milestones and benchmarks to chart progress along the way

7. Changing Systems and Structures
   Altering staffing, training, appraisal, communication, and reward systems, as well as roles and reporting relationships, to ensure that they complement and reinforce change

---

experienced pilots. Yet they offer no new insights. Instead, they make existing knowledge more visible and accessible, ensuring that all essential steps are followed. Discipline, not discovery, is the goal of the checklist—just as with CAP, which teaches a familiar and widely recognized change process. According to Kerr: "It's basic stuff, but people don't do it every time. With CAP, they do it every time." Still, there are subtleties and refinements. For example, the process is not as linear as it first appears:

> When we say these steps happen in sequence, there's a tendency
> for managers to respond, "Okay, I did number one. Let's go on to

number two." They're great at starting stuff, but don't stay with it. They have the organizational equivalent of attention deficit disorder.

So to teach CAP, we use the metaphor of the circus act with the spinning plates. You start the first one. Then you start the second, then the third. By now, the first plate is wobbly, so you go back and spin it some more. In other words, you don't stop Shaping a Vision or Mobilizing Commitment to start Making Change Last. You have to keep them all going at once.

To help participants apply the framework, CAP includes a comprehensive set of tools and techniques. There are thirty-nine in all, although few teams use more than half a dozen. Most are staples of the change literature and have been culled from long-forgotten sources; a number are GE innovations. They are spread across the seven steps in the process and come in two varieties: tools for diagnosing an organization's readiness for change and tools for managing change more effectively.

Representative tools include the Calendar Test, the Elevator Speech, and Stakeholder Analysis. The Calendar Test, which is associated with the first step in the change process, Leading Change, is a simple audit of time spent. It teaches two powerful lessons: that leaders must invest time in their projects if they hope to succeed and that managers' stated priorities seldom match their actual commitments. Participants identify four to five important work or personal objectives and then review their calendars for the preceding thirty to sixty days to determine the percentage of time they actually devoted to these activities. The discrepancies are invariably stark—as one observer put it, "people are just weeping in the aisles because of the disconnect"—and team members then discuss how to ensure more efficient allocations as they move forward. To avoid slippage, many coaches repeat the test at regular intervals as the change process unfolds.

The Elevator Speech is associated with the third step in the process, Shaping a Vision. It is a response to an important dilemma facing all teams—how to communicate the essence of the desired change to colleagues back home but in a limited amount of time. Consider a typical scenario. A CAP team member has returned from training and has a

FIGURE 4-2

STAKEHOLDER ANALYSIS

Names	−2 Strongly Against	−1 Moderately Against	0 Neutral	+1 Moderately Supportive	+2 Strongly Supportive
Tony			X ──────→		O
Sally		X ──→ O			
Harry				X ──────→	O
Joan	X ──────────────────		──→ O		

X = current position
O = required position

chance meeting with a senior vice president in an empty elevator. As the doors close, she turns and says: "I understand that you've just come back from Crotonville. What happened?" Her office is on the sixth floor, so the elevator ride will last less than ninety seconds. How should the team member respond? Participants work to craft a concise, compelling response during CAP classes; before departing, they rehearse until they have committed it to memory. Most speeches use the same four-part design: "Here's what our project is about . . . ; here's why it's important to do . . . ; here's what success will look like . . . ; and here's what we need from you. . . . " The result is a common, consistent message that is continually replayed by all members of the CAP team.

Stakeholder Analysis is helpful for assessing an organization's political landscape. It is used in the fourth step of the process, Mobilizing Commitment, and positions individuals according to their likely reactions to the proposed change. The resulting diagram (see Figure 4-2) has obvious implications for action. Kerr described the process:

> We start by asking people, "For your change to be successful, who has to be involved?" They put down names. "There's Tony, there's Sally, there's Harry, there's Joan." Then we ask, "Where are they now? From minus two, 'strongly against,' to 'neutral,' which is zero,

to plus two, 'strongly supportive.'" Then we say, "Where do they have to be?" Some people have to be positive. Some just have to be neutral. Then we say, "What are the strategies for getting people to where they have to be? Who interacts with whom? Who do you have who's positive and can affect so-and-so?" And they build action plans to communicate and market their ideas to these people.

Today, the entire CAP course, including the framework and all associated tools, is taught in an intensive, three-day session. Seven to ten teams, drawn from diverse GE businesses, are invited to attend. By the time they arrive at Crotonville, they have already done substantial work, identifying the problem to be solved, meeting with their sponsor and their coach to clarify expectations and develop working relationships, and profiling their business's past change efforts to see where they have been strong or weak. The latter is an especially important step. Teams not only become acquainted with the basic CAP model but often discover that they have systematic biases: they have omitted the same stages in the process in several failed projects. They therefore arrive at Crotonville with considerable motivation to improve. GE Supply, for example, found that a number of past change efforts had failed because headquarters staff had dictated new approaches to the field, rather than mobilizing the commitment of line managers. By the time they came to Crotonville, team members knew exactly where they needed help.

A typical day in the program begins with a two-hour "content burst" that introduces one or two steps in the CAP framework. All teams attend these large sessions. Formats are diverse and include lectures, discussions, sharing of best practices, and "buzz sessions" in which teams tackle a brief exercise and then share their conclusions with others. All sessions are "coproduced." Rather than rigidly following a uniform syllabus, courses vary according to the needs of participants. If, for example, groups feel that they need little help shaping a vision, instructors will move quickly to another, more demanding step in the process.

Teams then disperse to separate breakout rooms, where, with the assistance of coaches, they spend the rest of the day working on their projects. New concepts and tools are applied immediately; they do not remain as abstract concepts but are quickly married to the problem at hand. Content and breakout sessions continue to alternate as the course unfolds, creating a comfortable rhythm. According to one participant: "It was a little bit of learning, a little bit of doing, a little more learning, and a little more doing, until the whole model came out." Eventually, each team develops an action plan to guide its activities back home. As Vierling observed, this is a crucial step, for it provides continuity and momentum:

> To ensure that the project doesn't stop when they leave Crotonville, we ask teams to identify a set of action steps that they are going to follow, with names and dates. Some projects will take one or two years, and it's important to drive home the fact that they have to keep moving forward. At every meeting they need to ask: When do we get together next? What do we have to do before we meet? Who is responsible, and what are the key deliverables and dates? We want them to start developing these habits while they're at Crotonville.

Plans are often extraordinarily detailed. GE Supply, for example, identified nearly one hundred separate actions that had to be taken by team members in the eight weeks following training. The result, one participant recalled, was "a seamless and logical transition from the workshop to the workplace." The project continued with hardly a pause, and needed changes were introduced within a few months.

CAP is obviously thoughtfully and carefully designed. It represents the very best of experiential learning, a blend of practical problems, motivated participants, and easy-to-apply concepts and tools (see Table 4-4). But does it impact the bottom line? The answer, in most cases, is a resounding yes. At GE Supply, the payoff was $16 million in additional sales, due, in large part, to a rise in "promises kept" from 65 to 95 percent. At GE Plastics Japan, the turnaround was even more dramatic. From 1989 to 1993, there were was nothing but red ink; in 1993 alone, the loss was $26 million. Managers signed up for CAP training as a last resort, after a new president announced that the alternative was shutting the business down. Classes were held in 1994; by the end of the year,

TABLE 4-4
EXPERIENTIAL LEARNING: LESSONS FROM CAP

1. Link learning to practical problems.

- Have business unit presidents or functional leaders select problems.
- Focus on problems that are strategically important and highly visible.
- Find problems that cannot be solved by current methods.
- Insist on projects that cannot be completed during training sessions and require further work at the home site.

2. Secure high-level sponsorship.

- Only accept sponsors with the power to act on recommendations.
- Require sponsors to select participants and provide ongoing oversight and support.

3. Send participants in teams.

- Select teams (natural, peer, or diagonal-slice) that best fit the problem at hand.
- Choose eight to twelve members for their knowledge, skills, credibility, and representativeness.
- Teach multiple teams simultaneously.

4. Assign coaches.

- Select coaches based on their process knowledge and facilitation skills and train them in advance.
- Choose coaches who are open-minded and do not have a point of view about the problem at hand.
- Assign coaches before training begins so that they can work with teams in advance of classes to scope out the problem and identify organizational challenges.
- Have coaches attend classes, facilitate discussions, and then return to their home sites to continue working with teams.

5. Alternate classroom work with applications.

- Schedule regular breakout sessions so that teams can apply lessons "just in time."
- Teach simple, generic approaches that can be tailored to individual problems.
- Support concepts and frameworks with easy-to-apply tools and techniques.
- Require fully developed action plans before teams leave training classes.

the business was breaking even. In 1995 net income was $18 million, and the company was on solid footing for the first time.

Programs like CAP represent the most active form of learning from experience. At times, these lessons arrive unconsciously as unintended by-products of repetitive activities. Learning and experience curves capture this effect. On other occasions, conscious reflection is involved, but only after the fact. Then, special forums or processes like AARs are needed to tease out important lessons. Experiential programs go a step further by actively coupling opportunities to learn with current, unfolding events. But in all three cases, learning deepens with increased familiarity, and skills improve with time. The old proverb is right after all. Practice does indeed make perfect.

5

Experimentation

Most approaches to learning accept the world as given. They begin with data that already exist—in the field, in the minds of customers, in accumulated experience—and then draw inferences and conclusions. The resulting lessons are often invaluable, as the previous two chapters have shown. But they are limited in an important respect. Because critical variables are taken at face value, with their ranges defined by natural variation, managers seldom consider the full array of alternatives or possible explanations. This is rarely a problem when challenges are conventional or a large knowledge base exists. But when unfamiliar concepts or unproven theories are involved, the desired data may first have to be produced. For real innovation to occur, active approaches to learning are essential. As Charles Kettering, the inventor of the copper-cooled engine, put it: "I have never heard of anyone stumbling on something sitting down."[1]

Usually, this requires some form of experimentation. The word has several meanings:

the action of trying anything, or putting it to proof . . . a tentative procedure; a method, system of things, or course of action, adopted in uncertainty . . . an action or operation undertaken to discover something unknown.[2]

All of these definitions argue for a "try-it-and-see" approach. First, conditions are modified or changes are introduced; then, the results are observed and new conclusions are drawn. Often, multiple trials are required to ensure success.

Scientists and engineers have long used this process to aid their work. But it is far less common among managers. Experimentation is surprisingly rare in most corporate settings—the obvious exceptions are in R&D labs and marketing research departments—largely because they require a change in mind-set and philosophy. For experiments to be effective, the focus must shift from justification and commitment (where the primary goal is making the case for one's preferred position) to skepticism and doubt (where the goal is keeping an open mind when faced with competing views).[3] Managers must regard knowledge as provisional, and conclusions as tentative. Otherwise, they will not subject prevailing views to testing, and experiments will exist in name only.

Managers, in fact, routinely misuse the term, applying it in a blanket fashion to any changes they have recently introduced.[4] But not all changes are experiments. Only those activities carefully and consciously designed to generate knowledge—normally through systematic trials and comparisons—qualify. For example, eliminating a layer of the organization for effi- ciency reasons is not an experiment. But testing new reporting relationships for possible rollout to other sites usually is. Experiments, it should be clear, are as much matters of intent as matters of proper design.

Inevitably, this approach involves a certain element of risk, since conditions are changed with no assurance of a positive outcome. Failure is always a possibility. Why, then, should managers experiment? Because in certain circumstances, other approaches to learning offer little help. They are simply incapable of generating the necessary data. When situations are novel, when experts disagree, or when multiple, difficult-to-disentangle alternatives exist, experimentation is often the only option.[5] Experience provides little guidance when "the state of knowledge is not well understood and must be continuously discovered."[6] Intelligence gathering normally produces ambiguous results when recognized experts disagree. And neither experience nor intelligence-gathering provides enough discriminating power when plausible alternatives coexist. In such settings, carefully constructed experiments are often the only way of distinguishing truth from fiction.

Unfortunately, it is easy to confuse experimentation with its close cousin observation. The latter is a largely passive act; it requires attentiveness and care but little change in the environment being studied. Astronomers and naturalists are the classic observers; they watch and wait as nature runs its course. Experimentation is a more intrusive activity; it involves the deliberate manipulation of conditions, often in a controlled environment. Chemists and physicists are devoted experimenters precisely because they can disentangle critical relationships only by subtly altering the status quo.

These same distinctions apply to business. Here, too, the "observer stands outside the course of events . . . and waits for nature to induce . . . changes . . . [while the] experimenter actively intervenes."[7] Both approaches are effective ways of gathering information but yield different insights. To learn more about customers, a department store manager might rely on observation, visiting competing stores in the hopes of picking up useful tips. Much would be learned about appealing floor layouts and customers' buying habits but little about unconventional displays or pricing practices not already in use. Alternatively, the manager might run a series of experiments, establishing pilot sites to explore novel selling approaches. Unfamiliar techniques could be tried and tweaked in real time. Banc One used this approach when it first developed Personal Investment Centers to package and cross-sell diverse financial services, while British Petroleum did the same with the first integrated food-and-fuel convenience sites it developed with Safeway.[8] In each case, a small number of pilot sites were created to test the original concept. Managers made changes as needed and collected additional data until the concept was deemed acceptable. Only then did full-scale rollout begin.

TYPES OF EXPERIMENTS

Experiments, of course, come in many varieties.[9] Two are of primary interest to managers: exploratory experiments and hypothesis-testing experiments. The former are designed for discovery, "to see what would happen if." Scientists use them to create a clearer map of an unknown territory, usually through determined but open-ended search. Researchers try a new technique or a new approach, then review results, and repeat the process with subtle variations. Sometimes, these steps are driven by preconceived ideas, but more often there is a large element of serendipity.

Such activity is hardly confined to scientists. Exploration is woven into the fabric of everyday life. It "is much of what an infant does when he explores the world around him, what an artist does when he juxtaposes colors to see what effect they make, and what a newcomer does when he wanders around a strange neighborhood."[10] The goal is to see what is out there, to collect impressions and develop a detailed picture of the surrounding world. These practices obviously extend to management. Most business examples involve a carefully constructed demonstration or test: an innovative product, process, or organization that stretches the boundaries of current practice and probes for reactions. GM created Saturn, a new division, to explore the benefits and risks of more cooperative labor relations, while Warner Cable and American Express established QUBE, a decade-long experiment in Columbus, Ohio, to explore customers' reactions to interactive television. Banc One and British Petroleum developed their pilot sites for similar reasons.

Hypothesis-testing experiments have different goals. They are designed to discriminate among alternative explanations and confirm (or discount) prevailing views. Here, proof is the desired end, not discovery. Two or more competing interpretations coexist; which one better fits the facts? Customers, for example, have stopped purchasing a popular product; is it because prices are too high, a competitor's offerings are superior, or a new advertising campaign is ineffective? A mixing process suddenly experiences a surge in defects; is it because of a bad batch of raw materials, inexperienced operators, or improper machine settings? Observation and exploration seldom provide complete answers; they normally produce descriptions and summary statistics that are consistent with diverse explanations.[11] Instead, a process of systematic elimination is usually required. Researchers alter one or more factors, while holding others constant; they record the results and rule out some explanations. The process is then repeated until only one possibility remains.[12]

Such efforts are designed to produce deep understanding, not superficial knowledge. At its simplest, the distinction is between knowing how things are done and knowing why they occur.[13] Knowing how is partial knowledge; it is rooted in norms of behavior, standards of practice, and settings of equipment. Knowing why is more fundamental; it captures underlying cause-and-effect relationships and accommodates exceptions, adaptations, and unforeseen events. The ability to control temperatures and pressures to align grains of silicon and form silicon steel is an example of knowing how; understanding the chemical and physical process that produces the alignment is knowing why.

Further refinements are possible. Scholars, in fact, have suggested that production and operating knowledge can be classified systematically into eight levels or stages of understanding (see Table 5-1).[14] At the lowest levels of knowledge, little is known other than the characteristics of a good product. Production remains an art, and there are few clearly articulated standards or rules. An example would be the construction of Stradivarius violins. Experts agree that they produce vastly superior sound, but no one can specify precisely how they were made because skilled artisans were involved. At intermediate levels of knowledge, understanding deepens, resulting in tighter specification and control. Recipes are developed, and well-defined processes ensure repeatable performance. An example would be a set of instructions for extruding plastic that includes both a complete list of raw materials and detailed machine settings. Finally, at the highest levels of manufacturing knowledge, all aspects of production are known and understood. All materials and processing variations are articulated and accounted for, with rules and procedures for every contingency. Here, an example would be a "lights out," fully automated factory that operates for many hours without any human intervention.

In this context, hypothesis-testing experiments foster learning by moving organizations up the hierarchy from lower to higher stages of knowledge. They lead to a more refined understanding of causal relationships, a more expansive list of critical variables, and a better appreciation of potential difficulties. Their cumulative impact can be enormous. In a few years, with limited capital investment but careful and systematic hypothesis testing, semiconductor companies are usually able to double their yields on new chip fabrication lines from below 40 percent to above 80 percent.[15]

TABLE 5-1

STAGES OF KNOWLEDGE

---

1. Recognizing prototypes (ability to determine what is a good product or service).

2. Recognizing attributes within prototypes (ability to define some conditions under which the process gives good output).

3. Discriminating among attributes (ability to distinguish those attributes that are important from those that are not).

4. Measuring attributes (ability to measure some key attributes using qualitative, quantitative, or relative metrics).

5. Controlling attributes locally (ability to achieve repeatable performance).

6. Recognizing and discriminating among contingencies (ability to mechanize process and monitor it manually).

7. Controlling contingencies (ability to automate the process).

8. Understanding procedures and controlling contingencies (ability to understand completely all aspects of the process).

Source: Adapted with permission from Ramchandran Jaikumar and Roger Bohn, "The Development of Intelligent Systems for Industrial Use: A Conceptual Framework," in Richard S. Rosenbloom, ed., Research on Technological Innovation, Management, and Policy, vol. 3 (Greenwich, CT: JAI Press, 1986), pp. 182–188.

EXPLORATION

Exploration has long been associated with the frontier. It conveys a sense of promise and opportunity that, even today, retains a powerful hold on our collective imaginations.[16] The frontier marks the boundary between the civilized world and the wilderness that lies beyond it: a vast, largely unpopulated region filled with unknowns. Originally, this meant large expanses of open, unsettled land; today, it applies equally well to untapped markets, untested technologies, and untried forms of organization. In all of these settings, exploration is essential to success. Scouting and reconnaissance are critical activities because so little is known about the territory ahead. The landscape is largely uncharted, with few signposts or maps. The inhabitants are unlikely to be familiar, and much that is encountered will be new. Agendas will be difficult to frame because few, clear-cut categories exist. As historians have observed, these challenges have long plagued pioneers: "[They] were faced with a succession of unique problems where past precedents did not apply; only by devising new techniques and gadgets were they able to exploit the riches about them fully. So they were quick to experiment and scornful of traditional practice."[17]

In formal terms, frontier environments are characterized by ambiguity and great uncertainty, with problems that are poorly structured.[18] Most essential information is lacking. Potential solutions are therefore difficult to identify, and the relationship between means and ends is unclear. An airline wants to shift to electronic ticketing; how should it design the supporting processes? A retailer wants to offer its products over the Internet; how should it market the site? A manufacturer wants to introduce state-of-the-art machine tools; how should it configure the factory? These are all challenges that lack clear answers or even easy-to-define options. According to scholars: "This is not the decision making under *uncertainty* of the textbook, where alternatives are given even if their consequences are not, but decision making under *ambiguity,* where almost nothing is given or easily determined."[19]

When ambiguity is high, the usual sources of knowledge provide limited insight. Market research, in particular, is often incomplete and misleading because consumers lack a firm basis for describing their preferences or predicting future behavior. This is especially true for radical, discontinuous innovations: products, such as cellular telephones, xerography, and optical fibers, that break completely with established offerings and create wholly new markets. The usual tools of marketing research assume that "the target market is known, the product form is fairly well known, and the timing is understood." A recent study of discontinuous innovations found that none of these assumptions was met.[20] The result, not surprisingly, was a series of misinterpretations, misjudgments, and misunderstandings.

In the mid-1970s, for example, cellular telephones were in the early stages of development. It would be nearly ten years before the first fully licensed commercial systems were sold. To explore this market, Motorola sent a mail survey to several hundred thousand potential users. It then combined the survey results with evidence from focus groups and census data, applied sophisticated methods of conjoint analysis, and ranked the leading market segments. The thirty-first most important group was salespeople. Yet they soon proved to be devoted users, who led the adoption process and purchased the product in large numbers. Corning was similarly misled in the late 1960s when it interviewed current customers about the potential of optical fibers. Both AT&T and ITT, the dominant players in the market, firmly rejected the idea, arguing that it was unnecessary and at least 30 to 40 years ahead of its time.[21]

The experiences of Motorola and Corning are hardly unique. Radically new products and technologies frequently befuddle experts, who fail to see their true potential. The combination of their own focused experiences and conventional sources of information lead to serious errors. These problems have recurred throughout history and have involved some of the best minds of the time, as the following examples suggest:

- "Drill for oil? You mean drill into the ground to try and find oil? You're crazy." Drillers when asked by Edwin L. Drake to enlist in his project to drill for oil, 1859.

- "The telephone has too many shortcomings to be seriously considered as a means of communication. The device is inherently of no value to us." Western Union, internal memo, 1876.

- "The phonograph . . . is not of any commercial value." Thomas Alva Edison, inventor of the phonograph, 1880.

- "Who the hell wants to hear actors talk?" H. M. Warner, Warner Brothers, 1927.

- "I think there is a world market for about five computers." Thomas J. Watson, chairman of IBM, 1943.

- "There is no reason anyone would want a computer in their home." Kenneth Olson, president, chairman, and founder of Digital Equipment Corporation, 1977.[22]

Given this sorry record, how should managers respond when faced with unfamiliar innovations? How can they collect the information they need for sound decision making, while avoiding the errors of their predecessors? The answer is exploration, or what scholars have termed the "probe-and-learn" process. When faced with novel technologies or markets, it is often the only reliable source of knowledge. Both Motorola and Corning used this approach to overcome the limitations of their early market research. GE did the same with CAT scanners, as did Searle with NutraSweet. In each case, "these companies developed their products by probing potential markets with early versions of the products, learning from the probes, and probing again. . . . Probing and learning is an iterative process . . . a process of successive approximation . . . each time striving to take a step closer to a winning combination.[23]

Often, early versions of the product were considerably off base. In fact, "in all four cases, the initial experience was mostly if not entirely negative."[24] Motorola's first cellular telephones were far too heavy and bulky, while GE's first CAT scanners had poor resolution and slow scanning times. None of the early versions fully met the needs of established customers or had the features necessary to appeal to untapped markets. But they were still invaluable because they provided feedback under real-world conditions. Each succeeding iteration was a step in the right direction, ensuring that the next version was that much more likely to hit the mark.

The Probe-and-Learn Process

This approach to exploration has four critical elements: a starting point, one or more feedback loops, a process for rapid redesign, and a stopping rule. The starting point must be "good enough." It need not be perfect but must generate enough interest among potential users to induce them to try the product or service and provide reactions. Once the first trial is underway, feedback loops are needed to collect information and funnel it to those who are capable of putting it to good use. A rapid redesign process is then required to ensure that useful feedback is immediately incorporated into the next iteration of the product or service. Finally, a stopping rule is needed to avoid endless fine-tuning and the fruitless pursuit of dead ends. Eventually, a decision has to be made. Either the innovation is ready for launch—despite any lingering imperfections—or managers must pull the plug because the project lacks promise.

The probe-and-learn process is not limited to product and service design. It is equally useful for exploring other uncharted domains. In fact, much entrepreneurial activity proceeds in this fashion, with new ventures being used to establish a toehold in unfamiliar domains. Once established, these ventures present managers, in the language of finance, with "real options" for proceeding further, which would not otherwise be available.[25] New markets, new technologies, new operating systems, and new organizational forms can all be pursued using this approach. Consider the following examples:

- Serengeti Eyewear, a maker of high-end sunglasses, has used "test launches" to explore the potential of new markets. Before entering Europe on a large scale, the company chose to sell for the first year in Finland only, a country somewhat outside the European mainstream but regarded as representative enough to provide cultural and institutional learnings. A relatively small number of retail outlets were involved in the hopes that competitors would fail to take notice. After a successful test launch, distribution was broadened to include other parts of the Continent.[26]

- Boeing used a similar process to evaluate the potential of composites, a new technology, for airframe manufacturing. Composites are formed by combining two or more complementary materials. They have the advantage of offering both great strength and light weight. But in the 1960s and 1970s their performance was still unproven. To begin, Boeing's engineers conducted a number of laboratory tests using large, composite panels; eventually, they found a promising material, a mixture of graphite and Kevlar. To explore its properties in the "real-world airline environment," the engineers then worked with a small number of airlines to conduct limited, in-service tests. Boeing fabricated structural parts, such as wing control surfaces or spoiler panels, using composites; had them installed on a plane then in production; and monitored the material's performance as the plane underwent normal use. These tests soon indicated a problem with water absorption in environments of high heat and humidity, such as Brazil. Further analysis suggested that adding a layer of fiberglass to the composite panels would solve the problem; engineers made the changes and continued monitoring to ensure that problems did not recur. When they did not, the decision was made to use composites to construct a variety of parts for the 767.[27]

- In 1986 Motorola formed Team Bandit to design and develop a highly automated assembly line. By employing robots, fault-tolerant computers, and a sophisticated material control system, the line was expected to produce customized versions of the new Bravo pager, in lot sizes of one, with exceptionally short cycle times and few if any defects. The project schedule was built around four prototype cycles; in each case, prototypes were to be assembled on the line, even if the computer system was not up and running. In the initial two cycles, the full line was not yet ready, so assembly was completed by hand. But the goal remained constant: to explore the fit between product and process and resolve difficulties as they emerged. The entire project took 18 months, and the automated line was introduced with minimal problems. Its performance quickly exceeded expectations, achieving the highest quality record in Motorola's history.[28]

- IDEO, a leading product design firm, has long had a culture that encourages experimentation. Brainstorming is widespread, and physical prototypes are constantly generated, distributed, reviewed, and revised. David Kelley, the CEO, recently extended this approach to structural change. In 1995 and 1996, he introduced a number of organizational innovations, including work teams and a smaller "company within the company." Kelley urged employees to view these arrangements the same way that they treated physical prototypes: as "temporary and reversible experiments" that could be refined and altered as needed.[29]

These examples suggest that the probe-and-learn process can be used to generate knowledge in a variety of settings. Its advantages should be obvious: immediacy, relevance, and the involvement of users under real-world conditions. The process also appears to be simple and straightforward. But it is easily misused. In particular, probe-and-learn techniques are poorly suited to settings that require continuous, error-free operation. It is difficult, for example, to imagine them being used to redesign air traffic control procedures or streamline the manufacturing process for pharmaceuticals.

It is equally important to recognize that probe and learn is not the same as unguided trial and error. The former requires careful planning and distinctive habits of mind; the latter is largely an ad hoc affair, with enormous inefficiency and findings that are often difficult to interpret. Perhaps the primary design skill in effective probe-and-learn processes is the ability to create prototypes that are simultaneously inexpensive and representative. A delicate balancing act is required. On the one hand, prototypes must be easy to modify, since repeated iterations are inevitable. This suggests the use of "quick-and-dirty" mock-ups, streamlined processes, inexpensive methods of construction, and low-cost materials such as cardboard and clay. On the other hand, prototypes must meet the test of fidelity. They must be close enough approximations of the final version of the product or process—matching it in form, fit, function, and features—that they provide insights into real-world performance and use.[30] Otherwise, experiments will be of little value, for generalizations will be impossible. Here, the pressures are in the opposite direction, suggesting the need for more inclusive designs, sophisticated processes, careful construction, and enduring materials such as metal and glass.

How can this dilemma be resolved? One approach is to rely on "incomplete" models that lack essential features but still capture enough of reality to provide useful data. Aircraft manufacturers have long used this approach in wind tunnel tests. Their prototypes have no interior design details (seats, aisles, or cockpit configurations) but are still valuable because those details are largely irrelevant when assessing aerodynamic properties such as wind resistance.[31] A second approach is to use computer simulation, creating digital prototypes that mimic the properties and performance of a proposed product or process. Automobile manufacturers have used this technique to explore the crashworthiness of new designs. Compared to physical models, digital prototypes offer equal fidelity at much lower cost. A typical computer "crash" costs less than $5,000; when the same crash involves a physical prototype, the cost is more than $300,000.[32] Computer simulations can also be easily and endlessly repeated, with minor modifications, allowing a wider range of options to be explored.

A third approach is to rely on intensive interactions with users to compensate for overly simple prototypes. This technique, which goes by the name of "participatory" or "cooperative" design, has deep roots in Scandinavia, where it was used successfully in the early 1980s to help Swedish trade unions shift from manual to computerized typesetting.[33] Because budgets were limited, real computers could not be purchased, and inexpensive prototypes were used to design the new process. Initially, typesetters interacted with Styrofoam and plywood mock-ups to map out the steps in page makeup. Later, they used slide projectors to project images that mimicked the way that text and pictures might appear on computer screens and then manipulated them to explore alternative compositions and formats.

Probe-and-learn processes must also be designed with repetition in mind. Managers must recognize that in ambiguous environments it is seldom possible—or even desirable—to "get it right the first time."[34] It is usually far too expensive and time-consuming to produce a perfect prototype. Instead, experiments should be conducted early and often. They should be as comprehensive and complete as possible, given the facts at hand. They should focus on interactions at the systems level, not purely local impacts. And they should lead to a gradual convergence over time as designers eliminate extraneous features, enhance critical functions, and define goals with greater clarity and precision. These improvements will be made only if prototypes are viewed as learning opportunities, rather than as simple go/no go decisions. According to a recent study of product development:

> The most successful teams . . . frequently and regularly built a variety of prototypes; started creating prototypes of the entire system very early in the development process; and made each successive model more closely approach the desired final product in terms of form, content, and the customer experience it provoked . . . The most successful teams also built multiple copies of each prototype so that everyone involved in the development and eventual production, sale, use, and servicing of the product (including suppliers, prospective customers, and dealers) could rapidly evaluate it and offer feedback. . . .
>
> But the projects that exploited prototypes in this manner were the exception. Indeed, most of the projects studied . . . failed to create enough prototypes. And often the prototypes they did build (1) were not created early enough to solve problems that took more time and resources to solve later; (2) focused on only one of two components and not on the entire system; (3) were not used to test the manufacturing processes that would produce the final product; and (4) were not widely tested in the field, meaning that an opportunity to glean potentially invaluable reactions from customers was missed.[35]

It is also essential to involve diverse observers. Multiple lenses and complementary perspectives help reduce bias and overcome problems of interpretation. Most exploratory experiments involve a limited number of trials and extremely small samples; in such settings, "meaning is not self-evident . . . [and] many different interpretations are both supportable and refutable."[36] Causality is difficult to determine, and some degree of guesswork is normally required. But the interpretative process can be made more robust by including observers with conflicting interests and varied functional backgrounds. Their presence provides a set of checks and balances and counteracts the natural tendency to discount surprises. "Because different individuals and groups experience . . . events differently, they learn different lessons from the same experience . . . reduc[ing] the standard confirmatory bias of experience."[37]

A final design issue concerns data collection. Effective probe-and-learn processes require baseline data. Researchers must first understand prevailing conditions in order to properly evaluate experiments; otherwise, the observed impact is as likely to be a statistical artifact as the result of a planned intervention. All too often, performance improvements that are thought to result from innovative programs or policies actually reflect preestablished trends or natural processes of maturation and growth.[38] Successful exploration therefore demands "skillful application of the measurement package before the change is introduced, so that it will be in place to 'capture'" the impact of the interaction.[39] An innovative service delivery system can be evaluated properly only by comparing customer satisfaction levels before and after the system is introduced, just as the impact of self-managing work teams can be assessed only by drawing on climate surveys that include periods before and after teams were formed. For truly comprehensive evaluations, the data must be even more inclusive. The "ideal measurement package . . . should be longitudinal, usually covering several years"; should include "roughly comparable areas where . . . the change will not be introduced"; "should involve a broad range of economic and behavioral measures"; and should be administered by an objective third-party "not actively involved in the change process."[40]

Probe-and-learn processes, it should be clear, demand careful planning (see Table 5-2). But design alone does not guarantee success. The process also requires distinctive personal qualities and habits of mind.

TABLE 5-2
DESIGNING EFFECTIVE PROBE-AND-LEARN PROCESSES

---

1. Create representative, inexpensive prototypes.

- Design prototypes that are appealing enough to induce users to try the product or service.
- Ensure that designs are accurate enough to ensure valid feedback about users' needs.
- Use materials and configurations that are cheap enough to permit multiple revisions.

2. Collect feedback directly from the market.

- Connect designers with users, suppliers, distributors, and service personnel.
- Keep cycles short so that market information remains current and up to date.
- Add new features and design characteristics as required, then return immediately to the market for further testing.

3. Expect to revise repeatedly.

- Treat early designs as works in progress.
- Don't try to produce the perfect prototype.
- Don't be disappointed by repeated rejections, especially if users are finding some features to be of interest.
- Expect the initial market research to be misleading.
- Stay attuned to unanticipated requirements and emerging needs.

4. Employ a comprehensive measurement package.

- Agree on objective measures before beginning the experiment.
- Collect data over time (before, during, and after) to capture the initial impact of the experiment as well as subsequent changes in designs.
- Use comparative data (on similar products, services, or sites) to isolate experimental effects.

5. Know when to stop.

- Establish guidelines in advance for evaluating success and failure.
- Allow enough time for experiments to produce representative results.

Explorers are seekers and searchers; they must be open to the unexpected and sensitive to their own biases and preconceptions. As Thomas Huxley, the famed British biologist and writer, put it: "My business is to teach my aspirations to conform themselves to fact, not to try to make facts harmonize with my aspirations."[41] Explorers must be equally skilled at teasing out patterns from fragmentary, incomplete data. The primary challenge is homing in on a target that in the early stages is only dimly understood—"to see," in the words of an experienced engineering manager, "what could be from what is." For this reason, and because reactions to early prototypes are seldom definitive, probe-and-learn processes require that practitioners learn to think longitudinally and developmentally, acquiring "a sense of how to cumulate questions, tests or experiments so that they build on one another in sequence."[42]

Surprisingly, scholarly values are equally important to success. Exploration demands discipline as well as inquisitiveness. Sound conclusions require a firm foundation; they cannot be based on speculation and wishful thinking but must rest on clear logic, untainted evidence, and techniques that are above reproach.[43] Otherwise, errors can quickly sneak in. To avoid them, a certain integrity and honesty is required, a bending over backwards to keep conclusions pure. Gordon Forward, the CEO of Chaparral Steel, an innovative minimill renowned for its commitment to exploratory learning, has provided an eloquent summary of the required mind-set:

> [W]hen you're trying to go one step beyond in research, one of the things you learn fast is that you can't fool yourself. . . . You've got to be open in your questioning. You can't play games. And you can't succeed by pretending you know things you really don't. You have to go find them out. You have to try an experiment here, an experiment there, make your mistakes, ask your questions, and learn from it all.[44]

Demonstration Projects

Exploration is especially difficult when large, complex systems are involved. Even when the individual pieces of such systems are well understood, their combined impact is almost impossible to predict. Parts and components are often tightly coupled, forced into confined spaces with multiple, shared connections. Because of the associated complexity, any number of things can go wrong: "unfamiliar or unintended feedback loops; many control parameters with potential interactions; indirect or inferential information sources; and limited understanding."[45] The nuclear power accident at Three Mile Island provides a vivid example of how complex systems can go awry in unexpected ways. Changing environments and diverse operating conditions only exacerbate the problem.

Particularly when human and technological systems are to be linked in novel ways, error-free operation requires an unusual degree of harmony and alignment of the underlying processes.

In these settings, the probe-and-learn process remains vital for effective exploration. But because experimenters must assess a much wider range of interactions than is usually the case with a new product or service, a distinctive approach is required. Prototyping is still necessary, but the focus shifts from marketing and design to operations and use. Now, the critical task is putting the system through its paces: seeing how it works under varied conditions, environments, and behaviors. Success, after all, requires components that work together smoothly, subsystems that are mutually supportive, technologies that are resistant to stress, and operators who are willing and able to follow procedures. All of these conditions must be demonstrated; they cannot be taken for granted or assumed to be true.

The associated experiments are best called demonstration projects. Most involve holistic, large-scale changes, introduced at a single site, that are undertaken with the goal of developing new organizational capabilities. Frequently, they are associated with breakthroughs in technology or fundamentally new operating philosophies. Because these projects represent a sharp break with the past, they are usually designed from scratch, using a "clean slate" approach. General Foods' Topeka plant, one of the first high-commitment work systems in this country, was a pioneering demonstration project initiated to introduce the idea of self-managing teams and high levels of worker autonomy. A more recent example, designed to explore environmentally sound operating methods and new approaches to energy conservation, is Wal-Mart's "green store."[46] The approach has also been used in the public sector. The 1978 Civil Service Reform Act gave the Office of Personnel Management the authority to conduct and supervise demonstration projects that explored innovative approaches to pay and job classification. Experiments were later conducted by groups as diverse as the U.S. Navy and the Department of Commerce, and successful approaches were incorporated in subsequent legislation.[47]

Demonstration projects normally take one of two forms: on-line experiments or large-scale simulations. The former involve fully functioning businesses, with real employees and customers, that present living examples of the system in action; the latter involve prototypical operations or systems, constructed of mock-ups or models, in which participants play out their roles over time so that designers can learn more about how their newly created processes and equipment are likely to work. Both approaches share a number of distinctive characteristics:

- They are usually the first projects to embody principles and approaches that the organization hopes to adopt later on a larger scale. For this reason, they are more transitional efforts than endpoints and involve considerable real-time readjustment and learning. Mid-course corrections are common.

- They implicitly establish policy guidelines and decision rules for later projects. Managers must therefore be sensitive to the precedents they are setting and must send strong signals if they hope to establish new norms.

- They often encounter severe tests of commitment from employees who wish to see whether the rules have, in fact, changed.

- They are normally developed by strong multifunctional teams reporting directly to senior management. (For projects targeting employee involvement or quality of work life, teams should be multilevel as well as multifunctional.)

- They tend to be developed by impassioned advocates who have difficulty communicating their vision to peers. Those peers may also be resentful of the attention that demonstration projects receive. For these reasons, projects tend to have only limited impact on the rest of the organization if they are not accompanied by explicit strategies for transferring learning.

All of these characteristics appeared in an on-line demonstration project launched by Copeland Corporation, a highly successful compressor manufacturer, in the mid-1970s.[48] Matt Diggs, then the new CEO, wanted to transform the company's approach to manufacturing. Previously, Copeland had machined and assembled all products in a single facility in Sidney, Ohio. Costs were high, and quality was marginal. The problem, Diggs felt, was too much complexity.

At the outset, Diggs assigned a small, multifunctional team the task of designing a "focused factory" dedicated to a narrow, newly developed product line. The team reported directly to Diggs and took three years to complete its work. Initially, the project budget was $10 million to $12 million; that figure was repeatedly revised as the team found, through experience and with Diggs' prodding, that it could achieve dramatic improvements. The final investment, a total of $30 million, yielded unanticipated breakthroughs in reliability testing, automatic tool adjustment, and programmable control. All were achieved through exploration and real-time learning.

The team set additional precedents during the plant's start-up and early operations. To dramatize the importance of quality, for example, the quality manager was appointed second-in-command, a significant move upward. The same reporting relationship was used at all subsequent plants. In addition, Diggs urged the newly hired plant manager to ramp up slowly to full production and resist all efforts to proliferate products. These instructions were unusual at Copeland, where the marketing department normally ruled. (They were especially surprising coming from Diggs, who had previously been the vice president of marketing.) Both directives were quickly tested; management held firm, and the implications were felt throughout the organization. Manufacturing's stature improved, and the company as a whole recognized its competitive contribution. One observer commented: "Marketing had always run the company, so they couldn't believe it. The change was visible at the highest levels, and it went down hard."

Once the initial focused factory was running smoothly—it seized 25 percent of the market in two years and held its edge in reliability for over a decade—Copeland built four more focused factories in quick succession. Diggs assigned members of the initial project to each factory's design team to ensure that early learnings were not lost; these people later rotated through operating assignments. Today, focused factories remain the cornerstone of Copeland's manufacturing strategy and a continuing source of its cost and quality advantages.

Perhaps the most important measure of success for projects like Copeland's is diffusion: the extent to which new policies, practices, and procedures spread to other parts of the organization. By this measure, focused factories fared extremely well. They quickly became part of daily operations. But all too often, new approaches run into massive resistance and are never accepted by the rest of the organization—even when they meet their initial targets. That was the fate of many of the early demon-stration projects that involved innovative work systems such as self-managing teams. Their difficulties are instructive, for they suggest several potential problems.

Projects may receive too much favorable publicity, resulting in "star-envy" and resentment by peers. Projects may suffer a loss of credibility over time, regressing in performance after the great enthusiasm and in-tense dedication of early operation. Projects may be viewed as one-time commitments by senior management, making it difficult to find the time, money, and experienced talent necessary to develop second-generation sites. And projects may have been framed with ideological purity rather than practical business needs as the primary motivation, creating hesi-tancy about their likely contribution in the minds of less committed outsiders.[49]

These problems, while common, are not insurmountable. They can be overcome if demonstration projects are designed with diffusion clearly in mind. They are, after all, supposed to be copied by others. If learning is not shared, projects will not have served their intended purpose. Low public profiles, well-defined business objectives, personal incentives that predispose managers toward transfers, aggressive goals and milestones that carry projects beyond start-up, and the active transfer of resources (both dollars and personnel) to second-generation sites are helpful in meeting these larger goals.[50]

Demonstration projects that involve simulations bring different chal-lenges. They are difficult to design because they face so many conflicting demands. Like all models, they must simplify reality without distorting it. They must be easy to construct, yet comprehensive enough to capture the complex links between systems design, human behavior, and opera-tional and financial performance. They must be adaptable and robust, capable of accommodating different styles, approaches, and behaviors. And they must be engaging enough to encourage high levels of operator and user involvement. The best simulations, in short, are flexible, func-tional, and fun. The latter requirement is particularly important, because a spirit of playfulness is often essential for encouraging creativity and imagination. Frequently, the deepest learning occurs when a freewheel-ing, inquisitive approach is coupled with periods of reflection so that participants can periodically step back and draw lessons from their turns at the "game."[51]

TIMKEN'S REDESIGN OF MANUFACTURING: EXPLORING THROUGH STORYBOARDING, CARDBOARD CITY, AND THE TRAINING MODULE

The Timken Company, America's leading manufacturer of tapered roller bearings, presents a dramatic example of exploration.[52] In 1988 Timken embarked on a bold project to revolutionize the production process for manufacturing customized bearings. Historically, its industrial customers had waited eight to ten months for Timken to fill their small, tailor-made orders; the new goal was to reduce the waiting period to weeks or days. To do so, Timken would have to develop leading-edge technology and pioneer radically new approaches to machining, hardening, gauging, and computer integration. Among the requirements were setup times less than ten minutes and equipment that made the first pieces of every production run without errors or defects. These requirements were difficult in themselves, but the problem was compounded by the extraordinarily tight tolerances required of bearings, which at times ran to the ten-thousandths of an inch. As Joe Toot, Jr., the company's president and CEO, observed: "We set out to do something that no one in manufacturing had done before, not simply in the bearing industry, but, to the best of our intelligence, no one in manufacturing." This challenge clearly demanded exploratory learning. According to Mike Arnold, the first plant manager: "There was no one to teach us. There were no classrooms to go to. There were no books to read. There were no manuals or models. So we had to learn as we went exactly what the right and wrong steps were."

Timken chose to tackle the problem in stages, breaking the task into smaller, more manageable parts. Complex, ambiguous problems are often far easier to solve once they have been parceled out, especially if tasks become progressively more concrete as the process unfolds. At Timken, four stages were involved; each was the responsibility of a different team (see Figure 5-1). The teams proceeded in

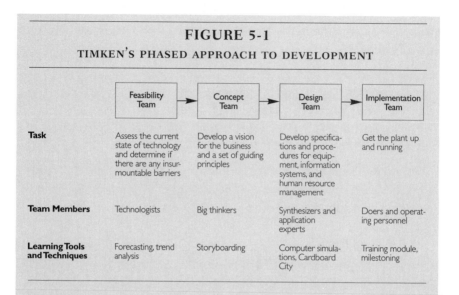

FIGURE 5-1

TIMKEN'S PHASED APPROACH TO DEVELOPMENT

	Feasibility Team	Concept Team	Design Team	Implementation Team
Task	Assess the current state of technology and determine if there are any insurmountable barriers	Develop a vision for the business and a set of guiding principles	Develop specifications and procedures for equipment, information systems, and human resource management	Get the plant up and running
Team Members	Technologists	Big thinkers	Synthesizers and application experts	Doers and operating personnel
Learning Tools and Techniques	Forecasting, trend analysis	Storyboarding	Computer simulations, Cardboard City	Training module, milestoning

sequence, with some overlap in membership and tenure. Each team had a distinct, defined assignment. The Feasibility Team was asked to assess the current state of technology and determine if there were any insurmountable barriers to success. The Concept Team was asked to develop an overarching vision of the business as well as a set of guiding principles. The Design Team was asked to develop precise specifications for equipment, information systems, and human resource management. And the Implementation Team was asked to get the plant up and running; its tasks included training operators, programming equipment, and testing the various components of the system to ensure that they worked together. This four-phased approach, it should be clear, is directly analogous to the use of "successive approximations" in the probe-and-learn process.

The teams used simulations extensively to generate insights. In each case, they proceeded in stages and evolved from high-level abstractions to detailed, concrete representations. The Concept Team, for example, relied heavily on storyboarding to develop a vision of the business. This technique has a long history in filmmaking and television production, where it is used to develop an outline of the core elements of a show or story. It has recently migrated to corporate settings, where it is used as a primitive prototyping process.[53] Key words and phrases are written on large index cards that can be easily reshuffled. They are then arranged in order to map out process flows and sequences of required activities. At Timken, members of the Concept Team began with topic cards describing key portions of the production process; then, underneath them they developed supporting concepts and ideas. According to a participant:

> The storyboard technique allowed us to capture the picture of a particular portion of the business in a very confined space. And then to create another picture, for another portion of the business, on another storyboard. We then put those pieces on the wall together and could begin to visualize the linkages, which to some degree illustrated how the business would operate. We could begin to see whether we had the right priorities for each portion of the business. We could begin to see patterns and sort ideas. And we could take the storyboards away from our little conference room, working independently in small teams of two or three to refine the ideas and then bring them back and post them on the wall again.
>
> It was a very dynamic process. The storyboards enabled us to create a vision of the business we were trying to build in a way that was very flexible. They allowed us to come back from time to time and revisit that vision based on new information we had gathered or learned, or new ideas that had come to the table.

The Design Team made even more extensive use of simulations. They began with computer programs that mimicked the proposed product flow, equipment layout, and plant capacity. They then explored a large number of alternative designs and compared the results. A cellular approach, with machines arranged in a horseshoe fashion, proved to be superior. But it was difficult to pin down the exact layout because the data came with a serious limitation: all of the simulations were two-dimensional. Each layout appeared only within the confines of a flat computer screen. Engineers therefore had little sense of the proper spacing of equipment or the desired timing of adjacent operations. There were a number of unanswered questions: Would the plant's machine operators have enough room to load and unload? Would the aisles be wide enough for impromptu problem-solving sessions? Would operators bump into one another while carrying work-in-progress from station to station? Would employees have the necessary line of sight to communicate should problems arise?

Cost was an issue as well. If the plant was too large, millions of dollars would be wasted on unnecessary space; if machines were poorly positioned, thousands of dollars would be spent on relocation. The grinders presented a special challenge. To ensure precision, they had to be absolutely immobile, set in a foundation of six feet of concrete. As the director of engineering wryly observed: "Once you laid that machine down, it was not a trivial task to move it to a new location."

To resolve these questions, the Design Team created Cardboard City, a three-dimensional model of a manufacturing cell. It was built out of cardboard and two-by-fours and included full-scale mock-ups of each piece of equipment, placed on casters so that they could be moved easily. The location was an empty portion of the R&D building—essentially a warehouse—and the total cost was $2,000. The real innovation, however, was the associated learning process, which included elements of both competition and cooperation. It ensured that Cardboard City produced a wide range of possible layouts and simulated a wide variety of production flows.

Three teams were formed. Each contained ten to fifteen people, largely engineers and designers with a sprinkling of operating personnel. Each team was given approximately one hour to arrange the "equipment" in Cardboard City to its satisfaction. Their challenge was to create the best material flows and best interaction among operators while using the minimum amount of space. There were a few constraints—maximum allowable facility size, operating parameters, and performance targets—but otherwise teams were given free rein to create their own preferred layouts. Operators then simulated a production run for each layout, loading and unloading machines and carrying cardboard versions of partially completed bearings from station to station. The results were recorded on videotape for later review. All teams then met together to debrief, discuss the alternatives, and vote on their preferences. They could draw on any of the approaches, not only their own. At this point, the group came to an important realization: none of the proposed layouts was obviously superior. According to a participant: "We decided that each team had elements that were unique and creative. And we recognized that choosing any one of the three solutions might not be the best approach."

So, after a presentation to senior management, a fourth team was formed; it consisted of volunteers drawn from the three original teams. This group's task was to use the "best of the best" from prior simulations, rearranging Cardboard City a final time. Again, operators were asked to simulate the production process, and the results were videotaped. After another review, this last layout was approved. It resulted in a compact, tightly focused factory and well-positioned machines. According to engineers: "We saved a bundle of money. The building is quite a bit smaller than we thought it was going to be. . . . Today, every machine is right in the spot where the simulations put it. Nothing's been rearranged."

Cardboard City shows simulations at their best. The process was cleverly designed to produce the maximum amount of learning. It was, to use an earlier phrase, flexible, functional, and fun—and cheap, to boot. Inexpensive, movable mock-ups encouraged participants to try out alternative designs. Competing, multifunctional teams ensured diverse perspectives and high levels of interest and involvement. The use of experienced operators to simulate production contributed realism and credibility. Combining voting with an open, reflective debriefing process guaranteed that all voices would be heard, while improving the odds that the best possible solution would emerge. As one engineer summed up the process: "This was a multimillion dollar project. And I think that Cardboard City was the best $2,000 we ever spent."

Timken's simulations did not end with Cardboard City. The Implementation Team went a step further, creating a training module at R&D to test out unproven machinery and equipment. It had two purposes: teaching inexperienced operators how to run the new equipment and fine-tuning the technology and associated systems. By starting in a simulated environment, operators were able to move up the learning curve without facing the usual pressures of daily production. They were, in the language of chapter 2, working in an environment that was "psychologically safe," which encouraged risk taking and experimentation. According to an operator: "Nobody was afraid because this wasn't actual production; it was simulated production. Nobody was actually waiting for the product. So if we messed up, we messed up."

Equally important was the ability to integrate the new equipment and computer systems into a seamless whole—before the factory began full-scale operation. If the process was to operate as planned, all of the pieces had to fit. Again, Timken proceeded in stages, using the training module as its laboratory. An engineer described the approach:

> This was something that we'd never done before. We knew we couldn't just jump in the middle and expect to be going down the road at a hundred miles an hour. So we started out slowly and then progressively upped the ante as we went through each phase.
>
> We used a concept called "milestoning." Each milestone had a specific objective: a product type, a level of systems integration, the number of machines that would be involved, and who would be running the machines. Each step was more difficult than the previous one, and after each milestone we conducted an assessment. Did we make what we set out to make? Did we accomplish what we wanted on the information systems side?

Once again, the learning process was incremental and involved a series of successive approximations. All milestones, in fact, were grouped into three broad categories: "crawl, walk, run." Crawling involved the easiest tasks: the ability to make basic, unadorned products. Here, the goal was to ensure that all elements of the operating system were in place and worked together smoothly. Walking involved an expanded product range: the ability to produce complex shapes and respond to special orders. Here, the goal was to stretch the capabilities of the operating system and ensure that it was both flexible and robust. Running involved optimization and efficiency: the ability to execute orders rapidly and at maximum productivity. Here, the goal was to ensure that operators and equipment were capable of achieving high throughput rates. Each phase, in the words of the first plant manager, involved a large number of exploratory experiments: a series of "test runs" that "took the individual pieces of the project, put them together, and gave us a chance to try and run the business."

On September 30, 1994, Timken opened its 21st Century bearings business plant in Asheboro, North Carolina.[54] It came on line smoothly, with few problems, a highly unusual event for a factory with such state-of-the-art technology. The company's staged, iterative process and heavy investment in simulations paid enormous dividends. The Concept Team's business design and guiding principles remained intact, with little substantive change. The Design Team's placement of machinery and equipment proved to be unerring, with no need for reshuffling. And the Implementation Team's approach to training and development produced knowledge and skills that were easy to apply in the real-world operating environment. Exploration—the process of "going down alleys to see which ones are blind"—ensured that Timken made its way successfully through previously uncharted territory.[55]

HYPOTHESIS TESTING

Hypothesis testing is quite different from exploration. It is deductive rather than inductive, disciplined rather than playful, targeted rather than open-ended. As noted earlier in this chapter, here the goal is proof, not discovery, and the approach is best used when there are competing views or explanations and less intrusive modes of learning are incapable of discriminating among them. Then, the only alternative is often to intervene actively in the environment, altering conditions until underlying cause-and-effect relationships become clear.

Such experiments are the bread-and-butter work of scientists. In any number of fields, they have played a vital role in generating data, validating theories, and ensuring that new ideas were accepted. Practicing scientists, in fact, are almost reverential in their regard for the process. According to a prize-winning researcher: "Ever since Bacon's day experimentation has been thought to be so deeply and so very necessarily a part of science that. . . . activities that are not experimental are often denied the right to be classified as sciences at all."[56] Yet for all its power, the

approach is seldom seen outside the laboratory. There are a number of
reasons why. Managers are not scientists; few have been trained in the
associated methods and techniques, which can be dauntingly complex.
The necessary conditions for success are often rigidly prescribed. Problems must be well structured; otherwise, experiments will be difficult to
design. Understanding must be deep enough to generate diverse views;
otherwise, there will be no basis for comparison. Environments must
permit the manipulation of selected variables; otherwise, their contribution will be impossible to assess. Participants must have at least a nod-
ding acquaintance with the processes of causal inference; otherwise,
conclusions will lack broad application. Clearly, hypothesis testing, in its
purest form, is not the simplest or easiest of tasks.

As if these challenges were not enough, there is an additional road-
block: the necessary mind-set is hard to come by. Hypothesis testing is of
value only if one's preferred position remains open to scrutiny—whatever
the outcome. Truth must be valued over advocacy, and considerable time
must be devoted to testing (and possibly undermining) one's preferred
explanation. The underlying philosophy has been well described by Richard Feynman, a Nobel Laureate in physics:

> It's a kind of scientific integrity, a principle of scientific thought that
> corresponds to a kind of utter honesty—a kind of leaning over back-
> wards. . . . [I]f you're doing an experiment, you should report every-
> thing that you think might make it invalid—not only what you think
> is right about it: other causes that could explain your results; and
> things you thought of that you've eliminated by some other experi-
> ment, and how they worked—to make sure the other fellow can tell
> they have been eliminated. Details that could throw doubt on your
> interpretation must be given, if you know them.[57]

Managers often find these recommendations hard to swallow. They
smack of ideological purity, while taking no account of organizational
politics. For similar reasons, managers are frequently uncomfortable with
the strict requirements that scientists insist are necessary for valid experiments. Two of the most obvious are control groups (comparable units
that do not receive an experimental treatment) and random assignment

(individuals or groups that, on a blind basis, are subjected to differing conditions).[58] Managers seldom employ these techniques when experimenting with new approaches because, in their eyes, they "fail to mesh with the realities of life in organizations."[59] Instead, the argument goes, considerations of equity should rule, with all customers or employees benefiting (or suffering) equally from a new policy or procedure. No one should be excluded simply to ensure a sound experimental design. And no new initiative should be delayed unnecessarily, especially if it promises substantial benefits. There are exceptions, of course—Dayton Hudson, the retail chain, developed REGARDS, a highly successful loyalty program, by first comparing the responses of a selected sample of frequent buyers with those of a carefully matched control group—but they are remarkably rare.[60]

A Way of Thinking

Fortunately, a compromise exists. Many of the benefits of experimentation can be obtained without a full-blown scientific approach. The underlying logic and principles remain the same, but the methods are subtly altered to accommodate the realities of the workplace. Practices and techniques are no longer rigidly prescribed. Instead, the associated reasoning process becomes paramount and is highlighted as the key to success. This approach goes by various names—quasi-experimentation, adaptive experiments, field experiments, the modus operandi method; all, however, are designed to make hypothesis testing less burdensome, while preserving its insights and discriminating power.[61]

Experimentation, after all, is as much a mind-set and philosophy as a set of rigid rules. Whether one is a detective, chemist, anthropologist, engineering troubleshooter, or manager, the goal remains the same: to select one explanation, from many possibilities, by drawing on disciplined data collection. According to this view:

> [E]xperimentation is a process of observation, to be carried out in a situation especially brought about for that purpose. . . . [T]he functions of an experiment . . . are no more—and no less!—than to provide occasions for "controlled observation." . . . What experi-

ments can do is to minimize the errors of observation that are inseparable from casual encounters, or at any rate from unplanned ones.[62]

To minimize these errors, experiments must meet two conditions.[63]
First, they must demonstrate, with a high degree of confidence, that a
change in one variable actually causes a change in another. This is simply
a fancy way of saying that a good experiment firmly establishes the relationship between cause and effect. Findings must hold up to careful
scrutiny; they must not be statistical artifacts or traceable to unknown,
yet-to-be measured causes. Second, results must generalize beyond the
experimental setting. They must apply to a wider set of circumstances,
not only the narrow, idealized environment used for testing. This is simply another way of saying that experiments are of little use if they are true
only for a particular person, place, or time. To be of value, they must have
more universal application.

These concepts can be readily adapted to real-world settings. The
reasoning process remains the same, and the desired features continue to
include controlled observation, careful measurement, logical inference,
and reproducible results. This process is especially useful on the
shop floor, where problems arise continuously and hypothesis testing
is often needed to zero in on the desired corrective action. Consider
these scenarios:

- A company shifts to a new supplier of components. When they are
  first employed in production, they cause a host of difficulties—
  slower machine speeds, defective output, improper fits with other
  parts—even though the exact same specifications and tolerances
  have been used. What is the problem?

- A company finds that a critical machine tool works perfectly well on
  some days, but experiences massive quality problems on others. The
  problems do not have an obvious pattern and cannot be attributed to
  a particular operator, order, or equipment setting. What is the explanation?

- A company purchases the latest robotics technology and attempts to
  shift the assembly of diverse products from less advanced equipment. The results are highly variable. Some transfers work flawlessly,

others require constant changes in settings and speeds, while still others will not work at all. What accounts for the differences?

Each of these challenges can be solved only if variables are manipulated selectively and the results are carefully observed. Experiments are essential. They must be based on systematic planning and forethought, the active pursuit of alternative explanations, and techniques that uncover underlying relationships. But pristine laboratory conditions and textbook experimental designs are seldom needed. Distinctive habits of mind, however, remain crucial. The odds of success improve dramatically when managers follow a few simple guidelines.

Conducting Experiments

These guidelines are not particularly complex (see Table 5-3). But they do require that the associated learning process be designed with care. The goal is to reduce or eliminate the most common errors in hypothesis testing—unfocused data collection, flawed reasoning, indeterminate findings—while improving discrimination and deepening understanding.

To begin, it is important to be clear about the purpose of the experiment. What exactly is the goal? What knowledge is being pursued? Which relationships are unclear? Unlike exploration, hypothesis testing is not an open-ended search (a "vacuum cleaner" approach to collecting data); rather, it is a focused inquiry that addresses tightly framed questions (more of a "directed telescope").[64] For this reason, it is essential to have one or more possible explanations in mind before starting out. These explanations, which scientists call *hypotheses,* guide the experimental process by dictating the information that must be collected. Typically, they take the form of "if . . . then" statements or predicted linkages that will be supported or undermined by the existence of certain evidence. Researchers thus know exactly what data to pursue. There is another, often unanticipated benefit of beginning with a hypothesis in mind. Observation is invariably more intelligent and insightful. Hypotheses offer focal points, evaluative frameworks that "help one see the significance of an object or event that would otherwise mean nothing." Such frameworks serve as guidance systems, leading the eye in certain directions. Surprisingly, benefits often accrue even when the initial explana-

TABLE 5-3

GUIDELINES FOR HYPOTHESIS-TESTING EXPERIMENTS

1. Be clear about the purpose of the experiment.
2. Begin with a hypothesis in mind.
3. Ensure that all needed measures (pretest and posttest) are in place.
4. Reproduce real-world conditions as closely as possible.
5. Manipulate a single variable at a time.
6. Use comparison groups or other natural controls.
7. Involve diverse, complementary observers.
8. Search for distinctive patterns.
9. Employ multiple, repeated trials.

tion is off the mark. Because they offer a way of structuring data, hypotheses can be helpful without being correct—as long as they are viewed as provisional and are not pursued beyond reason.[65]

The best hypotheses share several characteristics. They are clear and unambiguous, describe a relationship or connection among variables, and are capable of being disproved. The last requirement is especially important. If potential cause-and-effect relationships have been framed so generally that there is no way of pinning down their truth or falsity, even the best-designed experiments will fail. Here, precision is a virtue. Attributing defective products to "variability in incoming materials" is virtually useless as a guide for action; linking mixtures with excess acidity to "chemicals that arrive every other month with greater than 15 percent impurities" provides much more direction and focus.

But even with well-framed hypotheses, experiments will be of value only if appropriate measures are also in place. Quantification is part and parcel of effective hypothesis testing, for it provides the glue linking cause and effect. There are three associated requirements: First, there must be unambiguous measures of successful outcomes. Second, there must be refined measures of the variables being manipulated. And third, there must be comprehensive data on the direction that variables were moving before the experiment was initiated. The first requirement is needed for determining whether the desired results have in fact been produced; the second requirement is needed for establishing the precise link between the changes made and the desired ends; and the third requirement is needed for ruling out spurious effects due to preestablished trends or random variation. All too often, reductions (increases) in a variable of interest are falsely ascribed to actions or interventions when the results were already moving in the desired direction. The same outcomes would have occurred if the status quo were left undisturbed. Changes may also be statistical in nature, for extreme events tend to be followed, over time, by values that are closer to average scores.[66] Without historical data, it is impossible to rule out these alternatives.

Experiments must also be carefully designed. There are five critical elements: the choice of environment or setting, the process of manipulating variables, the inclusion of comparisons or controls, the selection of participants, and the confirmation of results. To begin, real-world conditions should be approximated as closely as possible; otherwise, findings are unlikely to be useful or representative. This means that if laboratory work is required, it should be combined with on-line experimentation to ensure that results remain equally true on the shop floor. To isolate presumed cause-and-effect relationships, only one or two variables should be manipulated at a time; otherwise, it is difficult to rule out alternative explanations.[67] Selectivity and forethought are essential. Before proceeding, experimenters should have some idea of the most likely patterns at work. They can then manipulate variables and search for expected patterns; if they do not appear, they can move quickly to another possible explanation. This is the process used by all good detectives, and it applies equally well to business.[68]

Several steps should be taken to avoid interpretative errors. Controls are essential; otherwise, it is easy to delude oneself about the true impact of an intervention or policy change. This does not mean that formal control groups are required. But it does suggest that experimenters should search actively for reference groups or points of comparison—departments with similar problems, factories with similar technologies, customers with similar needs—to contrast their behavior with that observed in the experimental setting. Often, the data is there for the taking. Few large, multinational corporations, for example, introduce new policies or programs at all sites around the world at exactly the same time. There are invariably leaders and laggards. Sites that are "late adopters" provide invaluable reference points, serving as implicit controls for evaluating the impact of a policy change.

To further reduce bias, multiple observers should be asked to review results. Whenever possible, they should represent different departments and competing points of view. Diversity provides checks and balances, creates divergent perspectives, and ensures that no single interpretation dominates. For example, shop-floor experiments should generally be reviewed by individuals from R&D, engineering, operations, and quality control. Each is likely to interpret the data in slightly different ways. Then, to validate the team's conclusions, multiple trials should be conducted. They ensure that critical findings hold up under diverse conditions—different operators, times of day, order sizes, and production sequences—and are not one-time events.

ALLEGHENY LUDLUM STEEL'S SYSTEM FOR EXPERIMENTATION: HYPOTHESIS TESTING ON THE 91 LINE

All of the factors that lend to effective hypothesis testing can be seen at work at Allegheny Ludlum Steel, an extremely successful manufacturer of specialty steel that has a long history of experimentation.[69] At Allegheny, experiments are routine rather than rare, the rule rather than the exception. According to Richard Simmons, chairman and CEO of the parent company: "This isn't something that you do twice a year at a meeting. It is something that you do every day of every week of every month of every year. After a while, it becomes part of the culture."

Twenty experiments are typically underway at any given time, with over one hundred per year in the alloy product line alone. To manage this volume, Allegheny has developed a comprehensive approach, with four key elements: a detailed measurement system, which provides the impetus for experiments and permits before-and-after comparisons; an innovative incentive system, which encourages managers to pursue improvements and take risks; a formal proposal mechanism, which structures and coordinates the work by requiring affected departments to agree to common goals, approaches, and outcomes; and a disciplined experimental process, which ensures rapid turnaround and valid, verifiable results (see Table 5-4). All of these elements work in concert to produce an integrated, reinforcing system.

Measurement. Allegheny has an extraordinarily complete tracking system that compares, for every grade of steel and every grade of equipment, current operating results with the very best productivity, quality, and costs that the company has ever obtained. Work is actually tracked to the individual coil level. Literally millions of standards have been developed, and the database can be exploded in any way that engineers believe to be of value: by grade, by product, by customer, even by thickness of the material. The resulting reports, which focus on variances from both the current target and the company's best-ever performance (known as the "Olympic standard"), are available on-line and in real time. They serve as the basis for daily, weekly, and monthly meetings that pinpoint potential areas for improvement and suggest possible experiments. The associated historical data play two additional roles: they are an invaluable source of information on potential cause-and-effect relationships, and they provide an implicit set of controls that eliminate statistical artifacts and flawed attributions.

Incentives. Allegheny uses its accounting system to encourage experimentation. Because all plant personnel are held responsible for operating margins (and are penalized for excess costs), they would normally have little incentive to experiment with novel, untested approaches. But once experiments are approved, they are moved to a separate account. Operating managers are no longer charged for the associated material and production costs; instead, those costs are assigned to technical services, a separate department consisting largely of metallurgists and process experts. (For the few elaborate experiments that are designed to commercialize new products—usually, no more than two or three per year—entire 100-ton heats are written down to scrap value immediately, removing them completely from the cost accounting system.) These changes in scorecards have the predictable effect of eliminating resistance due to incompatible incentives. And because all managers commit themselves annually to aggressive improvement targets, which typically involve shared goals (e.g., "increase melt shop capacity by $x\%$"), they

TABLE 5-4

ALLEGHENY LUDLUM'S SYSTEM OF EXPERIMENTATION

	Description	Purpose	Key Elements
Measurement System	Tracks productivity, quality, and costs at the level of individual coils and pieces of equipment	Identifies potential areas of improvement, suggests possible experiments, helps evaluate the impact of experimental changes	On-line, real-time reporting of variances, compared to current targets as well as best-ever performance
Incentives	Separates the costs of experiments from day-to-day operating expenses	Removes experiments from the scorecards used to evaluate operating managers, reducing their resistance	Separate budgets for small and large experiments
Proposals and Work Plans	Specifies the purpose, procedures, and personnel involved in experiments	Obtains approvals in advance, ensures interdepartmental coordination, and clearly specifies the nature of experiments and the desired results	Brief, two- to three-page documents that contain all critical information
Experimental Process	Generates plausible hypotheses and tests them systematically	Determines underlying cause-and-effect relationships	Manipulation of variables one at a time, alternating between the shop floor and laboratory as needed, drawing on the expertise of multifunctional teams

have a positive interest in designing and executing successful experiments.

Proposals and Work Plans. At Allegheny, all operational experiments are documented using the same, simple format. Each experiment is given its own name and number and is described in a brief proposal. The initial document is two or three pages long, and includes seven sections: objective, background, procedure, evaluation, responsibility, prepared by, and approvals (see Table 5-5). This approach serves several ends. First, by requiring prework and preparation, it ensures that all experiments have been thought through. Spur-of-the-moment initiatives and poorly conceived flashes of inspiration seldom qualify. Second, by carefully laying out the experiment's rationale and goals, as well as the procedures and measures to be employed, it ensures that learning is disciplined and focused. Third, by explicitly assigning responsibility to and requiring sign-offs from all parties likely to be affected by experiments, it ensures that the process does not take place in a vacuum. As one metallurgist put it: "Everybody is on the same page." And because upstream and downstream impacts have been taken into account, unanticipated problems are rare.

The sign-offs are especially important. As Robert Miller, vice president of technical services, observed, the primary difference between laboratory and shop-floor experiments is that the former have much simpler logistics:

> When you go into the laboratory, everything you need is sitting there waiting for you. But when you go onto the manufacturing floor, that is generally not the case. You have to bring people, machines, and material together in the right place at the right time. You have to have good communication and coordination to make sure that the right things happen.

The documentation process ensures that the necessary coordination has occurred and that both operators and equipment are prepared for the proposed experiment.

TABLE 5-5
PLANNING FOR EXPERIMENTS AT ALLEGHENY LUDLUM

Objective. This section describes the purpose of the experiment—the operational problems it is designed to solve or the commercial ends it is designed to serve.

Background. This section describes the evolution of the experiment—how it came about, any relevant experience, and the critical operating issues that must be addressed.

Procedure. This section explains how the experiment will be conducted, paying special attention to the required activities on the shop floor and how they will differ from normal practice.

Evaluation. This section describes how the results of the experiment will be evaluated, including how success will be judged.

Responsibility. This section contains a list of the primary departments affected by the experiment and the individuals who have been assigned responsibility in each one.

Prepared by. This section names the person—typically, a metallurgist—who prepared the documentation for the experiment and orchestrated the experimental process.

Approvals. This section contains the names and signatures of those middle or senior managers who have approved the experiment. Four or five sign offs are normally required, typically from individuals one or two levels above those who have been assigned responsibility for actually conducting the experiment.

The Experimental Process. Allegheny applies a disciplined approach to the design, development, and deployment of experiments. The challenges may be diverse, but the process remains remarkably consistent in format and style. Typically, experiments begin with a review of historical data, shift to shop-floor activities that manipulate one or two variables at a time, migrate to the laboratory if deeper insights are required, and then return to the shop floor for final testing and confirmation. Each step is carefully designed to rule out measurement error or other spurious explanations. The steps are also carefully sequenced, so that early diagnostic activities are separated from later efforts to optimize performance. Throughout, managers are guided by a simple, golden rule: "First we make it right, then we make it cheaper." This process has obvious parallels to the guidelines for effective experimentation described earlier in the chapter. To see them in action, it is best to draw on a real-world example: a series of experiments that Allegheny conducted in 1996 to transfer a difficult-to-manufacture grade of steel from an older, slower annealing line to one using the latest, most up-to-date technology.

THE PROCESS IN ACTION:
ANNEALING 304DA ON THE 91 LINE

Annealing is a process that softens steel so that it can be fabricated and shaped more easily by customers. For many years, Allegheny relied on its number 45 line for annealing. The equipment was relatively old and slow but continued to yield high-quality output. One product long produced on the line was 304DA, used by customers to make expensive, highly polished pots and pans. This product differed from Allegheny's usual products in an important respect. Rather than involving coils or sheets of pure stainless steel, 304DA ("double armor") was a metal sandwich, composed of two outer layers of stainless steel and an inner layer of carbon steel.

This combination posed special challenges. After considerable experimentation, Allegheny had learned how to anneal 304DA on the 45 line to the softness required by a demanding customer. Then, in early 1996, the customer placed an unexpectedly large order. It came with very short lead times; worse yet, the 45 line was already fully scheduled and was without spare capacity. The only way that Allegheny could fill the order would be to anneal 304DA on its newer 91 line. But that line bore only a passing resemblance to its predecessor. It was four times longer, ran four times faster, and incorporated state-of-the-art heating and cooling technology. Moreover, the equipment had been in place for only a year, and its capabilities were still not fully understood. Managers therefore faced a difficult task. Could they make the required volume of 304DA on the 91 line—at double the usual production rate—while still meeting the customer's demanding standards?

To find out, they launched a series of experiments (see Figure 5-2). The process began with a review of past successful transfers from the 45 to the 91 line. All had involved pure stainless products, and all had required little more than a simple, one-to-one matching of temperatures and machine settings. The same approach was used for 304DA. The 91 line's furnace was set to the identical temperature used for the product

FIGURE 5-2

LEARNING TO ANNEAL 304DA ON THE 91 LINE

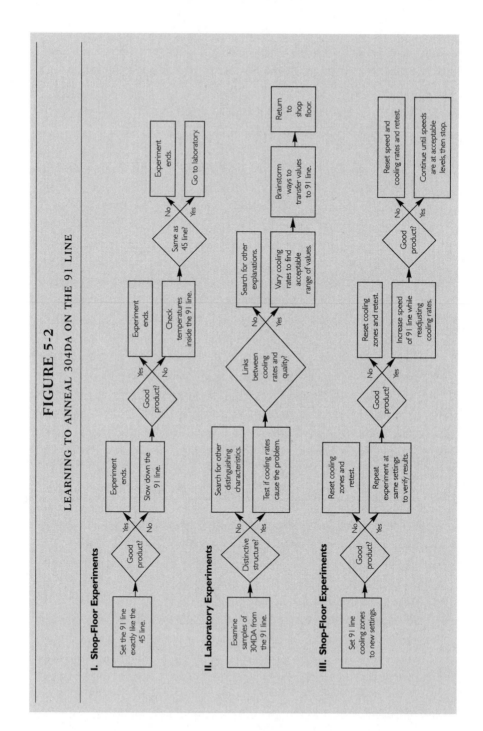

on the 45 line, and a small amount of material was annealed. The experiment could have ended right there if the steel came out soft enough. But the results were disappointing. As one participant recalled: "We got thrown a curve. The properties weren't close to those we were getting from the 45 line." The steel was far too hard. This time, a straightforward transfer of equipment settings had failed to produce the desired results. The question was, why?

Managers quickly launched a learning process that, within a few short weeks, produced the knowledge needed to successfully anneal 304DA on the 91 line. To begin, they tried to reproduce the old process *exactly*, slowing the 91 line down so that its speed was identical to that of the 45 line. This is an important step in real-world experiments: replicating, as closely as possible, the conditions that were previously successful in producing good product, but with new equipment, material, or operators. In essence, the goal is to mimic the old with the new—and, in the process, to isolate critical causal factors. Unfortunately, in this case the results were no better than before. The steel was still too hard.

So managers ran another experiment, taking the idea of replication a step further. Perhaps, they reasoned, the equipment's heating cycles— the time the lines took to heat up and hold a given temperature—were different despite the identical furnace settings. Their gauges and instruments might not be telling the whole story. Machine settings, after all, do not always capture actual operating conditions, nor do identical readings on different machines always reflect the same internal environments. To find out, managers would have to look inside the equipment. By opening up the "black box" of production, they would learn more about how the process really worked. They therefore attached a temperature probe directly to the unprocessed steel and ran it through the furnace, taking readings along the way. Unfortunately, here again there were few differences. The internal temperature of the 91 line was, in fact, 1,850 degrees—just like the 45 line. And the two lines' heating cycles were nearly identical.

Far from being solved, the mystery had only deepened. Managers were stumped. They could think of no other shop-floor experiments to conduct. At the same time, there were growing pressures to find a solution. Producing soft-enough 304DA was not a theoretical problem to be solved at leisure, but one with significant bottom-line implications. According to a participant: "The customer understood that we were going through a learning process. But their patience was becoming short. We needed to solve the problem immediately."

Further progress required even deeper analysis. At Allegheny, this meant shifting from the shop floor to the laboratory. A researcher was briefed about the early experiments. He then reviewed the accompanying data, requested samples of 304D from the 91 line, and examined them under a powerful microscope. He had definite ideas about where to look for clues: the carbon steel in the sandwich, since it was the primary factor distinguishing 304DA from the stainless products that had earlier been transferred without problems. On close examination, the carbon steel samples displayed a distinctive pattern (called a microstructure) that occurred only under certain conditions. According to the researcher:

> There are normally three critical variables that cause this kind of microstructure—how fast you heat the material, how long you hold it at that temperature, and how fast you cool it. They had already done experiments that showed the heating rate and the time at temperature had no effect on the material. So the only other thing that needed to be done was to determine if there was a third or a fourth variable that was not yet taken into account.

The researcher therefore focused his detective work still further. He conducted a series of experiments, heating and cooling small strips of 304DA on a tabletop version of a production line. It soon became clear that the cooling rate was the cause of the problems. But because it was difficult to meet a precise cooling target with large production equipment, the researcher broadened his experiments. Now his goal was to identify a "window" of opportunity—a range of cooling rates that would still produce acceptable softness. He used the cooling rate of the 45 line as a lower bound, since it was known to yield good results. By increasing the cooling rate in small increments until the steel finally became too hard, he came up with a range of values that would meet the customer's demands.

With these findings, the laboratory experiments came to an end. They were a resounding success but would have been far less effective—and far more time-consuming—without the initial work on the shop floor. Even though the early experiments did not solve the immediate problem, they helped rule out alternative explanations. They show that experimentation is a cumulative process in which even negative findings can be of value. As the laboratory researcher discovered, it is generally easier to "find the unknown . . . by . . . narrowing down the possibilities than by making direct but blind guesses."[70]

Yet even with the suggested cooling rates in hand, the problem was not fully solved. Managers still had to get the 91 line to act like the tiny, tabletop version used in the laboratory. Unfortunately, the translation from laboratory to shop floor is seldom straightforward. As a metallurgist observed:

> Lab work is done in a closed environment, where you can set parameters exactly as you like them. In a production facility, that isn't the case. You can approximate where you'd like to be, but there are some variables that cannot be set exactly. So the lab work gives you a direction, but it doesn't always give you the absolute values you need on the line.

At Allegheny, the problem was compounded by the fact that managers had no way of monitoring exactly what went on inside the 91 line's three cooling zones. For technical reasons, they could not attach a probe to the metal and send it through the equipment, as they had done with the furnace. The entire cooling section was sealed and impenetrable. All they could do was take the steel's temperature when it went in hot and again when it came out cool. The rest was guesswork—and experience.

Engineers and technical specialists therefore met as a group to discuss ways of meeting the cooling targets set in the laboratory. Thankfully, they had a range of values to shoot for rather than a single number and could adjust each of the cooling zones independently. As a first step, they decided to shut down the first zone, cut back the second, and leave the third on full. A few coils of 304DA were annealed using the new settings. Samples were rushed to quality control, where they were tested for softness. This time, the steel came out just right. But to confirm the results, managers ran several additional coils at exactly the same settings. When they too passed the tests for softness, the customer was informed. The new settings were then written up as standard operating procedure.

Surprisingly, the experimental process did not end there. Now the goal shifted to optimization: raising the speed of the 91 line without compromising the newly achieved softness. This is a time-honored practice at Allegheny. According to Simmons: "If we can experiment to make it better, then we should—and we do—experiment to make it more efficiently." Here, too, managers proceeded incrementally, running a series of experiments that steadily speeded up the line while simultaneously adjusting cooling rates. The critical variables were now well understood; the challenge was to keep them in balance. After considerable tinkering, the process was optimized. Today, Allegheny's 91 line produces three times more soft steel per day than it did at the start.

Nor was this the only benefit of the experiments. Because they produced deep, enduring knowledge about both product and process, there were several additional applications. Managers used their new knowledge to increase the 45 line's productivity when annealing 304DA and the 91 line's effectiveness when annealing other products. They were able to do so because they had moved, in the language of this chapter, from lower to higher stages of knowledge. They had progressed from "knowing how" to "knowing why."

As this story suggests, Allegheny has mastered the process of experimentation. A quick review of Table 5-3 shows that managers followed all of the guidelines for hypothesis-testing experiments. They began with clear goals, developed a definite set of hypotheses, drew on comprehensive measures, used diverse observers, and employed effective controls. They proceeded selectively, variable by variable, searching for patterns until the causes of the problem were well understood. They moved smoothly from the shop floor to the laboratory and then back to the shop floor, repeating experiments to ensure that their findings were valid. Throughout, they relied on a structure, format, and set of incentives that coordinated efforts and kept all parties aligned.

Equally important was the company's underlying philosophy. At Allegheny, experiments are valued for business reasons, not simply because they are fun to do. As Simmons observed:

> Experimentation is an investment, no different than an investment in a rolling mill, a melt furnace, or a refining vessel. It is an investment that you expect to get a return on. The fact that we don't solve every problem the first time is irrelevant. It is the learning process that creates a culture of continuous improvement, wanting to get better and outperforming your competition.

It should come as no surprise that the company has a sterling record of productivity improvement. In good years, the gains are as much as 7 to 8 percent—two or three times the national average and well ahead of peers. Experimentation deserves much of the credit.

III

THE LEADERSHIP
CHALLENGE

6

Leading Learning

Today managers and leaders are considered to be very different.[1] Managers are action-oriented; they spend their days doing, delegating, and deciding. Their eyes are on the present, and they measure success by skilled execution and effective implementation. Consistency and stability are the primary goals. Leaders, on the other hand, focus on the future; they spend their time setting targets, developing strategies, communicating vision, and aligning individuals and departments. Change is the primary objective, and the challenge is to get all parts of the organization moving in the desired direction at a rapid enough rate. Clearly, companies need both managers and leaders to succeed, for together they ensure attention to both short- and long-term goals.

Yet according to the preceding chapters, enduring success requires that both groups broaden their horizons. Both need to add a new goal, "improving organizational learning," to their already lengthy agendas. Managers, for example, need to master approaches like Allegheny Ludlum Steel's to ensure operational excellence, while leaders need to craft processes like Xerox 2000 to ensure that their organizations are targeting the right segments and strategies. Superior intelligence gathering, experiential learning, and experimentation are all required. Otherwise, atrophy and drift are inevitable. The challenge is great and becomes ever more pressing with time:

> When organizations and societies are young, they are flexible, fluid, not yet paralyzed by rigid specialization and willing to try anything once. As the organization or society ages, vitality diminishes, flexibility gives way to rigidity, creativity fades and there is a loss of capacity to meet challenges from future directions.[2]

It is for this reason that learning is the key to long-term survival and growth and that organizational effectiveness is so intimately linked to adaptability and flexibility.

Scholars have responded to the need for adaptable, flexible, learning organizations by suggesting that executives devote more of their time to teaching.[3] As one expert put it: "An organization cannot become a learning organization without first becoming a 'teaching' organization."[4] To that end, executives are urged to share their distinctive perspectives about their companies' strategies, purposes, and values. They are told to develop a "teachable point of view" that captivates and enlightens, communicating it to employees through stories and parables. They are instructed to lead management development sessions in which they share their own successes and failures and diffuse their favored approaches throughout the organization. Such prominent CEOs as Roger Enrico of PepsiCo, Jacques Nasser of Ford, and Andy Grove of Intel have taken up this challenge, spending weeks of their time in face-to-face meetings with direct reports and other high-potential managers. There, they tell war stories, describe their personal philosophies, and teach others to use their favorite tools and techniques.

This new role is vitally important. It provides a broad base of knowledge and understanding, gives purpose and meaning to organization members, and ensures commitment to common goals. But it remains incomplete—especially in environments that are changing rapidly and unpredictably. To succeed in those settings, the focus must broaden from teaching to leading learning. The difference is more than mere semantics; it reflects a fundamental shift in perspective and approach.[5]

TEACHING AND LEARNING

Teaching puts the instructor front and center. Concepts and ideas flow from the top down or the center out, and the focus is on knowledge transfer. Teachers are the experts; their role is to deliver content, communicate clear messages, and instill better ways of working. Students are regarded as novices; their role is to absorb and accept. The effectiveness of the process is usually measured by the degree to which important information makes the trip from the first group to the second without distortion or loss. Unfortunately, all too often a completed trip results in little more than "inert ideas . . . that are merely received into the mind without being utilized, or tested, or thrown into fresh combinations."[6] Knowledge is repackaged and repositioned, but deeper learning is not achieved. As a noted business school professor observed over fifty years ago: "It can be said flatly that the mere act of listening to wise statements and sound advice does little for anyone....We cannot efficiently use the knowledge of others; it must be our own knowledge and insight that we use."[7]

A process designed to foster learning is quite different. New ways of thinking become the desired ends, not facts or frameworks. Discussion and debate replace ex cathedra pronouncements. Questions become as important as answers. And success, to use a currently popular phrase, is measured by the degree to which students "learn how to learn." Because the focus shifts from transferring knowledge to developing organizational skills and capabilities, executives' roles must change as well. They become shepherds of learning, responsible for creating supportive environments, probing for insights and deeper thinking, and constructing settings where employees can collect, interpret, and apply information. This, in turn, requires a significant shift in mind-set and attitudes. According to Charles Peirce, the pragmatist philosopher:

> In order that a man's whole heart may be in teaching he must be thoroughly imbued with the vital importance and absolute truth of what he has to teach; while in order that he may have any success in

learning he must be penetrated with a sense of the unsatisfactoriness of his present condition of knowledge.[8]

For these reasons, executives who are adept at communicating their own opinions and views are seldom equally skilled at shaping and participating in learning processes. To succeed at the latter task, most need to broaden their portfolio of skills. They need to develop a more comprehensive understanding of the elements and conditions that lead to effective intelligence gathering, experiential learning, and experimentation. They need to recognize that each mode of learning involves common activities—data collection, dialogue, and decision making—and that each provides an opportunity for interaction and the cultivation of cognitive and social skills. They need to become sensitive to the risks and barriers that impede learning. And, perhaps most important, they need to shift their attention from content to process.

Learning, after all, is simply another organizational process, not all that different from strategy formulation, product development, or order fulfillment. Like other processes, it unfolds over time, has inputs and outputs, involves diverse departments and levels, and consists of interconnected activities and steps.[9] And like other processes, it must be crafted and led. The concept of a "process owner" is as relevant to intelligence gathering, experiential learning, and experimentation as it is to better-known operational and business processes—and for many of the same reasons: lack of attention, diffused responsibility, fragmentation, and inefficiency. According to an expert on reengineering: "Why did we design inefficient processes? In a way, we didn't. Many of our procedures were not designed at all; they just happened."[10] It is no coincidence that the learning processes described in the preceding chapters all reflect planned, holistic approaches that were developed under the guidance of senior executives. They involve learning skills that were carefully cultivated, often in the face of formidable barriers.

There are three primary tasks. First, leaders and managers must create opportunities for learning by designing settings and events that prompt the necessary activities. Second, they must cultivate the proper tone, fostering desirable norms, behaviors, and rules of engagement. Third, they must personally lead the process of discussion, framing the debate, posing questions, listening attentively, and providing feedback and closure. Done properly, these three tasks go a long way toward building an organization's enduring capacity for learning.

CREATING THE OPPORTUNITY

Today's managers and employees are inundated with work. They have far too much to do and far too little time to do it. Head counts are down, while workloads continue to rise. Products and services are proliferating, markets are globalizing, and technology is forcing radical changes. The pressure to produce is high and unrelenting. In such settings, the urgent frequently drives out the important, and learning, as chapter 1 observed, becomes an unnecessary frill. It is easily postponed in the face of more immediate demands.

Learning Forums

To raise its visibility, executives need to create learning forums—assignments, activities, and events whose primary purpose is to foster learning. Think, by way of analogy, of the ancient Roman forum, a central gathering place where citizens discussed the great issues of the day. Organizations are equally in need of public and private settings where they can wrestle collectively with difficult questions. Several have already been discussed: Xerox 2000, which brought together senior managers to examine the company's changing competitive environment and desired product portfolio, technology, and market positioning; L.L. Bean's two-day gathering at Pinkham Notch, which brought together field testers, marketers, product designers, and suppliers to compare products and experiences and to develop a clearer picture of user needs; and the U.S. Army's After Action Reviews, which brought together soldiers and their commanders immediately after missions or training exercises to explore the reasons for success or failure. Each of these forums exposed participants to raw, unfiltered data and then offered time for reflection and interpretation, leading to improved understanding as well as concrete actions and plans.

Learning forums can take many other forms. They include systems audits, which review the health of large, cross-functional processes and delivery systems; internal benchmarking projects, which identify and compare best-in-class activities within an organization; and study missions, which dispatch employees to leading organizations around the world to better understand their performance and distinctive skills. All, it should be clear, involve a well-defined learning agenda and complete, compressed learning cycles. A small group of people is assembled and given a learning task; first-hand information is collected and alternative interpretations are explored; and implications are developed and quickly deployed.

All of these examples involve activities that are separate from daily work. They exist apart from employees' normal responsibilities, and learning is the primary, if not the sole, goal. But forums need not be one-of-a-kind events or assignments. Nor do they necessarily demand dedicated task forces. Even routine meetings and get-togethers—weekly telephone calls, monthly staff meetings, quarterly off-sites—can serve as learning forums, providing they are properly designed and led. The trick is to ensure that learning goals are well defined, decisions are deferred until ideas mature, and leaders steer participants toward insights as well as action. Improvements in collective understanding must be viewed as a prelude to bottom-line gains.

In more formal terms, executives must shift from a pure performance orientation—in which results are all that matter—to one that balances performance and learning goals. According to scholars, when people find themselves in settings such as the classroom or the workplace, they typically display one of two orientations.[11] Some focus primarily on performance; their goal is to gain favorable evaluations from superiors and perform well relative to peers. Others focus primarily on learning; their goal is to increase their competence and skills and develop increased mastery of the task at hand.

A performance orientation is desirable because it produces hard work. But it has a number of unfortunate side effects. When people evaluate themselves strictly on their current rankings and results, they are much more likely to shun difficult challenges, sacrifice potential learning opportunities, and avoid situations where there is a high risk of error. People with a learning orientation, on the other hand, tend to persist in the face of obstacles. They willingly assume challenges that broaden their portfolio of skills, even if errors are likely. Over time, they gain both competence and confidence, and their results improve. Put succinctly, a performance orientation ensures that people will work hard in order to look good; a learning orientation ensures that they will work smart in order to perform better.

While the two orientations are to some degree ingrained, they also reflect the surrounding environment. Psychologists have found that when teachers focus exclusively on results, respond negatively to errors, and praise students for their innate abilities, they tend to encourage a performance orientation. When they pay attention to personal development, use errors as opportunities for improvement, and praise students for their effort and hard work, they tend to encourage a learning orientation. The analogy to management should be obvious. Just as teachers are responsible for the environments of their classrooms, leaders are responsible for the climates of their organizations. For both short- and long-term success, they must attend to more than results alone. A performance orientation remains vital—otherwise, employees will engage in activity for activity's sake, with little direction or design—but its impact can be magnified when coupled with efforts to stimulate more of a learning orientation.

Chad Holliday, for example, the CEO of DuPont, works personally to improve his organization's skill at intelligence gathering. Every other week, he holds a telephone conference with twenty top managers from around the globe. The group is expected to stay on top of changes in customers, competitors, and local economies and politics by sharing the latest insights from the field. Sessions are highly interactive, with Holliday taking the lead. Not by giving answers, however, but by asking questions: "What's happening to our customers and their customers? To the political will of local leaders to deal with the downturn? To the changing competitive rules? What do we need to do now?" His goal is to help members of the group educate one another by learning more about critical issues in the marketplace. In his words: "By hearing the answers simultaneously from their peers, they broaden their perspective of the global landscape."[12]

Successful forums like Holliday's share several characteristics. They increase participants' exposure to information by introducing new, previously untapped sources of data. They encourage divergent thinking by cultivating a range of interpretations and views. They engage participants by assigning topics and themes that prompt open discussion without stirring up traditional functional and divisional loyalties. They counteract common learning disabilities by employing a variety of "debiasing" techniques.[13] And they stimulate exploratory thinking by injecting counter-intuitive and unexpected perspectives into discussions. At heart, these are little more than clever techniques for overcoming the pressures and prejudices of daily work that so often short-circuit learning.

Planning meetings, for example, frequently operate on automatic pilot. They seldom encourage active engagement or new thinking. In many cases, senior managers arrive armed with the latest competitive or customer information and then report it to subordinates, who are expected to relay the same data to others with little or no embellishment. In other cases, participants arrive having read the same memo or report; they then compare notes and choose among prespecified alternatives, usually by giving a simple thumbs-up or thumbs-down. Discussion normally proceeds predictably, with few surprises and limited learning. Yet the process does not have to be so confining. More active, stimulating approaches are possible; typically, they involve pooling information from diverse sources and continually challenging, testing, and debating.

Chuck Knight, the CEO of Emerson Electric, has long embedded learning in his company's planning reviews. Division general managers submit their plans in advance, knowing that their presentations will be interrupted by difficult, often unsettling questions. All proposals are vetted, however carefully they have been constructed and designed. "The concept," according to a senior corporate officer, "is to disagree with the thesis being presented, irrespective of the thesis."[14] Why? Because Knight's primary goal is to establish the depth and quality of the supporting analysis, not simply approve proposals. He does so by probing each and every argument to uncover unfounded assumptions and logical flaws. This not only improves his understanding of the plans but also sharpens the thinking of division managers as well.

Exploratory Assignments

Of course, meetings need not be contentious and argumentative to produce deep learning. Sometimes, the same results can be achieved simply by bringing together participants around a common challenge and setting aside enough time and space so that real thinking can occur. This is especially true when problems are ambiguous or poorly defined. Then, broad exploratory assignments, open-ended questions, and an atmosphere of give and take seem to work best. Jack Welch used this approach when he first introduced Work-Out at GE. He structured the two-day meetings of his Corporate Executive Council (CEC) as forums for sharing best practices and accelerating progress. The CEC is composed of the heads of GE's fourteen major businesses. For many months, Work-Out was virtually the only topic on its agenda. Moreover, the format and approach of CEC meetings were designed to foster collaboration and experiential learning. The setting was informal; meetings were run like workshops; all participants were expected to come with experiences to share, based on their successes and failures with Work-Out; formal presentations were not allowed; and sessions were highly interactive, with Welch guiding the discussion.[15]

John Fahey of Time Life used a similar approach to foster thinking by his senior team about multimedia products and the best use of the company's master file, editorial staff, and other shared assets. In 1992 he appointed a Corporate Strategy Committee, consisting of Time Life's three division heads as well as key functional leaders, to consider ways that the books, music, and video and television divisions might work together more productively. At the time, there was little interdivisional cooperation; the company, in Fahey's view, was little more than "a loosely confederated conglomerate." He therefore began by giving the group a wide-open assignment, designed to break down barriers and free up thinking rather than solve immediate problems. Members were asked to consider the meaning and possible extent of "strategic integration"; they met several times, away from the workplace and under the guidance of a trained facilitator, to brainstorm possible interpretations. A few weeks later, Fahey asked each member of the committee to prepare two brief documents: a vision of Time Life in the year 2002 and a description of what the corporate strategy statement should and should not be. These topics were also cleverly selected to encourage dialogue and discussion; they were chosen for their ability to stimulate thinking, not produce solutions or tangible outputs. Meetings continued for several months. By that time, the group had progressed to the point where they had developed a common vocabulary and shared understanding; then, and only then, did Fahey ask them to come up with a detailed agenda, including a small number of strategic goals and several significant organization changes. The final result was a tightly knit senior team, more efficient operations, an improved approach to multimedia products, and increased profitability.[16]

Shared Experiences

At times, especially when radical changes are required, senior executives may find it necessary to put managers and employees through a learning process that mimics one they have personally experienced. Otherwise, they may fail to understand the rationale and need for new behaviors. Here, a common problem is surface agreement that cloaks deep uncertainties and doubts. Members of the organization may have heard the words but do not yet understand the music. Craig Weatherup, the president and CEO of Pepsi-Cola North America, overcame these barriers with a carefully crafted learning process. In September 1990, after several months of reviewing financial data, interviewing customers and employees, and visiting field operations, he launched a massive change process. Pepsi was facing pressure on several fronts because of shifting competitive requirements. According to Weatherup:

> In the late 1980s, we made a $4 billion bet, buying up many of our independent bottlers to gain control over distribution. Almost overnight, we went from a company with 600 customers—the franchised bottlers—to a company with 600,000 customers. And we moved aggressively into a wide range of alternative beverages, such as juices and teas, and added lots of new packaging. All of a sudden, we had an explosion of complexity in various shapes, forms, and sizes.
>
> At the same time, we were still a company with a "big event" marketing mentality. Our entire mindset was geared to superstar entertainers such as Michael Jackson and Ray Charles. However, we now had several hundred thousand customers, and we weren't spending enough time thinking about them. The complexity was a huge challenge and drove us to this compelling commitment: to devote as much time, energy, and passion to operations and service as we had historically devoted to marketing.[17]

To communicate these new priorities, Weatherup began with a four-day meeting of his direct reports, designed to introduce them to the new demands facing the company and win acceptance of the need for change. After considerable discussion, they accepted the challenge and began crafting a vision. But there were questions about how the rest of the organization would react. The business was still profitable and successful; Weatherup was anticipating problems, not responding to current difficulties. He and his team therefore designed a learning process to ensure that the new needs were better understood. Every three months they worked with a different group, starting with the 70 people who were on the rung below the senior team, moving to larger groups of 400 and 1,200, then to a huge meeting of 5,500 in Dallas, and finally to a one-day video presentation to all 20,000 frontline employees.

Each group followed the same format. After a three-day kickoff meeting, participants were given ninety days to complete assigned activities, which included interviewing customers, charting work processes, and designing and leading the three-day enrollment meeting for the next group of employees. As Weatherup observed, these ninety-day cycles were based on an explicit model of learning:

> We ended up calling it "head, heart, hands" because we believed that for change to occur, people had to do three things: develop a conceptual understanding of the rationale and proposed direction of change, internalize and commit emotionally to the new vision, and acquire new skills to ensure that the vision would be realized.[18]

In essence, Weatherup was requiring others in the organization to undergo a learning process similar to the one that he had personally experienced, but to do so in a vastly compressed period. Like Fahey, he was also triggering a process of "unlearning," dislodging long-established patterns of behavior by challenging ways of thinking that had worked successfully in the past.[19] It succeeded admirably, producing a new mind-set, improved service, more efficient operations, a new organization structure, and, over the course of eight years, a doubling of revenues and a tripling of operating income.[20]

Weatherup, Fahey, Welch, Knight, and Holliday were all able to devise processes that encouraged others in the organization to learn in new and different ways. All five executives designed or constructed settings that caused managers and employees to adopt, at least temporarily, more of a learning orientation. Participants shared information, pooled insights, explored innovative ideas, stretched their imaginations, and broadened their experiences to a degree that they would not have otherwise. In the process, they managed to keep traditional business concerns firmly in their sights. The results were both hard and soft gains: measurable improvements in bottom-line performance, as well as more knowledgeable, involved employees.

SETTING THE TONE

All of these examples also show the importance of setting the proper tone. As chapter 2 observed, learning is a difficult and delicate process: it will flower only if the climate is right. Participants face considerable uncertainty and risk. Politics and gamesmanship often impede the smooth flow of information. Partisanship can easily derail discussions. Learning, after all, is seldom an unmixed blessing. There are normally competing interests at stake, and some parties will benefit at the expense of others. Executives must therefore work hard to encourage objective, open-minded inquiry. Otherwise, even the best-designed forums will produce only limited insight.

There are several requirements. The atmosphere must be one of challenge, skepticism, and doubt, so that easy, pat solutions are not accepted until they have been subjected to careful scrutiny. Participants must feel a sense of security, so that they can stretch themselves in new directions without fear of failure, and incentives must support experimentation and risk taking. A sense of fairness must prevail, with no group feeling that its ideas are getting short shrift. And the rules of engagement must encourage the sharing of knowledge, so that information is pooled and becomes common property. Cultivating such climates requires special sensitivities: extraordinary attention to context and tone, the ability to draw people out, and a deep familiarity with the forces that drive learning. In the words of Bob Galvin, the former CEO of Motorola, the focus shifts from deciding and directing "to creat[ing] and maintain[ing] an evocative situation, stimulating an atmosphere of objective participation, keeping the goal in sight, recognizing valid consensus, inviting unequivocal recommendation, and finally vesting increasingly in others the privilege to learn through their own decisions."[21]

Challenge and Dissent

This does not mean that executives should strive to create "warm and fuzzy" cultures that lack tension or pressure. Learning must be channeled and directed; otherwise, "the result is likely to be a series of random walks to personal enlightenment that do little for overall performance."[22] Ensuring that employees deal with difficult business issues is a vital part of the leader's role.[23] But challenges must be framed in ways that encourage inquiry and foster a learning orientation. Tough questions can be raised, but they must be framed in ways that draw participants into the problem. Neither stinging critiques nor fiery speeches are necessary. Instead, effective interventions typically take one of three forms: (1) tentative, partially developed proposals that stimulate discussion; (2) novel, unexpected questions that prompt new thinking; or (3) changes in processes and procedures that introduce contrary, dissenting views.

Galvin used the first approach in 1983, when, at the company's biennial meeting of top officers, he rose to deliver his usual summary speech and instead made an unexpected request: that managers take a fresh look at the structure of their organizations. He urged them to consider the possibility of shifting to smaller, more focused business units, decreasing the many layers of management while bringing executives closer to products and markets. He concluded with an invitation and a promise:

> I see a welling up of the evidence of need and today I think the window is open. So I decided to express my concern and my conviction to you, confident that you share my insights and that together we will find our way to an organized effort of change. When we come together in two years, we will report and share the changes made and the lessons learned.[24]

Galvin's remarks were unscripted and deliberately vague; they were designed to surface an important concern, not resolve it. This was very much in keeping with his concept of his own role—as one who stirs the pot, raising important but overlooked issues, even though he lacks immediate answers. Galvin's brief, provocative speech prompted a multiyear process of soul searching by Motorola's managers, as well as extensive discussions of the current structure. In time, they led to several innovative experiments, a new program for organizational effectiveness, and significant improvements in speed and responsiveness.[25]

Harvey Golub, the CEO of American Express, has long relied on the second approach to set tone. He pushes hard on the reasoning process, forcing managers to think creatively and in unexpected ways. Often, a subordinate observed, he "comes at things from a different angle" to ensure that conventional approaches are not accepted without first being examined deeply. In Golub's words:

> I am far less interested in people having the right answer than in their thinking about issues the right way. What criteria do they use? Why do they think the way they do? What alternatives have they considered? What premises do they have? What rocks are they standing on?[26]

Such questions are not designed to lead to a particular answer but are aimed at generating truly open-minded discussion. There is an important difference between Golub's style of probing, which is designed to broaden thinking, and a Socratic approach, in which the endpoint is known and novices are led by the nose until they arrive at the desired conclusion. Members of the senior team at American Express clearly recognize the distinction:

> I can't remember Harvey ever telling anyone what to do. He pays more attention to *how* you think than anything else. He is always testing your thinking process. If he finds that you have thought about something really well, you get to do it. If not, you get coached.
>
> Harvey really has only two questions in business unit reviews: "How did you think about that? And how would it be different if you thought about it this way instead?"
>
> Harvey is the best counterintuitive thinker I have ever seen. If everyone agrees on something, he will ask, "Why?" For example,

when everyone agreed that we should lower credit card fees, he spent two days with us discussing his counterproposal—that maybe we should raise them. I don't think he meant it seriously, but he certainly taught us how to think about fees.[27]

Such interactions, it should be clear, produce in-depth discussions without the emotional fallout that so often accompanies barbed questions from the CEO. They also produce deep learning on multiple fronts—substantively, about the issue at hand, as well as cognitively, about how to approach problems better in the future.

President Kennedy used the third approach to create an atmosphere conducive to learning. After his disastrous experience with the Bay of Pigs, in which interdepartmental politics sharply restricted learning, he redesigned the national security decision-making process to ensure that dissenting views were encouraged and difficult issues were aired. Kennedy began by establishing new ground rules. Senior advisers were told that pure partisanship would no longer be acceptable. All assumptions would now be tested. Intelligence information would be regularly updated and shared, without filtering by intermediaries.

Then, Kennedy assigned new roles. Every participant was asked to function as a "skeptical generalist," assuming a broad integrated perspective rather than the narrow focus of his or her agency or department. Robert Kennedy and Theodore Sorensen, two of Kennedy's most trusted advisers, were asked to be "intellectual watchdogs," with the goal of "pursu[ing] relentlessly every bone of contention in order to prevent errors arising from too superficial analysis of the issues."

Finally, Kennedy tackled the process itself, reconfiguring it to open up debate. The usual rules of protocol were suspended so that respect for hierarchy no longer squelched discussion. New advisers were routinely brought into meetings to inject fresh views. Separate subcommittees were used to flesh out alternative positions. Kennedy deliberately absented himself from preliminary discussions to ensure that his personal views did not limit the alternatives generated by advisers. Together, these changes introduced far more challenge and breadth into the decision-making process. The new approach was quickly tested during the Cuban missile crisis, where it served the president to great effect.[28]

Security and Support

Challenge alone, however, is not enough to guarantee learning. Individuals also need a sense of security if they are to throw off old ways of thinking and acting. As a noted educator observed: "Learning means leaving the known for the unknown—an exhilarating, but scary venture."[29] Fear of failure creates personal risk and vulnerability; both make it difficult to move forward. Some level of support is therefore required if the process is ever to get off the ground. Here, senior executives play a vital role, for they can personally shape the environment in ways that provide protection and support.

Linda Doyle, the president and CEO of Harvard Business School Publishing (HBSP), has long tried to create a secure, supportive environment—in her words, "a clearing where it is safe to talk about hard issues." In 1994 Doyle inherited a fragile organization that was still emerging from difficult, uncertain times. HBSP was only two years old, having been stitched together from several previously independent groups. Employees were struggling to find an identity and common goals. In addition, most members of the organization had a strong critical bent. HBSP was populated with editors and academics; bright people who by temperament and training had a critical cast of mind, enjoyed finding holes in arguments, and were skilled at explaining why new ideas would not work. The typical discussion, Doyle observed, often resembled a "skeet shoot. Someone would yell 'pull,' there would be a deafening blast, and the idea would be in pieces on the ground."

To create a more supportive setting, she took several reinforcing steps. (The goal, she later recalled, was to help people learn to "disagree without being disagreeable.") To begin, Doyle sent clear signals about the desired tone, intervening in meetings to halt overheated or nonproductive discussions. She sent the same messages privately during managers' performance reviews. Next, she set strict ground rules for strategy development, insisting that no one criticize ideas during the initial brainstorming process. Finally, she hired a consultant to introduce and train members of the organization in the use of Edward de Bono's "six thinking hats." De Bono is a leading expert on creativity; he developed the six thinking hats as a way of categorizing the types of comments that people make and the roles and positions they frequently take in discussions. A "white hat" comment is neutral or factual; a "red hat" comment is emotional or judgmental; a "yellow hat" comment is positive or constructive; a "black hat" comment is negative or critical; a "green hat" comment is creative or innovative; and a "blue hat" comment is process- or discussion-focused.[30] Doyle's goals in introducing this approach were to help people vary their own thinking styles and become more receptive to different types of thinking. She also wanted to open up and broaden discussion, giving people permission to express feelings or make negative comments while softening their effect. Over time, these interventions had a significant cumulative impact. They produced an environment that was more tolerant of dissent, more supportive of experimentation, and more committed to shared discussion and learning. They also led to sharp increases in growth and net contribution.[31]

An equally effective way of providing security is to give learners help when they first venture into the unknown. Like any high-wire act, learning is far less stressful when a safety net is near. Risks are greatly reduced when one works side by side with an experienced expert or can bounce ideas off a knowledgeable superior. Errors may still occur, but they are a lot less damaging. This principle has long been the mainstay of apprenticeship programs; it is easily adapted to other corporate settings. Managers at Chaparral Steel, for example, have developed a practice that they call "vice-ing." When a foreman or supervisor is absent, the most senior operator or craftsman is temporarily promoted to take his place. He becomes a "vice foreman," with expanded responsibilities. But his superiors ensure that he has help in the new role. A vice-foreman is always assisted by the foreman from the previous shift, who works extra hours at his usual pay level, but as second-in-command. He becomes a subordinate and a security blanket. This approach meets several goals simultaneously. It stretches and challenges employees, transfers expertise, avoids risky errors, and creates a supportive learning environment.[32]

Zaki Mustafa, vice president and general manager of Serengeti Eyewear, a division of Corning, used a similar approach to foster learning. Rather than delegating the task to others, he took personal responsibility for giving employees the needed sense of security. In part, he did so out of necessity, because there were few other resources available. In 1984, after years of weak sales and profits, Corning had decided to exit the sunglasses business; only a last-minute appeal from Mustafa, who was then operations manager, succeeded in keeping it afloat. After assuming the role of general manager, he began to create a new environment that would expand employees' knowledge and skills. His goals were developmental—to build the business by building the skills of the few remaining employees. The resulting process relied heavily on collaboration and hand-holding, as well as conscious efforts to reduce risk. As Mustafa described the process:

> People would come to me with a problem—say, expanding our distribution system. I would talk with them, and they would arrive at "a recommendation." I would say, "That's really your decision, so go do it." They wanted it to be my decision, but I wouldn't let it be. Gradually, a pattern evolved, with people coming to me to help them "think things through." Then, after awhile, they stopped coming to me for advice [either].
>
> My goal has been to get people to aspire to do more than they thought they could. Once they have experienced that, the sky's the limit. But they need to know that it's not exploitation for the sake of business. They have my support all the way, and if something goes wrong, I'll take the rap for it.

Using this approach, and with only limited additional investment, Mustafa succeeded in turning the business around and then growing it substantially. Serengeti's sales expanded more than tenfold between 1984 and 1992. By the end of the period, it was one of Corning's most profitable divisions.[33]

Open Communication

A final element of tone is open access to information. Executives must send the signal that knowledge is to be shared, not hoarded, especially among peers. They are, after all, invaluable sources of insight, since they usually face similar problems and opportunities. As Ralph Waldo Emerson, the American essayist, noted over a hundred years ago: "I pay the schoolmaster, but 'tis the schoolboys that educate my son."[34] This is a concept that receives lip service at most corporations today but is surprisingly rare in practice. Why? Because knowledge is power, and shared knowledge usually means less power. To overcome the problem, leaders have three main options. They can alter incentives, rewarding individuals if they share knowledge with others. They can redesign work processes, legitimizing knowledge sharing as a form of behavior. And they can impose policies and directives that require managers to seek help from others in order to complete their assignments.

The first approach can be seen at Ernst & Young, which evaluates and compensates consultants on their contributions to companywide databases and other knowledge repositories.[35] The second approach can be seen at British Petroleum, which employs a knowledge-sharing process called Peer Assists. It brings together engineers, geologists, and other experts from around the globe to help divisions and departments solve difficult problems. Reciprocity becomes part of daily work, since as many as 3 to 5 percent of the people in a unit may be involved in assists at any given time.[36] The third approach can be seen at Rank Xerox, which recently asked a central group to compile a list of best practices in sales and marketing from all parts of Europe. Country managers were then told to choose four items from the list and adopt them without alteration. Because no single country was represented by more than one practice, most sales and marketing personnel found themselves serving as both teachers and learners, overcoming the one-way flow that so often impedes effective knowledge sharing.[37]

Finally, senior executives must remember to model personally the desired attitude and tone. The tenor and style of their communications matter a great deal. An open, inviting approach is essential; it is far more likely to be effective than one in which content is tightly controlled.[38] In fact, a well-tuned communication process is often the key to learning. According to social psychologists: "[T]he way the group 'utilizes' its resources and the procedures it employs for communicating essential information are as important, if not more important than 'knowledge' of the problem for determining its performance."[39] For example, routinely acknowledging that information has been received not only encourages greater information sharing but also leads to fewer errors. In addition, information can be solicited in many different ways, with widely varying impact. Some executives issue commands ("Ask the marketing department to collect information on customers"), others make observations ("I think we should ask the marketing department to collect information on customers"), and still others pose inquiries ("Why don't we ask the marketing department to collect information on customers?"). The resulting responses are not always the same, and the accompanying environments often differ dramatically in their levels of coordination and information exchange.[40]

LEADING THE DISCUSSION

Once leaders have created the desired climate, learning can begin in earnest. Whether the focus is intelligence gathering, learning from experience, or experimentation, some discussion is usually involved. In fact, virtually every example in this book—Xerox 2000, L.L. Bean's use of field testers, the Center for Army Lessons Learned and After-Action Reviews, GE's Change Acceleration Process, Timken's Cardboard City, and Allegheny Ludlum's experiments with 304DA—involved intensive discussions at several points along the way. Findings were seldom self-evident. Meaning often had to be constructed, and participants usually found it necessary to engage actively with the material and with one another, debating alternatives until they reached a decision or conclusion.

Such discussions seldom proceed smoothly or of their own accord. They can easily derail, resulting in entrenched positions, superficial debate, finger-pointing, miscommunication, and an inability to move forward. For real progress to occur, considerable shaping and direction are required. Someone has to lead the process. Skilled executives recognize that this is one of their primary responsibilities. As Linda Doyle put it, describing her efforts to gain acceptance for centralized marketing from the heads of the largely autonomous units that been melded into Harvard Business School Publishing:

> Until people began to see the vision of what might be and could live it and breathe it, they were never going to give up control. If I had forced the issue, it would just have driven them underground. What

I had to do was lead the case discussion, so they would see the need for themselves.[41]

To succeed at this process, executives need skills in three broad areas: questioning, listening, and responding.[42] All are tools of effective discussion leaders. And all can be used equally effectively in corporate settings.

Questioning

Questions, for example, are enormously powerful tools for leading learning. They are the motive and force that gives shape to inquiry. Unfortunately, managers often treat questions as second-class citizens and regard them as a badge of ignorance. They prefer bold assertions and strong statements because they convey a sense of mastery and control. Yet questions are vital for moving groups forward. Peter Drucker, in fact, has argued that "the most common source of mistakes in management decisions is the emphasis on finding the right answer rather than the right question."[43] Good questions get to the heart of a matter; they force deep thinking and reflection. They must therefore be formulated with care and applied with a deft, sensitive touch. Just as surgeons should not wield scalpels blindly or without proper training, managers should not use questions without first developing a clearer sense of their strengths, weaknesses, benefits, and risks.

To begin, it is important to recognize that not all questions are alike. They come in many forms and play diverse roles. There is no single best type of question; the preferred form depends on the situation and current needs. Questions can be used to:

- frame issues,
- offer instructions,
- solicit information,
- probe for analysis,
- draw connections,
- seek opinions, and
- ratify decisions.[44]

Framing, for example, is critical for defining and structuring problems properly. A manager's opening question often shapes the task for the group by setting boundaries and providing a context for discussion ("Why don't we consider this proposal in light of the likely responses of current and future competitors?"). At the same time, questions can be used to issue instructions. With a bit of imagination, leaders can use them to set the agenda and assign roles, while simultaneously focusing the group's attention ("Could we begin by having Larry discuss the most recent intelligence he collected on U.S. Industrial, since they seem to pose the greatest challenge going forward?"). Soliciting information and probing for analysis are two sides of the same coin; both are essential if leaders hope to deepen understanding and move the group beyond superficial arguments ("Do we have any evidence that supports this hypothesis? Are there other possible reasons why the 91 line might be producing steel that is too hard?"). Questions are equally effective at building bridges among participants and linking comments in constructive ways. They allow executives to create a sense of camaraderie and collaboration, while moving the debate forward ("Aren't Fred and Mary really saying the same thing— that we need to involve all operating units in our efforts to achieve an 85 percent learning curve?"). Finally, managers can use questions to test for agreement or disagreement and ultimately to bring discussions to a close ("Are we all in accord on this strategy? Does everyone understand their new assignments?").

Clearly, one implication of this list is that executives need to broaden the range of questions they employ. Excessive use of a single approach is unlikely to produce the greatest possible learning. But even after expanding their repertoires, most managers need to take additional steps to ensure that they are using questions most effectively. They need to adopt a few rules of thumb, since certain questioning styles are preferable if the aim is to encourage learning. For example, open questions, which allow for a variety of possible responses and do not point respondents in a particular, prespecified direction, are normally better than closed questions. Typically, they invite greater involvement and participation, and produce a wider range of options and alternatives. Designers at L.L. Bean, for example, are likely to learn a great deal more by asking field testers, "Why do you prefer this design?" than by asking them, "Do you prefer this parka because of its large pockets or drawstring hood?" The first question invites a range of possible answers; the second virtually dictates the response. According to a skilled practitioner:

> The open question is broad, the closed question narrow. The open question allows the interviewee full scope; the closed question limits him to a specific answer. The open question invites him to widen his perceptual field; the closed question curtails it. The open question solicits his views, opinions, thoughts, and feelings; the closed question usually demands cold facts only. The open question may widen and deepen the contact; the closed question may circumscribe it. In short, the former may widen the door to good rapport; the latter usually keeps it shut.[45]

In a similar fashion, questions should be designed to draw out assumptions and ensure that people are talking *to* one another rather than past each other. Discussions often founder needlessly because of unstated differences in meaning. Especially when groups span geographies or are composed of members with diverse backgrounds and experiences, even the simplest communication presents a challenge. Common problems include different uses of the same terms and different reference points. Lucent Technologies, for example, had considerable difficulty with a large software development project because programmers in New Jersey and Massachusetts used the word "test" so differently.[46] Lucent is hardly alone. Misinterpretation is distressingly common, as two classic studies of communication found:

> The one thing people tend to take for granted when talking to others is that they understand each other. It is rare, indeed, in a meeting to have someone hold up his own argument long enough to say, "I think you said . . . Did you?" or "Was I right in thinking you meant . . . ?" We found people ever so eager to parry what a man says without ever wondering whether *that* is what the man said.[47]
>
> People often think they disagree when actually they simply are not talking about the same experiences. In such cases they do not draw each other out far enough to realize that, although they are using the same *words,* they are thinking about different *experiences.*[48]

Such problems would disappear if discussion leaders, as well as participants, probed more actively for the roots of differing positions.

Questions are also powerful tools for overcoming the biases and learning disabilities described in chapter 2. By injecting contrary, divergent views into discussions, they broaden participants' field of view and counteract common errors. Groups are less likely to be blindsided by unforeseen events if they have tried to consider them in advance; individuals are less likely to be overconfident if they have faced humbling feedback or contradictory evidence.[49] Questions that produce such insights may take a variety of forms—counterfactuals, hypotheticals, even the illogical alternatives posed by Chuck Knight in his planning reviews. Here, a particularly useful questioning technique is the "pre-mortem," in which participants are asked to imagine, *before* a policy or practice is formally adopted, that time has elapsed, the approach has been introduced, and the results are extremely disappointing. They must then explain why. Researchers have found that this approach generates a longer list of potential weaknesses than traditional analysis, as well as more robust plans going forward. Looking back to the future—with what scholars call "prospective hindsight"—leads groups to imagine flaws more easily while generating richer, more concrete, often unanticipated insights.[50]

How, then, should executives develop these skills? Few managers are naturally talented at questioning; their training normally points them in other directions. To acquire the needed expertise, they have three main options: seeking instruction, learning through observation, and engaging in deliberate practice. Xerox used all three approaches in 1992. After a massive reorganization, members of the Corporate Office were having difficulty framing questions for the newly appointed business heads. They continued to delve into the same kinds of operational challenges as they had previously, even though they now needed to provide more strategic direction. To learn to ask the right questions, they requested that the director of strategy canvass the best strategic thinkers he could find—at leading consulting firms, as well as respected corporations—and ask them to identify the questions and frameworks they used when reviewing strategies, assessing markets, and evaluating competitors. Armed with these findings, they worked to develop an expanded vocabulary and better strategic insights. They then began to ask new and different questions of the business unit heads, leading to sharp improvements in their plans.[51]

Listening

Of course, skilled questioning is not enough to ensure that discussions are productive. If real learning is to occur, there must also be active listening. The two go hand in hand, like the blades of a scissors. Questioning generates the needed raw material, while listening ensures that it is put to good use. As chapter 3 pointed out, listening is a demanding process that requires attentiveness; it is not "just the act of keeping still."[52] Since this will occur only if one is "genuinely interested in what matters to the other person," attitude is as important as skill.[53] But like questioning, listening can usually by improved by following a few, simple guidelines.

Perhaps the most important is practicing patience. All too often, managers interrupt before others have finished, short-circuiting the learning process. They jump to conclusions, assuming that they have understood someone's position before receiving a full briefing. Or they project so much of their own thinking into the conversation that the original message is lost. This problem is hardly confined to business. A study of seventy-four medical interviews found that over two-thirds of the patients were interrupted by their doctors within the first eighteen seconds of beginning to explain what was wrong with them. Only one got to finish. Most doctors assumed that the first complaint they heard was the most important and designed their treatment accordingly. Yet when patients were given the chance to say everything on their mind, their third complaint was actually the most troubling.[54] The analogy to managers, particularly when they interact with subordinates and peers, should be clear. They too must remember that it is difficult to hear words that are left unsaid.

In the same spirit, executives must learn to listen for "disconnects" during discussion. Effective communication requires a strong link between source and receiver. As the writer Henry David Thoreau put it: "It takes two to speak truth—one to speak and another to hear."[55] But these connections take work, as well as empathy and rapport. Members of a group must be willing to suspend their preconceptions long enough to internalize what others are actually saying. Here, a useful technique for leaders is to insist that participants repeat what they have just heard and then to ask the original speaker to verify that his or her point has been correctly stated. Only after participants have agreed that the message has been heard is debate allowed to begin.

It should be clear that effective discussions require leaders who are able to listen at multiple levels. They must learn to attend—simultaneously—to *what* is being said and *how* it is stated. They must listen for affect and tone—"the tremulous voice, the stereotyped role . . . the angry, belittling response"—as carefully as they listen to content.[56] They must be vigilant in rooting out personal attacks that so often accompany substantive disagreements. Otherwise, discussions will quickly lose their value, and inquiries will become inquisitions. Unfortunately, "many people seem not to realize that it is possible to quarrel on an issue without . . . doubting another's sincerity or casting aspersions on his integrity."[57] It is up to leaders to make sure that the line is not crossed.

For similar reasons, they must remain on the lookout for nonparticipants—voices not heard—and must find ways of bringing them into the dialogue. Silence is not always a sign of assent; it can just as easily signal apathy or disaffection. Here, it is wise to heed the advice of Bob Galvin, who defined his role, in part, as "look[ing] for the unattended, the void, the exception that my associates are too busy to see."[58] Listening to these voices provided him with a window into his company's most pressing problems.

Responding

If leaders did no more than ask questions and listen for answers, many discussions would eventually bog down. Executives must also be able to respond—usually, on the spot and in real time. An issue is raised, an opinion is ventured, an argument breaks out, and all eyes turn to the most senior person in the room. How should she react if she hopes to stimulate learning? There are an almost infinite variety of choices, and many paths to success. But there are also a few practices that should be avoided at all costs because they are extremely damaging. Some create high levels of uncertainty and risk, others discourage dissenting or contradictory views, while still others condition speakers to clam up in the future. The results, in each case, are impediments to future participation.

Two of the most pernicious practices are "depreciation-of-the-learner" and "drowning-of-the-learner."[59] The former asserts an executive's superiority by dumping cold water on anyone else's comments; the latter asserts his expertise by responding to simple queries with prolonged, mind-numbing lectures. In both cases, further contributions are unlikely to be forthcoming. Dialogue disappears, and learning is severely hampered. This problem is not merely theoretical or confined to the classroom; it has been observed in a variety of real-world settings, with severe consequences. Studies of cockpit crews, for example, have found that insensitive, intimidating captains create a form of trained incapacity in their copilots and crew—an unwillingness to speak up even when faced with potentially dangerous situations. Several fatal crashes have been the result.[60]

To avoid these problems, executives need to broaden their repertoires. They need to approach responding as they approach questioning, with an arsenal of skills. No one technique is best, and each has its place. The possibilities can be arrayed on a spectrum, ranging from responses that are more reflective and speaker-centered to those that are more intrusive and interventionist (see Figure 6-1).[61] At one extreme are responses like silence, restatement, and clarification; they keep the focus on the speaker and encourage a more extended presentation. At the other end of the spectrum are responses like ridicule, denial, and threat; they involve the open use of power and invariably put distance between leaders and followers. Responses like encouragement and suggestion are somewhere in the middle; they remain upbeat and supportive in tone but inject a point of view. Also in the middle are responses like disagreement and criticism; they too inject a point of view but one that is opposed to the speaker's. The choice among these approaches is both situational and cultural; it reflects the issues at hand, as well as an organization's characteristic ways of acting and interacting. GE and Emerson Electric have flourished under leaders with a scrapping, combative style; Pepsi-Cola and Serengeti Eyewear have profited from leaders with a more supportive, accepting style. In general, however, when the goal is fostering

FIGURE 6-1

A SPECTRUM OF RESPONSES IN LEADING DISCUSSIONS

Response	Characteristic	Position on Spectrum
• Silence • Restatement • Clarification	Keeps the focus on the speaker	Reflective, facilitative
• Encouragement • Suggestion	Injects a supportive point of view	
• Disagreement • Criticism	Injects a negative point of view	
• Ridicule • Denial • Threat	Involves the open use of power or authority	Intrusive, interventionist

learning, executives should strive for more frequent use of responses at the reflective, facilitative end of the spectrum. Combative styles can be effective, but unless they are applied with great skill, they run the high risk of demoralizing employees.

Used properly, questioning, listening, and responding can generate discussions of real power. Learning blossoms in such settings, as the examples of Xerox, L.L. Bean, Allegheny Ludlum Steel, and the other organizations described earlier in this book suggest. In each case, group leaders strove to produce genuine thinking and debate, at the same time cultivating a collegial, collaborative atmosphere. The former kept ideas bubbling and in constant ferment, while the latter ensured that groups remained cohesive and were able to act decisively on their conclusions. As chapter 1 pointed out, both elements—reflection and action—are defining features of learning organizations. The combination is hard to find, for it requires discussions that are at once comfortable and contentious. David Hume, the Scottish philosopher, made much the same point over two hundred years ago, when he observed that "truth springs from arguments amongst friends."[62]

FROM ORGANIZATIONAL TO INDIVIDUAL LEARNING

We are left with a paradox. The preceding chapters have focused primarily on organizations and the processes they use to cultivate learning. Most examples have featured groups and teams but have said little about individuals. Yet, without individuals who learn, there can be no learning organizations.[63] They are necessary for success.[64] Typically, those individuals—operators, technicians, customer service representatives, supervisors, and managers—look to their leaders for models to imitate, especially when it comes to learning, where attitude and tone are set at the top. If senior executives are committed to personal improvement and growth, their employees are likely to feel much the same way. But if they shun new ideas and stick with outdated views, employees are likely to be closed and unyielding. As with all attempts to shape behavior, leaders must walk the talk if meaningful changes are to occur.

Unfortunately, in all too many organizations, those at the top stopped learning long ago. They continue to travel the same well-trod path. As a leading organizational consultant put it, only partly in jest: "Too many senior executives who have been on the job thirty years don't necessarily have thirty years of experience—they have more like one year of experience, thirty times."[65] For these executives, the first step in building a learning organization is a personal one: they need to develop their own skills as learners. There are four main requirements: openness to new perspectives, an awareness of personal biases, immersion in unfiltered data, and a growing sense of humility.

Openness to New Perspectives

Openness requires that leaders accept the provisional nature of knowledge. Even long established truths must eventually be revised and replaced. This principle has long been a staple of the sciences, and it applies equally well to business. In most cases, the best that we can expect from a theory—whether it is a cornerstone of biology or the foundation of a marketing strategy—"is that it should hold together long enough to lead us to a better one."[66] Such impermanence suggests the importance of repeatedly revisiting underlying assumptions. It also explains why executives need to be curious, open-minded learners. To remain current, they must continuously seek out competing concepts and evidence, wrestle with surprising and unfamiliar ideas, and consider new and unpopular points of view. Many executives think that they behave this way but fail to do so in practice. They suffer from a common problem: an excessively optimistic view of their own openness. As William James, the pragmatist philosopher, slyly observed: "A great many people think they are thinking when they are merely rearranging their prejudices."[67]

A good indicator of openness is one's attitude toward challenging questions. Do executives encourage subordinates to air dissenting views? Do they readily accept unsolicited suggestions? Do they carefully consider opposing positions? The presence of such dissonance is an important contributor to learning. But it should not be overdone. "Rates of disagreement and antagonism that are too high are sure indicators of trouble. Apparently, when ill feeling rises above some critical point, a 'chain reaction' or 'vicious circle' tends to set in."[68] Moderate levels of disagreement, which produce a manageable amount of debate, typically produce superior discussions. They are desirable for another reason as well. By increasing the amount of timely, diagnostic feedback, they contribute directly to improved performance. Leaders, however, must usually solicit that feedback, since it seldom arises spontaneously. In fact, a willingness to seek feedback from others is one of the hallmarks of experts in a variety of fields.[69]

A study of pilots found that those who were rated as outstanding "felt more strongly that first officers should be encouraged to question their decisions and that first officers should question decisions other than those that threaten the safety of flight. Pilots with below average performance held the opposite attitudes." In addition, superior pilots recognized that their decision-making abilities deteriorated in emergencies, increasing the likelihood that they would "become more receptive to inputs from others" when faced with stressful situations. Below average pilots were less receptive: they felt that there was no difference between their decision-making abilities in emergencies and routine conditions.[70] Again, the analogy to management should be clear. A genuine acceptance of differing views provides a lifeline in difficult times.

Another indicator of openness is the amount of exposure one has to unfamiliar, thought-provoking environments. Effective executives seek out these opportunities; they do not wait for challenging environments to come to them. As GE's businesses expanded globally, Jack Welch embarked on a series of around-the-world trips, where, for weeks at a time, he immersed himself in foreign cultures and climates. John McCoy of Banc One met personally with the heads of virtually all of the leading Internet portals before launching Wingspan, the company's foray into electronic banking. John Browne of British Petroleum joined the board of Intel to experience personally the ethos and decision-making style of Silicon Valley. Countless executives carry out benchmarking visits to see how other companies, often in radically different businesses and markets, conduct their work. Even participation in training programs, rotations, and special assignments can open managers' eyes if they stay long enough in challenging settings to question long-established routines.[71]

Awareness of Personal Biases

A second requirement for effective learning is an awareness of one's personal biases. These biases may appear as distinctive cognitive styles or as pervasive learning disabilities. The former are unique to individuals, while the latter are common to all. Each of us, for example, has our own, idiosyncratic cognitive style. It is neither right nor wrong but predisposes us to think in particular ways. In business settings, a cognitive style is simply "the way in which an executive . . . defines his informational needs for purposes of making decisions. . . . [It] also refers to his preferred ways of acquiring information from those around him and making use of that information, and to his preferences regarding advisers and ways of using them in making decisions."[72]

Some of us, for example, are readers, who like to absorb material in written form; others are talkers, who flesh out ideas by discussing them. Readers tend to prefer memos, while talkers tend to prefer meetings.[73] Some of us enjoy being immersed in the details; others are more interested in the big picture. Detail-oriented people tend to prefer reports that dig into the nitty-gritty, while big-picture people tend to prefer broad, sweeping narratives. Some of us are comfortable juggling many topics simultaneously; others like to stay focused on a single subject. Jugglers tend to prefer rich, multifaceted agendas, while focused individuals tend to prefer narrower, targeted meetings.[74] None of these approaches is inherently superior. But each comes with predictable strengths and weaknesses. At a minimum, leaders need to be aware of their preferred styles and should try to ensure that they fit well with the tasks at hand. Otherwise, their learning is likely to be extremely inefficient.

Nor are these the only biases that affect learning. Leaders must also strive consciously to counteract the common disabilities discussed in chapter 2. All of us are flawed statisticians, who commit a wide range of interpretative errors. We have trouble separating signals from noise, do a poor job estimating probabilities, rely on misleading rules of thumb, and are overcertain of our own understanding and skills. To combat these errors and improve the accuracy and quality of learning, experts use a variety of techniques that could be easily adopted by managers. They keep running lists of their predictions to overcome hindsight bias. They solicit critical feedback to combat overconfidence. They review flawed choices to uncover hidden assumptions. They enlist the help of coaches and third-party observers to ensure that their words match their deeds. They compile extensive experience banks to enrich their repertoire of analogies and increase their skill at pattern recognition. They use formal decision aids to calibrate their judgments and improve consistency.[75] All of these techniques are designed to heighten awareness and develop a more refined understanding of how decisions are actually made. Harvey Golub of American Express has long pursued the same goal. In his words:

> When you make a decision, you explain how you made it. . . . You do not rely on unconscious competence. I do everything inductively, so I have to force myself to become deductive in order to explain things. The struggle is to tease out the reasoning process and make it clear.[76]

Exposure to Unfiltered Data

A third requirement for leaders wishing to improve their learning is greater contact with raw, unfiltered data. Many executives are distressingly detached from the realities of their organizations. They rely on information that is prepackaged and highly compressed, making it difficult to interpret. According to a noted student of leadership:

As organizations (and societies) become larger and more complex, [those] at the top . . . depend less and less on first-hand experience, more and more on heavily "processed" data. Before reaching them, the raw data—what actually goes on "out there"—have been sampled, screened, condensed, compiled, coded, expressed in statistical form, spun into generalizations and crystallized into recommendations. . . .

But what does the information processing system filter out? It filters out all sensory impressions not readily expressed in words and numbers. It filters out emotion, feeling, sentiment, mood and . . . those intuitive judgments that are just below the level of consciousness. . . .

That is why every top executive . . . should periodically emerge from his world of abstractions and take a long unflinching look at unprocessed reality.[77]

Managers need to take charge of this process by finding ways of confronting, directly and experientially, the realities of organizational life: the stuff that goes on "out there." They need to tour factories, drop in on service centers, meet with disgruntled employees, and talk with customers. They need to "staple themselves to an order" or follow a product development process from beginning to end to see how the work really gets done.[78] They need to track, on a daily or weekly basis, bookings, billings, backlogs, receivables, inventory, and other real-time operational data, not simply aggregated financials.[79] Learning often improves markedly when executives return to the front lines and confront data in these tangible, concrete forms.

Why are these activities so important? Because, as Harvey Golub observed, "the first task of a leader is to define reality."[80] And leaders can do so only if they already possess a grounded, granular view of the challenges and opportunities facing their organizations. To develop that perspective, they often need to expose themselves to the same unwelcome story again and again. Repetition is a remarkably powerful technique for improving one's hearing.

It is for this reason that Zaki Mustafa, the vice president and general manager of Serengeti Eyewear, for many years spent about a third of his time on the road. Of that, 40 percent was spent visiting customers,

40 percent visiting suppliers, and the balance visiting Serengeti employees in the field. Other members of the senior team had similarly hectic
travel schedules. In addition, every four to six weeks, sales staff invited
different retailers to join them at Serengeti headquarters. All employees,
from Mustafa on down, were invited as well. The purpose of these meetings was to learn as much as possible about customers' products, organization, people, and needs, while also uncovering Serengeti's weaknesses.
Discussions were frank and covered a broad range of topics: What is your
business? What does your company do? How do you do it? What does
Serengeti do well? What does Serengeti need to improve on? Mustafa
was quite clear on the reasons why it was necessary to expose himself,
and others in the organization, to so much unfiltered data: "Our
presumption is that if you're going to make a decision, you need to
have first-hand information, because we want first-hand ownership and
results."[81]

A Sense of Humility

Finally, if they are to progress as learners, leaders need to develop a sense
of humility.[82] They must recognize that they do not have all the answers.
They must acknowledge that superior insights lie elsewhere—outside
their offices, and at times outside their organizations. They must become
skilled at defining the limits of their own knowledge. Learning, after all, is
a profession of faith in the future, an admission that progress is possible.
Senior managers at Xerox made this point explicitly when they observed,
in the midst of a lengthy change process, that "we are no longer the
organization we used to be and we are not yet the organization we intend
to be." The same can be said of most companies—and most executives.
Learning is the best way for both of them to bridge the gap.

Notes

Chapter 1: From Individual to Organizational Learning

1. See, for example, Erik H. Erikson, *Identity and the Life Cycle* (New York: W. W. Norton, 1980); Daniel J. Levenson et al., *The Seasons of a Man's Life* (New York: Ballantine Books, 1978); Morgan W. McCall, Jr., Michael M. Lombardo, and Ann M. Morrison, *The Lessons of Experience* (Lexington, MA: D. C. Heath, 1988); and Dennis O'Connor and Donald M. Wolfe, "From Crisis to Growth at Midlife: Changes in Personal Paradigm," *Journal of Organizational Behavior* 12 (1991): 323–340.

2. Allen Tough, *The Adult's Learning Projects,* 2d ed. (Toronto: The Ontario Institute for Studies in Education, 1979). Tough's samples were small but exceedingly broad, including professors, politicians, lower-level white-collar men, lower-level white-collar women, factory workers, teachers, and mothers. Such diversity suggests that learning projects are not confined to a single sector of the population. Subsequent studies have found somewhat lower numbers—three learning projects per year, each lasting fifty hours annually—but still support his basic finding of the pervasiveness of adult learning. See Ron Zemke and Susan Zemke, "Adult Learning: What Do We Know for Sure?" *Training* (June 1995): 31–40 for an update.

3. Edward Prewitt, "What Managers Should Know about How Adults Learn," *Management Update* 2 (January 1997): 5.

4. See, for example, Ronald Henkoff, "Companies That Train Best," *Fortune,* 22 March 1993, 62–75; Jeanne C. Meister, *Corporate Quality Universities* (Burr Ridge, IL: Richard D. Irwin, 1994); and Bruce A. Pasternack, Shelley S. Keller, and Albert J. Viscio,

"The Triumph of People Power and the New Economy," *Strategy & Business* 2d quarter (1997): 26–39.

5. Gordon R. Sullivan and Michael V. Harper, *Hope Is Not a Method* (New York: Times Business/Random House, 1996), 192.

6. Charles Handy, *The Age of Unreason* (Boston: Harvard Business School Press, 1989), 142.

7. Peter M. Senge, *The Fifth Discipline* (New York: Doubleday, 1990), 1.

8. Ikujiro Nonaka, "The Knowledge-Creating Company," *Harvard Business Review* 69 (November/December 1991): 97.

9. Aaron Wildavsky, "The Self-Evaluating Organization," *Public Administration Review* 32 (September/October 1972): 509, 513.

10. Ross Henderson, "A Management Program for Expedition and Control of Process Plant Startups," *Proceedings No. 52*, Institute of Electronic and Radio Engineers, December 1981, 127–145; Ross Henderson, "Prediction of Plant Startup Progress, Duration, and Lost Capacity," *International Journal of Operations and Production Management* 2 (1981): 14–28; and Ross Henderson, "Achieving Quality During Plant Startup," *Quality Progress* (May 1985): 36–40.

11. Gabriel Szulanski, "Intra-Firm Transfer of Best Practices Project: Executive Summary of the Findings," (Fontainebleau, France, and Houston, Texas: INSEAD and American Productivity & Quality Center, October 1994), photocopy; and Gabriel Szulanski, "Exploring Internal Stickiness: Impediments to the Transfer of Best Practice within the Firm," *Strategic Management Journal* 17 (Winter Special Issue, 1996): 27–43.

12. Craig S. Galbraith, "Transferring Core Manufacturing Technologies in High-Technology Firms," *California Management Review* (Summer 1990): 56–70.

13. Joseph Bower and Clayton M. Christensen, "Disruptive Technologies: Catching the Wave," *Harvard Business Review* 73 (January/February 1995): 43–53.

14. Michael Tushman and Charles A. O'Reilly III, "The Ambidextrous Organization," *California Management Review* 38 (Summer 1996): 1–3.

15. Andrew S. Grove, *Only the Paranoid Survive* (New York: Doubleday, 1996), 11–23.

16. This same point has been made, using different language, in James C. Collins and Jerry I. Porras, *Built to Last* (New York: HarperBusiness, 1994), especially ch. 4, 7.

17. Warren G. Bennis, "Toward a 'Truly' Scientific Management: The Concept of Organizational Health," *Industrial Management Review* (MIT) 4 (1962): 9.

18. Because of these diverse views, there is a long academic tradition of reviewing the literature on organizational learning. Well-known reviews include Chris Argyris and Donald A. Schön, *Organizational Learning: A Theory of Action Perspective* (Reading, MA: Addison-Wesley, 1978), 319–331; George P. Huber, "Organizational Learning: The Contributing Processes and the Literatures," *Organization Science* 2 (February 1991): 88–115; Barbara Levitt and James G. March, "Organizational Learning," *Annual Review of Sociology* 14 (1988): 319–340; Anne S. Miner and Stephen J. Mezias, "Ugly Duckling No More: Pasts and Futures of Organizational Learning Research," *Organization Science* 7 (1996): 88–99; and Paul Shrivastava, "A Typology of Organizational Learning Systems," *Journal of Management Studies* 20 (1983): 7–28.

19. Noel M. Tichy and Ram Charan, "Speed, Simplicity, and Self-Confidence: An Interview with Jack Welch," *Harvard Business Review* 67 (September/October 1989): 118.

For further details on Work-Out, see Noel M. Tichy and Stratford Sherman, *Control Your Own Destiny or Someone Else Will* (New York: HarperBusiness, 1994), 237–259.

20. Some of these litmus tests first appeared in P. Ranganath Nayak, David A. Garvin, Arun N. Maira, and Joan L. Brager, "Creating a Learning Organization," *Prism* 3d quarter (1996): 28–29.

21. David Nadler, "Even Failures Can Be Productive," *New York Times,* 23 April 1989, section 3, p. 3.

22. Myra M. Hart and Hugo Uyterhoeven, "Banc One–1993," Case 9-394-043 (Boston: Harvard Business School, 1993), 4.

Chapter 2: The Learning Process

1. The concept of routines, also known as "standard operating procedures," has long been associated with the behavioral theory of the firm. See, for example, Richard M. Cyert and James G. March, *The Behavioral Theory of the Firm* (Englewood Cliffs, NJ: Prentice-Hall, 1963), 101–103; Barbara Levitt and James G. March, "Organizational Learning," *Annual Review of Sociology* 14 (1998): 319–340; and James G. March and Herbert A. Simon, *Organizations,* 2d ed. (Cambridge, MA: Blackwell, 1993), 160–161.

2. These frameworks go by various names, including perceptual filters, organizational frames of reference, and mental models. See, for example, William H. Starbuck and Frances J. Milliken, "Executives' Perceptual Filters: What They Notice and How They Make Sense," in Donald C. Hambrick, ed., *The Executive Effect* (Greenwich, CT: JAI Press, 1988), 35–65; Paul Shrivastava and Ian I. Mitroff, "Nonrationality in Organizational Actions," *International Studies of Management & Organization* 17 (1987): 90–109; and Peter M. Senge, *The Fifth Discipline* (New York: Doubleday, 1990), ch. 10.

3. The quotation is from Albert Szent-Gyorgyi, who won a Nobel Prize for studies showing that vitamin C prevents oxidation, and is cited in Robert Scott Root-Bernstein, *Discovering* (Cambridge: Harvard University Press, 1989), 186.

4. For example, scholars have described the learning process in the following terms: scanning, interpretation, and learning; hypothesizing, exposure, encoding, and integration; generating, integrating, interpreting, and acting; and observing, assessing, designing, and implementing. These examples are taken, respectively, from Richard L. Daft and Karl E. Weick, "Toward a Model of Organizations as Interpretation Systems," *Academy of Management Review* 9 (1984): 284–295; Stephen J. Hoch and John Deighton, "Managing What Consumers Learn from Experience," *Journal of Marketing* 53 (1989): 1–20; Nancy Dixon, *The Organizational Learning Cycle* (London: McGraw-Hill International, 1994), ch 4; and Daniel H. Kim, "The Link between Individual and Organizational Learning," *Sloan Management Review* (Fall 1993): 37–50. Other studies with similar descriptions of the learning process include David A. Kolb, *Experiential Learning* (Englewood Cliffs, NJ: Prentice-Hall, 1984), ch. 2; Arie de Geus, *The Living Company* (Boston: Harvard Business School Press, 1997), ch. 4; Stephan H. Haeckel and Richard L. Nolan, "Managing by Wire," *Harvard Business Review* 71 (September/October 1993): 122–132; and Charles Handy, *The Age of Unreason* (Boston: Harvard Business School Press, 1989), ch. 3.

5. For representative definitions, see Roberta Wohlstetter*, Pearl Harbor: Warning and Decision* (Stanford, CA: Stanford University Press, 1962), 1–3; Roger E. Bohn, "Learning by Experimentation in Manufacturing," working paper 88-001, Harvard Business

School, Boston, MA, 10; and Starbuck and Milliken, "Executives' Perceptual Filters," 40–46.

6. Wohlsetter, *Pearl Harbor*, 386–387.

7. Ibid., 387–388.

8. Diane Vaughan, "The Trickle-Down Effect: Policy Decisions, Risky Work, and the *Challenger* Tragedy," *California Management Review* 39 (Winter 1997): 86–87. For a more detailed discussion, see Diane Vaughan, *The Challenger Launch Decision* (Chicago: University of Chicago Press, 1996), especially ch. 7.

9. Roger E. Bohn, "Noise and Learning in Semiconductor Manufacturing," *Management Science* 41 (January 1995): 31, 38. See also Roger E. Bohn, "The Impact of Process Noise on VLSI Process Improvement," *IEEE Transactions on Semiconductor Manufacturing* 8 (August 1995): 228–238.

10. Starbuck and Milliken, "Executives' Perceptual Filters," 40.

11. For discussions of the role of hypotheses in information acquisition, see Berndt Brehmer, "In One Word: Not from Experience," *Acta Psychologica* 45 (1980): 223–241; Hoch and Deighton, "Managing What Consumers Learn from Experience," 3–6; and Judith E. Tschirgi, "Sensible Reasoning: A Hypothesis about Hypotheses," *Child Development* 51 (1980): 1–10.

12. Sara Kiesler and Lee Sproull, "Managerial Response to Changing Environments: Perspectives on Problem Sensing from Social Cognition," *Administrative Science Quarterly* 27 (1982): 559.

13. Rohit Deshpande and Gerald Zaltman, "Factors Affecting the Use of Market Research Information: A Path Analysis," *Journal of Marketing Research* 19 (February 1982): 14–31; Rohit Deshpande and Gerald Zaltman, "A Comparison of Factors Affecting Researcher and Manager Perceptions of Market Research Use," *Journal of Marketing Research* 21 (February 1984): 32–38; and George S. Day, "Continuous Learning about Markets," *California Management Review* 39 (Summer 1994): 9–31.

14. Karl E. Weick and Richard L. Daft, "The Effectiveness of Interpretation Systems," in K. S. Cameron and D. A. Whetten, eds., *Organizational Effectiveness* (New York: Academic Press, 1983), 74.

15. For introductions to schemas, scripts, and other interpretive frameworks, see Daft and Weick, "Toward a Model of Organizations as Interpretation Systems," 284–295; Dennis A. Gioia, "Symbols, Scripts, and Sensemaking," in Henry P. Sims Jr., Dennis A. Gioia, and associates, eds., *The Thinking Organization* (San Francisco: Jossey-Bass, 1986) 49–75; Kiesler and Sproull, "Managerial Responses to Changing Environments," 556–558; Starbuck and Milliken, "Executives' Perceptual Filters," 51–52; James P. Walsh, "Managerial and Organizational Cognition: Notes from a Trip Down Memory Lane," *Organization Science* 6 (May/June 1995): 280–321; and Weick and Daft, "The Effectiveness of Interpretation Systems," 84–85.

16. Peter F. Drucker, "The Theory of the Business," *Harvard Business Review* 72 (September/October 1994): 95–104.

17. Weick and Daft, "The Effectiveness of Interpretation Systems," 76.

18. Ibid., 82–87.

19. David A. Garvin, "How the Baldrige Award Really Works," *Harvard Business Review* 69 (November/December 1991): 93.

20. Grove, *Only the Paranoid Survive*, 20–21.

21. Lee S. Sproull and Kay Ramsay Hofmeister, "Thinking about Implementation," *Journal of Management* 12 (1986): 58.

22. Claudia H. Deutsch, "Competitors Can Teach You a Lot, but the Lessons Can Hurt," *New York Times*, 18 July 1999, sec. 2, p. 4.

23. Michael E. Porter, *Competitive Strategy* (New York: Free Press, 1980), 59.

24. Shaker A. Zahra and Sherry B. Chaples, "Blind Spots in Competitive Analysis," *Academy of Management Executive* 7 (1993): 9–12. For a discussion of other blind spots in competitive decision making, including capacity expansion and new business entry decisions, see Edward J. Zajac and Max H. Bazerman, "Blind Spots in Industry and Competitor Analysis: Implications of Interfirm (Mis)Perceptions for Strategic Decisions," *Academy of Management Review* 16 (1991): 37–56.

25. Scholars have named this phenomenon the "threat-rigidity effect." See Barry M. Staw, Lance E. Sandelands, and Jane E. Dutton, "Threat-Rigidity Effects in Organizational Behavior: A Multilevel Analysis," *Administrative Science Quarterly* 26 (1981): 501–524.

26. Hugo Uyterhoeven, "Phil Knight: Managing Nike's Transformation," Case 9–394-012 (Boston: Harvard Business School, 1993), 2.

27. Starbuck and Milliken, "Executives' Perceptual Filters," 40–46.

28. Charles G. Lord, Lee Ross, and Mark R. Lepper, "Biased Assimilation and Attitude Polarization: The Effects of Prior Theories on Subsequently Considered Evidence," *Journal of Personality and Social Psychology* 37 (1979): 2098–2109.

29. Karl E. Weick, "The Vulnerable System: An Analysis of the Tenerife Air Disaster," *Journal of Management* 16 (1990): 583–585.

30. Thomas H. Davenport, Robert G. Eccles, and Laurence Prusak, "Information Politics," *Sloan Management Review* 34 (Fall 1992): 53–65.

31. Jack L. Engledow and R. T. Lenz, "Whatever Happened to Environmental Analysis?" *Long Range Planning* 18 (April 1985): 98–99.

32. Levitt and March, "Organizational Learning," 323.

33. The problem is certainly not confined to managers. Clinical psychologists and doctors, for example, suffer from many of the same biases. Even statisticians are not immune. For a summary of the findings on the first two groups, see Lewis R. Goldberg, "Simple Models or Simple Processes? Some Research on Clinical Judgments," *American Psychologist* 23 (1968): 483–496. For a series of experiments involving statisticians, see Hillel J. Einhorn and Robin M. Hogarth, "Confidence in Judgment: Persistence of the Illusion of Validity," *Psychological Review* 85 (1978): 395–416.

34. On illusory correlation and illusory causation, see Kiesler and Sproull, "Managerial Responses to Changing Environments," 553–554; and David L. Hamilton and Terrence L. Rose, "Illusory Correlation and the Maintenance of Stereotypical Beliefs," *Journal of Personality and Social Psychology* 39 (1980): 832–845. On the illusion of validity, see Einhorn and Hogarth, "Confidence in Judgment," 395–416; and Goldberg, "Simple Models or Simple Processes?" 483–496. On framing effects, see Amos Tversky and Daniel Kahneman, "Rational Choice and the Framing of Decisions," *Journal of Business* 59 (1986), part 2, S254–S257. On categorical bias, see J. M. Feldman, "Beyond Attribution Theory: Cognitive Processes in Performance Appraisal," *Journal of Applied Psychology* 66 (1981): 127–148; and Hamilton and Rose, "Illusory Correlation

and the Maintenance of Stereotypical Beliefs," 832–845. On availability bias, see Amos Tversky and Daniel Kahneman, "Judgment under Uncertainty: Heuristics and Biases," *Science* 185 (1974): 1127–1128. On regression artifacts, see Donald T. Campbell, "Reforms as Experiments," *American Psychologist* 24 (1969): 409–429; and Thomas D. Cook and Donald T. Campbell, *Quasi-Experimentation* (Boston: Houghton Mifflin, 1979), 99–103. On hindsight bias, see Baruch Fischhoff, "Hindsight ≠ Foresight: The Effect of Outcome Knowledge on Judgment under Uncertainty," *Journal of Experimental Psychology: Human Perception and Performance* 1 (1975): 288–299; and Baruch Fischhoff and Ruth Beyth, "'I Knew It Would Happen': Remembered Probabilities of Once-Future Things," *Organizational Behavior and Human Performance* 13 (1975): 1–16.

35. S. Oskamp, "Overconfidence in Case-Study Judgments," *Journal of Consulting Psychology* 29 (1965): 264. Italics in original.

36. Ed Bukszar and Terry Connolly, "Hindsight Bias and Strategic Choice: Some Problems in Learning from Experience," *Academy of Management Journal* 31 (1988): 635, 637.

37. Fischhoff and Beyth, "'I Knew It Would Happen,'" 13.

38. "Jack Welch's Lessons for Success," *Fortune*, 25 January 1993, 88.

39. Chris Argyris and Donald Schön, *Theory in Practice* (San Francisco: Jossey-Bass, 1974), 7.

40. Frank Friedlander, "Patterns of Individual and Organizational Learning," in Suresh Srivastava and associates, *The Executive Mind* (San Francisco: Jossey-Bass, 1983), 192–220.

41. Janet Simpson, Lee Field, and David Garvin, "The Boeing 767: From Concept to Production (A)," Case 9-688-040 (Boston: Harvard Business School, 1988), 9.

42. Charles F. Knight, "Emerson Electric: Consistent Profits, Consistently," *Harvard Business Review* 70 (January/February 1992): 62.

43. Kathleen M. Eisenhardt, Jean L. Kahwajy, and L. J. Bourgeois III, "Conflict and Strategic Choice: How Top Management Teams Disagree," *California Management Review* 39 (Winter 1997): 42–62; and Kathleen M. Eisenhardt, Jean L. Kahwajy, and L. J. Bourgeois III, "How Top Management Teams Can Have a Good Fight," *Harvard Business Review* 75 (July/August 1997): 77–85.

44. For an introduction to these techniques, see David M. Schweiger, William R. Sandberg, and James W. Ragan, "Group Approaches for Improving Strategic Decision Making: A Comparative Analysis of Dialectical Inquiry, Devil's Advocacy, and Consensus," *Academy of Management Journal* 29 (1986): 51–71.

45. Irving Janis, *Victims of Groupthink* (Boston: Houghton Mifflin, 1972), 147–149.

46. Jack Feldman, "On the Difficulty of Learning from Experience," in Sims, Gioia, and associates, *The Thinking Organization*, 281.

47. Hart and Uyterhoeven, "Banc One–1993," 11.

48. These results were achieved between 1983 and 1992. In the mid-1990s, Banc One changed its approach, moving to a more centralized model to take advantage of the scale economies and consolidations that were reshaping the banking industry. For updates, see Saul Hansell, "Banc One Lives Up to Its Name," *New York Times*, 12 May 1995, D1, D4; Thomas N. Urban and James L. Heskett, "Banc One–1996," Case 9-396-315 (Boston: Harvard Business School 1996); and Matt Murray, "After Long

Overhaul, Banc One Now Faces Pressure to Perform," *Wall Street Journal,* 10 March 1998, A1, A10.

49. Dixon, *The Organizational Learning Cycle,* 96–97.

50. William Keenan Jr., "How GE Stays on Top of Its Markets," *Sales & Marketing Management* (August 1994): 61. Also see Richard J. Babyak, "Marketing with a Vision," *Appliance Manufacturer* (July 1995): GEA-8–GEA-10.

51. Gordon E. Forward, "Wide-Open Management at Chaparral Steel," *Harvard Business Review* 64 (May/June 1986): 96–102; Dorothy Leonard-Barton, "The Factory as a Learning Laboratory," *Sloan Management Review* 34 (fall 1992): 23–38; and "Chaparral Steel (Abridged)," Case 9-687-045 (Boston: Harvard Business School, 1987).

52. Joe McGowan, "How Disney Keeps Ideas Coming," *Fortune,* 1 April 1996, 131–134.

53. Robin Cooper and M. Lynne Markus, "Human Reengineering," *Sloan Management Review* 36 (Summer 1995): 46.

54. Edgar H. Schein, "How Can Organizations Learn Faster? The Challenge of Entering the Green Room," *Sloan Management Review* 34 (Winter 1993): 89. Also see Amy Edmondson, "Psychological Safety and Learning Behavior in Work Teams," *Administrative Science Quarterly* 44 (Summer 1999): 350–383.

55. Robert I. Sutton and Andrew Hargadon, "Brainstorming Groups in Context: Effectiveness in a Product Design Firm," *Administrative Science Quarterly* 41 (1996): 706.

56. Thomas A. Stewart, "3M Fights Back," *Fortune,* 5 February 1996, 94–99.

57. Feldman, "On the Difficulty of Learning from Experience," 283.

58. Lisa Belkin, "How Can We Save the Next Victim?" *New York Times Magazine,* 15 June 1997, 44. The quotation is from David Woods, a professor of cognitive systems engineering at Ohio State University.

59. Warren Bennis and Burt Nanus, *Leaders* (New York: Harper & Row, 1985), 76.

60. Amy C. Edmondson, "Learning from Mistakes Is Easier Said Than Done: Group and Organizational Influences on the Detection and Correction of Human Error," *Journal of Applied Behavioral Science* 32 (March 1996): 5–28.

61. Michal Tamuz, "The Impact of Computer Surveillance on Air Safety Reporting," *Columbia Journal of World Business* 22 (1987): 69–77; and Charles Perrow, *Normal Accidents* (New York: Basic Books, 1984), 168–169.

62. Atul Gawande, "When Doctors Make Mistakes," *The New Yorker,* 1 February 1999, 40–55.

63. Peter J. Frost, "Crossroads: Bridging Academia and Business: A Conversation with Steve Kerr," *Organization Science* 8 (May/June 1997): 335.

Chapter 3: Intelligence

1. P. B. Medawar, *Advice to a Young Scientist* (New York: Harper Colophon, 1979), 18.

2. There are strong parallels between this progression and the distinction that scholars have made between "exploitation" and "exploration." Much of that discussion has appeared in comparisons of evolutionary and revolutionary change. See, for example, Michael L. Tushman and Charles A. O'Reilly III, *Winning through Innovation* (Boston: Harvard Business School Press, 1997).

3. Richard E. Combs and John D. Moorhead, *The Competitive Intelligence Handbook* (Metuchen, NJ: Scarecrow Press, 1992), 3. Combs and Moorhead focus primarily on collecting publicly held information but also discuss a number of other broader definitions.

4. For brief histories, see Allen Dulles, *The Craft of Intelligence* (New York: Harper & Row, 1963), ch. 2 and 3; and Richard Eels and Peter Nehemkis, *Corporate Intelligence and Espionage* (New York: Macmillan, 1984), ch. 2.

5. Herbert O. Yardley, *The American Black Chamber* (Indianapolis: Bobbs-Merrill, 1931).

6. Dulles, *The Craft of Intelligence*, 71, 75–76; and Eels and Nehemkis, *Corporate Intelligence and Espionage*, 30.

7. Shari Caudron, "I Spy, You Spy," *Industry Week*, 3 October 1994, 35–40; and "They Snoop to Conquer," *Business Week*, 28 October 1996, 172–176.

8. Larry Kahaner, *Competitive Intelligence* (New York: Simon & Schuster, 1996), 15.

9. Francis Joseph Aguilar, *Scanning the Business Environment* (New York: Macmillan, 1967), 19–20; Sumantra Ghoshal, "Environmental Scanning: An Individual and Organizational Level Analysis" (Ph. D. diss., Sloan School of Management, MIT, May 1985), 205–206; and Sumantra Ghoshal, "Environmental Scanning in Korean Firms: Organizational Isomorphism in Action," *Journal of International Business Studies* (Spring 1988): 72.

10. Aguilar, *Scanning the Business Environment*, ch. 4; John P. Kotter, *The General Managers* (New York: Free Press, 1982), ch. 4; and Henry Mintzberg, *The Nature of Managerial Work* (New York: Harper & Row, 1973), ch. 3.

11. For lists of potential sources, see Leonard M. Fuld, *Monitoring the Competition* (New York: John Wiley & Sons, 1988), ch. 2; and Kahaner, *Competitive Intelligence*, ch. 6.

12. On Coors, see Kahaner, *Competitive Intelligence*, 58–59. On the food-packaging company, see Richard S. Teitelbaum, "The New Race for Intelligence," *Fortune*, 2 November 1992, 106.

13. Herbert E. Meyer, *Real-World Intelligence* (New York: Grove Weidenfeld, 1987), 60–61.

14. Kahaner, *Competitive Intelligence*, 24; and Teitelbaum, "The New Race for Intelligence," 104–105.

15. Ghoshal, "Environmental Scanning in Korean Firms," 75–77.

16. Allen C. Bluedorn et al., "The Interface and Convergence of the Strategic Management and Organizational Environment Domains," *Journal of Management* 20 (1994): 211–219; Sumantra Ghoshal, "Environmental Scanning: An Individual and Organizational Level Analysis," 213–215; and Kathleen M. Sutcliffe, "What Executives Notice: Accurate Perceptions in Top Management Teams," *Academy of Management Journal* 37 (1994): 1360–1378.

17. "They Snoop to Conquer," 172. The estimate comes from David H. Harkerload, director of business intelligence for the Futures Group, Inc.

18. Aguilar, *Scanning the Business Environment*, 60.

19. Meryl Reis Louis and Robert I. Sutton, "Switching Cognitive Gears: From Habits of Mind to Active Thinking," *Human Relations* 44 (1991): 55–76.

20. Jack L. Engledow and R. T. Lenz, "Whatever Happened to Environmental Analysis?" *Long Range Planning* 18 (1985): 99. For additional evidence, see Subhash C. Jain,

"Environmental Scanning in U.S. Corporations," *Long Range Planning* 17 (1984): 126–127.

21. The Xerox story is drawn primarily from personal interviews conducted in 1992 and 1993 with Xerox's senior managers and internal company documents. I am especially grateful to William Buehler, senior vice president, for arranging and coordinating my visits and providing essential background information (11 May 1992 and 16 June 1992), and to Roger Levien, Xerox's vice president of corporate strategy during the 1980s and 1990s, for interviews (16 June 1992, 4 August 1992, and 29 April 1997) and access to unpublished material. The few public accounts focus on Xerox '92 and Xerox '95. They include Carol Kennedy, "Xerox Charts a New Strategic Direction," *Long Range Planning* 22 (1989): 10–17; Roger E. Levien, "Making Strategic Concepts Work," in Kenneth C. Laudon and Jon A. Turner, eds., *Information Technology and Management Strategy* (Englewood Cliffs, NJ: Prentice Hall, 1989), ch. 4; and David A. Nadler, *Champions of Change* (San Francisco: Jossey-Bass, 1998), ch. 8.

22. Because the studies were forward-looking, they were named for the year at the end of the decade ahead, not the year in which the study was conducted. Thus, Xerox '92 was conducted in 1982, Xerox '95 was conducted in 1985, etc.

23. The conceptual model involved two equations:
    Aggregate market size = economics + demographics ± social forces + technology
    and
    Xerox revenues and share of market = aggregate market size ± government policy – competition
    Plus signs indicated a positive influence on market size or revenues, minus signs indicated a negative influence, and plus/minus signs indicated that the influence might go in either direction, depending on the particular forces or policies at work. The entire analysis was conducted by products and regions, showing expected growth and revenues in a more segmented fashion.

24. There are two competing descriptions of the BMW option. Both are from insiders. The one included here follows Levien; it is drawn from my interview notes plus a brief discussion in Kennedy, "Xerox Charts a New Strategic Direction," 16. A second version appears in Nadler, *Champions of Change*, 167–168; it focuses more on technological superiority. From these accounts, it is impossible to tell which version is correct.

25. This problem appears in many settings. For example, a leading political scientist has observed of foreign policy disputes that "participants in these policy debates may not be fully aware of the fact that their specific disagreement over a policy rests fundamentally on different images of the opponent. When this is the case, participants in the policy discussion may fail to come to grips with the root issue." See Alexander L. George, *Presidential Decisionmaking in Foreign Policy* (Boulder, CO: Westview Press, 1980), 71.

26. Scholars have drawn similar conclusions. Students of strategic planning, for example, have argued that "most strategy differences are caused by differences in fundamental assumptions about the nature of the problem—not facts about the viability of a particular solution." See James R. Emshoff and Ian I. Mitroff, "Improving the Effectiveness of Corporate Planning," *Business Horizons* (October 1978): 55.

27. Irving L. Janis, *Crucial Decisions* (New York: Free Press, 1989), ch. 2.

28. T. Wonnacott and R. Wonnacott, *Introductory Statistics for Business and Economics,* 3d ed. (New York: John Wiley, 1984), 4.

29. Jeffrey Durgee, "New Product Ideas from Focus Groups," *Journal of Consumer Marketing* 4 (Fall 1987), 58.

30. Jeffrey A. Trachtenberg, "Listening, the Old-Fashioned Way," *Forbes,* 5 October 1987, 204.

31. For discussions of research designs and alternative approaches to data collection, see David A. Aaker and George S. Day, *Marketing Research,* 2d ed. (New York: John Wiley & Sons, 1983); and Gilbert A. Churchill Jr., *Marketing Research: Methodological Foundations,* 5th ed. (Chicago: Dryden Press, 1991).

32. For an example of a poorly worded questionnaire that includes many of these problems, see Philip Kotler, *Principles of Marketing,* 3d ed. (Englewood Cliffs, NJ: Prentice-Hall, 1986), 106–107.

33. These terms are drawn from marketing research. Both approaches are discussed at length in Aaker and Day, *Marketing Research,* 49–51; and Churchill, *Marketing Research: Methodological Foundations,* 128–130. Note that both texts also list a third approach, causal research, which is used to determine cause-and-effect relationships. It is discussed at length in chapter 5 of this book, when experimental methods are introduced.

34. John Koten, "You Aren't Paranoid If You Feel Someone Eyes You Constantly," *Wall Street Journal,* 29 March 1985, 1, 22.

35. Durgee, "New Product Ideas from Focus Groups," 57–59.

36. Howard Gardner, *Leading Minds* (New York: Basic Books, 1995), ch. 1–3; Roger Schank, *Virtual Learning* (New York: McGraw-Hill, 1997), 20–22, 32–33; and Helen B. Schwartzmann, *Ethnography in Organizations* (Newbury Park, CA: SAGE, 1993), 60–63.

37. Schwartzmann, *Ethnography in Organizations,* 54–63.

38. Mason Haire, "Projective Techniques in Marketing Research," *Journal of Marketing* 14 (April 1950): 650.

39. Ibid., 649–656.

40. Herman B. Leonard, "With Open Ears: Listening and the Art of Discussion Leading," in C. Roland Christensen, David A. Garvin, and Ann Sweet, eds., *Education for Judgment* (Boston: Harvard Business School Press, 1991), 139.

41. Norman R. Augustine, *Augustine's Laws* (New York: Penguin, 1987), 465.

42. The L.L. Bean story is drawn primarily from interviews conducted with nearly a dozen researchers, marketers, and product developers in February and March 1997, as well as unpublished company documents. Several discussion groups and work sessions were observed and filmed during the same period. Excerpts from that footage appear in the videotape *Working Smarter: Redesigning Product/Service Development* (Boston: Harvard Business School Video, 1997).

43. Eric von Hippel, "Lead Users: A Source of Novel Product Ideas," *Management Science* 32 (June 1986), 796.

44. Scholars use the term "triangulation" to describe the combining of research techniques when studying the same phenomenon. See Todd D. Jick, "Mixing Qualitative and Quantitative Methods: Triangulation in Action," *Administrative Science Quarterly* 24 (1979): 602–611.

45. The technique was originally described by Gary Burchill in his MIT doctoral disserta-

tion and draws heavily on earlier work in total quality management by Professors Noriaki Kano, Jiro Kawakita, and Shoji Shiba of Japan. Today, the term is a trademark of the Center for Quality of Management (CQM). Burchill worked for CQM and served as a consultant to L.L. Bean during the company's first experiences with concept engineering; design teams at Bean have subsequently refined and modified the approach. See Gary M. Burchill, "Concept Engineering: An Investigation of TIME vs. MARKET Orientation in Product Concept Development," (Ph.D. diss., Sloan School of Management, MIT, June 1993); and Center for Quality of Management, *Concept Engineering* (Cambridge, MA: Center for Quality of Management, 1995).

46. Clifford Geertz, *The Interpretation of Cultures* (New York: Basic Books, 1973), 28.

47. Technically, the team is constructing an "affinity diagram." For a complete description of the approach, including the silent clustering of ideas, see Michael Brassard, *The Memory Jogger Plus+*™ (Methuen, MA: GOAL/QPC, 1989), ch. 1.

48. Dorothy Leonard and Jeffrey F. Rayport, "Spark Innovation through Empathic Design," *Harvard Business Review* 75 (November/December 1997): 105–107.

49. Michael Polanyi, *The Tacit Dimension* (New York: Anchor Books, 1966), 4.

50. John Seely Brown, "Research That Reinvents the Corporation," *Harvard Business Review* 69 (January/February 1991): 108.

51. Paul Cornell and Pam Brenner, "Field Test Learning . . . Creating Knowledge," <http://www.steelcase.com>.

52. Brigitte Jordan, "Notes on Methods for the Study of Work Practices" Palo Alto, CA (Institute for Research on Learning and Xerox Palo Alto Research Center, undated, photocopy); Louise H. Kidder and Charles M. Judd, with Eliot R. Smith, *Research Methods in Social Relations*, 5th ed. (New York: Holt, Rinehart & Winston, 1986), ch. 8; Maurice Punch, *The Politics and Ethics of Field Work* (Beverly Hills, CA: SAGE, 1986), ch. 1 and 2; Leonard Schatzman and Anselm L. Strauss, *Field Research* (Englewood Cliffs, NJ: Prentice-Hall, 1973); James P. Spradley, *Participant Observation* (New York: Holt, Rinehart & Winston, 1980); and William Foote Whyte, *Street Corner Society*, 3d ed. (Chicago: University of Chicago Press, 1981), appendix A.

53. Schatzman and Strauss, *Field Research*, 22. Italics in original.

54. Yogi Berra, *The Yogi Book* (New York: Workman, 1998), 95. Berra was a baseball player renowned for his humorous, inconsistent, and often redundant sayings.

55. W. I. B. Beveridge, *The Art of Scientific Investigation* (New York: Vintage Books, 1957), 132.

56. Ibid., 69.

57. Schatzman and Strauss, *Field Research*, 54.

58. Ibid., 54.

59. Whyte, *Street Corner Society*, 303.

60. Kidder and Judd, *Research Methods in Social Relations*, 171–173; Schatzman and Strauss, *Field Research*, 58–63; and Spradley, *Participant Observation*, 58–62.

61. Lance Ealey and Leif G. Soderberg, "How Honda Cures 'Design Amnesia,'" *McKinsey Quarterly* (Spring 1990), 7.

62. Koten, "You Aren't Paranoid If You Feel Someone Eyes You Constantly," 22.

63. Karen Holtzblatt and Sandra Jones, "Contextual Inquiry: A Participatory Technique for System Design," in Douglas Schuler and Aki Namioka, eds., *Participatory Design* (Hillsdale, NJ: Lawrence Erlbaum, 1993), ch. 9.

64. Jonathan West and David A. Garvin, "Serengeti Eyewear: Entrepreneurship within Corning Inc.," Case 9-394-033 (Boston: Harvard Business School, 1993), 6.

65. Punch, *The Politics and Ethics of Field Work,* 17.

66. The CALL story is drawn primarily from interviews conducted with Colonel Orin A. Nagel, director, Center for Army Lessons Learned, in November 1994 and December 1995, and U.S. Army, "A Guide to the Services of CALL," 29 February 1996 <http://call.army.mil/call/handbook/96-2/calltoc.htm>. Portions of the second Nagel interview, plus footage from CALL's activities in Haiti and Bosnia, appear in the videotape *Putting the Learning Organization to Work: Learning After Doing* (Boston: Harvard Business School Video, 1996). Other sources include Lloyd Baird, John C. Henderson, and Stephanie Watts, "Learning from Action: An Analysis of the Center for Army Lessons Learned (CALL)," *Human Resource Management* 36 (1997): 385–395; John C. Henderson and Stephanie A. Watts, "Creating and Exploiting Knowledge for Fast-Cycle Response: An Analysis of the Center for Army Lessons Learned," (Boston, MA, Boston University, undated, photocopy); Thomas E. Ricks, "Army Devises System to Decide What Does and Does Not Work," *Wall Street Journal,* 23 May 1997, A1, A10; and Gordon R. Sullivan and Michael V. Harper, *Hope Is Not a Method* (New York: Times Business/Random House, 1996), 204–210.

Chapter 4: Experience

1. Bertrand Russell, *The Problems of Philosophy* (London: Oxford University Press, 1912), 73–74.

2. John Dewey, *Experience and Education* (New York: Collier, 1938), 25.

3. John Dewey, *Democracy and Education* (New York: Free Press, 1916), 154.

4. Reginald W. Revans, *The Origins and Growth of Action Learning* (Lund, Sweden: Studentlitteratur, 1982).

5. Gordon H. Bower and Ernest R. Hilgard, *Theories of Learning,* 5th ed. (Englewood Cliffs, NJ: Prentice-Hall, 1981), 9–11.

6. John Seely Brown, Allen Collins, and Paul Duguid, "Situated Cognition and the Culture of Learning," *Educational Researcher* (January/February 1989): 32–42; Robert Glaser, "Education and Thinking: The Role of Knowledge," *American Psychologist* 39 (1984): 93–104; and J. Willems, "Problem-Based (Group) Teaching: A Cognitive Science Approach to Using Available Knowledge," *Instructional Science* 10 (1981): 5–21.

7. Lauren B. Resnick, *Education and Learning to Think* (Washington, DC: National Academy Press, 1987), 18.

8. Wesley M. Cohen and Daniel A. Levinthal, "Absorptive Capacity: A New Perspective on Learning and Innovation," *Administrative Science Quarterly* 35 (1990): 128–152.

9. K. Anders Ericsson and Neil Charness, "Expert Performance: Its Structure and Acquisition," *American Psychologist* 49 (1994): 725–747; and K. Anders Ericsson and Robert J. Crutcher, "The Nature of Exceptional Performance," in Paul B. Baltes, David L. Featherman, and Richard M. Lerner, eds., *Life-Span Development and Behavior,* vol. 10 (Hillsdale, NJ: Lawrence Erlbaum, 1990), 187–217.

10. The ten year rule was originally discovered among chess players but has since been observed in other settings as well. See Herbert A. Simon and William G. Chase, "Skill in Chess," *American Scientist* 61 (1973): 394–403.

11. Morgan W. McCall Jr., *High Flyers* (Boston: Harvard Business School Press, 1998), 65–79; and Morgan W. McCall, Jr., Michael M. Lombardo, and Ann M. Morrison, *The Lessons of Experience* (Lexington, MA: D. C. Heath, 1988).

12. McCall, *High Flyers*, 64, 76. Italics in original.

13. Neil A. Hayes and Donald E. Broadbent, "Two Modes of Learning for Interactive Tasks," *Cognition*, 28 (1988): 249–276; Arthur S. Reber, "Implicit Learning and Tacit Knowledge," *Journal of Experimental Psychology: General* 118 (1989): 219–235; and Richard M. Shiffrin and Susan T. Dumais, "The Development of Automatism," in John R. Anderson, ed., *Cognitive Skills and Their Acquisition* (Hillsdale, NJ: Lawrence Erlbaum, 1981), 111–140.

14. In their early writings, engineers and economists distinguished "learning curves" from "progress functions." Technically, learning curves focus on direct labor learning and measure the relationship between experience and direct labor costs, while progress functions include both direct and indirect labor learning and measure the relationship between experience and all manufacturing costs. For simplicity, the former term will be used here to describe both relationships.

15. The relationship was discovered by the engineer Theodore P. Wright in the 1920s and 1930s and was first reported in his article "Factors Affecting the Cost of Airplanes," *Journal of Aeronautical Science*, 3 (1936): 122–128. The same discovery was made independently by the commander of Wright-Patterson Air Force Base at roughly the same time. The seminal theoretical treatment within economics is Kenneth J. Arrow, "The Economic Implications of Learning by Doing," *Review of Economic Studies* 29 (1962): 155–173.

16. John M. Dutton, Annie Thomas, and John E. Butler, "The History of Progress Functions as a Managerial Technology," *Business History Review* 86 (1984): 204–233: and Louis E. Yelle, "The Learning Curve: Historical Review and Comprehensive Survey," *Decision Sciences* 10 (1979): 302–328.

17. William J. Abernathy and Kenneth Wayne, "Limits of the Learning Curve," *Harvard Business Review* 52 (September/October 1974): 110–111.

18. Nathan Rosenberg, *Inside the Black Box: Technology and Economics* (Cambridge: Cambridge University Press, 1982), ch. 6.

19. The Boston Consulting Group, *Perspectives on Experience* (Boston: The Boston Consulting Group, 1970).

20. Pankaj Ghemewat, "Building Strategy on the Experience Curve," *Harvard Business Review* 63 (March/April 1985): 146.

21. Winfred B. Hirschmann, "Profit from the Learning Curve," *Harvard Business Review* 42 (January/February 1964): 125–139. Also see David L. Bodde, "Riding the Experience Curve," *Technology Review* (March/April 1976): 53–57.

22. Armen Alchian, "Reliability of Progress Curves in Airframe Production," *Econometrica* 31 (1963): 679–693.

23. Marvin B. Lieberman, "The Learning Curve and Pricing in the Chemical Processing Industries," *Rand Journal of Economics* 15 (1984): 221–222.

24. Linda Argote, Sara L. Beckman, and Dennis Epple, "The Persistence and Transfer of Learning in Industrial Settings," *Management Science* 36 (1990): 150–151.

25. Bodde, "Riding the Experience Curve," 54.

26. Argote, Beckman, and Epple, "The Persistence and Transfer of Learning in Industrial Settings," 144–146; and Dennis Epple, Linda Argote, and Rukimini Devadas, "Organizational Learning Curves: A Method for Investigating Intra-Plant Transfer of Knowledge Acquired through Learning by Doing," *Organization Science* 2 (1991): 68–69.

27. Ghemewat, "Building Strategy on the Experience Curve," 147–149.

28. Matthew Hayward, "Acquiror Learning from Acquisition Experience: Evidence from 1985–1995" (London Business School, undated, photocopy), 22. Forthcoming in 1999, Academy of Management, Business Policy and Strategy Division, *Best Paper Proceedings.*

29. Jerayr Haleblian and Sydney Finkelstein, "The Influence of Organizational Acquisition Experience on Acquisition Performance: A Behavioral Learning Perspective," *Administrative Science Quarterly* 44 (1999): 29–56.

30. Ghemewat, "Building Strategy on the Experience Curve," 149.

31. Hirschmann, "Profit from the Learning Curve," 137.

32. Gerald B. Allan and John S. Hammond, "Note on the Use of Experience Curves in Competitive Decision Making," Case 9-175-174 (Boston: Harvard Business School, 1975), 4.

33. J. M. Juran, *Juran on Leadership for Quality* (New York: Free Press, 1989), 136–141.

34. Tracy Kidder, *The Soul of a New Machine* (Boston: Atlantic-Little Brown, 1981), 217.

35. James G. March, Lee S. Sproull, and Machal Tamuz, "Learning from Samples of One or Fewer," *Organization Science* 2 (1991): 1–13.

36. Sim B. Sitkin, "Learning through Failure: The Strategy of Small Losses," in B. M. Staw and L. L. Cummings, eds., *Research in Organizational Behavior,* vol. 14 (Greenwich, CT: JAI Press, 1992), 231–266.

37. Modesto A. Maidique and Billie Jo Zirger, "The New Product Learning Cycle," *Research Policy* 14 (1985): 299, 306, 309.

38. For a methodology describing how to develop and write "learning histories," see Art Kleiner and George Roth, "How to Make Experience Your Company's Best Teacher," *Harvard Business Review* 75 (September/October 1997): 172–177.

39. Michael A. Cusumano and Richard W. Selby, *Microsoft Secrets* (New York: Free Press, 1995), 331–339; and Julie Bick, *All I Really Need to Know in Business I Learned at Microsoft* (New York: Pocket Books, 1997): 9–10.

40. The quotation is from Fred Moody's book *I Sing the Body Electronic* and is cited in David Stauffer, "What You Can Learn about Managing from Microsoft," *Harvard Management Update* (September 1997): 3.

41. Janet Simpson, Lee Field, and David Garvin, "The Boeing 767: From Concept to Production (A)," Case 9-688-040 (Boston: Harvard Business School, 1988), 5–6.

42. These patterns are sometimes called "life themes." See Len Schlesinger, "How to Hire by Wire," *Fast Company,* November 1993, 86–91.

43. Robert Kelley and Janet Caplan, "How Bell Labs Creates Star Performers," *Harvard*

Business Review 71 (July/August 1993): 128–139; and Robert E. Kelley, *How to Be a Star at Work* (New York: Times Business, 1998).

44. Robert W. Johnson, "Theory and Policy of Post Audit," in Frank G. J. Derkinderen and Roy L. Crum, eds., *Readings in Strategy for Corporate Investment* (Boston: Pitman, 1981), 135–145.

45. Frank R. Gulliver, "Post-Project Appraisals Pay," *Harvard Business Review* 65 (March/April 1987): 128–132.

46. Gabriel Szulanski, "Intra-Firm Transfer of Best Practices Project: Executive Summary of the Findings," (Fontainebleau, France, and Houston, Texas: INSEAD and American Productivity & Quality Center, October 1994), photocopy, 4.

47. John Krafcik, "Learning from NUMMI," International Motor Vehicle working paper, MIT, Cambridge, MA, 15 September 1986, photocopy, 14–16.

48. Andrew M. Pettigrew, "Longitudinal Field Research: Theory and Practice," *Organization Science* 1 (1990): 270.

49. The AAR story is based primarily on interviews conducted in December 1995 and January 1996 with General Gordon R. Sullivan, chief of staff of the U.S. Army; Colonel Orin A. Nagel, director, Center for Army Lessons Learned; and various commanders and officers who had recently returned from Haiti and were participating in exercises and AARs at the National Training Center at Fort Polk, Louisiana (Lieutenant Colonel Michael Trahan, Colonel Ray Fitzgerald, Colonel Sharp, Major Patrick MacGowan, Captain Favio Lopez, Sergeant Dawson, and Lieutenant Fogg). Portions of these interviews, as well as excerpts from the AARs at the National Training Center, appear in the videotape *Putting the Learning Organization to Work: Learning After Doing* (Boston: Harvard Business School Video, 1996). Other sources include an interview with Captain Andrew D. Clarke, a former observer-controller at the National Training Center, in September 1998; and Baird, Henderson, and Watts, "Learning from Action," 385–395; William Blankmeyer and Terry Blakely, "Leaders Conducting After-Action Reviews Often Deliver Substandard Feedback," *ARMOR* (November/December 1998): 15–18; Henderson and Watts, "Creating and Exploiting Knowledge for Fast-Cycle Response"; Richard Pascale, "Fight, Learn, L*E*A*D," *Fast Company* (August/September 1996): 65–69; Richard Pascale, Mark Millemann, and Linda Gioja, "Changing the Way We Change," *Harvard Business Review* 75 (November/December 1997): 127–139; Thomas E. Ricks, "Army Devises System to Decide What Does and Does Not Work," *Wall Street Journal*, 23 May 1997, A1, A10; Gordon R. Sullivan and Michael V. Harper, *Hope Is Not a Method* (New York: Times Business/Random House, 1996), 189–203; and U.S. Army, "A Leader's Guide to After-Action Reviews," Training Circular 25-20, 30 September 1993, photocopy.

50. Pascale, Millemann, and Gioja, "Changing the Way We Change," 137. Italics in original.

51. This principle has long been recognized by the quality movement. See, for example, John Guaspari, *I Know It When I See It* (New York: AMACOM, 1985).

52. Roger Schank, *Virtual Learning* (New York: McGraw-Hill, 1997), ch. 3.

53. Ron Zemke and Susan Zemke, "Adult Learning: What Do We Know for Sure?" *Training* (June 1995): 31–40.

54. Dewey, *Experience and Education,* 20.

55. Gina M. Walter, *Corporate Practices in Management Development* (New York: The Conference Board, 1996), 16.

56. K. Patricia Cross, "A Proposal to Improve Teaching or What 'Taking Teaching Seriously' Should Mean," *American Association for Higher Education* (September 1986).

57. On GE, see James L. Noel and Ram Charan, "GE Brings Global Thinking to Light," *Training & Development* (July 1992): 32–33. On Whirlpool, see Paul Froiland, "Action Learning: Taming Problems in Real Time," *Training* (January 1994): 32. On Motorola, see Timothy T. Baldwin, Camden Danielson, and William Wiggenhorn, "The Evolution of Learning Strategies in Organizations: From Employee Development to Business Redefinition," *Academy of Management Executive* (November 1997): 47–58.

58. David T. Kearns and David A. Nadler, *Prophets in the Dark* (New York: HarperBusiness, 1992), 214–215.

59. Charles J. Margerison, "Action Learning and Excellence in Management Development," *Journal of Management Development* 7 (1988): 44.

60. Froiland, "Action Learning: Taming Problems in Real Time," 29.

61. Schank, *Virtual Learning,* 35.

62. Eric O. Wheatcroft, *Simulators for Skill* (London: McGraw-Hill, 1973), 26.

63. H. Clayton Foushee, "Dyand and Triads at 35,000 Feet," *American Psychologist* (August 1984): 891–892. Italics in original.

64. Jeanne C. Meister, *Corporate Quality Universities* (Burr, IL: Richard D. Irwin, 1994), 115–117.

65. Roy E. Butler, "LOFT: Full-Mission Simulation as Crew Resource Management Training," in Earl L. Wiener, Barbara G. Kanki, and Robert L. Helmreich, eds., *Cockpit Resource Management* (San Diego: Academic Press, 1993), 235.

66. Schank, *Virtual Learning,* 30–33, 41–42.

67. Rick Becker, "Taking the Misery Out of Experiential Training," *Training* (February 1998): 80. For a complete description of BARNGA, see Sivasailam Thiagarajan, *Simulation Games by Thiagi,* 6th ed. (Bloomington, IN: Workshops by Thiagi, 1997).

68. Charles E. Watson, *Management Development through Training* (Reading, MA: Addison-Wesley, 1979), 178–186.

69. Ronald Henkoff, "Companies that Train Best," *Fortune,* 22 March 1993, 73.

70. Schank, *Virtual Learning,* 87–88.

71. Watson, *Management Development through Training,* 186–195.

72. Jane C. Lindner, "War Games: How Polaroid Links Knowledge to Innovation," in *The Knowledge Advantage: A Summary of the 1994 Colloquium on Organizational Knowledge* (Boston: Ernst & Young Center for Business Innovation, 26–27 September 1994), 79–86.

73. Peter J. Frost, "Crossroads: Bridging Academia and Business: A Conversation with Steve Kerr," *Organization Science* 8 (May/June 1997): 340.

74. Walter, *Corporate Practices in Management Development,* 21–22.

75. William Wiggenhorn, "Motorola U: When Training Becomes an Education," *Harvard Business Review* 68 (July/August 1990), 75.

76. Nancy Foy, "Action Learning Comes to Industry," *Harvard Business Review* 55 (September/October 1977): 158–168; Joseph A. Raelin, "Action Learning and Action Sci-

ence: Are They Different?" *Organizational Dynamics* (Summer 1997): 21–33; and Revans, *The Origins and Growth of Action Learning*, 629–630.

77. The CAP story is based primarily on interviews conducted in January and February 1996 with Steve Kerr, vice president, corporate leadership development; Jacquie Vierling, manager, Work-Out, Best Practices, and Change Acceleration; and selected members of CAP teams from GE Supply (Frank Billone and Paul Slattery) and GE Plastics Japan (Nani Beccalli, Greg Adams, Masao Fukuda, and Mr. Kimura). Portions of these interviews, as well as excerpts from CAP sessions at GE's Crotonville training facility, appear in the videotape *Putting the Learning Organization to Work: Learning While Doing* (Boston: Harvard Business School Video, 1996). Other sources include John A. Byrne, "Jack: A Close-Up Look at How America's #1 Manager Runs GE," *Business Week*, 8 June 1998, 90–111; Frost, "Bridging Academia and Business," 332–347; Richard M. Hodgetts, "A Conversation with Steve Kerr," *Organizational Dynamics* (Spring 1996): 68–79; Noel M. Tichy, "GE's Crotonville: A Staging Ground for Corporate Revolution," *Academy of Management Executive* 3 (1989): 99–106; Noel M. Tichy and Ram Charan, "Speed, Simplicity, and Self-Confidence: An Interview with Jack Welch," *Harvard Business Review* 67 (September/October 1989): 112–120; Noel M. Tichy and Stratford Sherman, *Control Your Destiny or Someone Else Will* (New York: Harper Business, 1994), and Dave Ulrich, "A New Mandate for Human Resources," *Harvard Business Review* 76 (January/February 1998) 124–134.

78. Joseph L. Bower and Jay Dial, "Jack Welch: General Electric's Revolutionary," Case 9-394-065 (Boston: Harvard Business School, 1993), 8.

79. The latest of GE's broad-based improvement program is Six Sigma, designed to sharply improve quality levels. It was introduced in the mid-1990s, a few years after CAP.

Chapter 5: Experimentation

1. Robert Scott Root-Bernstein, *Discovering* (Cambridge: Harvard University Press, 1989), 409.

2. *Oxford English Dictionary*, 2d ed. (Oxford: Oxford University Press, 1991), 550.

3. Martin Landau, "On the Concept of a Self-Correcting Organization," *Public Administration Review* 33 (1973): 533–542; and Aaron Wildavsky, "The Self-Evaluating Organization," *Public Administration Review* 32 (1972): 509–520.

4. Malcolm Warner, *Organizations and Experiments* (Chichester: Wiley, 1984), 8.

5. William R. Dill, Wallace B. S. Crowston, and Edwin J. Elton, "Strategies for Self-Education," *Harvard Business Review* 43 (November/December 1965): 124.

6. Sim B. Sitkin, Kathleen M. Sutcliffe, and Roger G. Schroeder, "Distinguishing Control from Learning in Total Quality Management: A Contingency Perspective," *Academy of Management Review* 19 (1994): 553.

7. Ron Harré, *Great Scientific Experiments* (Oxford: Oxford University Press, 1981), 21–22.

8. On Banc One, see Myra Hart and Hugo Uyterhoeven, "Banc One—1993," Case 9-394-043 (Boston: Harvard Business School, 1993), 15. On British Petroleum, see Steven E. Prokesch, "Unleashing the Power of Learning: An Interview with British Petroleum's John Browne," *Harvard Business Review* 75 (September/October 1997): 160.

9. For discussions of the many different types of experiments, see Roger E. Bohn, "Learning by Experimentation in Manufacturing," working paper 88-001, Harvard Business School, Boston, MA, June 1987; photocopy; Abraham Kaplan, *The Conduct of Inquiry* (San Francisco: Chandler, 1964), ch. 4; P. B. Medawar, *Advice to a Young Scientist* (New York: Harper & Row, 1979), ch. 9; and Donald A. Schön, *The Reflective Practitioner* (New York: Basic Books, 1983), 141–156.

10. Schön, *The Reflective Practitioner,* 145.

11. There are exceptions to this rule. Occasionally, "natural experiments" arise that include enough variation to draw firm conclusions even without manipulating critical variables. American Airlines, for example, took advantage of already existing differences in the time it took cabin crews to open an airplane's doors after gate arrival. It measured these times and then followed up with telephone surveys to assess passengers' perceptions of on-time performance. Managers found that perceptions improved dramatically if the doors were opened less than 25 seconds after gate arrival. See George S. Day, "Continuous Learning about Markets," *California Management Review* 36 (Summer 1994): 15.

12. W. I. B. Beveridge, *The Art of Scientific Investigation* (New York: Vintage Books, 1957), 21.

13. Raghu Garud, "On the Distinction Between Know-How, Know-Why, and Know-What," in James P. Walsh and Ann Huff, eds., *Advances in Strategic Management,* vol. 14 (Greenwich, CT: JAI Press, 1997), 81–101.

14. Roger E. Bohn, "Measuring and Managing Technological Knowledge," *Sloan Management Review* 36 (Fall 1994): 61–73, and Ramchandran Jaikumar and Roger Bohn, "The Development of Intelligent Systems for Industrial Use: A Conceptual Framework," in Richard S. Rosenbloom, ed., *Research on Technological Innovation, Management, and Policy,* vol. 3 (Greenwich, CT: JAI Press, 1986), 182–188.

15. Bohn, "Measuring and Managing Technological Knowledge," 61.

16. Frederick Jackson Turner, *The Frontier in American History* (New York: Henry Holt, 1920).

17. Ray Allen Billington and Martin Ridge, *Westward Expansion,* 5th ed. (New York: Macmillan, 1982), 689.

18. Sven Ove Hansson, "Decision Making under Great Uncertainty," *Philosophy of the Social Sciences* 26 (1996): 369–386; and Eric Von Hippel and Marcie Tyre, "How Learning by Doing Is Done: Problem Identification in Novel Process Equipment," *Research Policy* 24 (1995): 1–12.

19. Henry Mintzberg, Duru Raisinghanii, and André Théorêt, "The Structure of 'Unstructured' Decision Processes," *Administrative Science Quarterly* 21 (1976): 251. Italics in original.

20. Gary S. Lynn, Joseph G. Morone, and Albert Paulson, "Emerging Technologies in Emerging Markets: Challenges for New Product Professionals," *Engineering Management Journal* 8 (1996): 23.

21. Gary S. Lynn, Joseph G. Morone, and Albert S. Paulson, "Marketing and Discontinuous Innovation: The Probe and Learn Process," *California Management Review* 38 (1996): 13–14.

22. Christopher Cerf and Victor Navasky, *The Experts Speak* (New York: Pantheon Books, 1984).

23. Lynn, Morone, and Paulson, "Marketing and Discontinuous Innovation: The Probe and Learn Process," 15, 19.

24. Ibid., 18.

25. Timothy P. Luehrman, "Strategy as a Portfolio of Real Options," *Harvard Business Review* 76 (September/October 1998): 89–99; and Rita Gunther McGrath, "Falling Forward: Real Options Reasoning and Entrepreneurial Failure," *Academy of Management Review* 24 (1999): 13–30. Others have argued that this process occurs more by happenstance than by design, with lower-level managers taking actions that over time are then recognized by senior-level managers and articulated as a new strategic direction. See Robert A. Burgelman, "Strategy Making as a Social Learning Process: The Case of Internal Corporate Venturing," *Interfaces* 18 (1988): 74–85, and Henry Mintzberg, Bruce Ahlstrand, and Joseph Lampel, *Strategy Safari* (New York: Free Press, 1998), ch. 7.

26. Jonathan West and David A. Garvin, "Serengeti Eyewear: Entrepreneurship within Corning Inc.," Case 9-394-033 (Boston: Harvard Business School, 1993), 5.

27. Janet Simpson, Lee Field, and David Garvin, "The Boeing 767: From Concept to Production (A)," Case 9-688-040 (Boston: Harvard Business School, 1988), 8.

28. Geoffrey K. Gill and Steven C. Wheelwright, *Motorola, Inc.: Bandit Pager Project,* Case 9–690-043 (Boston: Harvard Business School, 1990), 4–5.

29. Robert I. Sutton and Andrew Hargadon, "Brainstorming Groups in Context: Effectiveness in a Product Design Firm," *Administrative Science Quarterly* 41 (1996): 704.

30. Bohn, "Learning by Experimentation in Manufacturing," 10–11, 30–34.

31. Stefan H. Thomke, "Managing Experimentation in the Design of New Products," *Management Science* 44 (1998): 745.

32. Stefan H. Thomke, "Simulation, Learning and R&D Performance: Evidence from Automotive Development," *Research Policy* 27 (1998): 66.

33. Susanne Bodker, Kaj Gronbaek, and Morten Kyng, "Cooperative Design: Techniques and Experiences from the Scandinavian Scene," in Douglas Schuler and Aki Namioka, eds., *Participatory Design: Principles and Practices* (Hillsdale, NJ: Lawrence Erlbaum, 1993), 157–175; Pelle Ehn and Morten Kyng, "Cardboard Computers: Mocking-it-up or Hands-on the Future," in Joan Greenbaum and Morten Kyng, eds., *Design at Work: Cooperative Design of Computer Systems* (Hillsdale, NJ: Lawrence Erlbaum, 1991), 169–195; and Robert Howard, "UTOPIA: Where Workers Craft New Technology," *Technology Review* 88 (April 1985): 42–49.

34. Thomke, "Managing Experimentation in the Design of New Products," 743–762; and Von Hippel and Tyre, "How Learning by Doing Is Done," 1–12.

35. Dorothy Leonard-Barton et al., "How to Integrate Work *and* Deepen Expertise," *Harvard Business Review* 72 (September/October 1994): 124.

36. James G. March, Lee S. Sproull, and Machal Tamuz, "Learning from Samples of One or Fewer," *Organization Science* 2 (1991): 6.

37. Ibid., 3, 8.

38. Donald T. Campbell, "Reforms as Experiments," *American Psychologist* 24 (1969): 409–429.

39. Edward E. Lawler III, "Adaptive Experiments: An Approach to Organizational Behavior Research," *Academy of Management Review* 2 (1977): 579.

40. Ibid., 579.

41. Quoted in Beveridge, *The Art of Scientific Investigation*, 68.

42. Dill, Crowston, and Elton, "Strategies for Self-Education," 126.

43. J. Richard Hackman, "Doing Research That Makes a Difference," in Edward E. Lawler III et al., *Doing Research That Is Useful for Theory and Practice* (San Francisco: Jossey-Bass, 1985), 148.

44. Gordon E. Forward, "Wide-Open Management at Chaparrel Steel," *Harvard Business Review* 64 (May/June 1986): 101.

45. Charles Perrow, *Normal Accidents* (New York: Basic Books, 1984), 85–86.

46. On General Foods, see David A. Whitsett and Lyle Yorks, "Looking Back at Topeka: General Foods and the Quality-of-Work-Life Experiment," *California Management Review* 25 (1983): 93–109. On Wal-Mart, see David M. Stipanuk and Jack D. Ninemeier, "Environmental Examples," *Cornell Hotel and Restaurant Administration Quarterly* (December 1996): 79–80.

47. David Hornestay, "Noble Experiments," *Government Executive* (October 1996): 56–59.

48. Artemis March and David A. Garvin, "Copeland Corporation: Evolution of a Manufacturing Strategy, 1975–1982 (A), (B), (C), and (D)," Cases 9–686-088, 9–686-089, 9–686-090, and 9–686-091 (Boston: Harvard Business School 1986).

49. Richard E. Walton, "The Diffusion of New Work Structures: Explaining Why Success Didn't Take," *Organizational Dynamics* (Winter 1975): 3–22.

50. Richard E. Walton, "Successful Strategies for Diffusing Work Innovations," *Journal of Contemporary Business* 6 (Spring 1977): 1–22.

51. William L. Anderson and William T. Crocca, "Engineering Practice and Codevelopment of Product Prototypes," *Communications of the ACM* 36 (1993): 49–56; Eran Carmer, Randall D. Whitaker, and Joey F. George, "PD and Joint Application Design: A Transatlantic Comparison," *Communications of the ACM* 36 (1993): 40–48; and Michael J. Muller, Daniel M. Wildman, and Ellen A. White, "Taxonomy of PD Practices: A Brief Practitioner's Guide," *Communications of the ACM* 36 (1993): 26–27.

52. The Timken story is based on internal documents and interviews conducted in August 1991, January 1992, August 1992, December 1995, and January 1996 with over a dozen members of the organization, including senior managers, representatives of the Feasibility Team, Concept Team, Design Team, and Implementation Team, operators, and project engineers. I am especially grateful to Joe Toot, Jr. (president and CEO), Peter Ashton (president of the bearings business), Jon Elsasser (head of the Design Team), and Mike Arnold (head of the Implementation Team, as well as the first plant manager) for their cooperation and support. Portions of the 1995 and 1996 interviews, as well as scenes from Cardboard City and the training module, appear in the videotape *Putting the Learning Organization to Work: Learning Before Doing* (Boston: Harvard Business School Video, 1996).

53. For an introduction to storyboarding, see Harry Forsha, *Show Me: The Complete Guide to Storyboarding and Problem Solving* (Milwaukee: ASQC Quality Press, 1995).

54. Six years may seem like an unusually long design period. At Timken, the reasons in part were economic. Because the market nose-dived unexpectedly in the middle of

the planning process, managers temporarily put the project on hold. Only after demand rose did planning resume. At least a year (and possibly more) was lost as a result.

55. The quotation is from Professor C. Roland Christensen of the Harvard Business School. He actually used it to define research, but it seems equally appropriate as a description of exploration.

56. Medawar, *Advice to a Young Scientist*, 69.

57. Richard P. Feynman, *Surely You're Joking, Mr. Feynman* (New York: Bantam Books, 1985), 311.

58. For a detailed discussion of these (and other) methodological requirements, see Thomas D. Cook and Donald T. Campbell, *Quasi-Experimentation* (Boston: Houghton Mifflin, 1979), ch. 1.

59. Lawler, "Adaptive Experiments," 577.

60. The Dayton-Hudson program is described at length in the videotape *Customer Loyalty: Measuring, Managing, Making Money* (Boston: Harvard Business School Video, 1995).

61. See, respectively, Cook and Campbell, *Quasi-Experimentation*; Lawler, "Adaptive Experiments"; Stanley E. Seashore, "Field Experiments in Formal Organizations," in William M. Evan, ed., *Organizational Experiments: Laboratory and Field Research* (New York: Harper & Row, 1971), 147–153; and Michael Scriven, "Maximizing the Power of Causal Investigations: The Modus Operandi Method," in G. V. Glass, ed., *Evaluation Studies*, vol. 1 (Beverly Hills, CA: Sage, 1976), 101–118.

62. Kaplan, *The Conduct of Inquiry*, 144, 147.

63. For detailed discussions of these conditions, which scientists call *internal* and *external validity*, see Campbell, "Reforms as Experiments," 410–412, and Barry M. Staw, "The Experimenting Organization: Problems and Prospects," in Barry M. Staw, ed., *Psychological Foundations of Organizational Behavior*, 2d ed. (Glenview, IL: Scott, Foresman, 1983), 421–437.

64. The distinction between a "vacuum cleaner" and "directed telescope" approach to collecting data was originally used to describe the approach of the Center for Army Lessons Learned. See John C. Henderson and Stephanie A. Watts, "Creating and Exploiting Knowledge for Fast-Cycle Response: An Analysis of the Center for Army Lessons Learned" (Boston, MA, Boston University, undated, photocopy), 5–6.

65. Beveridge, *The Art of Scientific Investigation*, 63.

66. This phenomenon is called "regression toward the mean." For further discussion, see Campbell, "Reforms as Experiments," 413–414, and Max Bazerman, *Judgment in Managerial Decision Making*, 4th ed. (New York: Wiley, 1998), 23–26.

67. Occasionally, experiments can be crafted so that several variables can be altered simultaneously while still isolating their impacts. This technique, called "design of experiments," requires considerable statistical sophistication but can yield impressive benefits. Ford, for example, was able to cut test-development time for a new heat-treatment process by 63 percent using this approach. See Jill F. Minner, "DOE Slashes Test-Development Time by 63%," *Quality* (December 1996): 61.

68. Scriven, "Maximizing the Power of Causal Investigations," 103–108.

69. The Allegheny Ludlum story is based primarily on internal documents and interviews

conducted in March and April 1997 with Richard Simmons, chairman and chief executive officer, Allegheny Teladyne; Robert Miller, vice president, technical; Thomas DeLuca, director, process metallurgy; James Liput, manager, process metallurgy; Roy Andrews, manager, product metallurgy; Thomas Nese, senior product metallurgist; Roger Walburn, metallurgist; T. L. Swigart, superintendent, annealing & pickling, normalizing & plate finishing; Frank Spiecha, manager, hot working; and Thomas Parayil, research associate. Portions of these interviews, as well as scenes recreating the experimental process and showing the two annealing lines in action, appear in the videotape *Redoubling Shop Floor Productivity* (Boston: Harvard Business School Video, 1997). Additional information can be found in Artemis March and David A. Garvin, "Allegheny Ludlum Steel Corporation," Case 9–686-087 (Boston: Harvard Business School, 1985).

70. Beveridge, *The Art of Scientific Investigation,* 21.

Chapter 6: Leading Learning

1. On management, see Colin P. Hales, "What Do Managers Do? A Critical Review of the Evidence," *Journal of Management Studies* 23 (1986): 88–115; F. Luthans, R. M. Hodgetts, and S. A. Rosenkrantz, *Real Managers* (Cambridge: Ballinger, 1988); Henry Mintzberg, *The Nature of Managerial Work* (New York: Harper & Row, 1973); and Henry Mintzberg, "The Manager's Job: Folklore and Fact," *Harvard Business Review* 53 (July/August 1975): 49–61. On leadership, and especially its differences from management, see Warren Bennis and Bert Nanus, *Leaders* (New York: Harper & Row, 1985); John P. Kotter, *The Leadership Factor* (New York: Free Press, 1988); John P. Kotter, *A Force for Change* (New York: Free Press, 1990); Abraham Zaleznik, "Managers and Leaders: Are They Different?" *Harvard Business Review* 55 (May/June 1977): 67–80; and Abraham Zaleznik, *The Managerial Mystique* (New York: Harper & Row, 1989).

2. John Gardner, *Self-Renewal* (New York: Harper & Row, 1964), 3.

3. Eli Cohen and Noel Tichy, "How Leaders Develop Leaders," *Training & Development* (May 1997): 58–73; Noel M. Tichy, with Eli Cohen, *The Leadership Engine* (New York: HarperBusiness, 1997); and Howard Gardner, *Leading Minds* (New York: Basic Books, 1995).

4. James Kelley, "Learning Is Not Enough," *Transformation* (Autumn 1998): 46.

5. Carl Rogers, *Freedom to Learn for the 80's* (Columbus, OH: Charles E. Merrill, 1983); and Christensen, Garvin, and Sweet, *Education for Judgment.*

6. Alfred North Whitehead, *The Aims of Education* (New York: Free Press, 1929), 1.

7. Charles Gragg, "Because Wisdom Can't Be Told," *Harvard Alumni Bulletin,* 19 October 1940.

8. Charles Hartshorne and Paul Weiss, eds., *Collected Papers of Charles Sanders Peirce,* vol. 5 (Cambridge: Harvard University Press, 1934), 405.

9. David A. Garvin, "The Processes of Organization and Management," *Sloan Management Review* (Summer 1998): 33–50.

10. Michael Hammer, "Reengineering Work: Don't Automate, Obliterate," *Harvard Business Review* 68 (July/August 1990), 110.

11. This distinction was first reported by social psychologists, drawing on studies of elementary school, junior high school, and high school students. See Carole Ames

and Jennifer Archer, "Achievement Goals in the Classroom: Students' Learning Strategies and Motivation Processes," *Journal of Educational Psychology* 80 (1988): 260–267; Carole S. Dweck and Ellen L. Leggett, "A Social-Cognitive Approach to Motivation and Personality," *Psychological Review* 95 (1988): 256–273; and Claudia M. Mueller and Carole S. Dweck, "Praise for Intelligence Can Undermine Children's Motivation and Performance," *Journal of Personality and Social Psychology* 75 (1998): 33–52. The findings were later expanded to business settings. See Harish Sujan, Barton A. Weitz, and Nirmalya Kumar, "Learning Orientation, Working Smart, and Effective Selling," *Journal of Marketing* 58 (1994): 39–52; and Ajay K. Kohli, Tasadduq A. Shervani, and Goutam N. Challagalla, "Learning and Performance Orientation of Salespeople: The Role of Supervisors," *Journal of Marketing Research* 35 (1998): 263–274.

12. Ram Charan, "Managing Through the Chaos," *Fortune,* 23 November 1998, 284.

13. Max Bazerman, *Judgment in Managerial Decision Making,* 4th ed. (New York: John Wiley, 1998), 168–170; and Alexander L. George, *Presidential Decisionmaking in Foreign Policy* (Boulder, CO: Westview Press, 1980), 58.

14. Seth Lubove, "It Ain't Broke, But Fix It Anyway," *Forbes,* 1 August 1994, 59.

15. Noel M. Tichy and Stratford Sherman, *Control Your Destiny or Someone Else Will* (New York: Harper Business, 1994), 190–194, 424–425.

16. Jonathan West and David A. Garvin, "Time Life Inc. (A)," Case 9-395-012 (Boston: Harvard Business School, 1994), 3–7.

17. David A. Garvin, "Leveraging Processes for Strategic Advantage," *Harvard Business Review* 73 (September/October 1995): 79.

18. Garvin, "Leveraging Processes for Strategic Advantage," 84.

19. Bo Hedberg, "How Organizations Learn and Unlearn," in Paul C. Nystrom and William H. Starbuck, eds., *Handbook of Organizational Design,* vol. 1 (Oxford: Oxford University Press, 1981), 3–27.

20. Don Sull and David A. Garvin, "Pepsi's Regeneration, 1990–1993," Case 9-395-048 (Boston: Harvard Business School, 1994); and Nikhil Deogun, "Pepsi's Mr. Nice Guy Vows Not to Finish Last," *Wall Street Journal,* 19 March 1997, B1, B5.

21. Mary Gentile and Todd D. Jick, "Bob Galvin and Motorola, Inc. (A)," Case 9-487-062 (Boston: Harvard Business School, 1987), 11.

22. Kelley, "Learning Is Not Enough," 46.

23. This is the essence of Heifetz's model of "adaptive leadership." See Ronald A. Heifetz, *Leadership Without Easy Answers* (Cambridge, MA: Harvard University Press, 1994); and Ronald A. Heifetz and Donald L. Laurie, "The Work of Leadership," *Harvard Business Review* 75 (January/February 1997): 124–134.

24. Gentile and Jick, "Bob Galvin and Motorola, Inc. (A)," 6.

25. Mary Gentile and Todd D. Jick, "Bob Galvin and Motorola, Inc. (B)," Case 9-487-063 (Boston: Harvard Business School, 1987); and Mary Gentile and Todd D. Jick, "Bob Galvin and Motorola, Inc. (C)," Case 9-487-064 (Boston: Harvard Business School, 1987).

26. Artemis March and David A. Garvin, "Harvey Golub: Recharging American Express," Case 9–396-212 (Boston: Harvard Business School, 1996), 6.

27. March and Garvin, "Harvey Golub," 5. Italics in original.

28. Irving Janis, *Victims of Groupthink* (Boston: Houghton Mifflin, 1972), 147–148; J. Richard Hackman and Richard E. Walton, "Leading Groups in Organizations," in Paul S. Goodman, ed., *Designing Effective Work Groups* (San Francisco: Jossey-Bass, 1986), 72–119; and Richard T. Johnson, *Managing the White House* (New York: Harper & Row, 1974), 136–147.

29. C. Roland Christensen, "Premises and Practices of Discussion Teaching," in C. Roland Christensen, David A. Garvin, and Ann Sweet, eds., *Education for Judgment* (Boston: Harvard Business School Press, 1991), 22.

30. Edward De Bono, *Six Thinking Hats* (Boston: Little, Brown and Company, 1985).

31. Artemis March and David A. Garvin, "Harvard Business School Publishing," Case 9-397-028 (Boston: Harvard Business School, 1996).

32. Dorothy Leonard-Barton, "The Factory as a Learning Laboratory," *Sloan Management Review* (Fall 1992): 33.

33. Jonathan West and David A. Garvin, "Serengeti Eyewear: Entrepreneurship within Corning Inc." Case 9-394-033 (Boston: Harvard Business School, 1993), and David A. Garvin, *Serengeti Eyewear: An Interview with Zaki Mustafa* (Boston: Harvard Business School Video, 1997). Despite Serengeti's success, Corning sold the division in February 1997 as part of a refocusing effort aimed at shedding all businesses not connected to telecommunications or computers. See Timothy Aeppel, "Corning's Makeover: From Casseroles to Fiber Optics," *Wall Street Journal*, 16 July 1999, B4.

34. Quoted in James Freedman, *Idealism and Liberal Education* (Ann Arbor, MI: University of Michigan Press, 1996), 63.

35. Artemis March and David A. Garvin, "A Note on Knowledge Management," Case 9-398-031 (Boston: Harvard Business School, 1997), 14.

36. Andris Berzins, Joel Podolny, and John Roberts, "British Petroleum (B): Focus on Learning," Case S-IB-16B (Palo Alto, CA: Stanford Business School, 1998); Nancy Dixon and Jonathan Ungerleider, "Lessons Learned," January 1998 <http://www.businessinnovation.ey.com/mko/index.html>; and Steven E. Prokesch, "Unleashing the Power of Learning: An Interview with British Petroleum's John Browne," *Harvard Business Review* 75 (September/October 1997): 146–168.

37. Gary Deutsch and Gabriel Szulanski, "Rank Xerox–Team C," Case 1997-001-1 (Philadelphia, PA: Wharton Business School, 1997).

38. Alexander L. George, *Presidential Decisionmaking in Foreign Policy* (Boulder, CO: Westview Press, 1980), 101–103.

39. J. T. Lanzetta and T. B. Roby, "The Relationship Between Certain Group Process Variables and Group Problem-Solving Efficiency," *Organizational Behavior and Human Performance* 11 (1960): 146.

40. H. Clayton Foushee, "Dyads and Triads at 35,000 Feet," *American Psychologist* (August 1984): 890.

41. March and Garvin, "Harvard Business School Publishing," 14.

42. These three skills were, to my knowledge, first spoken of collectively by Professor C. Roland Christensen, who used them as part of his seminar on case method teaching at the Harvard Business School. For further discussion, see Louis B. Barnes, C. Roland Christensen, and Abby J. Hansen, *Teaching and the Case Method*, 3d ed. (Boston: Harvard Business School Press, 1994), 62–63; and Christensen's essays in Christensen, Garvin, and Sweet, eds., *Education for Judgment*, ch. 2, 6, and 9.

43. Peter F. Drucker, *The Practice of Management* (New York: Harper & Row, 1954), 351.

44. For discussions of questions and the various roles they play, see Barnes, Christensen, and Hansen, *Teaching and the Case Method*, 62–63; James Austin, with Ann Sweet and Catherine Overholt, "'To See Ourselves as Others See Us:' The Rewards of Classroom Observation," in Christensen, Garvin, and Sweet, eds., *Education for Judgment*, 156–163; and Thomas P. Kasulis, "Questioning," in Margaret Morganroth Gullette, ed., *The Art and Craft of Teaching* (Cambridge, MA: Harvard-Danforth Center for Teaching and Learning, 1982), 38–48.

45. Alfred Benjamin, *The Helping Interview*, 2d ed. (Boston: Houghton Mifflin, 1974), 67.

46. Thomas Petzinger Jr., "With the Stakes High, A Lucent Duo Conquers Distance and Culture," *Wall Street Journal*, 23 April 1999, B1.

47. Irving J. Lee, *How to Talk with People* (New York: Harper & Row, 1952), 11. Italics in original.

48. Robert F. Bales, "In Conference," *Harvard Business Review* 32 (March/April 1954): 49. Italics in original.

49. Jayashree Mahajan, "The Overconfidence Effect in Marketing Management Predictions," *Journal of Marketing Research* 29 (1992): 329–342.

50. On pre-mortems, see Gary Klein, *Sources of Power* (Cambridge: MIT Press, 1998), 71–72; and Gary Klein et al., "Decision Skills Training," in *Proceedings of the 41st Annual Meeting of the Human Factors and Ergonomics Society* (Santa Monica, CA: Human Factors and Ergonomics Society, 1997). On prospective hindsight, see Deborah J. Mitchell, J. Edward Russo, and Nancy Pennington, "Back to the Future: Temporal Perspective in the Explanation of Events," *Journal of Behavioral Decision Making* 2 (1989): 25–38.

51. A. Barry Rand, executive vice president, Xerox Corporation, interview 25 February 1993.

52. Charles I. Gragg, "Teachers Must Also Learn," *Harvard Educational Review* 10 (1940): 30–47.

53. Richard Farson, *Management of the Absurd* (New York: Touchstone, 1996), 62.

54. Daniel Goleman, "All Too Often, the Doctor Isn't Listening, Studies Show," *New York Times*, 13 November 1991, C1, C15.

55. Quoted in Lee, *How to Talk with People*, 11.

56. David A. Garvin, "A Delicate Balance: Ethical Dilemmas and the Discussion Process," in Christensen, Garvin, and Sweet, eds., *Education for Judgment*, 301. Also see "Handling Q&A: The Five Kinds of Listening," *Harvard Communications Update* (February 1999): 6–7.

57. Lee, *How to Talk with People*, 6.

58. Gentile and Jick, "Bob Galvin and Motorola, Inc. (A)," 2.

59. Gragg, "Teachers Must Also Learn," 32–38.

60. Foushee, "Dyads and Triads at 35,000 Feet," 888.

61. Benjamin, *The Helping Interview*, ch. 7.

62. Quoted in Charles Handy, *The Age of Unreason* (Boston: Harvard Business School Press, 1989), 67.

63. Daniel H. Kim, "The Link between Individual and Organizational Learning," *Sloan Management Review* (fall 1993): 37.

64. They are not, however, sufficient. If an organization is made up of individuals who learn but has not developed the associated processes for capturing and retaining knowledge, it does not meet the litmus tests of chapter 1 and therefore does not qualify as a learning *organization*.

65. Farson, *Management of the Absurd,* 117.

66. Norman H. Mackworth, "Originality," *American Psychologist* 20 (1965): 60.

67. Quoted in *Leo Rosten's Carnival of Wit* (New York: Plume, 1996), 483.

68. Bales, "In Conference," 46.

69. Gary Klein, "Developing Expertise in Decision Making," *Thinking and Reasoning* 3 (1997): 337–352; and James Shanteau, "Psychological Characteristics and Strategies of Expert Decision Makers," *Acta Psychologica* 68 (1988): 203–215.

70. Karl E. Weick, "The Vulnerable System: An Analysis of the Tenerife Air Disaster," *Journal of Management* 16 (1990): 582.

71. Edgar H. Schein, "Management Development as a Process of Influence," *Industrial Management Review* (May 1961): 69–72.

72. George, *Presidential Decisionmaking in Foreign Policy,* 147.

73. Peter F. Drucker, "Managing Oneself," *Harvard Business Review* 77 (March/April 1999): 67–68.

74. Robert J. Sternberg, *Thinking Styles* (Cambridge, England: Cambridge University Press, 1997).

75. Bazerman, *Judgment in Managerial Decision Making,* 168–170; George, *Presidential Decisionmaking in Foreign Policy,* 58; Klein, "Developing Expertise in Decision Making," 347–348; Shanteau, "Psychological Characteristics and Strategies of Expert Decision Makers," 208; and James Shanteau, "Competence in Experts: The Role of Task Characteristics," *Organizational Behavior and Human Decision Processes* 53 (1992): 252–266.

76. March and Garvin, "Harvey Golub," 5.

77. Gardner, *Self-Renewal,* 97–98.

78. Benson P. Shapiro, Kash Rangan, and John J. Sviokla, "Staple Yourself to an Order," *Harvard Business Review* 70 (July/August 1992): 113–122.

79. This is one feature that distinguishes firms that are rapid decision makers (and also rapid learners) from those that move more slowly. See Kathleen M. Eisenhardt, "Making Fast Strategic Decisions in High-Velocity Environments," *Academy of Management Journal* 32 (1989): 543–576.

80. March and Garvin, "Harvey Golub," 1.

81. West and Garvin, "Serengeti Eyewear: Entrepreneurship within Corning Inc.," 7, 13.

82. For a discussion of the links between humility and scholarship, see Wayne C. Booth, "The Scholar in Society," in Booth, *The Vocation of a Teacher* (Chicago: University of Chicago Press, 1988), 73.

Index

About the Author

DAVID A. GARVIN is the Robert and Jane Cizik Professor of Business Administration at the Harvard Business School, where he teaches general management in the M.B.A. and Advanced Management programs. He has also taught in many corporate executive programs and has consulted with companies around the world on organizational learning and strategic change. He is the author or coauthor of eight books, including *Education for Judgment* and *Managing Quality*; twenty-five articles, including "The Processes of Organization and Management," "Building a Learning Organization," and "Quality on the Line"; and four videotape series, including *Working Smarter* and *Putting the Learning Organization to Work*.

Garvin is a three-time winner of the McKinsey Award, given annually for the best article in the *Harvard Business Review*, and a winner of the Beckhard Prize, given annually for the best article on planned change and organizational development in the *Sloan Management Review.* From 1988–1990 he served as a member of the Board of Overseers of the Malcolm Baldrige National Quality Award, and from 1991–1992 he served on the Manufacturing Studies Board of the National Research Council.